Legal Research Demystified

Legal Research Demystified

A Step-by-Step Approach

Eric P. Voigt
RESEARCH AND WRITING ASSOCIATE PROFESSOR OF LAW
FAULKNER UNIVERSITY
THOMAS GOODE JONES SCHOOL OF LAW

CAROLINA ACADEMIC PRESS
Durham, North Carolina

Library of Congress Cataloging-in-Publication Data

Names: Voigt, Eric P., author.
Title: Legal research demystified : a step-by-step approach / by Eric P.
  Voigt.
Description: Durham, North Carolina : Carolina Academic Press, LLC, [2019]
Identifiers: LCCN 2019003158 | ISBN 9781531007836 (alk. paper)
Subjects: LCSH: Legal research--United States.
Classification: LCC KF240 .V53 2019 | DDC 340.072/073--dc23
LC record available at https://lccn.loc.gov/2019003158

e-ISBN 978-1-5310-0784-3

Carolina Academic Press
700 Kent Street
Durham, North Carolina 27701
Telephone (919) 489-7486
Fax (919) 493-5668
www.cap-press.com

2021 Printing
Printed in the United States of America

To my wife, Julie:
Thank you for your unconditional love.

To my children, Annie, Jacob, Emma, and Bennett:
You are precious gifts from God.

Contents

Preface

Legal Research Demystified introduces first-year law students to legal research. Through a step-by-step approach, this book offers a real-world approach to finding and understanding the law.

As a legal research and writing professor, I have developed my approach in response to my students' frustrations with legal research. Most textbooks focus on the bibliographic features of various sources, not legal research as a process. As a result, my first-year law students had a difficult time applying their "academic" knowledge about sources of law to the skill of legal research. Students have embraced my research steps, thanking me for clarifying the research process and for giving them an "edge" over other summer associates. And attorneys who have attended my CLE presentations have appreciated my practical approach to research.

Overview

Part I of *Legal Research Demystified: A Step-by-Step Approach* introduces students to the laws created by the three branches of government and explains where these laws are published in print and online. Parts II and III are organized around legal issues. Part II sets forth eight steps to research common law issues, and Part III guides students through ten steps to research statutory issues. Each chapter in Parts II and III discusses a single research step and identifies research strategies and the information the step should yield. Every chapter includes charts, diagrams, and screen captures to illustrate the research steps and finding tools. Each chapter concludes with a summary of key points that reinforces important concepts from the chapter.

Although the book discusses cost-effective online databases, it focuses on Westlaw Edge and Lexis Advance. Students who can navigate the research steps on those two platforms can transfer their knowledge to other online platforms. The book also examines print sources, including secondary sources, reporters, digests, and annotated statutory codes. This text highlights the benefits and limitations of researching with print and electronic sources.

Of course, the process of legal research is not linear. This book constantly reminds students of the recursive nature of legal research, and it identifies specific situations when they may deviate from the research steps. From each chapter, students should take away this key point: legal research requires critical thinking; thus, they should not mechanically follow the steps for every research assignment but rather should use them as a guide.

Key Distinguishing Features

This book attempts to demystify the legal research process for students. With a conversational tone, it breaks down the research process into "bite-size" pieces for novice researchers, minimizing the frustration often associated with learning a new skill. Additionally, the book provides students with information on a need-to-know basis to avoid overwhelming them with unnecessary information too early in the process. For example, students learn effective methods for locating all relevant statutes and statutory definitions (Step 3, Chapter 15); then they discover how to validate relevant statutes with citators, how to check the effective dates of relevant statutes, and how to identify the language of amendments (Step 4, Chapter 16); and then students learn effective methods for finding cases that interpret the controlling statutes (Step 7, Chapter 19).

Legal Research Demystified differs from existing texts in other important aspects. This book

- sets forth eight distinct methods to identify and retrieve secondary sources (instead of merely addressing how to navigate a particular source);

- contains a chart identifying binding cases in almost every situation (e.g., state law issue in federal court and federal law issue in state court);

- discusses in detail how to find cases on Lexis Advance using its headnote system (instead of only addressing the Key Number System);

- explains six different methods to find cases that interpret and apply relevant statutes;

- has a chapter devoted to reading relevant statutes critically;

- examines in detail the differences between using citators for cases and statutes;

- has three chapters on finding persuasive authorities for common law and statutory issues; and

- provides self-grading online research exercises.

Assessment Tools

This book provides students and professors with multiple assessment tools. Each chapter ends with true-false and multiple-choice questions that test students' understanding of chapter content. These questions are replicated on the book's companion website, Core Knowledge. Students may answer these end-of-chapter questions, as well as more advanced questions, on Core Knowledge and receive immediate feedback, including an explanation of why the answer is correct or incorrect. Professors can generate reports to track students' performance. Professors will then know whether to review a topic in more detail or to move to the next topic. (New books contain an access code to Core Knowledge; students purchasing used books can buy an access code separately.)

Core Knowledge offers yet another assessment tool: interactive research exercises. These online exercises walk students through the research steps on Westlaw and Lexis Advance, giving professors the option to "flip" the classroom. Through many screen captures and tips, students can navigate both research platforms outside of class, allowing students and professors to dig deeper into the material during class. Each research exercise simulates a real-world research experience and contains self-grading questions. For example, in one exercise, students research on Westlaw to determine whether the client could recover emotional distress damages against a neighbor for the death of the client's dog. To answer the client's question, students must complete the research steps, including finding and reviewing secondary sources on Westlaw, using the Key Number System and KeyCite, and performing keyword searches.

In sum, *Legal Research Demystified* helps students learn to find and understand the law with as little frustration as possible. I welcome input from you and your students.

Eric Voigt

February 26, 2019

Acknowledgments

Of course, I did not write this book alone. I am very grateful for the time and support of my colleagues, students, friends, and family. I appreciate the great suggestions from Gigi Panagotacos, a reference librarian at my law school. I somehow convinced her to read almost every chapter; as a result, this book contains much fewer errors. I am also appreciative for the helpful feedback from the following persons: Joan Malmud Rocklin, Christine Coughlin, Sandy Patrick, Donna Spears, Jennifer DeBoer, Stephanie Hauenstein, and Emma Mitchell.

I want to thank all the people at Carolina Academic Press (CAP) who assisted on this project. They include Carol McGeehan, Keith Moore, Ryland Bowman, and Susan Trimble. I appreciate Carol and the CAP acquisition team for believing in my idea and providing me with the opportunity to write a legal research book that differs from existing ones.

Most importantly, I am thankful to my family—especially my beautiful wife, Julie—for their amazing love. Thank you, Julie, for your encouragement and patience. Thank you for caring for our wonderful kids (Annie, Jacob, Emma, and Bennett) while I spent hours away from home to write this book. I did not like hearing our kids ask, "Daddy, do you have to work again?" I love you all very much.

Last, I would like to thank the publishers and authors listed below for granting me permission to reprint their materials.

Figure 3.4: Unpublished Case Retrieved on Westlaw.
Reprinted from Westlaw with the permission of Thomson Reuters.

Figure 3.5: Unpublished Case Retrieved on Lexis Advance.
Reprinted from Lexis Advance with the permission of LexisNexis.

Figure 3.6: Anatomy of Case Retrieved on Westlaw.
Reprinted from Westlaw with the permission of Thomson Reuters.

Figure 3.7: Anatomy of Case Retrieved on Lexis Advance.
Reprinted from Lexis Advance with the permission of LexisNexis.

Figure 4.2: Excerpt of Table of Contents for Title 42 of the U.S.C.A.
Reprinted from Westlaw with the permission of Thomson Reuters.

Figure 4.3: Excerpt from 42 U.S.C.A § 12112 on Westlaw.
Reprinted from Westlaw with the permission of Thomson Reuters.

Figure 4.4: Case Annotations for 42 U.S.C.S. § 12112.
Reprinted from Lexis Advance with the permission of LexisNexis.

Figure 4.6: Excerpt of Table of Contents for Title 47 of Page's Ohio Revised Code Annotated.
Reprinted from Lexis Advance with the permission of LexisNexis.

Figure 4.7: Statutory Text of Section 4705.01 of Page's Ohio Revised Code Annotated.
Reprinted from Lexis Advance with the permission of LexisNexis.

Figure 6.1: Excerpt from American Jurisprudence 2d.
Reprinted from Westlaw with the permission of Thomson Reuters.

Figure 6.2: Excerpt from Georgia Jurisprudence.
Reprinted from Westlaw with the permission of Thomson Reuters.

Figure 6.3: Excerpt from Alabama Pattern Jury Instructions.
Reprinted from Westlaw with the permission of Thomson Reuters and the Alabama Pattern Jury Instructions Committee.

Figure 6.4: Excerpt from Dobbs' The Law of Torts.
Reprinted from Westlaw with the permission of Thomson Reuters.

Figure 6.5: Excerpt from Texas Practice: Contract Law.
Reprinted from Westlaw with the permission of Thomson Reuters.

Figure 6.6: A.L.R. Annotation (81 A.L.R. 5th 563).
Reprinted from Westlaw with the permission of Thomson Reuters.

Figure 6.7: Excerpt from Florida Bar Journal.
Reprinted with the permission of The Florida Bar and Alan Bryce Grossman, Esq.

Figure 6.8: Excerpt from Minnesota Law Review.
Reprinted from Westlaw with the permission of Thomson Reuters and the Minnesota Law Review.

Figure 6.9: Georgia Secondary Sources on Westlaw.
Reprinted from Westlaw with the permission of Thomson Reuters.

Figure 6.10: Georgia Secondary Sources on Lexis.
Reprinted from Lexis Advance with the permission of LexisNexis.

Figure 6.12: Partial List of Subjects Covered in Georgetown's Treatise Finder.
Reprinted from the Georgetown University Law Library website with permission.

Figure 6.13: Partial List of Treatises on Contract Law in Georgetown's Treatise Finder.
Reprinted from the Georgetown University Law Library website with permission.

Figure 6.14: Excerpt of LibGuide by Washington and Lee University School of Law. Washington and Lee University grants a non-exclusive, royalty free license to Carolina Academic Press and Eric P. Voigt to use this image, containing a registered mark for the Washington and Lee University School of Law, only for purposes of this publication in hard copy and digital form. The University provides no further permission for use of said image/mark without express advance written consent.

Figure 6.15: Results from Online Library Catalog. Reprinted from the Mercer Law Library website with permission.

Figure 6.16: Excerpt of Table of Contents of a Practice Manual on Westlaw. Reprinted from Westlaw with the permission of Thomson Reuters.

Figure 7.1: Headnotes with Rules of Law. Reprinted from Westlaw with the permission of Thomson Reuters.

Figure 7.2: Headnote with Application of Rule to Facts. Reprinted from Westlaw with the permission of Thomson Reuters.

Figure 7.3: Print Reporter: Headnotes from Case of Freedom from Religion Foundation. Reprinted from Federal Reporter 3d with the permission of Thomson Reuters.

Figure 7.4: Headnotes for Topic "Constitutional Law" and Key Number 1378. Reprinted from Federal Practice Digest 5th with the permission of Thomson Reuters.

Figure 7.5: Excerpt from Key Number Outline for Topic "Constitutional Law." Reprinted from Federal Practice Digest 5th with the permission of Thomson Reuters.

Figure 7.6: Excerpt from 16A Am. Jur. 2d, Constitutional Law, § 436. Reprinted from American Jurisprudence 2d with the permission of Thomson Reuters.

Figure 7.7: Excerpt from Pocket Part of Volume 103. Reprinted from Federal Practice Digest 5th with the permission of Thomson Reuters.

Figure 7.8: Westlaw: Headnotes from Case of Freedom from Religion Foundation. Reprinted from Westlaw with the permission of Thomson Reuters.

Figure 7.9: Westlaw: Navigating the Key Number System. Reprinted from Westlaw with the permission of Thomson Reuters.

Figure 7.11: Headnotes from Harder v. Edwards, 174 So. 3d 524 (Fla. Dist. Ct. App. 2015). Reprinted from Lexis Advance with the permission of LexisNexis.

Figure 7.12: Topic Summary for False Imprisonment.
Reprinted from Lexis Advance with the permission of LexisNexis.

Figure 7.13: Results Page for "More Like This Headnote" Feature.
Reprinted from Lexis Advance with the permission of LexisNexis.

Figure 8.1: Shepard's Report for Rogers v. Runfola & Assocs., Inc.
Reprinted from Lexis Advance with the permission of LexisNexis.

Figure 8.2: KeyCite Report for Rogers v. Runfola & Assocs., Inc.
Reprinted from Westlaw with the permission of Thomson Reuters.

Figure 8.3: Shepard's (Lexis): Filtering by Jurisdiction and Court.
Reprinted from Lexis Advance with the permission of LexisNexis.

Figure 8.4: KeyCite (Westlaw): Filtering by Jurisdiction and Court.
Reprinted from Westlaw with the permission of Thomson Reuters.

Figure 8.5: Shepard's (Lexis): Filtering by Discussion and Headnotes.
Reprinted from Lexis Advance with the permission of LexisNexis.

Figure 8.6: KeyCite (Westlaw): Filtering by Depth of Treatment and Headnotes.
Reprinted from Westlaw with the permission of Thomson Reuters.

Figure 8.7: Lexis Advance: Headnote 3 of Rogers.
Reprinted from Lexis Advance with the permission of LexisNexis.

Figure 8.8: Westlaw: Headnote 4 of Rogers.
Reprinted from Westlaw with the permission of Thomson Reuters.

Figure 8.9: Shepard's (Lexis): Filtering by Keywords.
Reprinted from Lexis Advance with the permission of LexisNexis.

Figure 8.10: KeyCite (Westlaw): Filtering by Keywords.
Reprinted from Westlaw with the permission of Thomson Reuters.

Figure 8.11: Graph Explaining KeyCite Overruling Risk.
Reprinted with the permission of Thomson Reuters.

Figure 8.14: KeyCite Report for Holsapple v. Smith.
Reprinted from Westlaw with the permission of Thomson Reuters.

Figure 9.2: Drop-Down Menu from Search Box on Westlaw.
Reprinted from Westlaw with the permission of Thomson Reuters.

Figure 9.3: Drop-Down Menu from Search Box on Lexis Advance.
Reprinted from Lexis Advance with the permission of LexisNexis.

Figure 9.4: Natural Language Search on Westlaw.
Reprinted from Westlaw with the permission of Thomson Reuters.

Figure 9.5: Boolean Search on Lexis Advance.
Reprinted from Lexis Advance with the permission of LexisNexis.

Figure 9.6: Segments on Lexis Advance for Cases.
Reprinted from Lexis Advance with the permission of LexisNexis.

Figure 9.7: Fields on Westlaw for Cases.
Reprinted from Westlaw with the permission of Thomson Reuters.

Figure 9.8: Post-Search Filtering Options for Cases on Lexis.
Reprinted from Lexis Advance with the permission of LexisNexis.

Figure 9.9: Post-Search Filtering Options for Cases on Westlaw.
Reprinted from Westlaw with the permission of Thomson Reuters.

Figure 10.1: Excerpt from Section 559 of Restatement (Second) of Torts.
Restatement of the Law Second, Torts copyright © 1977 by The
American Law Institute. Reproduced with permission. All rights re-
served. And reprinted from Westlaw with the permission of Thomson
Reuters.

Figure 10.2: Google Scholar's "Cited By" Feature for Published Cases.
Google and the Google logo are registered trademarks of Google LLC,
used with permission.

Figure 10.3: Google Scholar's "Cited By" Feature for Unpublished Cases.
Google and the Google logo are registered trademarks of Google LLC,
used with permission.

Figure 11.1: Headnote 2 from Hall v. Rental Mgmt., Inc., 913 S.W.2d 293 (Ark.
1996).
Reprinted from Westlaw with the permission of Thomson Reuters.

Figure 11.2: Excerpt of Headnotes for Key Number 1231.
Reprinted from Westlaw with the permission of Thomson Reuters.

Figure 14.1: Fifth Circuit's Pattern Criminal Jury Instructions.
Reprinted from Westlaw with the permission of the Committee on
Pattern Jury Instructions and Thomson Reuters.

Figure 14.2: Excerpt from CLE Materials from State Bar of Texas.
Reprinted from the State Bar of Texas with the permission of Joseph
F. Cleveland, Jr., J. Heath Coffman, and Jared Wilkinson. And
reprinted from Westlaw with the permission of Thomson Reuters.

Figure 14.3: Excerpt from Looseleaf Service by Thomson Reuters.
Reprinted with the permission of Thomson Reuters.

Figure 15.1: Excerpt from General Index for the U.S.C.S.
Reprinted from U.S.C.S. with the permission of LexisNexis.

Figure 15.2: Table of Contents for Chapter 126 of Title 42 of U.S.C.A.
Reprinted from U.S.C.A. with the permission of Thomson Reuters.

Figure 15.4: Cross References from the U.S.C.A.
    Reprinted from U.S.C.A. with the permission of Thomson Reuters.

Figure 15.5: Excerpt of Popular Name Table for the U.S.C.A.
    Reprinted from U.S.C.A. with the permission of Thomson Reuters.

Figure 15.6: Excerpt of Table of Contents on Westlaw.
    Reprinted from Westlaw with the permission of Thomson Reuters.

Figure 15.7: Available Fields for Codes on Westlaw.
    Reprinted from Westlaw with the permission of Thomson Reuters.

Figure 15.8: Available Segments for Codes on Lexis Advance.
    Reprinted from Lexis Advance with the permission of LexisNexis.

Figure 15.9: Excerpt of Table of Content of Official Code of Georgia Annotated on
    Lexis Advance.
    Reprinted from Lexis Advance with the permission of LexisNexis.

Figure 15.10: Searching the Table of Contents of a Code on Lexis Advance.
    Reprinted from Lexis Advance with the permission of LexisNexis.

Figure 15.11: Searching the Table of Contents of a Code on Westlaw.
    Reprinted from Westlaw with the permission of Thomson Reuters.

Figure 16.3: KeyCite Report for Ga. Code Ann. § 40-5-55.
    Reprinted from Westlaw with the permission of Thomson Reuters.

Figure 16.4: Shepard's Preview for Ga. Code Ann. § 40-5-55.
    Reprinted from Lexis Advance with the permission of LexisNexis.

Figure 16.5: Shepard's Report for Ga. Code Ann. § 40-5-55.
    Reprinted from Lexis Advance with the permission of LexisNexis.

Figure 16.6: Shepard's Report for Cal. Rev. & Tax Code § 7094.
    Reprinted from Lexis Advance with the permission of LexisNexis.

Figure 16.7: Editorial Summary on Lexis Advance for Ala. Code § 13A-11-231.
    Reprinted from Lexis Advance with the permission of LexisNexis.

Figure 16.8: Editorial Summary on Westlaw for Ala. Code § 13A-11-231.
    Reprinted from Westlaw with the permission of Thomson Reuters.

Figure 16.9: Source Credits on Westlaw for Ga. Code Ann. § 40-6-320.
    Reprinted from Westlaw with the permission of Thomson Reuters.

Figure 16.10: History Notes on Lexis Advance for 42 U.S.C.S. § 12112.
    Reprinted from Lexis Advance with the permission of LexisNexis.

Figure 16.11: History Notes on Lexis Advance for Ala. Code § 13A-11-231.
    Reprinted from Lexis Advance with the permission of LexisNexis.

Figure 16.12: Credits on Westlaw for Ala. Code § 13A-11-231.
Reprinted from Westlaw with the permission of Thomson Reuters.

Figure 16.13: Depiction on Lexis Advance of Language Added to Ala. Code § 13A-11- 231 by a 2017 Session Law.
Reprinted from Lexis Advance with the permission of LexisNexis.

Figure 16.14: Depiction on Westlaw of Language Added to Ala. Code § 13A11-231 by a 2017 Session Law.
Reprinted from Westlaw with the permission of Thomson Reuters.

Figure 16.15: Statute Compare Feature on Westlaw Edge.
Reprinted from Westlaw with the permission of Thomson Reuters.

Figure 17.1: Excerpt of Table of Contents from Ohio Revised Code Annotated.
Reprinted from Westlaw with the permission of Thomson Reuters.

Figure 18.1: Excerpt from Page 32221 of Volume 83 of the Federal Register.
Reprinted from Westlaw with the permission of Thomson Reuters.

Figure 18.2: Table of Contents of Title 21 of the C.F.R.
Reprinted from Lexis Advance with the permission of LexisNexis.

Figure 19.1: Case Annotations for 42 U.S.C.A. § 12102.
Reprinted from Westlaw with the permission of Thomson Reuters.

Figure 19.2: Notes of Decisions (Westlaw) for Minn. Stat. Ann. § 347.22.
Reprinted from Westlaw with the permission of Thomson Reuters.

Figure 19.3: Case Notes (Lexis) for Minn. Stat. Ann. § 347.22.
Reprinted from Lexis Advance with the permission of LexisNexis.

Figure 19.4: Fastcase's Annotations for Minn. Stat. § 347.22.
Reprinted with the permission of Fastcase, Inc.

Figure 19.5: Filtering Options for a Shepard's Report.
Reprinted from Lexis Advance with the permission of LexisNexis.

Figure 19.6: Filtering Options for a KeyCite Report.
Reprinted from Westlaw with the permission of Thomson Reuters.

Figure 20.5: Excerpt from House Report No. 101-485 (Part II).
Reprinted from Westlaw with the permission of Thomson Reuters.

Figure 20.6: Source Credits on Westlaw for 42 U.S.C.A. § 12112.
Reprinted from Westlaw with the permission of Thomson Reuters.

Figure 20.7: History Notes on Lexis Advance for 42 U.S.C.S. § 12112.
Reprinted from Lexis Advance with the permission of LexisNexis.

Figure 21.1: Tables of Contents for Westlaw's Uniform Laws Annotated Database and Uniform Arbitration Act.
Reprinted from Westlaw with the permission of Thomson Reuters.

Figure 21.2: Citations to Uniform Arbitration Act in Adopting States.
Reprinted from Westlaw with the permission of Thomson Reuters.

Table 1: Binding vs. Nonbinding Cases (Appendix A).
Adapted from the chart in the document "Which Court Is Binding?
(Binding vs. Persuasive Cases)" by The Writing Center at Georgetown
University Law Center.

Part I

The United States Legal System

Introduction:
What You Should Know About Legal Research

This textbook guides you through the world of legal research—the process of finding and understanding the law to answer legal questions. As you practice law, your clients will seek your advice and depend on you to resolve their legal problems. One client may want to recover damages against another motorist who rear-ended the client's automobile. A second client may hire you to draft an agreement for its employees to protect its confidential information. And another client may ask whether the police violated her constitutional rights by searching her home without a search warrant. To answer those and other questions, you must know how to perform legal research.

Researching the law is exciting but challenging. Do not equate performing legal research with searching the internet. A few Google searches will rarely yield an accurate answer to a legal question, just like several searches on WebMD will rarely lead to a correct medical diagnosis. If clients could resolve their own legal issues and save on legal fees using Google or another search engine, they would.

The law does not exist in a neatly gift-wrapped box waiting to be found and opened. Even in the midst of this information age, you cannot jump on the internet and find one law that clearly answers a client's question. Multiple laws usually need to be researched. Additionally, you must consider which sources to use because the same laws can be found in more than one location. A print source in the library might be the best option for one research assignment, but an online database might be a better choice for another project.

To demonstrate this challenging process, suppose a driver of a government automobile was traveling under the posted speed limit but hydroplaned after a rainstorm and unexpected road hazard, damaging your client's vehicle. You would not find a specific law requiring the driver or the government to pay for the client's damages under those exact circumstances. You would need to locate and review multiple laws

1

to predict the client's likelihood of success. You may need to research laws enacted by Congress and your state legislature (known as statutes) and laws located in written decisions by federal and state courts (known as caselaw). You must also confirm that every law you have found has not been changed or repealed.

Although the complexity of legal research can be frustrating, you have a roadmap to navigate through the process—this textbook. This book directs you through the many steps and micro-steps needed to find and understand the relevant laws. It identifies why and when a particular research tool should be used; it illustrates every step and tool with charts, diagrams, and screen captures; and it explains how to maneuver around the inevitable potholes of the research journey. With that knowledge, you will reap the rewards of resolving the legal questions of future clients. In short, this book demystifies the research process for you.

Chapter 1

The Federal and State Systems:
Three Branches of Government

Each United States resident is governed by two primary sets of laws: federal and state. Before embarking on your research journey, you must understand the federal and state legal systems, how they create laws, and the types of laws they create. This chapter reminds you of what you learned in high school civics class and builds on that knowledge.

The United States Constitution organizes the federal government into three separate branches: Legislative, Executive, and Judicial. Each state has adopted its own constitution that creates the structure of government for that state. The states generally model their structure based on the federal system and thus have the same three branches of government and create laws in a similar manner. **Figure 1.1** depicts the similarities and differences between the federal system and a typical state system.

Each federal branch creates laws that regulate conduct throughout the nation, and each state branch creates laws covering the state's geographic sphere. The three branches at the federal and state levels create these types of laws:

- Statutes (Legislative Branch)
- Administrative Regulations (Executive Branch)
- Caselaw (Judicial Branch)

The United States Constitution is the source from which all our laws derive and is the "supreme Law of the Land."[1] Thus, all laws—whether federal or state and regardless of the originating branch—must be consistent with the federal Constitution. Any law conflicting with the United States Constitution is invalid and unenforceable. To illustrate, a state constitution may not strip a defendant of the Fourth Amendment right to be free from unreasonable searches or the Seventh Amendment right to a jury trial, but a state constitution may grant additional protections to defendants.

At the state level, each state's constitution is the supreme law for that state. Every state law—whether a statute, a regulation, or caselaw—must be consistent with the

---

1. U.S. Const. art. VI, cl. 2.

Figure 1.1: Federal System and Typical State System

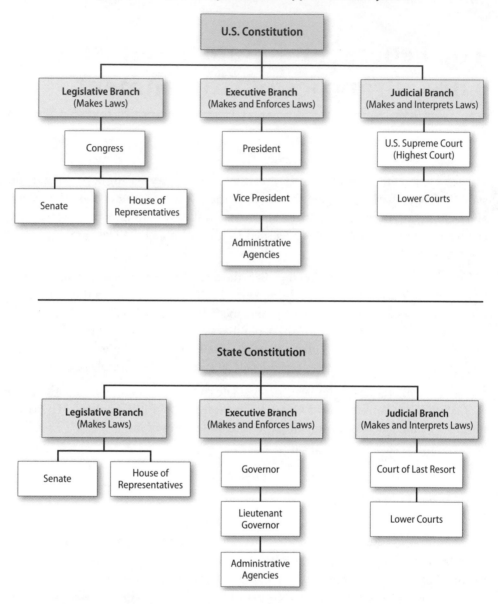

state's constitution to be enforceable. Many state constitutions provide more protections against the government than the federal Constitution.[2] A state law that provides more protections to its citizens, such as greater religious liberties, does not conflict with the United States Constitution or other federal laws and is valid. For example, a state law

---

2. *See, e.g., Odenthal v. Minn. Conference of Seventh-Day Adventists,* 649 N.W.2d 426, 442 (Minn. 2002) ("The Minnesota Constitution affords greater protection to the exercise of religious liberty than does the federal constitution.").

requiring a person to do something that violates the person's religious beliefs may be valid under the federal Constitution but invalid under a state constitution.

In short, at the federal and state levels, four types of laws exist: constitutions, statutes, administrative regulations, and caselaw. The next three sections discuss how the federal and state legislative, executive, and judicial branches create statutes, administrative regulations, and caselaw, respectively.

A. The Legislative Branch: Statutes

Article I, Section I of the federal Constitution creates the legislative branch, vesting power in "a Congress of the United States" that consists of a Senate and House of Representatives. Congress has authority to enact laws called **statutes**. Congress has power to enact statutes for many purposes, including to collect taxes, regulate interstate commerce, and criminally punish conduct crossing state lines.[3]

The life of a proposed statute starts as a bill. Any member of Congress may introduce a bill in the Senate or House of Representatives. The bill is then sent to at least one Congressional committee, which may hold a hearing on the bill. After passing in committee, Congress debates the bill on the floor and then votes on it. If the Senate and House pass the same bill and the President signs it, then the bill becomes a law called a statute. If the President vetoes a bill, however, then the bill does not become law unless both chambers of Congress override the veto by a two-thirds vote.[4]

You probably know about several federal statutes. For instance, the Civil Rights Act of 1964 prohibits an employer from discriminating against an employee based on the person's "race, color, religion, sex, or national origin."[5] The Americans with Disabilities Act of 1990 requires employers to provide their employees with "reasonable accommodations."[6] And the Fair Debt Collection Practices Act regulates the methods in which a creditor may attempt to collect a debt from a consumer, such as prohibiting the use of "any false, deceptive, or misleading representation."[7]

All states (except Nebraska) have a legislative branch with two legislative bodies, and most states, like Congress, call these bodies the senate and house of representatives. State constitutions establish the process by which a legislative bill becomes a statute. The process in almost every state is very similar to the federal process, except that the governor of the state (not the President) signs or vetoes bills. Thus, once you know the federal process, you can understand the process for your state.

---

3. *See* U.S. Const., art. I, § 8.
4. U.S. Const. art. I, § 7, cl. 2.
5. 42 U.S.C.A. § 2000e-2(a) (Westlaw through Pub. L. No. 115-253).
6. *Id.* § 12112(a), (b)(5)(A).
7. 15 U.S.C.A. § 1692e.

For assistance, you should see whether a law library has created an online guide—usually called a LibGuide—that describes the legislative process for your state.

Any power not granted to Congress is expressly "reserved" to the states or the people.[8] Thus, state statutes regulate many actions. State statutes govern all types of conduct and disputes, including crimes (robbery), commercial matters (trade secrets), and consumer disputes (defective products).

State and federal statutes are not mutually exclusive. They may co-exist and regulate the same conduct, as long as compliance with both statutes is possible and as long as both statutes do not require different conduct from a person. For example, a federal statute that prohibits kidnapping a person from one state to another for a ransom[9] does not conflict with a state statute that prohibits kidnapping with an intent to inflict harm.[10] Nonetheless, a conflict with federal law would exist if a state statute prohibited all employers from providing "reasonable accommodations" to employees with disabilities. That statute would be invalid because the Americans with Disabilities Act requires the opposite conduct: covered employers *must* provide "reasonable accommodations to … an otherwise qualified individual with a disability."[11]

This book discusses statutes and how they are enacted in more detail in Chapters 4 and 15.

B. The Executive Branch: Regulations

Article II, Section I of the United States Constitution creates the executive branch, vesting power in the "President of the United States of America" and the Vice President.[12] The executive branch also includes the President's inner advising circle called the "Cabinet." The Cabinet members lead their respective departments: the Attorney General heads the Department of Justice, the Secretary of Education heads that department, and the Secretary of Homeland Security heads that department.

The executive branch also includes federal administrative agencies, which Congress creates. The federal government has hundreds of agencies at its disposal. Some familiar ones include the Food and Drug Administration (FDA), the Environmental Protection Agency (EPA), and the Internal Revenue Service (IRS). Agencies are experts in their respective fields, and courts often defer to their expertise on specific subjects.

---

8. *See* U.S. Const. amend. X.

9. 18 U.S.C.A. § 1201.

10. *Cf.* Fla. Stat. Ann. § 787.01 (West, Westlaw through 2017 First Regular Session and Special "A" Session of the 25th Legislature).

11. *See* 42 U.S.C.A. § 12112(b)(5)(A).

12. U.S. Const. art. II, § 1, cl. 1.

You already know that the executive branch executes or enforces the statutes enacted by Congress, but it might surprise you that this branch also creates laws called **regulations** and **rules** through administrative agencies.[13] Any agency's authority to adopt regulations, however, is limited. Before an enforceable regulation can be adopted, Congress must enact a statute that authorizes the agency to adopt regulations and that delegates rulemaking authority to the agency (the "authorizing statute"). Each regulation must comply with the authorizing statute; if not, the regulation is invalid and unenforceable. To illustrate, the IRS has no authority to adopt regulations governing clean water, and any such regulation would be unenforceable. Congress may, at any time, invalidate any existing regulation or eliminate an agency's authority to adopt regulations.

Because of their expertise, agencies promulgate regulations that are detailed and specific. Here is an example that will help you understand the relationship between an authorizing statute and a regulation. The Civil Rights Acts of 1964 makes it unlawful for an employer to discriminate on the basis of an employee's "race, color, religion, sex, or national origin."[14] The Act authorizes the Equal Employment Opportunity Commission (EEOC) to enforce the statute and to adopt regulations.[15] The Act provides a broad definition of "religion,"[16] but the EEOC has adopted a regulation to fill in the gaps left by Congress. Under the EEOC regulation, a religious practice includes "moral or ethical beliefs as to what is right and wrong which are sincerely held with the strength of traditional religious views," but a belief does not need to be accepted by a "religious group" for the belief to be covered by the Act.[17]

The structure of the executive branch at the state level is similar to its federal counterpart. For each state, the head of the executive branch is the state's governor who, like the President, must faithfully enforce the laws. Additionally, each governor heads the state's many administrative agencies. Common state agencies include the department of motor vehicles, department of education, and department of labor. State agencies, like their federal counterparts, create laws called **rules** or **regulations** that implement statutes enacted by the state legislature. These state regulations, like federal ones, are limited by their authorizing statute. If an agency adopts a regulation that conflicts with the authorizing statute, it is unenforceable.

The chief lawyer in each state is called the attorney general. An attorney general is tasked with fighting crime, protecting consumers, and representing the state and

---

13. Another source of law is an "executive order." The President of the United States may issue executive orders "to direct or instruct the actions of executive agencies or government officials, or to set policies for the executive branch to follow." *Executive Order, Black's Law Dictionary* (10th ed. 2014). One executive order can have a profound impact in the United States, such as President Harry S. Truman's order in 1948 that desegregated the military.

14. 42 U.S.C.A. §2000e-2(a).

15. *Id.* §§2000e-4, 2000e-5.

16. *Id.* §2000e(j).

17. 29 C.F.R. §1605.1 (2018).

its agencies in court. An attorney general also drafts advisory opinions on the meaning of statutes or regulations, but the opinions do not constitute law.

This book discusses federal agencies and the rulemaking process in much greater detail in Chapter 18.

C. The Judicial Branch: Caselaw

Article III, Section I of the United States Constitution creates the judicial branch, vesting power in one Supreme Court and "such inferior Courts as the Congress may from time to time ordain and establish." For each state, the state's constitution establishes the judicial branch and the court system. Courts in the federal and state judicial systems create laws called **caselaw** when they decide legal issues and write judicial opinions. Courts make caselaw in two primary ways.[18]

First, caselaw consists of the law created when courts interpret and apply constitutions, statutes, or administrative regulations. A legislature may enact a statute without defining a key term or with terms having an ambiguous application to a particular factual situation. For example, assume that a state statute prohibits "vehicles" from entering public parks but fails to define "vehicles." It would be unclear whether the term "vehicles" includes only motorized objects (automobiles) and excludes all non-motorized objects (bicycles). When a court interprets the term "vehicles," its decision adds to the body of law in that state.

Second, caselaw consists of the common law, which is a body of law created in the absence of a statute, administrative regulation, or other enacted law. As part of the common law, a court may create an entirely new law or create law by interpreting existing law and applying it to a new set of facts. For instance, suppose a tenant was injured in the common areas of an apartment building when a third party entered the building and assaulted her, and the tenant wants to recover damages from the landlord. Without a federal or state statute, the court must decide whether the state should hold landlords liable for the criminal acts of third parties. If the court recognizes that claim against landlords, the court would have made a new law that becomes part of the common law and that would apply to future tenants and landlords. Now, suppose one year later, another court in the same state must decide whether a landlord is liable to a tenant who is attacked in the common areas after the landlord's security cameras failed. The court would take the existing law (landlords can be liable for the criminal acts of third parties) and apply it to the new facts involving a broken camera system. The resulting decision would create law that would become part of the common law.

All caselaw is not created equally. Decisions from the United States Supreme Court on a federal issue, for instance, are more authoritative than decisions from state courts.

---

18. These two categories of caselaw are derived from David S. Romantz & Kathleen Elliott Vinson, *Legal Analysis: The Fundamental Skill* 6–7 (2d ed. 2009).

Figure 1.2: Structure of Federal Court System

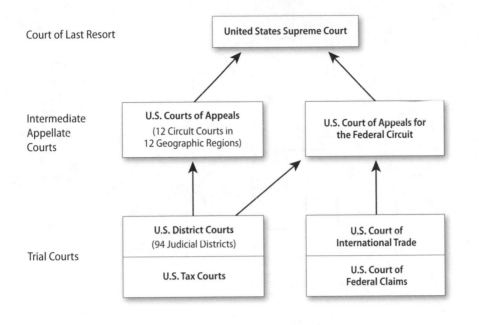

You must understand the hierarchical structure of the courts in the federal and state systems to know what is the best authority to answer your client's legal questions.

1. Structure of the Federal Court System

The United States Constitution authorizes Congress to create lower courts. Congress has established two distinct levels of courts below the U.S. Supreme Court: trial and intermediate appellate courts. **Figure 1.2** shows the structure of the federal court system.

The federal trial courts are the lowest court in the federal system and are called United States District Courts. This court is where most lawsuits in the federal system begin, whether civil or criminal. These trial courts hear a range of disputes from claims for violations of the United States Constitution, to violations of federal statutes, to violations of state law. Here, the parties present evidence through witnesses, documents (photographs), and physical evidence (a weapon); a judge or jury weighs the evidence and decides for or against the plaintiff.

The United States has 94 federal district courts located in 94 judicial districts. Each state has at least one district court located in one judicial district, but heavily-populated states like Florida and Texas have three or four district courts.

The courts immediately above the district courts are called the United States Courts of Appeals and are commonly referred to as United States Circuit Courts. A litigant

Figure 1.3: Geographic Regions for United States Courts of Appeals

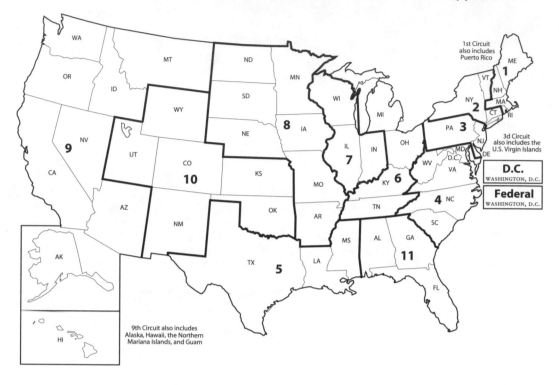

who is unhappy with a decision of a district court (a trial court) may appeal to a federal circuit court, which must hear the appeal. Unlike district courts, circuit courts do not convene juries, hold trials, or hear testimony from witnesses. For most appeals, three-judge panels are assigned to review a district court's procedures and decisions to determine whether the trial court or jury complied with the law.

The federal circuit courts (except one) are arranged based on geography. The 94 judicial districts containing the 94 district courts are organized into 12 geographic regions; each region has one circuit court (eleven numbered ones and the District of Columbia Circuit). A circuit court hears appeals from the district courts located within its geographic boundaries and from decisions by federal agencies. For instance, a case originating from a district court located in Florida must be appealed to the United States Court of Appeals for the Eleventh Circuit, which covers Alabama, Georgia, and Florida.[19] **Figure 1.3** shows the geographic boundaries of the twelve federal circuit courts.

---

19. On October 1, 1981, the United States Court of Appeals for the Fifth Circuit was divided into two circuits: the Eleventh Circuit and the new Fifth Circuit. *Bonner v. City of Prichard*, 661 F.2d 1206, 1207 (11th Cir. 1981). All decisions from the former Fifth Circuit that were issued on or before September 30, 1981, are "binding as precedent in the Eleventh Circuit," as well as the district courts located in the circuit. *Id.*

Figure 1.4: Structure of Typical State Court System

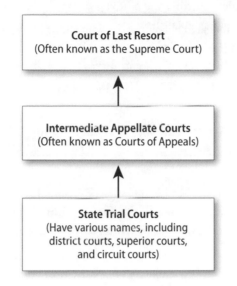

The one circuit court that is not limited by geography is called the Court of Appeals for the Federal Circuit. It has jurisdiction to hear cases on specific subjects, including patents, trademarks, and money damages against the United States government.

The highest court in the federal system is the United States Supreme Court. If you lose at the Supreme Court—the court of last resort on federal laws—you have no other court to hear your grievance. Nine justices sit on the Court: one Chief Justice and eight Associate Justices, all of whom are nominated by the President and confirmed by the Senate.

Although a few types of cases can originate at the Supreme Court (*e.g.*, a dispute between the United States and State of Florida), the Court usually hears cases on appeal from a lower court, such as the Sixth Circuit Court of Appeals or the supreme court of a state. The Court is not required to hear most appeals; each year, the Court declines to review over 7,000 cases that are appealed from lower courts. It grants and hears oral arguments in only about eighty cases.

2. Structure of State Court Systems

State courts are organized in a similar manner as the federal system and usually have three levels of courts (see **Figure 1.4**).

The courts at the lowest level are the trial courts and are where most civil and criminal lawsuits begin. The trial courts are divided into courts of limited and general jurisdiction. Courts of limited jurisdiction, such as small claims court, have authority to decide only certain types of disputes (*e.g.*, probate or family matters) or to award a maximum amount of damages (usually between $3,000 to $10,000). Courts of gen-

> ### Understanding the Court System in Your State
>
> Before starting a legal research assignment, you should review the court structure in your jurisdiction (*i.e.*, your state). You probably could locate a concise guide online by entering these terms into an internet search engine:
>
> [name of your jurisdiction] court system structure
>
> Scan the list of results and look for a link that will take you to a reliable site, such as the website of a law school or the state's administrative office of courts.

eral jurisdiction, however, decide a wide range of criminal and civil disputes, including murder, robbery, personal injuries, and breach of contract. Depending on the state, a trial court may be called a district court, circuit court, court of common pleas, or superior court.

In most states, the court immediately above the trial court is the intermediate appellate court. A party dissatisfied with a trial court's decision has a legal right to appeal to the intermediate appellate court. In some states, parties must appeal directly to the state's highest court. (Sparsely-populated states like Montana, where the animals outnumber the people, do not have intermediate appellate courts.) Like their federal counterpart, state appellate courts resolve questions of law and do not hold trials or hear testimony from witnesses.

The highest court in most states is called the supreme court and is the final decision-maker on the meaning of the state constitution, state statutes, and other state laws. In states having an intermediate appellate court, the highest court usually has discretion to hear an appeal. Thus, the intermediate appellate court is often, as a practical matter, the court of last resort for parties.

D. Primary Authority vs. Secondary Authority

Legal authority is divided into two broad categories: **primary authorities** and **secondary authorities**. Each type is discussed next.

The first category of legal authority is "primary authority." This authority is the law because it "issues directly from a law-making body."[20] Thus, any law created by the legislative, executive, or judicial branch is primary authority. Sources of primary authority include constitutions, statutes, administrative regulations, and caselaw.

---

20. *Primary Authority*, *Black's Law Dictionary* (10th ed. 2014).

The second category of legal authority is "secondary authority," which is not issued from a law-making body. It is authority that explains and summarizes the law "but does not itself establish it."[21] Secondary authorities are written by attorneys and law professors and include legal encyclopedias, treatises, and legal articles. While they are very helpful to you as a researcher, you usually will not cite secondary authority in documents filed with a court or in legal memoranda.[22]

An analogy from literature will help to explain the difference between primary and secondary authority. Pretend that Shakespeare's *Macbeth* is "primary authority" and that a study guide such as *CliffsNotes* or *SparkNotes* is "secondary authority." The study guide explains the meaning of *Macbeth* (and we all need help deciphering it), but it is not the actual play. Likewise, a legal secondary authority explains the law, but it is not the actual law.

Here is a legal example to further help you distinguish between primary and secondary authority. Assume that you found the following Florida statute prohibiting reckless driving: "Any person who drives any vehicle in willful or wanton disregard for the safety of persons or property is guilty of reckless driving."[23] You then found a Florida legal encyclopedia that explains "wanton" as acting with a "conscious and intentional indifference to consequences and with knowledge that damage is likely to be done to persons or property."[24] The statute is primary authority and is the law (enacted by the Florida legislature). But the encyclopedia is a secondary source explaining the law; it is not the actual law.

E. Summary of Key Points

The federal and state legal systems are organized into three branches, and each branch creates different types of laws. The legislative branch creates laws called **statutes**. Congress enacts statutes regulating conduct throughout the nation, and state legislatures enact laws covering the state's geographic sphere. Additionally, the executive branch, through administrative agencies, adopts laws called **rules** and **regulations**. Last, the judicial branch makes **caselaw**. This court-made law includes law created when courts interpret enacted laws (*e.g.*, statutes and regulations) and when courts resolve legal disputes governed by the common law.

Although the structure of most state court systems is similar to the federal court system, differences do exist. **Figure 1.5** summarizes key similarities and differences between federal and state courts.

---

21. *Secondary Authority*, *Black's Law Dictionary* (10th ed. 2014).
22. Chapter 6 discusses secondary sources in detail.
23. Fla. Stat. Ann. § 316.192(1)(a).
24. 4A *Fla. Jur. 2d Automobiles and Other Vehicles* § 548 (2d ed. 2017).

Figure 1.5: Comparisons Between Federal and State Courts

	Federal Courts	State Courts
Subject Matter Jurisdiction[1]	U.S. Constitution	U.S. Constitution (some provisions)
	Federal statutes and regulations	Federal statutes and regulations (some exceptions)[2]
	State constitution (limited)[3]	State constitution
	State statutes and regulations (limited)	State statutes and regulations
	State common law (limited)	State common law
Trial Courts	U.S. District Courts	Various names, including • circuit courts • courts of common pleas • district courts • superior courts
Intermediate Appellate Courts	U.S. Courts of Appeals (also known as U.S. Circuit Courts)	Various names, including • courts of appeals • court of civil appeals • court of criminal appeals • superior courts
	Hear appeals from lower courts	Hear appeals from lower courts
Courts of Last Resort (Highest Courts)	U.S. Supreme Court	Various names, including • supreme court (most states) • court of appeals (*e.g.*, New York)
	Not required to hear appeals	Not required to hear appeals (most states)

[1] When a court has subject matter jurisdiction over a legal issue, it has a legal right or authority to resolve the issue.

[2] Federal courts have exclusive jurisdiction over some federal matters, such as copyright and military issues.

[3] Federal courts have limited subject matter jurisdiction over state laws. They may resolve only those legal issues authorized by the United States Constitution or federal statutes.

F. Review Questions on Three Branches of Government

At this point, you should understand the three branches of government and the laws they create. To test your comprehension, answer the true-false and multiple-choice questions on this book's companion website, Core Knowledge. It will identify the correct answers and provide clear explanations for each question. The same questions are reproduced below.

1. Congress and state legislatures enacted laws called statutes.

    a. True

    b. False

2. Administrative agencies create laws called statutes.

    a. True

    b. False

3. Administrative agencies create laws called regulations.

    a. True

    b. False

4. Courts create laws called caselaw.

    a. True

    b. False

5. A United States Court of Appeals is also referred to as a United States Circuit Court.

    a. True
    b. False

6. Primary authority includes caselaw, statutes, and administrative regulations.

    a. True

    b. False

7. Secondary authority includes legal encyclopedias, legal articles, and treatises.

    a. True

    b. False

8. Identify the name of the highest court in most states.

    a. Supreme court

    b. Court of appeals

    c. Superior court

    d. District court

9. The United States Court of Appeals for the Eleventh Circuit covers which states?

    a. Alabama and Georgia

    b. Alabama, Georgia, and Florida

    c. Alabama, Georgia, Florida, and Louisiana

    d. None of the above

10. A state court has subject matter jurisdiction and the legal right to resolve disputes involving claims based on which laws?

    a. Federal statutes (most)

    b. State statutes

    c. Common law

    d. All of the above

Chapter 2

Binding and Nonbinding Legal Authorities

All legal authority, whether primary or secondary, does not have the same persuasive value. This fact should not surprise you. If you were reviewing articles about an automobile that you planned to purchase, you would discount articles drafted by authors with no expertise in the automotive industry and give more weight to articles by mechanics and independent organizations like Consumer Reports. Similarly, courts do not treat all legal authorities the same. A well-reasoned judicial decision, for instance, would be highly persuasive on a deciding court.

Legal authority is divided into two camps: binding and nonbinding. Understanding this distinction is vital in deciding which authority to rely on when answering a client's legal question.

Binding authority, sometimes called "mandatory authority," falls within the first camp. A decision-maker, which is often a court, is required to follow and apply binding authority. For instance, an Ohio statute is mandatory in Ohio, and an Ohio court faced with that law must apply the language of the statute to the parties before it. Even if the application of the statute would result in an unfair outcome, the court must enforce the statute as written.

Nonbinding authority, commonly called "persuasive authority," falls within the second camp of legal authority. For this type of authority, a court *may* follow and rely on it in reaching a decision, but the court is not *required* to do so. To illustrate, for a common law claim of negligence, a Georgia court may rely on a Texas case as persuasive authority or may wholesale reject the out-of-state case. The likelihood that the Georgia court would be persuaded to follow the Texas case depends on several factors, including its reasoning and the level of court issuing the opinion.

Primary authority, such as a statute or caselaw, may fall within the binding or nonbinding camp. Secondary authority—unlike primary authority—is never binding on a deciding court. Thus, a court is never required to follow statements made in legal encyclopedias, treatises, legal articles, or other secondary materials. The rationale is simple: secondary authority is not the actual law.

A. Constitutions, Statutes, and Regulations

As explained in Chapter 1, the United States Constitution is the highest authority in our nation. Thus, all laws—whether federal or state and regardless of the originating branch—must comply with the federal Constitution. Similarly, each state's constitution is the highest authority in that state. Any state law, such as a statute, that conflicts with the state's constitution is invalid and unenforceable.

The primary authorities immediately below constitutions are statutes and administrative regulations. Federal statutes and regulations apply throughout our nation and bind all federal and all state courts. State statutes and regulations, however, apply only within their geographic jurisdiction (with rare exceptions). Statutes enacted by the Texas Legislature bind Texas courts but not California ones. To further illustrate, residents of Texas must comply with Texas statutes but not California statutes.

Because federal and state statutes are mandatory authorities, courts cannot deviate from a statute or re-write it. For instance, suppose a court must construe the following Florida statute: "Any person who drives any vehicle in willful or wanton disregard for the safety of persons or property is guilty of reckless driving."[1] Even if the better policy would be to limit the reach of the statute to defendants who drive with an "intent to cause serious bodily injury to others," the court must enforce the statute as written and cannot add that phrase to the statute.

Additionally, Congress or a state legislature may enact statutes that replace or modify the common law or that supersede a court's prior interpretation of a statute. In fact, if a legislature disagrees with a court's decision, the legislature may enact a new statute or amend an existing one. The newly-enacted statute, and not the original court decision, would bind future courts and parties. To illustrate, suppose a state's court of last resort concluded that a driver of an automobile who is partially at fault cannot recover damages on a common law negligence claim, but one year later the state legislature enacted a statute allowing at-fault drivers to recover damages. Future courts must follow the statute, which would replace the prior common law rule.

B. Cases from Federal and State Courts

This section discusses the concepts of "controlling jurisdiction" and "controlling law," explains general principles on weight of authority for judicial decisions (caselaw), and discusses when one court must follow the decisions of other courts in resolving a legal dispute.

---

1. Fla. Stat. Ann. § 316.192(1)(a) (West, Westlaw through 2017 First Regular Session and Special "A" Session of the 25th Legislature).

1. Controlling Jurisdiction vs. Controlling Law

The court systems in the United States are divided into one federal jurisdiction and fifty state jurisdictions where each state is considered a different jurisdiction.[2] Attorneys and professors often use the term "jurisdiction" interchangeably with "state." So if your client has brought a claim in a court located in Florida, your supervisor may refer to Florida as the jurisdiction.

When researching a legal issue, your professors and supervisors may ask you to find judicial decisions from courts in the "controlling jurisdiction" or "governing jurisdiction." These phrases have different meanings in different contexts. Sometimes, your professor or boss intends to limit your research to only *binding* decisions from courts in your state. Sometimes, the term "controlling jurisdiction" means all decisions, whether binding or nonbinding, from all state courts located in the same state as the deciding court. Other times, the term is used even more broadly to refer to decisions, whether binding or nonbinding, from state and federal courts located in the same state as the deciding court.[3] For example, if your client brought a claim in a Florida trial court, the controlling jurisdiction may include all Florida state courts, all federal district courts located in Florida, and the United States Court of Appeals for the Eleventh Circuit.

What is the controlling *jurisdiction* is a different question than what is the controlling *law*. The "controlling law" is the law that the deciding court must apply to the legal dispute. The controlling law and the jurisdiction often coincide but may be different. If a Florida court is interpreting a Florida statute, Florida would be the jurisdiction and the controlling law. Now, assume that a Florida court is addressing a federal statute. Although Florida would still be the jurisdiction, the federal statute would be the controlling law.

Do not think you have to read your professor's or supervisor's mind to determine the intended meaning of the term "controlling jurisdiction" or "governing jurisdiction"; when in doubt, simply ask.

2. Doctrine of *Stare Decisis*

The determination of whether cases from a jurisdiction or particular court is binding or nonbinding is complicated and based on the doctrine of *stare decisis*, which means "let the decision stand." Under *stare decisis*, courts generally follow prior judicial decisions based on the maxim of justice that similar cases ought to be similarly

---

2. The District of Columbia is a separate jurisdiction with its own court system. The trial court is the Superior Court of the District of Columbia, and the sole appellate court is the District of Columbia Court of Appeals.

3. *Cf. Douglass v. Delta Air Lines, Inc.*, 897 F.2d 1336, 1344 (5th Cir. 1990) (interpreting the term "controlling jurisdiction" in ethical rules and admonishing attorney for failing to cite a decision from a Texas federal district court on Texas state law).

decided. This respect for the past also promotes stability in the law. As a result, parties and attorneys can predict whether conduct is lawful or unlawful.

The doctrine of *stare decisis* applies only to a federal or state court's *holding*. A holding is the part of a judicial opinion necessary to resolve the legal questions before the court.[4] Courts are not bound to follow dictum. Dictum is the part of a judicial opinion "that is not essential to the decision."[5]

Federal courts are the final decision-makers on federal issues. Based on *stare decisis*, a federal court must follow the decisions of higher courts in the United States judicial system when faced with similar legal issues and facts. For example, a decision by a federal circuit court on federal law binds all federal district courts (lower trial courts) within the geographic region of the circuit. Higher courts, however, are not bound by rulings of lower courts.

State courts have the final say on state issues. A decision by a state's highest court on state law binds lower courts in that jurisdiction, including the intermediate appellate courts and the trial courts. And in many states, rulings from a state's intermediate appellate court bind all trial courts in that state. Of course, exceptions exist. Some states like Ohio divide their intermediate appellate courts into geographic districts (similar to federal circuit courts) in which each appellate district encompasses one or more counties in the state. For these states, the trial courts must follow only the decisions from the particular appellate court that encompasses the trial court's location (with few exceptions). Last, state courts from different jurisdictions, such as California and Texas, are never bound by the other's decisions but may treat an out-of-state decision as persuasive authority.

You are probably wondering about weight of authority for courts at the same level (just nod). Courts at the same level are sometimes, but not always, bound by their decisions. Trial courts bind the parties involved but do not bind other trial courts, even when the prior decision was from the same trial court. To illustrate, the District Court for the Southern District of Florida is not bound by its earlier rulings. At the appellate level, however, a three-judge panel from a federal circuit court must follow decisions by other panels from the same circuit (recall each circuit court has multiple panels deciding cases), but the entire court (*en banc*) can overrule a prior panel decision. And although the U.S. Supreme Court usually follows its prior decisions, as a court of last resort, it may change its previous ruling. As previously stated, the weight of authority for caselaw can be complicated!

3. Two-Step Approach to Binding Caselaw

To know whether caselaw from a particular court is binding, you need to follow a two-step approach. First, you must determine the controlling law. Your client's legal issues may be governed by only federal law, only state law, or both federal and state

---

4. *See Holding, Black's Law Dictionary* (10th ed. 2014).
5. *Judicial Dictum, Black's Law Dictionary* (10th ed. 2014).

law. Second, you must determine what court will decide your issues. For the same controlling law, the binding authority will be different if your client is before a trial court versus a court of last resort or before a federal court versus a state court.

Table 1 (Binding vs. Nonbinding Cases) in Appendix A provides further guidance on the two-step approach and identifies the specific courts that are either binding or merely persuasive for federal and state law issues. As you read the following examples on binding and persuasive authority, review **Table 1**, starting with the far left column. This table has been reproduced in Section C below.

Here is a simple example to explain the two-step approach. Assume your client brought a claim under the Family and Medical Leave Act in the District Court for the Eastern District of Texas, a federal trial court located within the Fifth Circuit Court of Appeals. For that federal statute, your District Court would be bound by decisions from the Fifth Circuit and U.S. Supreme Court (cell G.2 in **Table 1**). Your District Court would not be bound by a decision from any other circuit courts, but those rulings would probably be highly persuasive (cell G.3 in **Table 1**). And your District Court would not be required to follow its prior rulings or those from other federal district courts, even if the prior decisions directly addressed the same federal statute.

Now, suppose your client injured a plaintiff's domesticated bear during a wrestling match, and the plaintiff seeks damages in state court based on an Oklahoma statute. Because you are before an Oklahoma trial court on a state law, the rulings from the intermediate appellate court (Court of Civil Appeals) and from the Supreme Court of Oklahoma would bind your court (cell A.2 in **Table 1**). If, however, you were before the Oklahoma Supreme Court on this same state issue, the intermediate appellate court (a lower court) would not bind your court (cell C.3 in **Table 1**). Under either scenario listed in this paragraph, no federal court ruling would be binding (cells A.2 and C.2 in **Table 1**) but would merely be persuasive authority (cells A.3 and C.3 in **Table 1**). Federal courts are not the final-decision makers on matters of state law.

Figure 2.1 depicts the hierarchy of the Oklahoma court system and federal system as they apply to the bear-wrestling statute.

Here is a more complicated example on the two-step process involving a federal court deciding state law. Say your client is litigating the same state statute on bear wrestling in the District Court for the Western District of Oklahoma, a federal trial court (cell D.1 of **Table 1**). (A federal court has jurisdiction to resolve a state issue when, among other reasons, the plaintiff and defendant are citizens of different states and the amount in controversy exceeds $75,000.) Because a state's court of last resort has the final say on state law, the decisions by the Supreme Court of Oklahoma would bind your District Court (cell D.2 of **Table 1**). Indeed, a question on the meaning of the bear-wrestling statute could be certified to the Supreme Court of Oklahoma. In short, if a conflict exists between a state's highest court and any federal court on state law, the state court ruling prevails. See **Figure 2.1**.

Figure 2.1: Oklahoma and Federal Court Systems

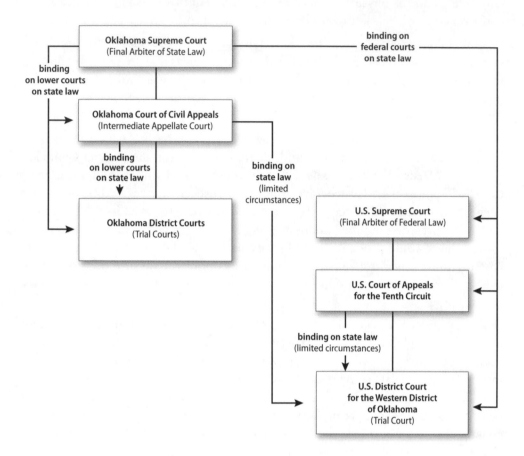

You might wonder what authority is binding if the sole court decision directly on point for your state issue is from the state's intermediate appellate court. In this situation, a federal district court must take the necessary steps to predict how the state's highest court—the final arbiter of state law—would rule.[6] Continuing with the bear wrestling statute, in the absence of a decision by the Supreme Court of Oklahoma, your District Court should follow a ruling by the Oklahoma intermediate appellate court, unless there is "convincing evidence that the highest court would decide otherwise."[7] So if your District Court predicts that the Supreme Court of Oklahoma (state's highest court) would disagree with the Oklahoma intermediate appellate court

---

6. *Santalucia v. Sebright Transp., Inc.*, 232 F.3d 293, 297 (2d Cir. 2000) (explaining that a federal court must "carefully predict how the state's highest court" would decide the state issue).

7. *See Black & Veatch Corp. v. Aspen Ins. (UK) Ltd.*, 882 F.3d 952, 967 (10th Cir. 2018). *Accord ADT Sec. Servs., Inc. v. Lisle-Woodridge Fire Prot. Dist.*, 672 F.3d 492, 498 (7th Cir. 2012) ("In the

decision, your District Court could disregard the appellate court decision.[8] See **Figure 2.1**.

But what decision a federal district court must follow becomes even murkier when the only state ruling on state law is the state's intermediate appellate court and that state ruling conflicts with a decision by a federal circuit court encompassing the district court. For the bear wrestling statute, if the Oklahoma intermediate court and the United States Court of Appeals for the Tenth Circuit (which encompasses Oklahoma) have issued conflicting rulings, the Tenth Circuit decision would bind your District Court.[9] On the other hand, some federal courts resolve the conflicting rulings by following, at least in theory, the decision of the state's intermediate appellate court (not the federal circuit court).[10] As a practical matter, federal district courts would likely rely on a decision by the federal circuit court encompassing it because the federal court, not the state's intermediate appellate court, has authority to reverse the district court's decision, even on a state law issue.

In short, when a state court interprets federal law or when a federal court construes state law, what authority is binding or persuasive is complicated, creating disagreement among the courts (and professors). In those circumstances, do not blindly rely on **Table 1** in Appendix A. Instead, use that table as a starting point, and then research cases from the courts in your jurisdiction to determine whether your court follows or deviates from the principles set forth in **Table 1**.

---

absence of guiding decisions by the state's highest court, we consult and follow the decisions of intermediate appellate courts unless there is a convincing reason to predict the state's highest court would disagree."); *Davis v. Nat'l Med. Enters., Inc.*, 253 F.3d 1314, 1319 (11th Cir. 2001) ("In applying state law, we adhere to decisions of the state's intermediate appellate courts absent some persuasive indication that the state's highest court would decide the issue otherwise.").

8. *See Greystone Constr., Inc. v. Nat'l Fire & Marine Ins. Co.*, 661 F.3d 1272, 1281 (10th Cir. 2011) (disregarding a ruling by the Colorado intermediate appellate court because the federal court predicted that the Supreme Court of Colorado would decide the issue differently).

9. *See Wankier v. Crown Equip. Corp.*, 353 F.3d 862, 866 (10th Cir. 2003) ("[W]hen a panel of this Court has rendered a decision interpreting state law, that interpretation is binding on district courts in this circuit, and on subsequent panels of this Court, unless an intervening decision of the state's highest court has resolved the issue."). *Accord Luna v. United States*, 454 F.3d 631, 636 (7th Cir. 2006) ("If a district court concludes that the intermediate state appellate courts have correctly answered a question this court botched, it should report [its] conclusions while applying the existing law of the circuit.") (internal quotation marks omitted; alteration in original).

10. *Kantor v. Hiko Energy, LLC*, 100 F. Supp. 3d 421, 427 (E.D. Pa. 2015) ("[W]hen the Pennsylvania intermediate appellate courts have ruled to the contrary [of the Third Circuit] and their decisions have not been overruled by the state's highest court, we are no longer compelled to follow the Third Circuit's prediction.").

C. Summary of Key Points

A particular primary authority could be binding (mandatory) authority or non-binding (persuasive) authority. Although enacted laws like statutes are generally referred to as binding authorities, whether a specific statute is mandatory authority depends on the circumstances. For example, for crimes committed in Alabama by Alabama residents, mandatory authorities include Alabama criminal statutes but exclude criminal statutes from other states. To further illustrate, if a client-landlord wants to evict a tenant in Ohio, the Ohio landlord-tenant statute would bind the parties, but Ohio criminal statutes would be irrelevant.

Determining which judicial decisions are binding can be more difficult. State courts resolving a state law issue must follow the decisions of higher courts in the same jurisdiction. Federal courts resolving a federal issue must follow the opinions of higher federal courts. For instance, decisions from the Fourth Circuit Court of Appeals, which covers North Carolina, bind all federal district courts located in North Carolina.

To identify binding cases, you should follow this two-step approach: (1) determine whether federal or state law applies; and (2) consider what court (*e.g.*, federal or state) and what level of court (*e.g.*, trial or appellate court) will decide the legal issue. Use **Table 1** (Binding vs. Nonbinding Cases) in Appendix A as a guide. It is also set forth below.

Table 1: Binding vs. Nonbinding Cases

	1	2	3
	(1) State or Federal Issue (2) State or Federal Court	**Binding (Mandatory) Cases**	**Nonbinding (Persuasive) Cases**
A	**State issue in state trial court**	• That state's highest court • That state's intermediate appellate courts	• U.S. Supreme Court • Federal circuit courts • Federal district courts • That state's trial courts
B	**State issue in state intermediate appellate court**	• That state's highest court • That state's intermediate appellate courts	• U.S. Supreme Court • Federal circuit courts • Federal district courts • That state's trial courts
C	**State issue in state's highest court**	• That state's highest court	• U.S. Supreme Court • Federal circuit courts • Federal district courts • That state's intermediate appellate courts • That state's trial courts

	1	2	3
	(1) State or Federal Issue (2) State or Federal Court	Binding (Mandatory) Cases	Nonbinding (Persuasive) Cases
D	State issue in federal district court	• That state's highest court • That state's intermediate appellate courts (limited circumstances) • Federal circuit court encompassing the district court (limited circumstances)	• U.S. Supreme Court • Other federal circuit courts • Federal district courts • That state's trial courts
E	State issue in federal circuit court	• That state's highest court • That state's intermediate appellate courts (limited circumstances) • That federal circuit court (limited circumstances)	• U.S. Supreme Court • Other federal circuit courts • Federal district courts • That state's trial courts
F	State issue in U.S. Supreme Court	• That state's highest court • That state's intermediate appellate courts (limited circumstances)	• U.S. Supreme Court • Federal circuit courts • Federal district courts • That state's trial courts
G	Federal issue in federal district court	• U.S. Supreme Court • Federal circuit court encompassing the district court	• Other federal circuit courts • That federal district court • Other federal district courts • All state courts
H	Federal issue in federal circuit court	• U.S. Supreme Court • That federal circuit court	• Other federal circuit courts • Federal district courts • All state courts
I	Federal issue in U.S. Supreme Court	• U.S. Supreme Court	• Federal circuit courts • Federal district courts • All state courts
J	Federal issue in state trial court	• U.S. Supreme Court • That state's highest court (limited circumstances) • That state's intermediate appellate courts (limited circumstances)	• Federal circuit courts • Federal district courts • That state's trial courts
K	Federal issue in state intermediate appellate court	• U.S. Supreme Court • That state's highest court (limited circumstances) • That state's intermediate appellate courts (limited circumstances)	• Federal circuit courts • Federal district courts • That state's trial courts
L	Federal issue in state's highest court	• U.S. Supreme Court • That state's highest court (limited circumstances)	• Federal circuit courts • Federal district courts • That state's intermediate appellate courts • That state's trial courts

D. Review Questions on Binding and Nonbinding Authorities

At this point, you should understand the difference between binding and nonbinding authorities. To test your comprehension, answer the true-false and multiple-choice questions on this book's companion website, Core Knowledge. It will identify the correct answers and provide clear explanations for each question. The same questions are reproduced below.

1. A case from the Supreme Court of Tennessee is secondary authority.

   a. True

   b. False

2. A treatise, such as *Corbin on Contracts* or *Murphy's Will Clauses*, is primary authority.

   a. True

   b. False

3. Secondary authority, such as a respected treatise on tort law, is sometimes binding on a court.

   a. True

   b. False

4. The common law includes rules from court cases decided in the absence of a statute or other enacted law.

   a. True

   b. False

5. Under the doctrine of *stare decisis*, courts generally follow prior judicial decisions based on the maxim of justice that similar cases ought to be similarly decided.

   a. True

   b. False

6. You are before the United States Court of Appeals for the Eleventh Circuit on a federal statutory issue. Which authority is generally binding on your court?

   a. *American Jurisprudence 2d*, a national legal encyclopedia.

   b. *Nimmer on Copyright*, a well-respected treatise.

   c. Cases from other panels from the Eleventh Circuit.

   d. Cases from other panels from the Eleventh Circuit and *Nimmer on Copyright*.

7. You are before a state trial court in Georgia on a claim for breach of contract, which is a state law issue. Which authority is binding on your court? Hint: Review **Table 1** (Binding vs. Nonbinding Cases) in Appendix A.

    a. Cases from the Supreme Court of Georgia.

    b. Cases from the United States Supreme Court.

    c. Cases from the Eleventh Circuit Court of Appeals (Georgia is located within the geographic area of this circuit).

    d. Cases from the United States Supreme Court and cases from the Supreme Court of Georgia.

8. You are defending a state law battery claim in the Hamilton County Court of Common Pleas, an Ohio trial court. Which authority is binding on your court for the elements of a battery claim? Hint: Review **Table 1** (Binding vs. Nonbinding Cases) in Appendix A.

    a. Cases from the Supreme Court of the United States.

    b. Cases from the Supreme Court of the United States and cases from the United States Court of Appeals for the Sixth Circuit. (Ohio is located in the Sixth Circuit.)

    c. Cases from an Ohio state trial court located in a different county.

    d. None of the above.

9. You are before the United States Court of Appeals for the Fifth Circuit on a claim that your client violated the Family Medical Leave Act, a federal statute. Which authority is binding on your court? Hint: Review **Table 1** (Binding vs. Nonbinding Cases) in Appendix A.

    a. Cases from the U.S. District Court for the Western District of Texas, a federal trial court located within the geographic area of the Fifth Circuit.

    b. Cases from the Supreme Court of Texas.

    c. Cases from other panels from the Fifth Circuit.

    d. Cases from all United States Courts of Appeals.

10. In Fulton County Superior Court, a Georgia trial court, you have filed a motion to suppress your client's confession, arguing that the police violated the Fourth Amendment to the U.S. Constitution. Which authority is binding on your court? Hint: Review **Table 1** (Binding vs. Nonbinding Cases) in Appendix A.

    a. Cases from the Supreme Court of the United States.

    b. Cases from the United States Court of Appeals for the Third Circuit.

    c. Cases listed in choices A and B are binding.

    d. None of the above.

11. You are before a U.S. District Court for the Middle District of Alabama on a claim for breach of contract under Alabama state law. Which authority is binding on your court? Hint: Review **Table 1** (Binding vs. Nonbinding Cases) in Appendix A.

    a. Cases from the Supreme Court of Alabama.

    b. Cases from the United States Court of Appeals for the First Circuit. (Alabama is located within the geographic area of the United States Court of Appeals for the Eleventh Circuit.)

    c. Cases listed in choices A and B are binding.

    d. None of the above.

12. In 1995, in Case A, the Supreme Court of Michigan ruled that punitive damages (damages to punish wrongful conduct) are recoverable for a common law negligence claim. In 2010, in Case B, the Supreme Court of Michigan reversed course and expressly allowed punitive damages. In 2012, the Michigan Legislature disagreed with both prior cases and enacted Statute Z that expressly precluded the recovery of punitive damages for a common law negligence claim. If your client filed a claim for negligence in a Michigan trial court, would punitive damages be recoverable under Michigan law?

    a. Yes, because Case A allowed recovery for a common law negligence claim.

    b. No, because Statute Z expressly precludes recovery for a common law negligence claim.

    c. It depends. The trial court has discretion to follow Case B or to follow Statute Z.

    d. None of the above.

Chapter 3

The Publication Process for Cases and the Anatomy of a Case

In Chapter 1, you learned that federal and state courts create laws called "caselaw" when resolving legal disputes. Caselaw includes the common law and the laws created when courts interpret enacted laws like statutes. Because courts' written decisions contain relevant laws, you must know how to find and analyze these decisions. But before researching judicial decisions, you need to understand a few basic things about them.

Thus, this chapter identifies where courts' written decisions are published, explains how to interpret citations to these decisions, and breaks down the different parts of an actual decision. This chapter will be only slightly more exciting than your art history or western civilization course in college. Nonetheless, as a required reading from your professor, you must march onward.

A. Where to Find Cases: Print Reporters and Online

The written decisions from federal and state courts are commonly called **cases** or **judicial decisions**. They are published in chronological order in books called **reporters**. The cases published in reporters are also available in electronic format for free on the deciding court's website or through a paid subscription to an online database, such as Westlaw and Lexis Advance. Not every written decision from a court, however, is published in a reporter; in fact, many cases never find their way into a print reporter and are available only in electronic format.

As to the federal court system, virtually all decisions by the highest court, the United States Supreme Court, are published in print reporters. The story is different for lower federal courts. Of all the cases by United States Courts of Appeals (intermediate appellate courts) and by United States District Courts (trial courts), only a small percentage are published in reporters. Most of the written decisions from those courts are available only electronically.

At the state level, almost all decisions by the court of last resort (often called the supreme court) are published in print reporters. But the percentage of cases located in reporters from the state intermediate appellate courts, which are immediately below a state's highest court, varies across the states. In some states (*e.g.*, Alabama, Georgia, and Florida), a substantial majority of the written decisions by the inter-

---

Westlaw and Lexis Advance

As Chapter 5 explains, the most robust and respected online legal research services are **Westlaw** and **Lexis Advance**. Their online databases contain judicial decisions from all federal and state appellate courts, as well as cases from trial courts. Law students have free, unlimited access to these research services, and many students enrolled in paralegal and legal studies programs also have access. Of course, these services are not "free" after graduation.

---

mediate appellate court are published in reporters. In other states (*e.g.*, Ohio and Texas), only some decisions by the intermediate appellate courts are published in print reporters, but many of these decisions are available electronically.

Most state trial courts do not publish their written opinions in reporters. In fact, these cases are very difficult to find in any format. (In several states, it appears that the trial judges "hide" their opinions in secret places, known only to a select few.) A few states like Florida and Ohio, however, do publish some trial court decisions.

Federal and state cases are published in **official** and **unofficial** reporters. Official reporters are published by governmental entities or under their direction. (Table T1.3 in *The Bluebook* and Appendix 1 in the *ALWD Guide* identify the jurisdictions that have official reporters.) Unofficial reporters are published by private companies, and the largest publisher is Thomson Reuters, formerly named West Publishing and West Group. One decision from a federal or state court may be located in just an official reporter, just an unofficial reporter, or both types of reporters. For virtually each case published in any reporter, an electronic version is also available in multiple locations—on Westlaw, Lexis Advance, the deciding court's website, and other online databases.

Difference Between Official and Unofficial Reporters

Despite the implication, a judicial decision published in an "official" reporter is not more authoritative than a decision located in an "unofficial" reporter. Indeed, the part of a case drafted by the deciding court—the opinion—is the same. The primary difference between the two reporters is that commercial editors add enhancements to each case published in their unofficial reporters, such as headnotes identifying the rules of law from the case. These editorial enhancements are explained later in this chapter.

B. West's National Reporter System

The largest collection of unofficial print reporters is West's National Reporter System. The written decisions of federal courts (all levels) and state courts (only appellate level) are published in the National Reporter System, which contains the full text of selected cases, as well as enhancements added by West's attorney editors. These cases are generally arranged in the reporters based on the date they were decided, not by topic or subject. A case published in volume 105 of a reporter would be newer than one published in volume 100 of the same reporter set.

1. Federal Cases

The level of court determines the reporter where a federal case is published in West's National Reporter System. Decisions from the United States Supreme Court, the United States Courts of Appeals, and the United States District Courts are located in different sets of reporters. In each reporter set, the volumes are numbered consecutively, and the numbering starts over when a new series is issued. To illustrate, the volume that follows volume 999 of the first series of the *Federal Supplement* reporter is volume 1 of the second series of the that reporter, and the volume that follows volume 999 of the second series of that reporter is volume 1 of the third series. Each series of the same reporter set covers different time periods. The first series of the *Federal Supplement*, for example, contains cases from 1932 to 1998.

Figure 3.1 identifies the names (and abbreviations) of the different reporters where federal cases are published. As shown in the chart, cases from the United States Supreme Court are published in West's *Supreme Court Reporter*, as well as other reporters; however, cases from the lower federal courts are published only in West reporters. The chart also shows that each set of West reporters contains only federal cases from the same level of court. All three series of the *Federal Reporter*, for instance, contain only the decisions by the United States Court of Appeals.

2. State Cases

In addition to federal cases, West's National Reporter System includes print reporters for cases from every state. This System divides the 50 states and the District of Columbia into seven national regions where each region has a reporter set: Atlantic, North Eastern, North Western, Pacific, South Eastern, South Western, and Southern. These regional reporters in the National Reporter System cover decisions from each state court of last resort and each intermediate appellate court (if one exists). But the regional reporters do not contain cases from state trial courts.

Figure 3.1: Federal Cases and Reporters

Federal Courts	West Reporters Series (Abbreviations)	Non-West Reporters (Abbreviations)
U.S. Supreme Court	*Supreme Court Reporter* First Series (S. Ct.)	*United States Reports* (U.S.) *United States Supreme Court Reports, Lawyers' Edition* (L. Ed. and L. Ed. 2d)
U.S. Courts of Appeals (U.S. Circuit Courts)	*Federal Reporter* First, Second, and Third Series (F., F.2d, and F.3d)	None
	Federal Appendix* First Series (F. App'x) * Select unpublished cases from 2001 to present	
U.S. District Courts	*Federal Supplement* First, Second, and Third Series (F. Supp., F. Supp. 2d, and F. Supp. 3d)	None
	Federal Rules Decision* First Series (F.R.D.) * Only cases interpreting the federal rules * Cases not reported in the *Federal Supplement*	

Even when a state appellate case is published in a West reporter, if the state has an official reporter, the same case would be published in it. Accordingly, for states with official reporters, the same case is published in two different reporters.

Citations to Official Reporters

When a state has an official reporter, the local rules of a court may require attorneys to cite the official reporter rather than the West reporter. Or the rules may require citations to both the official and West reporter (known as a parallel citation). You should comply with your court's rules.

Figure 3.2 identifies the names of the seven sets of West regional reporters where state appellate cases are located and the jurisdictions covered by each reporter set. The volumes for these regional reporters are arranged into series like the reporters for federal cases. **Figure 3.2** also provides the name of the West reporters that publish cases from the intermediate appellate courts in California and New York.

Figure 3.2: State Cases and West Reporters

Jurisdictions	West Reporters Series (Abbreviations)
Atlantic: Connecticut, Delaware, District of Columbia, Maine, Maryland, New Hampshire, New Jersey, Pennsylvania, Rhode Island, and Vermont	*Atlantic Reporter* First and Second Series (A. and A.2d)
California	*West's California Reporter* First, Second, and Third Series (Cal. Rptr., Cal. Rptr. 2d, Cal. Rptr. 3d)
New York	*New York Supplement* First and Second Series (N.Y.S., N.Y.S.2d)
North Eastern: Illinois, Indiana, Massachusetts, New York (limited coverage), and Ohio	*North Eastern Reporter* First, Second, and Third Series (N.E., N.E.2d, and N.E.3d)
North Western: Iowa, Michigan, Minnesota, Nebraska, North Dakota, South Dakota, and Wisconsin	*North Western Reporter* First and Second Series (N.W. and N.W.2d)
Pacific: Alaska, Arizona, California (limited coverage), Colorado, Hawaii, Idaho, Kansas, Montana, Nevada, New Mexico, Oklahoma, Oregon, Utah, Washington, and Wyoming	*Pacific Reporter* First, Second, and Third Series (P., P.2d, P.3d)
South Eastern: Georgia, North Carolina, South Carolina, Virginia, and West Virginia	*South Eastern Reporter* First and Second Series (S.E. and S.E.2d)
South Western: Arkansas, Kentucky, Missouri, Tennessee, and Texas	*South Western Reporter* First, Second, and Third Series (S.W., S.W.2d, S.W.3d)
Southern: Alabama, Florida, Louisiana, and Mississippi	*Southern Reporter* First, Second, and Third Series (So., So. 2d, So. 3d)

C. Unpublished and Non-Precedential Cases

As previously noted, federal and state courts write many opinions that are not published in print reporters. Each federal and state court establishes its own rules for designating a case "for publication" in a reporter, and a case's publication status often determines its precedential value. Courts consider various criteria in deciding to publish a judicial decision in a reporter: whether the decision establishes a new

---

Identifying Unreported and Unpublished Cases

You can identify an unpublished case in an online database in two ways. An unpublished case should contain the designation "not for publication," "unpublished," "not reported," "memorandum opinion," or "non-precedential." In addition, an unpublished case will lack any mention of a reporter (unless the case is located in the *Federal Appendix*).

---

rule of law, whether it applies an existing rule to a novel factual situation, or whether it involves a legal issue important to the public.[1]

Decisions not published in any print reporter are referred to as **unreported, unpublished**, or **non-precedential** cases. Although not contained in a reporter, these "unpublished" cases are often published in electronic format and available to students and attorneys through online databases. You can find them on a court's website, Westlaw, or Lexis Advance, making the term "unpublished" misleading. To complicate matters more, since 2001, Thomson Reuters (West) has published in a reporter federal cases that have been designated "not for publication" or "non-precedential." Specifically, a select number of these decisions from the United States Courts of Appeals (known as federal circuit courts) are located in the West reporter *Federal Appendix*.

The rules for the federal and state courts determine the weight of authority for cases designated "for publication" or "not for publication." A decision by a higher court that has the "for publication" designation is binding authority. Unlike those published decisions, a case that the deciding court designates "not for publication" or "non-precedential" is generally not binding.[2] For instance, the unpublished decisions from the federal circuit courts are not binding.[3] Even the "unpublished" cases printed in the *Federal Appendix* are not binding because attorney editors, not the deciding circuit courts, select cases for that reporter. Nonetheless, in some states like Ohio, select unpublished decisions from the appellate courts are binding on lower courts.[4] In those states, it is imperative that you find those binding unpublished cases.

---

1. *See, e.g,* 6th Cir. R. 32.1; Cal. R. Ct. 8.1105(c).

2. *See, e.g.,* Ga. Ct. App. R. 33.2(b) ("A decision that is not officially reported is neither physical nor binding precedent....").

3. *See, e.g.,* 8th Cir. R. 32.1A (providing that unpublished decision "are not precedent"); *United States v. Izurieta,* 710 F.3d 1176, 1179 (11th Cir. 2013) ("Unpublished opinions are not binding precedent.").

4. *See, e.g.,* Ohio Rep. Op. R. 3.2 ("All opinions of the courts of appeals issued after May 1, 2002 may be cited as legal authority and weighted as deemed appropriate by the courts without regard to whether the opinion was published or in what form it was published.").

The rules of the federal and state courts also determine whether parties may cite an "unpublished" case in a court filing. In the federal circuit courts, for example, parties may cite and rely on any unpublished circuit case "issued on or after January 1, 2007."[5] But for unpublished circuit decisions issued prior to that date, some circuit courts restrict and others allow litigants to cite them.[6]

In short, you should walk away with four important points about "published" and "unpublished" cases. First, each case printed in a West reporter (other than the *Federal Appendix*) is published and citable. Second, if you found a published and unpublished case for the same rule of law, you should cite and rely on the published decision. Third, if you cannot find any published case for a disputed legal issue, review Chapter 10 for tips on researching unpublished decisions. Although unpublished cases are generally not binding, citing one authority to support your argument is better than citing none. Last, check the local rules of the court deciding your client's issues to determine the persuasive value and citability of unpublished decisions. If the local rules prohibit citations to unpublished cases, do not waste time—and the client's money—researching them.

D. Deciphering Case Citations

The citation of a case identifies its "home address." Thus, once you know the citation to a federal or state case, you can easily retrieve the full text of the decision in print or through an online database.

Additionally, a proper citation to a judicial decision provides you and your reader with vital information about the cited case. A case citation informs a researcher of whether the case is published in a reporter or unpublished, the jurisdiction of the deciding court (*e.g.*, Ohio), and the specific state or federal court issuing the decision (*e.g.*, Supreme Court of Ohio). With that information, you know whether the case is binding or nonbinding on the court deciding your legal issue.

1. Citations to Reported Cases

Citations to federal and state cases in reporters identify the name of the parties involved in the case; the title, volume, and page number of the reporter containing the case; the deciding court; and the year of decision. **Figure 3.3** demystifies those basic parts. The parts of a citation for a federal case and state case published in a reporter are substantially the same. For example, the number preceding the abbreviated reporter title is always the volume number, and the number immediately after the abbreviated reporter title is always the starting page of the case.

---

5. *See* Fed. R. App. P. 32.1.
6. *See, e.g.*, 7th Cir. R. 32.1 (restricting citations); 10th Cir. R. 32.1 (permitting citations).

Figure 3.3: Parts of Citations to Cases in West Reporters

Federal Appellate Case: *United States v. Tobin*, 923 F.2d 1506 (11th Cir. 1991)					
Name of Parties	Volume of Reporter	Name of Reporter and Series	First Page of Case	Deciding Court	Year of Decision
United States v. Tobin	923	F.2d = *Federal Reporter*, Second Series	1506	11th Cir. = U.S. Court of Appeals for the Eleventh Circuit	1991

Federal Trial Case: *McKally v. Perez*, 87 F. Supp. 3d 1310 (S.D. Fla. 2015)					
Name of Parties	Volume of Reporter	Name of Reporter and Series	First Page of Case	Deciding Court	Year of Decision
McKally v. Perez	87	F. Supp. 3d = *Federal Supplement*, Third Series	1310	S.D. Fla. = U.S. District Court for the Southern District of Florida	2015

State Appellate Case: *Custer v. Coward*, 667 S.E.2d 135 (Ga. Ct. App. 2008)					
Name of Parties	Volume of Reporter	Name of Reporter and Series	First Page of Case	Deciding Court	Year of Decision
Custer v. Coward	667	S.E.2d = *South Eastern Reporter*, Second Series	135	Ga. Ct. App. = Court of Appeals of Georgia	2008

2. Citations to Unpublished Cases

Most parts of a citation to an "unpublished" case are similar to the parts of a citation to a case published in a reporter. The primary difference is that an unpublished case will contain no abbreviation for a reporter but instead will usually contain a unique identifier so that others can quickly find it online. As shown in **Figures 3.4** and **3.5**, Westlaw and Lexis Advance provide different identifiers for the same unpublished case; the Westlaw identifier is "2016 WL 6524394" and the Lexis Advance identifier is "2016 U.S. Dist. LEXIS 152360."

Because the various online databases provide different identifiers, the citation to an unpublished case changes based on where the researcher retrieved the case. If you retrieved the unpublished case from **Figure 3.4** on Westlaw, you would cite it as follows: *Howard v. Sunniland Corp.*, No. 2:16-cv-321-FtM-99MRM, 2016 WL 6524394

(M.D. Fla. Nov. 3, 2016). On the other hand, if you retrieved the same case on Lexis Advance, you would replace "2016 WL 6524394" with the Lexis unique identifier. See **Figure 3.5**.

Unlike citations to unpublished decisions, the citation to a case published in a reporter is not database dependent. So if you retrieved the published case of *Smith v. Jones* on Westlaw and Lexis Advance, the case will have the same citation, because both electronic versions are based on the same print version.

Figure 3.4: Unpublished Case Retrieved on Westlaw

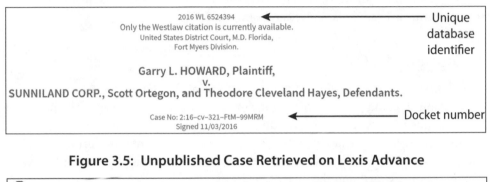

Figure 3.5: Unpublished Case Retrieved on Lexis Advance

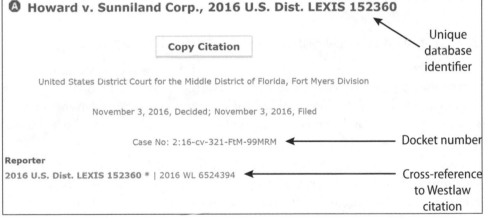

E. Dissecting Parts of a Case Found on Westlaw and Lexis Advance

Not every part of a case found on Westlaw and Lexis Advance is drafted by the deciding court. As mentioned earlier, editors of Thomson Reuters (West) and LexisNexis add enhancements to judicial decisions soon after being released by the deciding courts.

The attorney editors of Thomson Reuters add enhancements to all cases published in West reporters, and the same enhancements are included on the electronic version on Westlaw. These editors also add enhancements to a select number of cases on Westlaw that the deciding courts have designated "not for publication."

The attorney editors of LexisNexis include similar enhancements to the cases on Lexis Advance. Enhancements are added to all cases on Lexis Advance that the deciding court has designated "for publication." Although a "published" case on Lexis Advance is also located in a West reporter, the enhancements to the case are different, because different editors from different companies create the enhancements. LexisNexis editors also include enhancements to a select number of "unpublished" cases on Lexis Advance.

Substantially all cases on Westlaw and Lexis Advance are divided into multiple parts, which is one type of enhancement. These parts are known as **fields** on Westlaw and **segments** on Lexis Advance. The five primary fields or segments include the caption, summary, headnotes, judge, and opinion.[7]

1. Caption of a Case

The first field or segment is located at the top of the initial page of a case and is the **caption**. It contains the information you need to construct a proper citation and to determine whether the case is binding. The caption includes the following information: name of the parties litigating; the citation to the print reporter(s) (for "published" cases) or the unique database identifier (for "unpublished" cases); the name of the deciding court; and the date of decision.

2. Synopsis and Case Summary ("Editorial Summaries")

The next field or segment is where the editors of Westlaw and Lexis Advance summarize the background facts, procedural history, legal questions and issues, and holdings or outcomes of the case. This editorial enhancement is commonly called a **synopsis** on Westlaw and a **case summary** on Lexis Advance, but it may also be referred to as an **overview** or **syllabus**.

Because a **synopsis** and **case summary** (collectively, "editorial summaries") provide vital information about a case, they are excellent tools for researching and choosing relevant cases. The editorial summaries usually identify both the legal questions in dispute and the court's answer to each question. Additionally, they often set forth the legally relevant facts—those facts the court relied on in answering the legal questions. The editorial summaries also describe the parties based on their legal significance. Instead of using the terms plaintiff, defendant, appellant, and appellee, the editors of Westlaw and LexisNexis use descriptive terms like landlord/tenant, insurer/insured, buyer/seller, and employer/employee.

Here is a tangible example showing the utility of the editorial summaries. Suppose you are researching the enforceability of a client's noncompetition agreement with her employer where the agreement prohibits her from working for a competitor

---

7. In Parts II and III of this book, you will learn in much greater detail how editorial enhancements help researchers find and understand relevant cases.

within a 50-mile radius of her employer. Specifically, you must research the reasonableness of that geographic limitation. Assume that you reviewed the excerpts of the
editorial summaries for four cases:

- *Case A*: Employer sought to enforce a noncompetition agreement covering a 40-
  mile radius. The court held that the geographic limitation was reasonable; thus,
  the agreement was enforceable against the former employee.

- *Case B*: Employer sought to enforce a noncompetition agreement covering a 60-
  mile radius. The court held that the geographic limitation was unreasonable;
  thus, the agreement was unenforceable against the former employee.

- *Case C*: Employer sought to enforce a noncompetition agreement covering a
  three-year period. The court invalidated the noncompetition agreement because
  it prevented the former employee from competing for three years, an unreasonable duration.

- *Case D*: Employer sought to enforce a noncompetition agreement covering a
  50-mile radius. The court held that the employer's claim for breach of the agreement was time barred by the statute of limitations.

By reviewing just the summaries, you would have identified two cases that are
legally on point and factually analogous to the client's situation. Both *Case A* and
Case B involved noncompetition agreements with similar geographic limitations (40
and 60 miles) and involved the same legal issue (reasonableness of the geographic
limitation). And by skimming just the summaries, you could quickly discard the irrelevant results of *Case C* and *Case D*. Those cases are not legally on point, because
the courts never answered the legal issue of whether the geographic limitation of
those agreements was reasonable (your client's narrow issue).

Do not walk away from this discussion with the false impression that you can rely
solely on the editorial summaries. They are not written by the deciding court. Instead,
for each case that appears relevant based on the summary, you must read—and rely
on—the court's actual opinion. No substitutions are allowed.

3. Headnotes of a Case

The next field or segment is the **headnotes**. Like editorial summaries, headnotes are
another type of enhancement to a case and are excellent research tools. The headnotes
contain concise rules of law from the case and appear in the same order in which they
appear in the case. The headnotes on Westlaw and Lexis Advance are created differently.
The Westlaw headnotes contain a paraphrase of the law from the case, but the Lexis
Advance headnotes contain actual quotes from the case. In Chapter 7, you will learn
about headnotes in great detail, including how they are used to organize cases by topic.

Although a useful research tool, you should never rely solely on a headnote or cite
a headnote in an office memorandum or court document. The editors of Thomson
Reuters and LexisNexis, not the deciding court, draft headnotes. You must read the
court's actual opinion to confirm the accuracy of the headnotes and must rely only
on the court's language—which represents the law.

4. Judges and Opinion

The fields or segments after the headnotes are **judges** and **opinion**. The opinion is the part of the case drafted by the deciding court, not a third party. You must carefully read the text of the opinion; it identifies the legal issues, the court's holdings on the issues, why the court reached those holdings (the reasoning), and the rules of law. Because the court writes the opinion, the text of the opinion is the same regardless of whether it is retrieved from a print reporter, on Westlaw, on Lexis Advance, or other online database.

The field or segment for judge identifies the author of the opinion. It may provide the full name of the judge or simply state the judge's last name, followed by the letter "J." For federal and state trial courts, one judge decides the legal dispute and writes the opinion. For federal and state intermediate appellate courts (*e.g.*, United States Court of Appeals for the Eleventh Circuit), a panel of three judges often vote to decide a legal matter. And for the court of last resort in most jurisdictions, five to nine judges vote to resolve the legal dispute. Although multiple judges vote, only one judge from the majority usually drafts the opinion.

5. Illustrations of Parts of Cases Found on Westlaw and Lexis Advance

Figures 3.6 and **3.7** illustrate the five primary fields and segments for a single case published in a West reporter and retrieved on Westlaw and Lexis Advance. While the text of the opinion is the same for both electronic versions, the headnotes and editorial

Figure 3.6: Anatomy of Case Retrieved on Westlaw

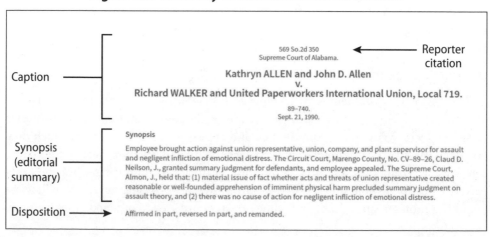

summaries are different. Remember the reason for the differences: commercial editors, not the deciding courts, add those editorial enhancements to cases.

Figure 3.6: *Continued*

West Headnotes (4)

Headnotes ⎯

1. **Assault and Battery** ⟶ Nature and Elements of Assault and Battery

   Words standing alone cannot constitute an assault; they may, however, give meaning to an act, and when both are taken together they may create well-founded fear of battery in mind of person at whom they are directed, thereby constituting assault.

   23 Cases that cite this headnote

2. **Judgment** ⟶ Tort cases in general

   Material issue of fact as to whether alleged threat by union representative that he would "whip employee anytime, anywhere," and alleged shaking of finger in employee's face could create reasonable or well-founded apprehension by employee of imminent physical harm precluded summary judgment in action for assault.

   4 Cases that cite this headnote

3. **Appeal and Error** ⟶ Summary Judgment

   When reviewing summary judgment, reviewing court must review evidence before trial court in light most favorable to nonmovant.

4. **Damages** ⟶ Negligent Infliction of Emotional Distress
   Damages ⟶ Intentional or Reckless Infliction of Emotional Distress; Outrage

   There is no action for negligent infliction of emotional distress; only intentional infliction of severe emotional distress is actionable.

   23 Cases that cite this headnote

Attorneys and Law Firms

*351 Collins Pettaway, Jr. of Chestnut, Sanders, Sanders, Williams & Pettaway, Selma, for appellants.

William J. Baxley and David McKnight of Baxley, Dillard & Dauphin, Birmingham, and Lynn Agee of UPIU Legal Dept., Nashville, Tenn., for appellees.

Opinion ⟵ Author of the opinion

ALMON, Justice.

Official opinion ⎯

The plaintiffs, Kathryn Allen and her husband, John Allen, appeal from a summary judgment for the defendants, Richard Walker and the United Paperworkers International Union, Local 719 ("the union"), in an action that involved claims of assault and negligence as to Kathryn. John alleged a loss of consortium. The Allens' complaint alleged that Walker had threatened Kathryn, and it included her employer, Gulf States Paper Company, and Herb Coley, the plant supervisor, as defendants. The complaint also stated numerous other theories of recovery that are not relevant to this appeal. The trial court dismissed Gulf States and entered a summary judgment for Coley. The Allens' appeal as to Gulf States and Coley was untimely and has been dismissed by this Court. This opinion will be restricted to a discussion of the Allens' allegations of assault and negligence against Walker and the union.

Assault

The Allens' claims of assault against Walker and the union[1] were based on the following facts:

Figure 3.7: Anatomy of Case Retrieved on Lexis Advance*

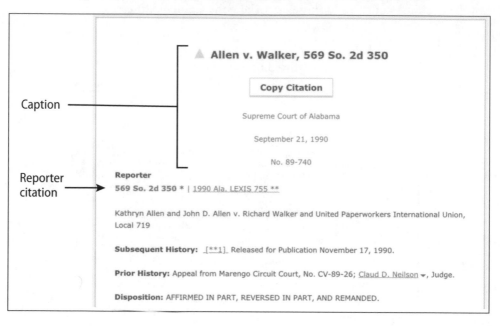

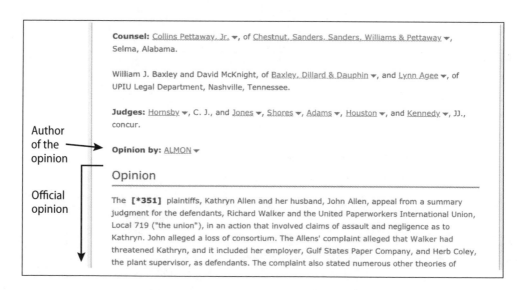

---

* The second and third screen captures had to be placed out of order. If you retrieved this case on Lexis, the opinion (the second screen capture) would appear after the case summary and headnotes (third screen capture).

Figure 3.7: *Continued*

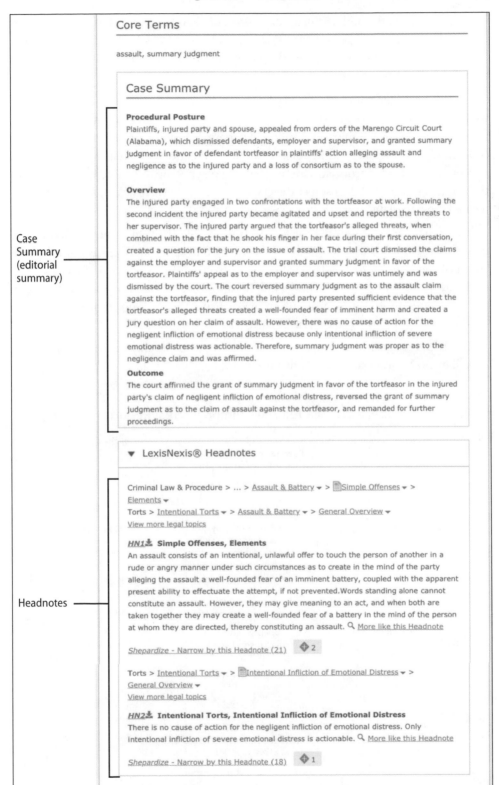

Core Terms

assault, summary judgment

Case Summary

Procedural Posture
Plaintiffs, injured party and spouse, appealed from orders of the Marengo Circuit Court (Alabama), which dismissed defendants, employer and supervisor, and granted summary judgment in favor of defendant tortfeasor in plaintiffs' action alleging assault and negligence as to the injured party and a loss of consortium as to the spouse.

Overview
The injured party engaged in two confrontations with the tortfeasor at work. Following the second incident the injured party became agitated and upset and reported the threats to her supervisor. The injured party argued that the tortfeasor's alleged threats, when combined with the fact that he shook his finger in her face during their first conversation, created a question for the jury on the issue of assault. The trial court dismissed the claims against the employer and supervisor and granted summary judgment in favor of the tortfeasor. Plaintiffs' appeal as to the employer and supervisor was untimely and was dismissed by the court. The court reversed summary judgment as to the assault claim against the tortfeasor, finding that the injured party presented sufficient evidence that the tortfeasor's alleged threats created a well-founded fear of imminent harm and created a jury question on her claim of assault. However, there was no cause of action for the negligent infliction of emotional distress because only intentional infliction of severe emotional distress was actionable. Therefore, summary judgment was proper as to the negligence claim and was affirmed.

Outcome
The court affirmed the grant of summary judgment in favor of the tortfeasor in the injured party's claim of negligent infliction of emotional distress, reversed the grant of summary judgment as to the claim of assault against the tortfeasor, and remanded for further proceedings.

▼ LexisNexis® Headnotes

Criminal Law & Procedure > ... > Assault & Battery ▾ > 🗎Simple Offenses ▾ > Elements ▾
Torts > Intentional Torts ▾ > Assault & Battery ▾ > General Overview ▾
View more legal topics

HN1⚖ Simple Offenses, Elements
An assault consists of an intentional, unlawful offer to touch the person of another in a rude or angry manner under such circumstances as to create in the mind of the party alleging the assault a well-founded fear of an imminent battery, coupled with the apparent present ability to effectuate the attempt, if not prevented. Words standing alone cannot constitute an assault. However, they may give meaning to an act, and when both are taken together they may create a well-founded fear of a battery in the mind of the person at whom they are directed, thereby constituting an assault. 🔍 More like this Headnote

Shepardize - Narrow by this Headnote (21) ◆ 2

Torts > Intentional Torts ▾ > 🗎Intentional Infliction of Emotional Distress ▾ > General Overview ▾
View more legal topics

HN2⚖ Intentional Torts, Intentional Infliction of Emotional Distress
There is no cause of action for the negligent infliction of emotional distress. Only intentional infliction of severe emotional distress is actionable. 🔍 More like this Headnote

Shepardize - Narrow by this Headnote (18) ◆ 1

Case Summary (editorial summary)

Headnotes

F. Summary of Key Points

If you snoozed through the prior discussion of reporters, case citations, and parts of a case, you should wake up for these important takeaways. (This author tried—but may have failed—to make this chapter more interesting than your art history or western civilization course.)

Federal and state courts decide legal disputes between parties and write opinions, which are commonly referred to as cases. Some cases are published in books known as reporters and added to various online databases. Of all print reporters, the largest collection is West's National Reporter System. This reporter system contains the full text of selected cases from all federal courts. West's Reporter System also contains the full text of selected decisions by every state court of last resort and every state intermediate appellate court (if one exists in the state).

Many cases are not selected for publication in any print reporter. In fact, courts designate many of their opinions as "not for publication" or "non-precedential." These "unpublished" cases are available only in electronic format, such as on Westlaw or Lexis Advance. While you may find a helpful unpublished case for your client's issue, before relying on it in a memorandum or court document, you need to review the local rules of your court to determine its persuasive value and its citability.

Figure 3.8 shows how a court's written opinion finds its way into a West reporter, as well as on Westlaw and Lexis Advance.

Figure 3.8: Publication of a Judicial Opinion in West Reporter and Online

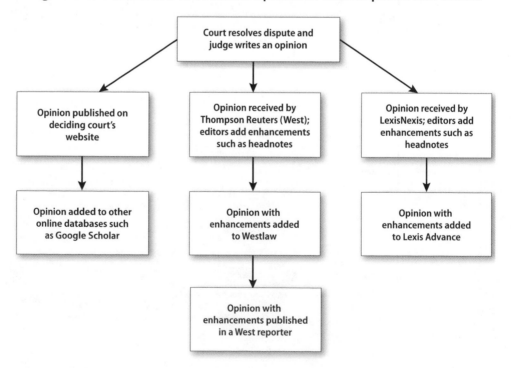

Last, the cases you retrieve on Westlaw and Lexis Advance are divided into multiple fields or segments. They include the caption, synopsis or case summary (collectively, "editorial summaries"), headnotes, judges, and opinion. The enhancements of editorial summaries and headnotes are added by commercial editors, not the deciding court. This is your final warning (at least for now): do not rely solely on those enhancements; you must carefully read the actual opinion of each case you plan to cite in any legal document.

G. Review Questions on Cases and Reporters

At this point, you should have a basic understanding of the publication process for cases and the parts of a case. To test your comprehension, answer the true-false and multiple-choice questions on this book's companion website, Core Knowledge. It will identify the correct answers and provide clear explanations for each question. The same questions are reproduced below.

1. Some written opinions of courts are published in books called reporters.

    a. True

    b. False

2. A written opinion that is published in a print reporter is not available in electronic format on Westlaw or Lexis Advance.

    a. True

    b. False

3. The second or third series of the *Southern Reporter* contains cases from the state trial courts of Alabama.

    a. True

    b. False

4. A case that a federal circuit court (*e.g.*, the United States Court of Appeals for the Eleventh Circuit) has designated "not for publication" or "non-precedential" is generally not binding.

    a. True

    b. False

5. The actual text of an opinion published in an official and unofficial reporter is different.

    a. True

    b. False

6. Cases found on Westlaw and Lexis Advance are divided into fields or segments, such as editorial summaries, headnotes, judges, and opinion.

    a. True

    b. False

7. How are cases organized in each volume of a print reporter?

    a. Organized by topic and subtopics.

    b. Organized by Key Numbers.

    c. Organized in chronological order.

    d. Cases are not published in print reporters.

8. The *Southern Reporter* contains cases from which states?

    a. Alabama, Florida, Louisiana, Mississippi.

    b. Alabama, Florida, and Louisiana.

    c. Alabama and Florida.

    d. Alabama, Florida, Georgia, and Louisiana.

9. Which reporter publishes decisions from the United States District Courts?

    a. *Federal Appendix*

    b. *Federal Supplement*

    c. *Federal Reporter*

    d. *United States Reports*

10. A case from the Supreme Court of North Carolina is published in which West reporter?

    a. *North Eastern Reporter*

    b. *Southern Reporter*

    c. *South Eastern Reporter*

    d. *Atlantic Reporter*

11. You found a case published in the third series of the *Federal Reporter* (F.3d). Which court issued that opinion?

    a. The United States Supreme Court

    b. A United States Court of Appeals

    c. A United States District Court

    d. None of the above

12. Peter has found relevant cases on Westlaw and Lexis Advance. What should he look for to determine whether the deciding courts have designated them "not for publication"?

   a. The designation "unpublished"

   b. The designation "not reported"

   c. The designation "non-precedential"

   d. All of the above

13. On Lexis Advance, Rachel has been reviewing just the case summaries for various cases and has identified one case that is almost factually identical to her client's situation. If pressed for time, what should she do next?

   a. She should save time and rely solely on the case summary because the deciding court wrote the case summary.

   b. She should save time and rely solely on the case summary because, even though the deciding court did not write the case summary, efficiency is more important than accuracy.

   c. She should carefully read the actual opinion because the deciding court did not write the case summary.

   d. She should carefully read the actual opinion because, even though the deciding court did not write the case summary, the deciding court reviews the summary and corrects any inaccuracy.

14. Which of the following fields (Westlaw) or segments (Lexis Advance) are written by commercial editors?

   a. Synopsis or case summary (collectively, "editorial summaries")

   b. Headnotes

   c. Opinion

   d. Both A and B

Chapter 4

The Publication Process for Statutes and the Anatomy of a Statutory Code

In Chapter 1, you learned that the legislative branch creates laws called **statutes**. Federal statutes are written and enacted by the United States Congress, and state statutes are written and enacted by state legislatures. Federal statutes regulate conduct throughout the United States, but the statutes enacted by a state legislature regulate only the conduct within that state. And both federal and state statutes may govern the same conduct.

Federal and state statutes are classified as either civil or criminal. **Criminal statutes** impose various types of penalties and punishments, including fines, probation, and imprisonment. Only the government may charge and prosecute an individual for violating a criminal statute. An attorney who brings criminal charges in court may be called a United States Attorney (federal), a prosecutor (federal or state), or district attorney (state). A defendant may violate a criminal law and be subject to punishment, even when there is no victim and no harm. For example, suppose Johnny drove his automobile on wet roads at speeds exceeding 100 miles per hour but did not damage property or harm any person. He may be convicted of the crime of driving recklessly, even though he caused no harm.

Civil statutes are different from criminal statutes in several respects. Civil statutes do not require the government to bring a lawsuit, do not authorize probation or imprisonment, and usually require some harm to property or a person before a potential plaintiff may recover damages. **Figure 4.1** highlights some key differences.

Both criminal and civil statutes at the federal and state levels govern almost all aspects of American society. They commonly prohibit conduct. No doubt, you are familiar with criminal statutes that prohibit assault, drunk driving, murder, and robbery. Civil statutes also prohibit a wide range of actions, including defamation, unfair consumer practices, dangerous conditions on land, and employment and housing discrimination. Some statutes require affirmative acts, subjecting individuals and entities to penalties or damages for an omission, such as requiring drivers to register their motor vehicles and sex offenders to register with a governmental entity.

In addition to prohibiting or requiring conduct, statutes may authorize conduct. These types of statutes permit, but do not require, particular acts or omissions, and they commonly contain the modal verb "may." A few examples include authorizing

Figure 4.1: Key Differences Between Criminal and Civil Statutes

Differences	Criminal Statutes	Civil Statutes
Charging Party/Plaintiff	Government (U.S. Attorney, prosecutor, or district attorney)	Individual, company, organization, or the government
Harm	Not required	Required (usually)
Victim/Injured Party	Not required	Required (usually)
Penalties/Damages for Violation	Fines, probation, and imprisonment	Compensatory damages, statutory damages, and punitive damages

a landlord to collect a security deposit and allowing an injured party to recover statutory or punitive damages.

An example of each type of statute is listed below.

- **Prohibiting Conduct:** "It is unlawful for any person to drive or to be in physical control of any automobile or other motor driven vehicle on any of the public roads and highways of the state ... while ... [t]he alcohol concentration in the person's blood or breath is eight-hundredths of one percent (0.08%) or more...."[1]

- **Requiring Conduct:** "[T]he adult sex offender shall appear in person and register all required registration information with local law enforcement in each county in which the adult sex offender resides or intends to reside, accepts or intends to accept employment, accepts or intends to accept a volunteer position, and begins or intends to begin school attendance."[2]

- **Allowing Conduct:** "A landlord may require a security deposit for each rental unit."[3]

In short, federal and state statutes, whether criminal or civil, represent the law. A court must follow and apply the language of a statute as written; it cannot deviate from its text, even if the court disagrees with the statute's purpose or policy. Because statutes reflect the law, you must find and analyze them when they apply to your client's situation.

This chapter explains how statutes are published, where statutes are published in print and online, and how to interpret citations to statutes. Although this chapter may not be very exciting or a "page turner," stay awake until the end. You must understand basic information about statutes before attempting to research them.

---

1. Tenn. Code Ann. § 55-10-401 (LEXIS through 2018 Reg. Sess.).
2. Ala. Code § 15-20A-10(a)(1) (LexisNexis, LEXIS through 2018 Reg. Sess.).
3. Mich. Comp. Laws Serv. § 554.602 (LexisNexis, LEXIS through 2018 Public Act 341).

A. Federal Statutes: From Bill to Law

Congress is comprised of the United States House of Representatives and United States Senate. Both chambers of Congress meet every year, which is part of a two-year session. For instance, the 115th Congress started its first session in 2017 and started its second session in 2018. That two-year session for the 115th Congress ended on December 31, 2018. The first session for the 116th Congress began in January 2019.

As explained in Chapter 1, a proposed federal statute begins its life in Congress as a bill.[4] After a bill passes both the United States House of Representative and Senate during a session, it is enrolled and sent to the President. If the **enrolled bill** is signed by the President or not vetoed within ten days, the bill becomes law. If the President vetoes the enrolled bill, however, both chambers of Congress must vote by a two-thirds majority to override the veto in order for the bill to become law.

When a bill becomes law, known as an **enacted law** or **statute**, it is assigned a **public law number**.[5] For each two-year session of Congress, public law numbers are assigned to new statutes in the order that they became law (*i.e.*, chronological order). The public law number identifies the session of Congress enacting the law and when the bill became law. For example, at the time of enactment, the Americans with Disabilities Act was assigned the number "Public Law 101-336" (abbreviated "Pub. L. No. 101-336"). That public law number means that the law was the 336th law enacted in the 101st Congress. The next bill that became law was assigned the number "Pub. L. No. 101-337." And the first law enacted in the 102nd Congress was assigned the number "Pub. L. No. 102-1."

B. Federal Statutes: Forms of Publication

Each enacted law or statute is made available to the public in print and online. Federal statutes are published in three different forms: (1) slip laws; (2) session laws; and (3) codes. The best source for researching statutes is a code, but you should know what happens to an enacted law before making its "home" in a code.

1. Slip Laws and Session Laws

Immediately after a bill becomes law, a government agency assigns a public law number to the new law. The newly-enacted law is then published in a paper pamphlet and is known as a **slip law**.[6] Slip laws are often published in electronic format within

---

4. The process for a bill becoming law is explained in great detail in a document published by the United States House of Representatives. The discussion in this section is based on that document. *See generally* John V. Sullivan, *How Our Laws Are Made*, House Doc. No. 110-49 (July 24, 2007).

5. Private laws apply only to specific individuals or entities and are not assigned a public law number.

6. The Office of the Federal Register publishes new laws as slip laws.

weeks of their enactment. The most updated—and free—websites to find newly-enacted laws are Congress.gov[7] and govinfo.gov.[8]

All slips laws—the newly-enacted laws—are compiled at the end of each session of Congress and published in books called the *United States Statutes at Large*. The collection of laws in the *Statutes at Large* is known as **session laws**. The session laws in the *Statutes at Large* are a verbatim reproduction of each slip law, arranged in chronological order as they have been enacted during a Congressional session. The session laws are not organized by topic or subject matter. When a newly-enacted law is assigned a public law number, it is also assigned a citation to the *Statutes at Large* that identifies the volume and page number where the law will appear. For instance, you can find the session law for the Americans with Disabilities Act on page 327 in volume 104 of the *Statutes at Large*, which is cited as "104. Stat. 327."

Session laws are available not only in print but also in electronic format. They are available to the public on Congress.gov and govinfo.gov.

2. Codes

You have finally arrived at the form of publication—**a code**—that will be the most useful research tool for finding federal and state statutes that apply to your client's situation. A code, whether for federal or state statutes, is a collection of all current laws. As a legislature enacts new statutes or repeals or amends existing ones, the additions, repeals, and amendments are reflected in a federal and state code. Additionally, a code organizes enacted laws by topic, making it possible for attorneys—at least those who have read this book—to locate relevant statutes.

Session Laws vs. Codes

You should not start a statutory research project by reviewing session laws. Session laws in the *Statutes at Large* or its counterparts for state statutes are arranged chronologically and are never updated to reflect amendments. Nonetheless, you need to understand what they are and where to find them, because you may need to review session laws for some research projects. Stay tuned for the juicy details in subsequent chapters.

---

7. Congress.gov is the official website for federal legislative information. To review recently-enacted laws, click "Public Laws" from the home page.

8. The govinfo.gov website is the official publication for all three branches of the federal government. To review new laws, from the home page, click on "Browse" and then "Public and Private Laws."

As explained next, all federal statutes are published in three different codes in print and online: one official code and two unofficial codes.

a. Official Code: United States Code

Federal statutes are codified in the *United States Code*, a multi-volume set of books. The *United States Code* is the official codification of all federal statutes currently in effect. **Codification** is a fancy term that means arranging session laws by **topic** and compiling them into a code. During the codification process, each new statute is also assigned a **section** number. The section contains the actual language of the statute.

The *United States Code* arranges federal statutes in over fifty broad topics called **titles**, which appear mostly in alphabetical order. For instance, the codified statutes on bankruptcy are under Title 11, the statutes on taxes fall under Title 26, and the statutes on war and national defense are under Title 50.

Each title is further divided into more specific topics. Most titles of the *United States Code* are divided into individual chapters, and some chapters are further divided into sub-chapters or parts. Under Title 11 (bankruptcy), for example, the statutes relating to liquidation are under Chapter 7, and the statutes addressing reorganization fall under Chapter 11. Regardless of the divisions of any particular title, the smallest division is a **section**. The code section contains the text of the statute.

To illustrate, the provisions of the Americans with Disabilities Act (ADA) that apply in the employment context have been codified in the *United States Code* under Title 42 ("Public Health and Welfare") and Chapter 126 ("Equal Opportunity for Individuals with Disabilities"), as shown in **Figure 4.2**. The statute that expressly prohibits discrimination on the basis of a disability is codified as section 12112 (which is referred to as 42 U.S.C. § 12112). An excerpt from that code section is shown in **Figure 4.3**.

The complete *United States Code* is accessible through many online databases. You can browse and search this federal code on several free websites, including Cornell Law School's Legal Information Institute (https://www.law.cornell.edu) and the Office of the Law Revision Counsel (http://uscode.house.gov).[9]

---

9. The Office of the Law Revision Counsel of the United States House of Representatives prepares and publishes the *United States Code*; as a result, the version on its website is very current. The *United States Code* on Cornell's website is more current than most other free electronic versions.

Figure 4.2: Excerpt of Table of Contents for Title 42 of the U.S.C.A.

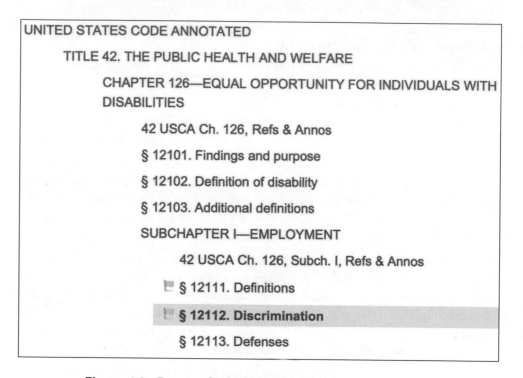

Figure 4.3: Excerpt from 42 U.S.C.A. § 12112 on Westlaw

Effective: January 1, 2009

42 U.S.C.A. § 12112

§ 12112. Discrimination

Currentness

(a) General rule

No covered entity shall discriminate against a qualified individual on the basis of disability in regard to job application procedures, the hiring, advancement, or discharge of employees, employee compensation, job training, and other terms, conditions, and privileges of employment.

b. Unofficial Codes: United States Code Annotated and United States Code Service

Federal statutes are also published in two **unofficial codes** published by commercial companies. (Similarly, judicial opinions are published in unofficial reporters.) Thomson Reuters (also known as West) publishes the *United States Code Annotated* (U.S.C.A.) and makes it available on Westlaw. Its competitor, LexisNexis, publishes the *United States Code Service* (U.S.C.S.) and makes it available on Lexis Advance. The federal statutes published in both unofficial codes are the same statutes located in the *United States Code.*

The organization of the two unofficial codes (U.S.C.A. and U.S.C.S.) mirrors the arrangement of the official *United States Code*. Both unofficial codes arrange federal statutes by topic and use the same title and section numbers as the official code. To illustrate, the official and unofficial codes use the same heading for Title 21 ("Food and Drugs"), and they all divide that title into the same twenty-seven chapters with the same section numbers.

Substantially all attorneys and judges research statutes with the unofficial codes for two primary reasons. First, the unofficial codes in print are updated with new statutes and amendments more frequently than the official code in print.

Second, both unofficial codes are enhanced, or **annotated**, by editors of Thomson Reuters and LexisNexis. (Remember from Chapter 3 that commercial editors also add enhancements to judicial opinions.) The **annotations** for a particular statute often contain references to related primary and secondary authorities. They may cite other related statutes, related administrative regulations, and legal articles discussing the statute. More importantly, the annotations include concise rules of law from judicial decisions that have interpreted the statutes, and the publishers organize these **case annotations** by topic. Nonetheless, you cannot rely solely on case annotations to discern the meaning of a statute; they are not drafted by legislators or courts. You must read the actual cases.

Figure 4.4 shows a few case annotations for the codified section of the Americans with Disabilities Act that prohibits employers from discriminating on the basis of a disability.

Figure 4.4: Case Annotations for 42 U.S.C.S. § 12112

175. Allowing double time to take exam

Where attorney sued Alabama State Bar for refusing to accommodate his disabilities of attention deficit disorder and dyslexia by refusing to allow him double time to take state bar examination, conflicting medical evidence as to whether his requested accommodations were reasonable under 42 USCS § 12112 created question of material fact precluding summary judgment in his favor. Cox v Ala. State Bar (2005, MD Ala) 392 F Supp 2d 1295.

176. Allowing employee to work at home

Employer may not deny otherwise reasonable accommodation because of past disciplinary action taken due to disability sought to be accommodated; thus, medical transcriptionist's request for accommodation of being allowed to work at home could not be denied because of her disciplinary record which consisted of warnings for tardiness and absenteeism caused by her obsessive compulsive disorder. Humphrey v Memorial Hosps. Ass'n (2001, CA9 Cal) 239 F3d 1128, 2001 CDOS 1295, 2001 Daily Journal DAR 1631, 11 AD Cas 765, cert den, motion den (2002) 535 US 1011, 152 L Ed 2d 509, 122 S Ct 1592, 12 AD Cas 1824.

Where relocation of state agency's office resulted in 90-minute commute for disabled employee, agency did not fail to reasonably accommodate employee by refusing to allow him to work at home, since agency had offered to accommodate employee by helping him to relocate or to find new job in old area, and there was evidence that all essential functions of job could not be adequately performed by employee at home. Kvorjak v Maine (2001, CA1 Me) 259 F3d 48, 12 AD Cas 160.

3. Comparison Between Public Laws (Session Laws) and Codified Statutes

Students often confuse the organizational scheme of a public law and statutes arranged in codes. The provisions in some public laws (session laws) are grouped together under broad topics known as titles. And all public laws contain sections in which each discrete provision is assigned a section number. A single public law may contain five sections or over twenty or fifty sections, depending on the number of provisions. For instance, as originally enacted, the Americans with Disabilities Act (ADA) was organized into five titles and contained over fifty different provisions with over fifty section numbers. As shown in the ADA's table of contents in **Figure 4.5**, the eight provisions (sections 101 through 108) that apply in the employment context fall under Title I. That is why employment lawyers refer to these provisions as Title I of the ADA.

Recall that every public law (session law) is then compiled and arranged by topic in the *United States Code*. During this codification process, provisions of the same public law may be placed in different locations in the federal code. Additionally, the title and section numbers of a public law are re-numbered when arranged in the code. Returning to the public law for the ADA, all eight provisions (sections 101 through 108) under Title I have been codified under Title 42 of the *United States Code*. The provision of the ADA setting forth definitions (section 101) and the prohibition against discrimination (section 102) have been assigned section numbers 12111 and 12112, respectively, in the federal code. You can see the newly-assigned section numbers in **Figure 4.2** above.

C. State Statutes: From Bill to Law

As discussed in Chapter 1, every state has a legislative branch with two legislative bodies (except Nebraska). Most state legislatures are comprised of a senate and house of representatives, which are collectively known as a general assembly (*e.g.*, "Tennessee General Assembly") or a legislature (*e.g.*, "Alabama Legislature"). State legislatures meet in regular sessions annually to introduce, debate, and vote on bills.[10] The process for a bill becoming a state statute is similar to the federal process. After a state legislature passes a bill, the governor of the state may either sign or veto the bill.

Because variations exists, before researching statutes from your jurisdiction, you should take a few minutes to learn about the legislative process in your state. A helpful research guide (*e.g.*, a LibGuide) may be posted on a website from a law library in

---

10. A few legislatures (*e.g.*, the Montana and Nevada Legislatures) do not meet in regular annual sessions.

Figure 4.5: Table of Contents for the ADA (Pub. L. No. 101-336)

PUBLIC LAW 101-336—July 26, 1990   104 STAT. 327

Public Law 101-336
101st Congress
                        An Act   July 26, 1990
                                                   [S. 933]
To establish a clear and comprehensive prohibition of discrimination on the basis of disability.

*Be it enacted by the Senate and House of
Representatives of the United States of America in Congress assembled,*

**SECTION 1. SHORT TITLE; TABLE OF
CONTENTS.**

   (a) SHORT TITLE.—This Act may be
cited as the "Americans with Disabilities Act
of 1990".
   (b) TABLE OF CONTENTS.—The table
of contents is as follows:

Sec. 1. Short title; table of contents.
Sec. 2. Findings and purpose.
Sec. 3. Definitions.

TITLE I—EMPLOYMENT

Sec. 101. Definitions.
Sec. 102. Discrimination.
Sec. 103. Defenses.
Sec. 104. Illegal use of drugs and alcohol.
Sec. 105. Posting notices.
Sec. 106. Regulations.
Sec. 107. Enforcement.
Sec. 108. Effective date.

TITLE II—PUBLIC SERVICES

Subtitle A—Prohibition Against
Discrimination and Other Generally
Applicable Provisions

Sec. 201. Definition.
Sec. 202. Discrimination.
Sec. 203. Enforcement.
Sec. 204. Regulations.
Sec. 205. Effective date.

your state or available on your state's legislative website. You could locate a guide by performing the following searches on an internet search engine:

[name of your state] legislative process LibGuide

[name of your state] legislature how a bill becomes law

D. State Statutes: Forms of Publication

State statutes, like federal ones, are organized chronologically (session laws) and topically (codes).

1. Session Laws

As with newly-enacted federal laws, all the enacted laws for a particular session of a state legislature are compiled and organized in chronological order and referred to as **session laws**. In most states, immediately after a bill becomes law, the Secretary of State's office assigns a session law number to the new law, just like Congressional bills that become law are assigned a public law number. This number is assigned based on when the bill became law during a legislative session, and the numbering usually restarts for each new session. The session law number may include a year and chapter number or just a chapter number. To illustrate, the first bill that became law during the 2015 session of the Tennessee General Assembly was numbered "Public Chapter No. 1," and the first bill that became law during the next legislative session has the same number.

In most states, at the conclusion of each legislative session, the Secretary of State's office compiles all the statutes enacted during the session and publishes them chrono- logically. Historically, all states have published the session laws in a multi-volume set of books (similar to the *United States Statutes at Large*). These print collections have various names, including "Acts of the Alabama Legislature," "Laws of Florida," and the "Tennessee Public Acts." Currently, some states (*e.g.*, Ohio) publish session laws only in electronic format.

The session laws for most states are available electronically. You can find them on Westlaw and Lexis Advance, as well as on the websites maintained by many secretary of state offices. For example, the session laws of Tennessee are published on the Ten- nessee Secretary of State's website.

2. Codes

The good news for researchers is that state statutes are not only arranged by date of enactment. State statutes, like federal ones, are also organized by topic in codes and assigned a section number. Because codification is the process of compiling and arranging enacted laws by topic, a law placed into a code is also known as a **codified statute** or **code section**.

A state code is a multi-volume set of books containing all the statutes for that state that are currently in force as of the date of publication. And codes are updated to reflect all amendments to codified statutes. A statute's date of enactment does not determine its inclusion in, or exclusion from, a code. So a statute that was enacted thirty years ago and another one enacted one year ago would both appear in a code, as long as the statutes have never been repealed (or otherwise invalidated).

Most states have codes organizing their statutes in titles.[11] Like the *United States Code*, each title represents one broad topic. A state code may have the following titles: "Animals," "Crimes," "Motor Vehicles," and "Taxation." Each title is further divided into sub-topics. The sub-topics could be known as chapters, articles, and sections. Regardless of the names of the divisions, the individual sections contain the actual language of the statute.

For instance, the Ohio statute prohibiting the unauthorized practice of law is codified under Title 47 ("Occupations") and Chapter 4705 ("Attorneys") of the *Ohio Revised Code*. The text of the statute is codified as section 4705.01. **Figures 4.6** and **4.7**, respectively, show where this statute is codified and the language of the statute.

Figure 4.6: Excerpt of Table of Contents for Title 47 of
Page's Ohio Revised Code Annotated

---

11. A small fraction of states (*e.g.*, California, New York, and Texas) do not have a single code divided into titles but have a different code per topic; for example, one code may cover family law issues, and another code may cover criminal laws. A few states (*e.g.*, North Carolina and Michigan) use "chapter" designations instead of titles.

Figure 4.7: Statutory Text of Section 4705.01 of *Page's*
Ohio Revised Code Annotated

---

§ 4705.01 Practice of law; prohibitions.

No person shall be permitted to practice as an attorney and counselor at law, or to commence, conduct, or defend any action or proceeding in which the person is not a party concerned, either by using or subscribing the person's own name, or the name of another person, unless the person has been admitted to the bar by order of the supreme court in compliance with its prescribed and published rules. Except as provided in <u>section 4705.09 of the Revised Code</u> or in rules adopted by the supreme court, admission to the bar shall entitle the person to practice before any court or administrative tribunal without further qualification or license.

All states have at least one code, and some states have more than one code. A state may have an official code, unofficial code, or both types of codes. An official code is published by or under the direction of the state government, and may contain annotations (unlike the official *United States Code*). Of all the unofficial codes, substantially all are compiled and published by Thomson Reuters (known as West) or LexisNexis, and all unofficial codes contain annotations. The annotations for state codes are similar to the ones contained in the unofficial codes for federal statutes in that they include references to primary and secondary authorities that address the codified statutes. Last, both official and unofficial codes contain the same statutory text, and their arrangements of the codified statutes mirror each other.

Names of Sources Publishing Enacted Laws

To identify the official name of the source containing a state's session laws, review Table T1.3 in *The Bluebook* or Appendix 1 in the *ALWD Guide*. That table and that appendix also identify the name of each state code. Some state codes exclude the word "code" from their names.

State codes are available electronically and in print. Westlaw and Lexis Advance have databases for all state codes. Electronic versions are also available for free on websites maintained by state legislatures or by LexisNexis (for states where it publishes the official code).

E. Deciphering Statutory Citations

The citation of a statute identifies its "home address." Thus, once you know the citation to a federal or state statute, you can quickly retrieve the full text of the statute in print or through an online database.

A citation to a federal and state statute published in a code contains similar information. As shown in **Figures 4.8** and **4.9**, all statutory citations include the abbreviated name of the code containing the statute, followed by the section number and a parenthetical identifying at least the year of print publication (or currency of an online database).

Citation Cheat Sheets

When citing statutes, you should review Table T1 in *The Bluebook* or Appendix 1 in the *ALWD Guide* for assistance. That table and that appendix identify the proper abbreviations for the names of federal and state codes, as well as identifying the other necessary information belonging in a statutory citation.

The format of a citation to a state code differs from the citation to a federal code in two respects. First, the name of the state code usually begins the citation, but the title number of a federal code always begins the citation. Second, the section number for a state statute often includes a reference to the title and chapter (or other heading) where the statute has been codified, but sub-divisions are not part of a section number for a federal statute. For instance, the code section number "15-10-7" for an Alabama statute identifies the following information:

- 15 = Title of Code (Criminal Procedure)
- 10 = Chapter of Code (Arrests)
- 7 = Section of Code (Arrests by Private Persons)

Figure 4.8 demystifies the parts of a citation to a federal statute found on Westlaw, and **Figure 4.9** breaks down the parts of a state statute found on Lexis Advance.

Figure 4.8: Parts of a Citation to a Federal Statute

18 U.S.C.A. § 521 (West, Westlaw through P.L. 115-221)					
Title Number	Name of Code	Section Number	Name of Publisher	Name of Online Database	Currency of Online Database
18	U.S.C.A. = United States Code Annotated	521	West (also known as Thomson Reuters)	Westlaw	P.L. 115-221 = The 221st law enacted in the 115th Congress

Figure 4.9: Parts of a Citation to a State Statute

Ala. Code § 15-10-7 (LexisNexis, LEXIS through end of the 2018 Reg. Sess.)				
Name of Code	Section Number	Name of Publisher	Name of Online Database	Currency of Online Database
Ala. Code = Michie's Alabama Code	15-10-7 ("15" is the title number; "10" is the chapter number)	LexisNexis	LEXIS = Lexis Advance	End of the 2018 Regular Session

F. Summary of Key Points

Congress and state legislatures enact laws known as statutes. Federal and state statutes may be civil or criminal in nature, and they often prohibit, require, or authorize conduct. Being the law, statutes must be followed by individuals, entities, and courts.

Federal and state statutes are published as session laws and in codes and are available in print and electronic format. Although you may need to review session laws for some research projects, you should start researching statutes in an annotated code. All codes are arranged by topic, not in chronological order. Annotated codes include the text of every statute currently in force, as well as having references to primary and secondary authorities. (In Chapter 15, you will learn to research using an annotated code.)

Figure 4.10 summarizes the similarities and differences between federal and state laws that are compiled and published as session laws and in codes.

Figure 4.10: Comparisons Between Federal and State Laws

Publication Forms	Federal Laws	State Laws
Session Laws: Names of Compilations	*United States Statutes at Large* (official)	Have various names, including • *Laws of Florida* • *Public Acts of the State of Tennessee* • *Statutes of California*
	United States Code Service Advance (unofficial)	
	United States Code Congressional & Administrative News (unofficial)	
Session Laws: Arrangement	Chronological by date of enactment	Chronological by date of enactment
Session Laws: Availability	Westlaw (fee-based)	Westlaw (fee-based)
	Lexis Advance (fee-based)	Lexis Advance (fee-based)
	Congress.gov (free) govinfo.gov (free)	Websites of secretaries of state (some exceptions) (free)
Codes: Names of Compilations	*United States Code* (official)	Have various names, including • *Official Code of Georgia Annotated* • *Michigan Compiled Laws Annotated* • *West's Florida Statutes Annotated*
	United States Code Annotated (unofficial) (Thomson Reuters)	
	United States Code Service (unofficial) (LexisNexis)	
Codes: Arrangement	Topics	Topics
Codes: Availability	Westlaw (fee-based)	Westlaw (fee-based)
	Lexis Advance (fee-based)	Lexis Advance (fee-based)
	Website of the Office of the Law Revision Counsel of the House of Representatives (free)	Websites of state legislatures (free)
	Website of Cornell's Legal Information Institute (free)	

Figure 4.11: Publication Process for Federal Statutes

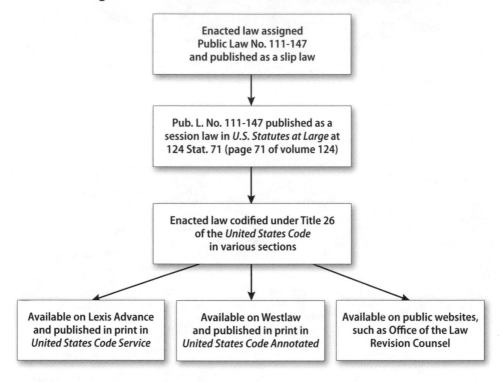

If you are confused by how a statute travels the path from slip law to session law to codification, review **Figure 4.11**. It shows the typical publication process for a federal statute enacted by Congress. The process for state statutes is similar in many states.

G. Review Questions on Statutes and Codes

At this point, you should have a basic understanding of the publication process for statutes and the parts of a code. To test your comprehension, answer the true-false and multiple-choice questions on this book's companion website, Core Knowledge. It will identify the correct answers and provide clear explanations for each question. The same questions are reproduced below.

1. If a bill has been assigned a public law number, the bill has become an enacted law.

    a. True

    b. False

2. The *United States Code* arranges federal statutes by topic.

    a. True

    b. False

3. The *Official Code of Georgia Annotated* organizes Georgia statutes based on the date of enactment.

    a. True

    b. False

4. Federal and state session laws are arranged based on the date of enactment.

    a. True

    b. False

5. A federal or state annotated code contains references only to secondary authorities and not primary authorities.

    a. True

    b. False

6. An individual section of a code contains the actual text of the statute.

    a. True

    b. False

7. A federal enacted law has been assigned the number "Public Law 110-42." What does that mean?
    a. The enacted law was the 110th law passed by the 42nd Congress.

    b. The enacted law was the 42nd law passed by the 110th Congress.

    c. The enacted law was published in the *United States Code* under Title 42.

    d. None of the above.

8. Identify the differences between a criminal and civil statute.

    a. A criminal statute does not require harm, but harm is usually required to violate a civil statute.

    b. Only the government may bring a charge under a criminal statute, but a private party may bring a claim under a civil statute.

    c. The violation of a criminal statute subjects a person to imprisonment, but imprisonment is not a penalty for a violation of a civil statute.

    d. All of the above.

9. Sarah has been tasked to research the Americans with Disabilities Act, a federal statute. In addition to finding the statutory text, she needs to find judicial decisions construing the Act. What source should Sarah consult?
    a. The Official *United States Code*

    b. The Unofficial *United States Code Annotated*

    c. A state code

    d. The Official *United States Statutes at Large*

10. Paul needs to research Texas statutes for a tax issue. As a beginner researcher, Paul wants to understand the legislative process in Texas and locate an online guide. Which of the following searches on an internet search engine would probably yield relevant results?

   a. Texas LibGuide legislative process

   b. Texas Legislature how a bill becomes law

   c. Both A and B

   d. None of the above

Part II

Eight Steps for Researching Common Law Issues

Introduction: What You Should Know About Researching the Common Law

After reading the previous chapters, you should know a few things about the United States legal system, including the structure of the federal and state court systems, the difference between binding and nonbinding authorities, and the publication process for cases. (If you skipped the first three chapters in Part I, that was a mistake; read them now.) You are ready to embark on the research journey. Part II examines the eight steps that students and attorneys should follow when researching a common law issue. The eight research steps discussed in the following eight chapters are summarized below.

Step 1: Create a Research Plan (Chapter 5)

Step 2: Research Every Unfamiliar Legal Issue with Secondary Sources (Chapter 6)

Step 3: Research Cases by Topic (Chapter 7)

Step 4: Use a Reliable Citator to Find Relevant Cases and to Confirm Their Validity (Chapter 8)

Step 5: Perform Keyword Searches in the Relevant Caselaw Databases (Chapter 9)

Step 6: Expand Your Research Within the Controlling Jurisdiction, If Necessary (Chapter 10)

Step 7: Research Cases from Outside the Controlling Jurisdiction, If Necessary (Chapter 11)

Step 8: Use a Reliable Citator to Re-Confirm the Validity of Each Relevant Case (Chapter 12)

Legal Research Is Not a Linear Process

Although the eight steps provide an excellent framework for common law issues, the process of legal research is *not* linear. Researching the law involves a constant process of evaluating and analyzing your authorities and legal conclusions. For some projects, you could skip one or more research steps. For many other projects, you should follow all eight steps but not necessarily in the exact order set forth above. The best path forward depends on your client's factual situation, the complexity of the law, the time constraints for the assignment, prior knowledge of the area of law being researched, the number of authorities on point, and other factors.

For every unfamiliar common law issue, you should follow—or at least consider—these eight research steps. These research steps are an excellent approach to maximize the likelihood that you will find all relevant cases applying to your client's situation. When faced with an unfamiliar legal question, you will have no idea the number of primary authorities addressing your issue. There might be only a handful of cases with a legal issue and facts like your client's circumstances, but they may be difficult to find. By following each research step and looking for cases using multiple research tools, it will be unlikely that you will miss an important case. Alternatively, there might be hundreds or even thousands of cases that indirectly touch on your issue, but they may not be directly relevant to the client's question. These steps will help you weed out irrelevant cases and keep you focused on finding binding cases so that you do not accidently rely on nonbinding cases that conflict with the binding ones. Your court must follow the binding precedent (see Chapter 2).

Additionally, these eight research steps for a common law issue are a great approach to reach a reliable answer on your client's legal question—one that accurately predicts the conclusion that the court deciding the legal issue will reach. It is insufficient to find just one or two cases; you must find and analyze all relevant cases for your research to be complete. This is especially true for common law issues, which are often fact-intensive. In contrast, when you fail to find the relevant authorities, you cannot accurately predict whether your client will win or lose. (Legal researchers rarely "stumble" upon the right answer.) The wrong answer at any time of your representation of a client could severely harm the client. Say your client has been offered $100,000 to settle her lawsuit against a company, but your boss rejects the settlement offer based on your memorandum predicting (wrongly) that your client will definitely prevail. If the client then loses at trial on every issue, the client would have lost at least $100,000.

To illustrate the non-linear research process, assume your law firm represents an employee against her employer. The partner has asked you to research whether the courts in your state recognize a common law claim against an employer who discharges an employee in retaliation for filing a lawsuit. Imagine, too, that you have background knowledge on claims for retaliation in the employment context but have not previously researched this specific issue. You could skip Steps 2 through 4 and begin with **Step 5** and perform a Google-like search in an online database. Through the keyword search, suppose you found one binding decision from an intermediate appellate court that expressly rejected a common law claim for retaliatory discharge. Although it appears you have a reliable answer, you should move back to **Step 2** (secondary sources), **Step 3** (research by topic), and **Step 4** (citators). By completing those research steps, you would discover whether the state supreme court has overruled the appellate decision and whether courts in subsequent decisions have carved out exceptions and allowed common law retaliation claims in limited circumstances.

In short, the purpose of the eight research steps is to provide you with a checklist for researching various legal issues, not to force you to mechanically follow each step for every assignment. If your professor or boss prefers that you deviate from one or more steps, then do so.

Chapter 5

Step 1:
Create a Research Plan

The first of the eight steps in researching a common law issue is to develop a research plan. If you needed surgery, you would really hope that your physician had an action plan *before* entering the operating room. Your clients will have similar expectations. For new legal issues, resist the urge to type "random" words into the search box of an online legal database in hopes that a computer algorithm will deliver the right answers. Many students have tried that method—and failed.

You cannot fully complete the research plan for a new and unfamiliar legal issue at the beginning stage of your research, so remember to update the research plan as you progress through the process. To illustrate, before reviewing a secondary source on a negligence claim, you would not know all possible defenses a defendant might assert against your injured client. After reviewing a secondary source on your state's negligence law, you might discover that the defendant has a good argument that the client assumed the risk of injury (which would relieve the defendant of liability). You should then revise your research plan to reflect the newly-discovered legal issue.

A. The Research Plan

A typical research plan (**Step 1**) includes the different parts discussed below. As you move through the research plan for an assignment, you should complete the Research Action Plan Form in Appendix C. An electronic version is also available on this book's companion website, Core Knowledge. It will keep your research plan organized.

1. Review the Client's Facts, and Identify the Governing Law

You should first gather and review the facts for your client's legal dispute and should then attempt to identify the law that applies to your client's factual situation. Initially, you should know the answers to the *who, what, where, when,* and *why* questions, including *who* are the parties and their relationship to each other (*e.g.,* landlord and tenant), *what* is the wrongful conduct and *what* person or thing caused the injury, *when* the injury occurred, *where* the injury occurred, and *why* your client wants to sue or is being sued. Those answers will help you determine the governing law. To illustrate, if both parties reside in Ohio and the wrongful conduct and injury occurred in Ohio, you know that Ohio state law applies. If the wrongful conduct and injury took place on a military base, you know that federal law applies.

Before reading secondary and primary authorities, you will not know the answer to multiple questions about your facts and the governing laws. As to the facts, you will not know which facts your court will consider in determining whether your client wins or loses on the disputed issue. As to the law, you will not know whether both federal and state laws govern. And you will not know whether your state allows a plaintiff to bring a claim under both a statute and the common law for the same conduct and injury. As you find those answers in relevant secondary sources (**Step 2**), make sure you update the research plan.

2. Identify the Legal Issues and Keywords

Next, you should identify your client's legal issues. Although you will not know all the potential issues and legally relevant facts initially, you should know enough information to sketch a preliminary statement of the issue. For example, suppose your client was attacked in Ohio by the neighbor's German Shepherd and wants to recover damages for his injuries. The client saw the dog running toward him and threw a few rocks at it, and then the dog bit him. Before performing any research, you could draft an issue statement similar to this one:

> **Preliminary Issue:** Under Ohio law, is a dog owner liable for damages when the owner's dog attacks a neighbor?

As you find more relevant laws throughout the research process, you will better understand what facts are relevant and will probably identify new legal issues. You should then revise your initial issue statement or draft additional ones. Suppose you reviewed a secondary source on Ohio dog-bite law and learned that a victim may bring a common law claim of negligence against a dog owner but that victims who assume the risk of a dog attack cannot recover damages. With this new information, you now know at least one claim to bring and understand that the fact about the rocks being thrown at the dog are legally relevant to the owner's possible defense of assumption of risk. You should revise the preliminary issue statement, such as stating this question (the added key terms appear in bold):

> **Revised Issue:** Under Ohio law, is a dog owner liable on a **negligence claim** when the owner's dog attacks a neighbor **after the neighbor threw rocks at the dog?**

Alternatively, you could divide your preliminary issue statement into two questions:

Broad Issue: Under Ohio law, is a dog owner liable on a negligence claim when the owner's dog attacks a neighbor?

---

and

Narrow Issue: Under Ohio law, does a dog-bite victim assume the risk of injury where the victim threw rocks at the dog immediately before the attack?

Once you have written down at least one issue statement, post it everywhere you plan to research the problem and especially next to your computer. That is no exaggeration. And remember to review the issue statements during the research process to avoid falling into the research "black hole."

After you have reviewed the client's facts, identified the governing law, and drafted an issue statement, you should create a list of relevant words and phrases (known as keywords) to use as you research your client's legal issues. A list of keywords is necessary to research in print and online and should include broad and specific terms. For example, for the dog-bite hypothetical, the broad and specific terms would include "pets," "animals," "dogs," and "German Shepherd." Start drafting your list by reviewing the answers to the *who*, *what*, *where*, *when*, and *why* questions. And as you review secondary and primary authorities, you will discover more legal terms applicable to your client's situation.

A great source for generating keywords is a legal dictionary or legal thesaurus. *Black's Law Dictionary* is a well-respected legal dictionary, and courts have cited it to define legal terms.[1] Cornell School of Law maintains a free version of a dictionary known as Wex (http://www.law.cornell.edu/wex). A good choice for a legal thesaurus is *Burton's Legal Thesaurus.*[2]

3. Identify the Binding and Most Relevant Authorities

Another part of the research plan is to identify binding authorities—the cases that the court deciding the client's issue must follow. When both binding and nonbinding authority exists for the same rule of law, you must cite the binding case in a legal document. If the nonbinding case further supports your argument, it could be cited as well. Citing just the nonbinding case, however, would mislead your reader to believe that binding authority does not exist.

---

1. It is available in print and on Westlaw.
2. For a further discussion of how to develop a list of keywords, see Chapter 9.

For common law issues (the focus of Part II of this book), judicial decisions are the only binding authorities.[3] As explained in Chapter 2, you should follow a two-step approach to know which decisions bind your court. You need to (1) determine whether federal or state law applies, and (2) consider what court (*e.g.*, federal or state) and what level of court (*e.g.*, trial court) will resolve the dispute. Recall that **Table 1** (Binding vs. Nonbinding Cases) in Appendix A helps you apply the two-step approach to your client's situation. For instance, imagine your client has brought a negligence claim (state law) in a Georgia trial court. **Table 1** informs you that the binding authority includes decisions from the Court of Appeals of Georgia (intermediate appellate court) and the Supreme Court of Georgia (cell A.2 of **Table 1**). As a result, you know to focus on researching decisions from those courts.

You may also need to research nonbinding judicial decisions. Their persuasive value primarily depends on what court issued the decision, the quality of the court's reasoning, and the similarities of the legal issues and facts to the client's situation. Returning to the negligence claim example, decisions from the United States Court of Appeals for the Eleventh Circuit or a federal district court in Georgia would, as a general rule, be highly or moderately persuasive authorities on a state trial court. But those designations are not static. A case would lose its "highly" or "moderately" persuasive status if it is poorly reasoned or conflicts with a binding case.

Of the cases falling in the binding and persuasive categories, remember to focus on finding judicial decisions in which the legal issues and facts are the same or similar to your client's situation. Because courts generally reach the same conclusion as prior decisions when faced with similar legal issues and facts (under *stare decisis*), those types of cases will be the most relevant and helpful in predicting how your court will resolve the client's issues.

Table 2 (Choosing the Best Authority) in Appendix B will help keep you focused on finding judicial decisions with similar legal issues and legally relevant facts. The table has three columns: "Best Authority," "Good Authority," and "Fair/Weak Authority." Of course, you should find cases falling in the "Best Authority" column—the decisions that closely align with the client's issues and facts. In reviewing **Table 2**, you should also consider whether a case falls near the top or bottom of a particular column (higher row is usually better authority), whether the case has been designated "for publication" (published decisions are usually better authority), the date the case was decided (recent decisions are usually better authority), and the court's reasoning.

But do not disregard cases falling in the "Good Authority" column. Many times, you should find and rely on those "Good Authority" cases. Your purpose for citing a case determines whether the "better" authority is the one that falls in the "Best Authority" or "Good Authority" column. For example, assume you need a case identifying the basic elements of a negligence claim in your jurisdiction. Further assume

---

3. If statutes and administrative regulations apply, the deciding court would also be bound by those laws.

that you found two cases for this purpose: a nonbinding case that is legally and factually similar ("Best Authority" column in **Table 2**) and a binding case that is legally similar but factually different ("Good Authority" column in **Table 2**). You should cite the binding case for the elements, even though it does not technically fall in the "Best Authority" column.

A hypothetical will help you navigate both **Table 1** and **Table 2**. Suppose you are researching Georgia law on whether a manager's derogatory, oral statements to a subordinate employee constitute "outrageous" conduct for a common law claim of intentional infliction of emotional distress ("IIED"). Assume also that the lawsuit is pending in a Georgia trial court and that you found three cases involving a claim for IIED:

- *Case A*: The Supreme Court of Georgia concluded that a co-worker's harsh, oral statements, alone, do not constitute outrageous conduct.

- *Case B*: The United States Court of Appeals for the Eleventh Circuit ruled that a co-worker's actions were outrageous when he physically harmed a cat in front of its owner, another co-worker.

- *Case Z*: The Supreme Court of Georgia concluded that plaintiff did not suffer severe emotional distress, which is a separate element than the element of outrageous conduct.

First, you should review **Table 1** (Binding vs. Nonbinding Cases) in Appendix A to know which authorities are binding and persuasive. *Case A* and *Case Z* are binding authorities because they are from the Supreme Court of Georgia (court of last resort); however, *Case B* is not binding, because a federal court cannot bind a state court on state law.

Second, you should determine where each case falls in **Table 2** to help you confirm whether you have found the most relevant cases for your issue. **Table 2** is reproduced below, and it identifies where the three cases fall. *Case A* falls in the "Best Authority" column (cell A.1) because it is binding and addresses the same legal issue (outrageous conduct) and similar facts (oral statements in the employment context) as the client's situation. *Case B* falls in the "Good Authority" column (cell B.2) because it is highly persuasive authority from the Eleventh Circuit and involves different, more extreme facts (physical harm instead of mere words).[4] *Case Z*, although from the Georgia Supreme Court, is the weakest authority. This case falls in the "Fair/Weak Authority" column (cell A.3) because it involves a different legal issue (severity of the emotional distress and not outrageous conduct).

As a warning, do not use **Table 1** and **Table 2** as substitutes for your own thinking and analysis. Instead, use both tables as guides and efficient ways to confirm whether your research is on the right track. No single chart can inform a researcher of the best authority for every circumstance because of the vast number of factual situations

---

4. If this Eleventh Circuit decision was based on weak reasoning, it would lose its "highly persuasive" status and fall on a lower row in **Table 2** (cell C.2).

Table 2: Choosing the Best Authority: Hypothetical on Outrageous Conduct

		1	2	3
		Best Authority	**Good Authority**	**Fair/Weak Authority**
	Weight of Authority (Refer to Table 1)	Higher Row in Same Column = Better Authority Better Reasoned Decision = Better Authority Recent Cases = Better Authority Published Cases = Better Authority		
A	**Binding Caselaw**	*Case A* Legal Issue: Same — outrageous conduct Facts: Similar — oral statements in the employment context	Legal Issue: Same or similar Facts: Different	*Case Z* Legal Issue: Different — severity of plaintiff's emotional distress, not outrageous conduct Facts: Different
B	**Nonbinding: Highly to Moderately Persuasive Caselaw**	Legal Issue: Same or similar Facts: Same or similar legally relevant facts	*Case B* Legal Issue: Similar — outrageous conduct Facts: Different — physical harm, not mere words	Legal Issue: Different but same area of law Facts: Different
C	**Nonbinding: Slightly Persuasive Caselaw**	Legal Issue: Same or similar Facts: Same or similar legally relevant facts	Legal Issue: Same or similar Facts: Different	Legal Issue: Different but same area of law Facts: Different

that exist and because the persuasive value of a nonbinding case correlates with the court's reasoning. You, therefore, should not spend hours antagonizing whether one case falls in the Best or Good Authority column of **Table 2** or whether a case falls in row B or C in a given column of **Table 2**. For instance, if the only cases you have found fall in the "Fair/Weak Authority" column of **Table 2**, you know to continue researching and to proactively look for judicial decisions that closely align with the client's legal issues and factual circumstances.

4. Consider the Appropriate Research Tools to Use

You should identify the research tools you expect to use online and in print to find all relevant secondary and primary authorities. The most popular and most respected online legal research services are **Westlaw** (owned by Thomson Reuters) and **Lexis Advance** (owned by LexisNexis). These fee-based commercial services essentially provide the "key" to the universe of law. Their online databases provide access to all federal and state constitutions, statutes, administrative regulations, and caselaw, as well as databases for many secondary authorities covering substantially all legal topics. Additionally, the proprietary computer algorithms on Westlaw and Lexis Advance are probably the most sophisticated in the legal research world.[5] If you cannot find any relevant legal authority for your assignment after researching on these sophisticated services, walk — or run — to a reference librarian or to your professor's office for help.

Recently, Thomson Reuters has introduced a new Westlaw platform called **Westlaw Edge**. This new platform has a fresh look and offers several exciting features, including improved artificial intelligence to minimize research time on some assignments. Despite the revamped interface, Westlaw's organization and search functionally are essentially the same. This book, therefore, refers to both platforms as "Westlaw." If a feature is available only on Westlaw Edge, it is noted. Students at most schools have access to Westlaw Edge. Attorneys can switch to Westlaw Edge for an additional fee; it is unclear how many attorneys will keep their current Westlaw or will upgrade to the new platform.

Although students have "free" access to Westlaw and Lexis Advance, these sophisticated services are expensive outside the law school bubble. Because some of your clients will be reluctant to pay for legal research, you should know about cost-effective alternatives to the fee-based services and should educate yourself on their limitations.

Casemaker and **Fastcase** are comprehensive online legal research services available to many attorneys as a benefit of bar membership, but the number of features pales in comparison to Westlaw and Lexis. Casemaker is available for free to members of almost 30 state and local bar associations (*e.g.*, Alabama and Ohio), and Fastcase is available for free to members of over 25 state and local bar associations (*e.g.*, Georgia and Florida). Their online libraries have good coverage of federal and state statutes, regulations, and cases. But both free research services lack significant coverage of secondary sources, although Fastcase provides access to some respected secondary sources for a fee.

A third alternative to Westlaw and Lexis is **Google Scholar** — a free service for every person with internet access.[6] It has extensive coverage of cases from federal and

---

5. A fairly new competitor to Westlaw and Lexis Advance is Bloomberg Law. Although this book does not focus on Bloomberg Law, the research skills you learn on Westlaw and Lexis transfer to other online providers like Bloomberg Law.

6. It is available at https://scholar.google.com.

state courts but has no database for any statute, whether federal or state. Google Scholar does not maintain a database for secondary sources; instead, it provides links to legal articles hosted on both free websites and fee-based databases.

The platforms just discussed make it easy to locate the full text of a judicial decision. Assume a secondary source provided this citation to a federal case: *United States v. Tobin*, 923 F.2d 1506 (11th Cir. 1991). You could retrieve it on Lexis Advance, Westlaw, Casemaker, Fastcase, or Google Scholar by entering the citation in the search box.

In short, if you need to minimize research costs, Casemaker, Fastcase, and Google Scholar are all good options. But use these free services to supplement, not supplant, Westlaw and Lexis Advance.

While a wealth of information is available online, you should also look for relevant secondary sources in print in a law library. Some excellent legal resources are available only in print (see Chapter 2), and some resources and research tools are easier to navigate and understand in print than online. In a nutshell, the printing press is not obsolete — yet.

5. Identify Any Constraints

You also need to identify the final work product expected, any limits on the time you can spend on the assignment, and the dollar amount in dispute. If you are drafting a motion for summary judgment or an appellate brief on a claim against your client for $500,000, you would spend many hours researching the law. You, however, would spend fewer hours researching the law for an office memorandum addressing a small-dollar claim.

B. Summary of Key Points

As you read the multiple parts to a good research plan, you should have realized that researching the law is more complicated than other types of research. To minimize mistakes and maximize efficiency, take time to create a research plan for your assignments. With a research plan in hand, you are ready to move to **Step 2** and find and review secondary sources covering your issues.

Remember two important points as you progress through the next research steps. You must update your research plan to reflect any new discoveries, such as new law that raises a new legal issue for the client. And track your research process. After researching for days or weeks and reading many authorities, you will forget which cases you read, which online databases you searched, and which methods you used to search online. You should track and organize your research by completing the Research Action Plan Form in Appendix C. That form is also posted on Core Knowledge.

C. Review Questions on Research Plans

At this point, you should understand how to create a research plan. To test your comprehension, answer the true-false questions on this book's companion website, Core Knowledge. It will identify the correct answers and provide clear explanations for each question. The same questions are reproduced below.

1. For the first part of your research plan, you should read court decisions discussing your client's legal issue.

   a. True

   b. False

2. You should consult **Table 1** (Binding vs. Nonbinding Cases) and **Table 2** (Choosing the Best Authority) to help you determine whether your research is on the right track.

   a. True

   b. False

3. After researching caselaw for one hour, if all the cases you have found fall in the "Fair/Weak Authority" column of **Table 2**, you should stop researching.

   a. True

   b. False

4. To determine whether a judicial decision falls in the "Best" or "Fair/Weak Authority" column of **Table 2**, you should consider whether the legal issue and facts are similar to your client's situation.

   a. True

   b. False

5. The most comprehensive and respected online legal research services are Westlaw and Lexis Advance.

   a. True

   b. False

D. Practice Completing a Research Plan

Like riding a bike, you cannot learn to research by merely reading about it; you must practice doing it. On this book's companion website, Core Knowledge, a few research assignments have been posted. The online assignments walk you through the steps for researching a common law issue on Westlaw and Lexis Advance, including how to develop research plans. For each assignment, you will research the law to resolve legal issues for your hypothetical client.

Chapter 6

Step 2:
Research Every Unfamiliar Legal
Issue with Secondary Sources

Step 2
(Secondary
Sources)

Step 3
(Cases
by
Topic)

In the previous chapter, you learned the importance of having a research plan in hand. Among other things, your research plan should identify the controlling law, client's legal issues, and the binding authorities. Remember to update the research plan as you complete this **Step 2** and subsequent research steps.

For **Step 2** of the eight steps in researching a common law issue, you should research each unfamiliar area of law using secondary sources. While not the actual law, secondary sources analyze and explain the law and legal concepts.[1] Law professors, attorneys, and judges author various secondary sources on legal topics in their fields of expertise. Those sources cover almost every legal topic, from criminal law, to family law, to contract breaches, to employment matters, to business disputes, to personal injury claims. Thus, there is no need to travel the research path as a lone wolf; you can — and should — tap into the knowledge of those experts.

Some students believe the myth that they will save time by diving into primary authorities and skipping secondary sources. The myth is based on the assumption that students can quickly sift through pages and pages of cases and understand an entire area of law by piecing together the rules of law and reasoning from those cases. Imagine you tried to bake a triple layer wedding cake not by reading cookbooks about cakes ("secondary sources") but by staring at individual ingredients ("primary sources"). Without assistance from cookbooks, it would be quite difficult to determine how the ingredients should be combined and how much to add; similarly, it would be difficult to understand and synthesize the rules of law and reasoning from multiple cases without assistance from experts in the legal field.

Step 5
(Keywords)

Step 6
(Expand)

Step 7
(Other States)

---

1. Secondary sources are sometimes referred to as secondary authorities or secondary materials.

A. Three Reasons to Research with Secondary Sources

To start your research journey, you should find and read several secondary sources on your client's legal issues (**Step 2**). These research tools are helpful for three primary reasons.

First, secondary sources summarize and explain the law. They describe all aspects of the law, from the basic (*e.g.*, elements of a claim) to the more complex (*e.g.*, proximate cause). Indeed, secondary sources often answer a threshold question important to any research project: whether federal or state law applies to the client's situation. Because both federal and state statutes can regulate the same conduct, you might need to research both laws. And secondary sources usually answer a second threshold question: whether a statute, the common law, or both laws govern the client's facts. In many states, a plaintiff can assert a claim under a state statute and a separate claim under the common law (*e.g.*, dog-bite cases). You need to know whether a plaintiff may bring statutory and common law claims, because they may have different standards of proof or may authorize different types of damages. You would also know to follow different research paths for the two claims. For the common law claim, you would follow the steps outlined in Part II, *Eight Steps for Researching Common Law Issues*. For the statutory claim, you would follow the steps set forth in Part III, *Ten Steps for Researching Statutory Issues*.

Additionally, by reviewing a summary of the relevant law in multiple secondary sources, you would discover other important information. You would have a better grasp of how the law applies to your client's factual situation and would better understand which facts are important, such as whether it is important in a dog-bite case that the dog had previously bitten another animal.

Second, secondary materials reveal important terminology and terms of art for an area of law. By knowing the terms of art, you can create a list of relevant search terms that will help you find additional authorities. For example, suppose you are researching Ohio law on whether a landlord may be liable for an injury caused by a tenant's dog. A secondary source would identify terms of art that a law student and new attorney would not know through intuition, such as "harborer," "keeper," and "vicious."

Third, secondary sources help you find primary authorities—binding and persuasive—that address your legal issues. When explaining the law, secondary sources cite primary authorities. Thus, these sources provide you with citations to primary authorities that help you analyze and potentially resolve your client's legal questions. Even if the primary authorities cited in a secondary source do not involve facts similar to your client's situation, those cited authorities can lead you to factually-similar authorities from the controlling jurisdiction.

In reviewing secondary sources for a common law issue, remember your ultimate goal: finding relevant cases to determine whether your client will prevail on the disputed legal issue. And remember to focus on finding cases that fall within the "Best Authority" and "Good Authority" columns in **Table 2** in Appendix B.

B. Major Categories of Secondary Sources

All secondary sources are not created equally. The usefulness of a particular type of secondary source depends on the controlling law and your client's legal issues and facts. The next sections discuss the five major categories of secondary sources that are available in print and online.[2]

1. Legal Encyclopedias

You probably consulted a traditional encyclopedia in elementary and middle school for science projects and history papers. **Legal encyclopedias** are similar to traditional ones but lack colorful pictures and are focused on legal topics.

A legal encyclopedia is a multi-volume set of books that provides a brief overview of almost *every* area of law, from broad legal issues (criminal law) to more narrow ones (liability of owners of wild animals). The legal topics are generally arranged in alphabetical order so that the first volume of a set includes the "A" topics (*e.g.*, "adverse possession") and the last volume includes the "Z" topic of Zoning.[3] A legal encyclopedia is a great place to start researching an unfamiliar topic because it will summarize the law and cite potentially relevant primary authorities. But a legal encyclopedia should not be your one-stop shop for secondary sources because of its limited discussion (often a few paragraphs) on any particular topic.

There are both national legal encyclopedias and state-specific ones. The two national encyclopedias are *American Jurisprudence 2d* (commonly called "Am. Jur.") and *Corpus Juris Secundum* (commonly called "C.J.S."). Each national encyclopedia addresses virtually all federal and state laws in over 100 volumes. State encyclopedias, however, discuss only the laws of a specific state; for instance, *West's Indiana Law Encyclopedia* covers only Indiana law, and *Texas Jurisprudence 3d* addresses only Texas law. Unfortunately, not every state has an encyclopedia explaining its laws. If your state has no encyclopedia, you could start a research project with a national encyclopedia, but remember to look for citations to primary authorities that discuss the law applicable to your client's issues.

---

2. Another frequently used secondary authority is the *Restatements of Law*. It is discussed in Chapter 10.

3. One volume of a legal encyclopedia may contain several topics or just one topic, depending on the breadth of the topic.

> ### Identifying State Encyclopedias
>
> A state-specific encyclopedia exists for about fifteen states. Many of these legal encyclopedias do not have the term "encyclopedia" in the title but instead have the word "jurisprudence" in the title.

Review **Figure 6.1** to see an entry from *American Jurisprudence 2d* (national encyclopedia), and review **Figure 6.2** to see an entry from *Georgia Jurisprudence* (state-specific encyclopedia).

Figure 6.1: Excerpt from *American Jurisprudence 2d*

3 Am. Jur. 2d Adverse Possession § 1

American Jurisprudence, Second Edition | August 2018 Update
Adverse Possession
Barbara J. Van Arsdale, J.D., Janice Holben, J.D. and Anne E. Melley, J.D., LL.M., of the staff of the National Legal Research Group, Inc.

I. In General

§ 1. Nature of adverse possession

Topic Summary | Correlation Table | References

West's Key Number Digest

- West's Key Number Digest, Adverse Possession ☞1

Trial Strategy

- Acquisition of Title to Property by Adverse Possession, 39 Am. Jur. Proof of Facts 2d 261

Forms

- Forms relating to effects and adverse possession, generally, see Am. Jur. Pleading and Practice Forms, Adverse Possession [Westlaw® Search Query]

Figure 6.1: *Continued*

§ 1.Nature of adverse possession, 3 Am. Jur. 2d Adverse Possession § 1

Adverse possession is a method whereby a person who was not the owner of property obtains a valid title to that property by the passage of time.[1] The concept of adverse possession allows a person to claim title to property presently titled in another[2] and permits one to achieve ownership of another's property by operation of law.[3] Adverse possession is thus recognized as a mode or method of acquiring title to property,[4] but it is not a favored one.[5]

CUMULATIVE SUPPLEMENT

Cases:

An adverse possession claim is really one for recognition of title and enforcement of the rights that accompany title. Roy v. Woodstock Community Trust, Inc., 2013 VT 100A, 94 A.3d 530 (Vt. 2014).

[END OF SUPPLEMENT]

Footnotes

1   Wallace v. Ayres, 228 Ark. 1007, 311 S.W.2d 758 (1958); USA Cartage Leasing, LLC v. Baer, 202 Md. App. 138, 32 A.3d 88 (2011), cert. granted, 425 Md. 227, 40 A.3d 39 (2012) and judgment aff'd, 429 Md. 199, 55 A.3d 510 (2012).
As to the operation and effect of adverse possession, see §§ 231 to 252.

2   Bynum v. Lewis, 393 S.W.3d 916 (Tex. App. Tyler 2013).

3   Recreation Land Corp. v. Hartzfeld, 2008 PA Super 76, 947 A.2d 771 (2008).

4   Tenala, Ltd. v. Fowler, 921 P.2d 1114 (Alaska 1996); Hart v. Sternberg, 205 Ark. 929, 171 S.W.2d 475 (1943); Cosgrove v. Young, 230 Kan. 705, 642 P.2d 75 (1982); Walling v. Przybylo, 7 N.Y.3d 228, 818 N.Y.S.2d 816, 851 N.E.2d 1167 (2006).

Figure 6.2: Excerpt from *Georgia Jurisprudence*

14 Ga. Jur. § 13:6

Georgia Jurisprudence | September 2018 Update
Personal Injury and Torts
Part Two. Specific Torts
Chapter 13. Assault and Battery
Christine M. G. Davis, J.D., LL.M.

I. Generally
B. Elements of Assault and Battery

§ 13:6. Battery

Chapter Summary | Correlation Table | Divisional References

West's Key Number Digest

- West's Key Number Digest, Assault and Battery 2

A.L.R. Library

- Secondary smoke as battery, 46 A.L.R.5th 813

The act of intentionally causing physical harm to another is actionable civilly as a battery.[1] Because of the importance of one's right of the inviolability of one's person, any unlawful touching,[2] or unauthorized offensive contact,[3] no matter how minimal, is actionable as a physical injury to a person.[4]

Practice Tip:

For purposes of battery, an offensive touching is one that proceeds from anger, rudeness, or lust. The test as to whether an assault and battery occurred is what would be offensive to an ordinary person not unduly sensitive as to such person's dignity.[5]

An actionable battery may be accomplished by an unauthorized caress as well as by an unauthorized blow.[6]

The intent to cause physical harm or injury to another is not the only basis for a claim of battery, however. Contact proceeding from rudeness is as offensive and harmful as that which proceeds from anger or lust and in law constitutes an assault and battery.[7]

The unlawful touching need not be direct, but may be indirect, such as by precipitation upon the body of a person of any material substance, for example, pipe smoke. Thus, it is enough that the defendant sets a force in motion that ultimately produces the result.[8]

Figure 6.2: *Continued*

Footnotes	
1	Ellison v. Burger King Corp., 294 Ga. App. 814, 670 S.E.2d 469 (2008); Hendricks v. Southern Bell Tel. & Tel. Co., 193 Ga. App. 264, 387 S.E.2d 593 (1989).
2	Ellison v. Burger King Corp., 294 Ga. App. 814, 670 S.E.2d 469 (2008); Metropolitan Atlanta Rapid Transit Authority v. Mosley, 280 Ga. App. 486, 634 S.E.2d 466, 20 A.L.R.6th 751 (2006); Lewis v. Northside Hospital, Inc., 267 Ga. App. 288, 599 S.E.2d 267 (2004).
3	Jarrett v. Butts, 190 Ga. App. 703, 379 S.E.2d 583, 53 Ed. Law Rep. 1008 (1989).
4	Ellison v. Burger King Corp., 294 Ga. App. 814, 670 S.E.2d 469 (2008); Metropolitan Atlanta Rapid Transit Authority v. Mosley, 280 Ga. App. 486, 634 S.E.2d 466, 20 A.L.R.6th 751 (2006); Darnell v. Houston County Bd. of Educ., 234 Ga. App. 488, 506 S.E.2d 385 (1998).
5	Lawson v. Bloodsworth, 313 Ga. App. 616, 722 S.E.2d 358, 277 Ed. Law Rep. 510 (2012); Ellison v. Burger King Corp., 294 Ga. App. 814, 670 S.E.2d 469 (2008); Metropolitan Atlanta Rapid Transit Authority v. Mosley, 280 Ga. App. 486, 634 S.E.2d 466, 20 A.L.R.6th 751 (2006).
6	Hendricks v. Southern Bell Tel. & Tel. Co., 193 Ga. App. 264, 387 S.E.2d 593 (1989).
7	Adams, Georgia Law of Torts § 2:2 (2012-2013 ed.).
8	Richardson v. Hennly, 209 Ga. App. 868, 434 S.E.2d 772 (1993), judgment rev'd on other grounds, 264 Ga. 355, 444 S.E.2d 317 (1994) and judgment vacated, 214 Ga. App. 364, 448 S.E.2d 91 (1994).

2. Model or Pattern Jury Instructions

Substantially all states have **model or pattern jury instructions** that trial courts rely on to instruct jurors about the law during trials. Most states have two sets of jury instructions: one set for civil claims and one set for criminal charges. Jury instructions summarize the elements and defenses for various claims, identify whether a plaintiff or defendant has the burden of proof, and cite a few primary authorities. Model or pattern jury instructions are reliable and almost always accurately restate the law. In fact, an inaccurate jury instruction is grounds for an appellate court to reverse a jury verdict. And many appellate courts highly recommend—or require—that the trial judges in their state rely on the state's model or pattern jury instructions.[4]

For most model or pattern jury instructions, the state's court of last resort or the state's bar association appoints a committee to draft the instructions. Because these instructions are directed at non-lawyers and written in "plain English," they simplify the law more than other secondary sources. Thus, they are a good place to start your research but should be supplemented with other secondary materials.

---

4. In civil actions in Florida, for example, trial judges must use the pattern jury instructions (with few exceptions). *See* Fla. R. Civ. P. 1.470(b) ("The Florida Standard Jury Instructions ... shall be used by the trial judges of this state in instructing the jury in civil actions to the extent that the Standard Jury Instructions are applicable, unless the trial judge determines that an applicable Standard Jury Instruction is erroneous or inadequate.").

Figure 6.3 is an example of a pattern jury instruction for a claim based on a slip and fall.

Figure 6.3: Excerpt from *Alabama Pattern Jury Instructions*

Alabama Pattern Jury Instructions Civil   December 2018 Update
Prepared by the Alabama Pattern Jury Instructions Committee-Civil

Chapter 31. Premises Liability [PL]

APJI 31.00 Premises Liability—Elements of
Liability Simple Slip and Fall or Trip and Fall [PL]

Plaintiff (name of plaintiff) says (he/she) was an invitee in defendant (name of defendant)'s (describe the premises, e.g. store, shop, warehouse, sidewalk, parking lot, etc.), and (he/she) was harmed when (describe the occurrence, e.g. slipped on _, tripped on or over _).

To recover damages on this claim, (name of plaintiff) must prove to your reasonable satisfaction all of the following:

1. That (name of plaintiff) was an invitee (in/on) (describe the premises);
(He/she) was an invitee if (he/she) was in (describe the premises) at the expressed or implied invitation of (name of defendant), and (name of plaintiff) was there for a business purpose or for (name of defendant)'s material benefit.

2. That the (describe the premises or area where the harm occurred) was not in a reasonably safe condition because (describe the condition);

3. That (name of defendant) (knew), or should have known about the condition, or (name of defendant) was at fault in not discovering the condition;

4. (Name of plaintiff) was harmed; and,

5. That (name of defendant)'s (negligent/wanton) failure to keep the (describe the premises) in a reasonably safe condition caused (name of plaintiff)'s harm.
If (name of plaintiff) proves these things you will find for (him/her) and determine what amount of money will fairly and reasonably compensate (him/her) for the harm. If (name of plaintiff) does not prove all of these things, you will find for (name of defendant).

Figure 6.3: *Continued*

Duty

The general duty of the store keeper to an invitee is to use reasonable care to keep the premises in a reasonably safe condition. <u>Vargo v. Warehouse Groceries Management, Inc., 529 So. 2d 986 (Ala. 1988)</u>. Whether a duty is owed is always a question for the trial court; therefore, it is not specifically defined in this or a separate instruction. Rather, it is set out in paragraph numbered 5 of the instruction. The Committee suggests that the jury not be told about duty as such, and that it be interwoven in the instruction.

If the trial judge believes the jury should be instructed about duty in greater detail, the Committee recommends the judge instruct the jury, as follows:

(Name of defendant) must keep (describe the premises) in a reasonably safe condition for invitees. (Name of defendant) must warn invitees about any dangers that (name of defendant) knows about or should know about and an invitee does not know.

Scope of the invitation.

A plaintiff's legal status changes when he or she exceeds the scope of the invitation. The scope of an invitation relates to area and it can relate to time. Generally, the status changes from invitee to licensee, and the corresponding duty of care changes. <u>Winn-Dixie, Montgomery, Inc. v. Cox, 284 Ala. 362, 224 So. 2d 908 (1969)</u>. See <u>APJI 31A.01</u>.

Rain water and snow cases.

When the plaintiff claims that he or she slipped on rainwater or snow on the floor and does not claim that the floor was defectively designed or built, the trial judge must supplement this instruction to fully explain the storekeeper's responsibility. This is because "[a] fall caused by snow or rain is distinguishable from a fall resulting from some other object as in the usual

---

3. Treatises and Practice Manuals

A **treatise** or **practice manual** is a single book or multi-volume set of books that usually provides a more detailed analysis of a legal subject than an encyclopedia. While a legal encyclopedia may provide a few paragraphs on a legal topic, a treatise or practice manual may contain an entire chapter on the same topic. Many treatises and some practice manuals do more than just explain the law; they may also evaluate the law, opining on the reasoning of various court decisions. Practice manuals are different from treatises in one primary respect: they focus on practical applications of the law and often include tools for practicing attorneys. A practice manual, for example, may contain a checklist of information to include in a complaint based on a personal injury claim and may contain a sample complaint for a negligence claim. In short, treatises and practice manuals not only provide citations to primary authorities but also help you analyze and understand those authorities.

While they do not cover as many different topics as legal encyclopedias, treatises and practice manuals can cover many areas of law. Some discuss both federal and state laws, but some examine only federal or only state laws. Additionally, a treatise or practice manual may cover one narrow topic (an employer's HIPPA obligations) or cover a broad topic (all aspects of employment law).

Review **Figure 6.4** to see an entry from *Dobbs' Law of Torts 2d* (national treatise), and review **Figure 6.5** to see an entry from *Texas Practice: Contract Law* (state-specific practice manual).

Figure 6.4: Excerpt from *Dobbs' Law of Torts*

Dan B. Dobbs, Paul T. Hayden and Ellen M. Bublick, The Law of Torts § 142 (2d ed.)

Dobbs' Law of Torts | June 2018 Update
Dan B. Dobbs, Paul T. Hayden, and Ellen M. Bublick

Part III. Negligent Physical Interference with Person or Property
Subpart A. The Negligence Claim and Its Elements
Chapter 13. Negligence: The Effect of Circumstances: Particularizing the Adjudication
Topic A. Considering Special Circumstances

§ 142. Emergency and unavoidable accident

Emergency as a circumstance to be considered. When an unforeseeable danger arises and alternative action is possible that requires quick judgment, courts often refer to the "emergency doctrine."[1] If an actor is confronted with a sudden and unforeseeable emergency not of the actor's own making, the jury is permitted to consider the emergency as one of the circumstances relevant in determining whether the actor behaved reasonably.[2] Put differently, even reasonable persons may conduct themselves in response to an emergency in ways that would not be reasonable if time permitted more thoughtful decision-making. Legal issues arise mainly because defendants frequently ask the trial judge to give an instruction specifically authorizing the jury to consider the emergency in determining negligence, or the related instruction that the defendant is not liable for unavoidable accident.[3]

Rationale. Although it is convenient to refer to this idea as the emergency doctrine, it is not, properly speaking, a doctrine at all. It is instead merely an application of the reasonable person standard, with the emergency as one of the circumstances to be considered in forming a judgment about the actor's fault.[4] That necessarily means that if the facts show grounds on which reasonable jurors could differ, the existence of an emergency is a jury question.[5] It also means that since emergency is merely a fact bearing on the reasonable person's care in the circumstance, the emergency doctrine is not a defense and the burden of proof does not shift.[6]

Figure 6.5: Excerpt from Texas Practice: Contract Law

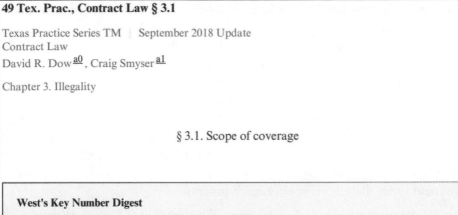

49 Tex. Prac., Contract Law § 3.1

Texas Practice Series TM | September 2018 Update
Contract Law
David R. Dow [a0], Craig Smyser [a1]

Chapter 3. Illegality

§ 3.1. Scope of coverage

West's Key Number Digest

- West's Key Number Digest, <u>Contracts</u> ☞ <u>103</u>, <u>108</u>, <u>136</u>

Legal Encyclopedias

- <u>C.J.S., Contracts §§ 195</u> to <u>200</u>, <u>213</u> to <u>218</u>, <u>269</u> to <u>270</u>, <u>272</u> to <u>273</u>, <u>277</u>, <u>280</u> to <u>281</u>, <u>296</u>

Because the very purpose of contract law is to give legal effect to voluntary agreements, the law generally permits parties to contract as they see fit. However, the law will not give effect to agreements that are illegal or against public policy. [1]

As a general rule, illegal contracts are void. [2] An illegal contract is an agreement in which parties undertake to do an act forbidden by the law of the place where the act is to be done. [3] Thus, a contract that does not violate the laws of the forum state but calls for violating the laws of another state or country will not be enforced in the forum state. [4]

Footnotes

[1] <u>Ellison v. Burger King Corp., 294 Ga. App. 814, 670 S.E.2d 469 (2008)</u>; <u>Hendricks v. Southern Bell Tel. & Tel. Co., 193 Ga. App. 264, 387 S.E.2d 593 (1989)</u>.

[2] <u>Ellison v. Burger King Corp., 294 Ga. App. 814, 670 S.E.2d 469 (2008)</u>; <u>Metropolitan Atlanta Rapid Transit Authority v. Mosley, 280 Ga. App. 486, 634 S.E.2d 466, 20 A.L.R.6th 751 (2006)</u>; <u>Lewis v. Northside Hospital, Inc., 267 Ga. App. 288, 599 S.E.2d 267 (2004)</u>.

[3] <u>Jarrett v. Butts, 190 Ga. App. 703, 379 S.E.2d 583, 53 Ed. Law Rep. 1008 (1989)</u>.

[4] <u>Ellison v. Burger King Corp., 294 Ga. App. 814, 670 S.E.2d 469 (2008)</u>; <u>Metropolitan Atlanta Rapid Transit Authority v. Mosley, 280 Ga. App. 486, 634 S.E.2d 466, 20 A.L.R.6th 751 (2006)</u>; <u>Darnell v. Houston County Bd. of Educ., 234 Ga. App. 488, 506 S.E.2d 385 (1998)</u>.

[5] <u>Lawson v. Bloodsworth, 313 Ga. App. 616, 722 S.E.2d 358, 277 Ed. Law Rep. 510 (2012)</u>; <u>Ellison v. Burger King Corp., 294 Ga. App. 814, 670 S.E.2d 469 (2008)</u>; <u>Metropolitan Atlanta Rapid Transit Authority v. Mosley, 280 Ga. App. 486, 634 S.E.2d 466, 20 A.L.R.6th 751 (2006)</u>.

[6] <u>Hendricks v. Southern Bell Tel. & Tel. Co., 193 Ga. App. 264, 387 S.E.2d 593 (1989)</u>.

[7] <u>Adams, Georgia Law of Torts § 2:2 (2012-2013 ed.)</u>.

[8] <u>Richardson v. Hennly, 209 Ga. App. 868, 434 S.E.2d 772 (1993)</u>, judgment rev'd on other grounds, <u>264 Ga. 355, 444 S.E.2d 317 (1994)</u> and judgment vacated, <u>214 Ga. App. 364, 448 S.E.2d 91 (1994)</u>.

4. American Law Reports (A.L.R.)

The *American Law Reports* ("A.L.R.") is a collection of legal articles on narrow legal topics. Each legal article, known as an **annotation**, analyzes a specific topic in depth and may even exceed 100 pages. An A.L.R. annotation also summarizes the rules of law from various cases and explains how courts have applied the law to many different factual situations, thus helping you understand the law for a particular topic in greater detail than an encyclopedia. Because A.L.R. annotations cover only narrow topics, you would not find one on the broad topic "Violations of the Fourth Amendment" but would find one on the specific topic "Permissibility Under Fourth Amendment of Detention of Motorist by Police, Following Lawful Stop for Traffic Offense, to Investigate Matters Not Related to Offense." In short, if an annotation is available, you should review it early in your research process.

An A.L.R. annotation collects cases from all or most jurisdictions that have addressed the topic. In addition to citing many court decisions, an annotation organizes the cases by jurisdiction. Thus, when reviewing a particular annotation, you can quickly locate all the cited cases from the controlling jurisdiction (or other jurisdiction). Further, A.L.R. annotations cite secondary sources, including similar A.L.R. annotations, treatises, and legal encyclopedias.

The A.L.R. books are published in seven series for state laws and three series for federal laws, and the volume numbers restart for each new series. The seven state series are designated "A.L.R.," "A.L.R.2d," "A.L.R.3d," and so forth, and the three federal series are designated "A.L.R. Fed.," "A.L.R. Fed. 2d," and "A.L.R. Fed. 3d." A new series (*e.g.*, A.L.R.5th) does not automatically supersede and replace all the annotations from a prior series (*e.g.*, A.L.R.3d). To illustrate, the annotation, "Attorney's fees as element of damages in action for false imprisonment or arrest, or for malicious prosecution," was originally published in 1968 in A.L.R.3d. That annotation from the third series still reflects current law, because the publisher continues to update it with

---

Relying on the Most Recent A.L.R. Annotation

The easiest method to confirm you are relying on the most recent A.L.R. annotation containing recent primary authorities is to access it on Westlaw or Lexis Advance. When you retrieve an annotation on either commercial service, it will indicate whether a new, superseding annotation exists; if a new annotation is available, Westlaw and Lexis Advance will link to it.

more recent court decisions, even though the A.L.R. books are in their seventh series. In other situations, however, an annotation from an earlier series will be superseded and replaced by an annotation in a later series.

Review **Figure 6.6** to view sample pages from an A.L.R. annotation on the admissibility of evidence involving dog tracking in criminal cases.

Figure 6.6: A.L.R. Annotation (81 A.L.R.5th 563)

II. IN GENERAL

§ 3. View that evidence admissible if foundation requirements are met

[Cumulative Supplement]

The courts in the following criminal cases have taken the view that evidence of the trailing by dogs of one charged with a criminal offense is admissible to prove the identity of the accused in a criminal prosecution, provided that a proper foundation is laid for the admission of such evidence.

Ala
Simpson v. State, 111 Ala. 6, 20 So. 572 (1896)
Little v. State, 145 Ala. 662, 39 So. 674 (1905)
Richardson v. State, 145 Ala. 46, 41 So. 82 (1906)
Hargrove v. State, 147 Ala. 97, 41 So. 972 (1906)
Gallant v. State, 167 Ala. 60, 52 So. 739 (1910)
Loper v. State, 205 Ala. 216, 87 So. 92 (1920)
Orr v. State, 236 Ala. 462, 183 So. 445 (1938)
Burks v. State, 240 Ala. 587, 200 So. 418 (1941)
Hodge v. State, 98 Ala. 10, 13 So. 385, 39 Am.St.Rep. 17 (1893)
Allen v. State, 8 Ala. App. 228, 62 So. 971 (1913)
Moore v. State, 26 Ala. App. 607, 164 So. 761 (1935)
Holcombe v. State, 437 So. 2d 663 (Ala. Crim. App. 1983)

Figure 6.6: *Continued*

Evidence of the conduct of a dog tracking a suspect may be introduced, providing a proper foundation is laid. McCray v. State, 915 So. 2d 239 (Fla. Dist. Ct. App. 3d Dist. 2005).

Evidence as to the conduct of dogs in following tracks should not be admitted until after a preliminary investigation in which it is established that one or more of the dogs in question were of a stock characterized by acuteness of scent and power of discrimination, and had been trained or tested in the exercise of these qualities in the tracking of human beings, and were in the charge of one accustomed to use them; it must also appear that the dogs so trained and tested were laid on a trail, whether visible or not, concerning which testimony has been admitted, and upon a track which the circumstances indicate to have been made by the accused. Johnson v. State, 293 Ga. App. 32, 666 S.E.2d 452 (2008).

Commonwealth satisfied foundational requirements for evidence that accelerant detection dog had alerted to the presence of ignitable liquids at trailer home fire scene, in trial for arson, assault, and manslaughter; national certified fire investigator to whom the dog was assigned testified to his qualifications for being a dog handler and to his Federal Bureau of Alcohol, Tobacco and Firearms (ATF) certification, testing, and training record in accelerant detection with the dog. Yell v. Com., 242 S.W.3d 331 (Ky. 2007), as modified, (Dec. 21, 2007).

Dog–tracking evidence is admissible provided a proper foundation has been laid. Com. v. Hill, 52 Mass. App. Ct. 147, 751 N.E.2d 446 (2001).

Dog tracking evidence was admissible in capital murder prosecution; qualifications of tracking dogs, as well as handlers, were well documented at trial, both dogs and their handlers had undergone various training and certification, although majority of dog's training was focused on narcotics, he performed human tracking or small article locates at least once per week, and regarding reliability, officer testified that dog had never failed in human tracking search. Hudson v. State, 977 So. 2d 344 (Miss. Ct. App. 2007), cert. denied (Miss. Mar. 20, 2008).

5. Legal Periodicals

A **legal periodical** is a fancy term to describe a collection of articles discussing the law. One type of a legal periodical is a bar journal. Bar journals are legal magazines published by state or local bar associations and other non-profit organizations. These journals are generally similar in look and length as non-legal magazines, such as *Consumer Reports*. The articles in bar journals usually span between five and fifteen pages, summarize recent state laws for the jurisdiction in which they are published, and cite primary authorities from that jurisdiction. Because practicing attorneys often draft these legal articles, they combine a discussion of the law with practical advice. You would find articles like "Ten Tips for Handling Complex Probate" and "A Checklist for Proving Negligence in Automobile Accident Cases."

A second type of a legal periodical is a law review or law journal. Every law school publishes at least one law review covering general legal topics, and some law schools publish specialized law reviews tailored to more narrow topics, such as *University of Miami Entertainment & Sports Law Review* and *Estate Planning & Community Property Law Journal.* Law review articles differ from bar journal articles in several respects. A law review article discusses a specific topic in more depth than a bar journal article, providing hundreds of citations to primary and secondary authorities in the footnotes. Further, while law review articles explain the current status of the law on a particular topic and provide historical background of a law, they primarily react to the law by critiquing the policies underlying statutes and cases and arguing for specific changes to the law. Last, they commonly discuss the United States Constitution and federal statutes and cases, not the law of a specific state.

Excerpts of a bar journal article and law review article are shown in **Figures 6.7** and **6.8**, respectively.

Figure 6.7: Excerpt from *Florida Bar Journal*

THE FLORIDA
BAR JOURNAL
Advertising Rates • Submission Guidelines • Archives • Subscribe • *News*

July/August, 2015 Volume 89, No. 7   Journal HOME

Termination of Residential Rental Agreements
by Alan Bryce Grossman

Page 77

A tenant's possession of a landlord's residential property in Florida begins with an agreement, oral or written. Typically, of course, that agreement will require the periodic payment of rent from the tenant to the landlord. If the tenant fails to pay the rent as agreed, the landlord has the right to evict the tenant and regain possession of the property.

Self-Help Evictions Abolished
Florida law has long abolished "self-help" evictions, that is, the forcible reentry by the landlord to remove the tenant outside of court procedure.[1] The process to properly remove a tenant from residential real property requires compliance with the Florida Residential Landlord and Tenant Act.[2] The starting gun for this process, and the key to whether an eviction can be successful, is the proper preparation and delivery of a three-day notice.[3] A proper three-day notice cannot be waived by the parties.[4]

Termination for Nonpayment of Rent
A landlord's action to remove a tenant from residential property for nonpayment of rent cannot begin until there is a proper termination of the tenancy.[5] Termination for nonpayment of rent is exclusively accomplished under the act by the service on all tenants of an accurate three-day notice.[6] "Termination of the tenancy is a prerequisite to an action for eviction and must be satisfied prior to filing the eviction action."[7] For a landlord who purchased the subject property at foreclosure, federal law[8] imposed an additional 90-day notice to all bona fide tenants, even if they were not named on the lease.[9] This was held as a condition precedent to eviction for such property.[10] However, as of this writing, the federal law was sunset on December 31, 2014, and further discussion regarding that law is beyond the scope of this article.

Figure 6.8: Excerpt from *Minnesota Law Review*

Article

The Free Speech Rights of University Students

Mary-Rose Papandrea[†]

In March 2014, University of Oklahoma President David Boren reacted swiftly when a video surfaced online revealing members of the SAE fraternity singing a racist song[1] on a bus. Two young men leading the singing were immediately expelled. Boren explained in a letter to the students that they had been expelled due to their "leadership role in leading a racist and exclusionary chant which has created a hostile educational environment for others."[2] Several prominent First Amendment scholars denounced the expulsions, arguing that the racist speech was entitled to constitutional protection.[3]

[†]   Associate Dean for Academic Affairs & Professor of Law, University of North Carolina School of Law. Copyright © 2017 by Mary-Rose Papandrea.

1.   The song is set to the tune of "If You're Happy and You Know It," and appears to contain the following lyrics:
There will never be a . . . SAE
There will never be a . . . SAE
You can hang 'em from a tree
But he'll never [inaudible—possibly "sign"] with me
There will never be a . . . SAE.
Matt Pearce, *Is University of Oklahoma Frat's Racist Chant Protected by 1st Amendment?*, L.A. TIMES (Mar. 10, 2015), http://www.latimes.com/nation/la-na-oklahoma-fraternity-explainer-20150310-story.html#page=1.

2.   Manny Fernandez & Erik Eckholm, *Expulsion of Two Oklahoma Students over Video Leads to Free Speech Debate*, N.Y. TIMES (Mar. 11, 2015), http://www.nytimes.com/2015/03/12/us/expulsion-of-two-oklahoma-students-leads-to-free-speech-debate.html?_r=0.

3.   *See, e.g., id.* (summarizing views of prominent First Amendment experts); Pearce, *supra* note 1 (quoting experts stating that the speech is protected); Eugene Volokh, *No, It's Not Constitutional for University of Oklahoma To Expel Students for Racist Speech [UPDATED in Light of Students' Expulsion]*, WASH. POST: VOLOKH CONSPIRACY (Mar. 10, 2015), http://www.washingtonpost.com/news/volokh-conspiracy/wp/2015/03/10no-a-public-university-may-not-expel-students-for-racist-speech.

C. Identifying and Retrieving Secondary Sources

Now, you will learn how to identify the names of secondary sources addressing your client's legal issues and how to retrieve the full text of each relevant source. This section discusses finding secondary materials both online and in print but has a heavy emphasis on electronic databases. While researching, remember to stay focused on the end goals: understanding the controlling law and finding citations to helpful primary authorities.

1. Two Excellent Methods to Find Secondary Sources on Westlaw and Lexis Advance

As expected, the commercial research services of Westlaw and Lexis Advance have a huge collection of the full text of secondary sources in their online databases.[5] The secondary sources in their databases cover virtually all areas of law and include legal encyclopedias, jury instructions, treatises and practice manuals, *American Law Reports*, and legal articles.

The two commonly-used methods to find secondary sources on Westlaw and Lexis Advance include (1) browsing by source or category, and (2) searching by keywords.

a. Browsing by Source or Category

One excellent method to locate secondary materials on Westlaw and Lexis Advance is to **browse by source or category**. (You have browsed in a similar manner outside the legal world, such as browsing online to see which movies or books are available through an Amazon Prime membership.) By browsing, you can retrieve a list of all secondary sources available on Westlaw and Lexis Advance for a specific jurisdiction like Alabama or Georgia. You can then scan the titles of those sources and access the full text of each relevant source with just a few clicks.

On Westlaw, for example, you can view all Georgia secondary sources using this method:

1. From the home page, select the "State Materials" tab to view a list of all states.

2. Click on "Georgia."

3. Scroll down and click "All Georgia Secondary Sources" on the next screen to view a list of secondary materials covering Georgia law.

---

5. As explained in the prior chapter, the leading cost-effective platforms of Casemaker and Fastcase have a small collection of secondary sources available as a benefit of bar memberships. Both platforms, however, provide access to some respected secondary sources for a fee.

As shown in **Figure 6.9**, Westlaw's databases have a Georgia legal encyclopedia and have treatises on employment law, landlord-tenant law, and torts.

Figure 6.9: Georgia Secondary Sources on Westlaw

- Georgia Employment Law ⓘ
- Georgia Employment Law Letter ⓘ
- Georgia Enforcement of Security Interests in Personal Property with Forms ⓘ
- Georgia Environmental Law Letter ⓘ
- Georgia Forms: Legal and Business ⓘ
- Georgia Guardianship & Conservatorship ⓘ
- Georgia Handbook on Foundations & Objections ⓘ
- Georgia Journal of International & Comparative Law ⓘ
- Georgia Jurisprudence ⓘ
- Georgia Juvenile Practice & Procedure with Forms ⓘ
- Georgia KeyRules - State Superior Court ⓘ
- Georgia Landlord & Tenant Breach & Remedies with Forms ⓘ
- Georgia Landlord & Tenant Lease Forms & Clauses ⓘ
- Georgia Law of Damages with Forms ⓘ
- Georgia Law of Torts ⓘ

On Lexis Advance, retrieving a list of Georgia secondary sources involves a similar process.

1. From the home page, select the "State" tab to view a list of all states.
2. Click on "Georgia."
3. Scroll down and click "All Georgia Treatises, Practice Guides & Jurisprudence" on the next screen to view a list of Georgia secondary materials.

Figure 6.10 displays the names of some secondary sources that you would find.

Figure 6.10: Georgia Secondary Sources on Lexis

General

Georgia Civil Practice | ℹ

Georgia Civil Procedure Forms | ℹ

Georgia Corporate Forms | ℹ

Georgia Criminal Law Case Finder | ℹ

Georgia Domestic Relations Case Finder | ℹ

Georgia Domestic Relations Forms | ℹ

Georgia DUI Law A Resource for Lawyers and Judges | ℹ

Georgia Estate Planning, Will Drafting and Estate Administration Forms | ℹ

Georgia Legal Malpractice Law | ℹ

Georgia Objections at Trial | ℹ

Georgia Real Estate Forms | ℹ

Kissiah & Lay's Georgia Workers' Compensation Law | ℹ

Labor and Employment in Georgia: A Guide to Employment Laws, Regulations & Practices | ℹ

> **Coverage of Secondary Sources**
>
> No single online database provides access to *all* secondary materials. If possible, you should browse secondary sources on both Westlaw and Lexis Advance, because their online databases contain different sources. Westlaw may have more secondary sources for your jurisdiction on a negligence claim, but Lexis Advance may have a more comprehensive collection of sources on a claim for breach of contract.

Additionally, you can browse by source or category to find all secondary materials covering a particular topic (instead of a specific jurisdiction). Both Westlaw and Lexis Advance have categorized their secondary sources by over 40 topics, such as contracts law, criminal law, and employment law. So if you click on the topic privacy law on Westlaw, you could browse the titles of over 40 secondary sources under that topic.

The following hypothetical demonstrates how you can quickly locate relevant secondary sources by browsing by source or category. Suppose you must research Georgia law on whether the client-landlord must pay for injuries to a tenant where the tenant fell after stepping in a hole under the carpet. (These facts implicate tort law, including premise liability.) If you browsed the names of Georgia secondary sources on Westlaw for just five minutes, you would find the sources identified in **Figure 6.11**.

b. Performing Keyword Searches

Unsurprisingly, you could locate secondary sources on Westlaw and Lexis Advance by **performing keyword searches**. This book uses the phrase "keyword search" to broadly include two types of electronic word searching: **natural language** and **terms and connectors**. If you are over ten years old, you have performed natural language searches using Google or other search engines. Nonetheless, you may be unfamiliar with a terms and connector search, which directs an online database to return only the results that exactly match the words and criteria you specify. To illustrate, you can direct the database to return only the sections of secondary sources in which "landlord" appears in the same sentence as "dog bite."[6]

---

6. Before researching secondary sources by executing keyword searches, you should review Chapter 9. That chapter discusses in detail how to perform keyword searches on Westlaw and Lexis Advance.

Figure 6.11: Browsing Georgia Secondary Sources on Westlaw

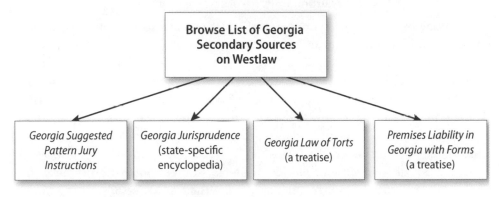

When performing a keyword search on Westlaw or Lexis Advance, you generally should not search all secondary sources in their databases. Instead, you should pre-filter your search to reduce the amount of irrelevant results. Two good options are available.

One approach is to search only within the database of secondary sources that discuss the controlling law. This approach will minimize the likelihood that you will read a treatise on Alaska law when Georgia law governs. Using this approach for a state law issue, you would select the pertinent jurisdiction (*e.g.*, Georgia), select the database for all secondary sources for that jurisdiction, and then run a keyword search. Returning to the hypothetical on landlord liability for physical defects, after selecting the database for just Georgia secondary sources, you could type these keywords into the search box on Westlaw:

landlord liability physical defects tenant premises

As you scroll through the results, you would see multiple secondary sources that discuss your client's legal issues.

Another method for keyword searching is to search only secondary sources categorized under a particular topic or practice area. Under this approach for the Georgia hypothetical, you could select all secondary sources on Westlaw (from the home page), click on the topic "Real Property," and then run the same keyword search listed above. There is a huge disadvantage with this approach: your search results will contain many secondary materials that do not discuss the controlling law (here, Georgia). On the flip side, you may have to rely on secondary sources outside your jurisdiction, such as when a state-specific source is unavailable; if so, you should narrow the secondary source database by topic instead of jurisdiction and then perform a keyword search.

> ### Caution on Keyword Searching
>
> Although performing a keyword search is the go-to method for students, when starting an assignment on an unfamiliar topic, you should browse the titles of the secondary sources on Westlaw or Lexis Advance *before* performing a keyword search. Imagine you are researching the standard to grant a motion to dismiss in Florida for a fraud claim. If you took a few minutes to browse all secondary materials in Florida, you would discover that Florida has four treatises and practice manuals on the rules of civil procedure. But if you searched all Florida secondary sources by keywords (*e.g.*, "rules of civil procedure"), you probably would not discover all four Florida secondary sources on civil procedure. In fact, all four of those sources are not listed in the top 100 results.

2. Four Additional Methods to Find Secondary Sources When Searching on Westlaw and Lexis Is Ineffective

The two methods just discussed—browsing by source and performing a keyword search—are not the only options that will lead you to relevant secondary sources on Westlaw and Lexis Advance. The methods of browsing and searching may actually present obstacles and frustrate you for some research assignments.

First, when browsing or searching, you might feel overwhelmed with the number of treatises and other secondary materials addressing the client's legal issues. Both Westlaw and Lexis Advance have over 200 secondary sources categorized under the topic "Labor and Employment." As a novice researcher, you do not know which of those hundreds of sources would be the most helpful. When faced with this obstacle on your research path, it is time to tap into the knowledge of legal experts. Law librarians, for instance, have created legal research guides compiling a list of respected and reliable secondary sources on various topics, including employment and tort law. A quick review of a research guide would inform you of the leading secondary materials on point, saving you from having to parse through hundreds of sources on Westlaw and Lexis Advance.

Second, when browsing or searching, you might feel underwhelmed with the lack of relevant secondary source on Westlaw and Lexis Advance (or other online database). Suppose you searched on both research platforms but found only one secondary source covering the controlling law for your client's negligence issue. Because it is doubtful that only one source exists for your tort issue, circumventing this obstacle requires help from a legal expert. If you spent five to ten minutes using a method discussed below, you most likely would identify additional secondary materials on point.

In short, you should not rely solely on the methods of browsing and performing a keyword search when faced with either of the previously-discussed obstacles. As explained in the next sections, you have four additional research tools for locating relevant and reliable secondary sources. To the delight of students, these tools are available online, making them accessible from the comforts of your cozy couch.

a. Online Treatise Finders

The first research tool is an **online treatise finder**. You can easily access this tool for free through the internet. The treatise finders on the websites of the Georgetown Law Library and Harvard Law School Library arrange treatises by over forty-five subjects and summarize their content. The treatises listed on those websites are respected and reliable; they were not drafted by a newly-minted attorney! After browsing either online treatise finder and locating a relevant secondary source, you should determine whether the full text of the source is accessible on a commercial service. For instance, imagine you reviewed Georgetown Law Library's online treatise finder and discovered the book *Law of the Internet*. To determine this treatise's availability on Westlaw or Lexis Advance, you could type the name of the treatise in the main search box on the home page and look for the name of the treatise in the drop-down list that appears.

Figure 6.12 shows some subjects covered in Georgetown Law Library's treatise finder, and **Figure 6.13** shows a partial list of treatises under the subject "Contract Law Treatises."

Figure 6.12: Partial List of Subjects Covered in Georgetown's Treatise Finder

- Computer Law Treatises
- Constitutional Law Treatises
- Consumer Law Treatises
- Contract Law Treatises
- Corporate Law Treatises
- Criminal Law Treatises
- Disability Law Treatises
- Education Law Treatises
- Elder Law Treatises
- Energy Law Treatises
- Entertainment, Art & Sports Treatises
- Environmental Law Treatises
- Estate Planning Treatises
- European Union Treatises
- Evidence Law Treatises
- Family Law Treatises
- Federal Practice & Procedures Treatises

Figure 6.13: Partial List of Treatises on Contract Law in Georgetown's Treatise Finder

Electronic Resources

Corbin on Contracts by Arthur L. Corbin Ⓛ

Long called the "classic treatise on contract law," Corbin's work has been revised by Joseph Perillo, but the unique Corbin style has been preserved. Containing more than 90 chapters, the major parts of this multi-volume treatise are: formation of contracts, statute of frauds, interpretation, parol evidence, avoidance and reformation, construction and legal operation of contracts, rights of third parties, breach of contracts, judicial remedies, discharge and impossibility, and contracts contrary to public policy. Supplementary volumes published annually.

Williston on Contracts 4th by Samuel Williston Ⓦ

This multi-volume treatise provides comprehensive coverage and analysis of all aspects of contract law. Williston discusses the law and the reasoning behind it, especially in judicial decisions, and includes historical underpinnings, majority and minority views, and current trends. An extensive forms collection is included in separate print volumes, as well as online. Updated annually.

Restatement of the Law Second. Contracts by American Law Institute Ⓦ

Contract law is analyzed by the practitioners, judges and legal scholars of the American Law Institute in this multi-volume treatise which contains black letter restatements, reporter's notes and commentaries. Updated with pocket parts and annual supplements.

b. Legal Research Guides

A second research tool to help you locate the titles of respected secondary sources is a **legal research guide**. Many law librarians have created free research guides — often designated **LibGuides** — and posted them on their law libraries' websites. LibGuides cover various federal and state laws and assist students and attorneys in locating relevant secondary materials. Like online treatise finders, LibGuides summarize the content of many secondary sources and identify the most respected ones for particular areas of law.[7]

---

7. Many LibGuides cover more sources of law for a legal topic than a treatise finder. LibGuides, for instance, provide citations to important primary authorities, such as statutes, administrative regulations, and caselaw.

To determine whether an online research guide exists for your topic, you should search on Google or other search engine with the term "LibGuide" or "legal research guide" and your topic. Suppose you want to find respected treatises and practice manuals on race and age discrimination in the employment context. You could type this search string in the Google search box:

employment race age discrimination LibGuide

By running that search, you would find an excellent LibGuide by Washington and Lee University School of Law. The LibGuide identifies multiple treatises and other books discussing anti-discrimination statutes, including The Civil Rights Act of 1964, The Civil Rights Act of 1991, and The Age Discrimination in Employment Act of 1967 (see **Figure 6.14**). Once you know the names of reliable treatises, you can then retrieve the full text of some sources on Westlaw or Lexis Advance.[8]

Figure 6.14: Excerpt of LibGuide by Washington and Lee University School of Law

Treatises and Overview Materials

Employment Discrimination by Arthur Larson; Lex K. Larson
Call Number: KF3464 .L37
ISBN: 0820516260
Publication Date: 1975 (updated 3 times annually)
In-depth analysis of relevant cases, statutes, and regulations, providing not only comprehensive coverage of current law, but also new developments. Chapters on employment-at-will, sex differentiation versus discrimination, bona fide occupational qualification exceptions, pre-employment recruiting practices, seniority, layoffs, equal pay and benefits. Also covers the ADA. NOTE: Print current through 1994 in W&L Law Library — Also available up-to-date in Lexis.

Employment Discrimination Law (5th ed.) by Barbara Lindemann; Paul Grossman; C. Geoffrey Weirich
Call Number: KF3464 .S34 2012
ISBN: 9781617460159
Publication Date: 2012
A leading treatise in two volumes on labor and employment issues related to workplace discrimination. NOTE: Print current through 2013 in W&L Law Library — Also available up-to-date on Bloomberg Law.

Employment Discrimination Law and Practice Hornbook by Harold S. Lewis; Elizabeth J. Norman
Call Number: KF3464 .L4862 2004
ISBN: 0314150129
Publication Date: 2004
Surveys the claims, defenses, procedures and remedies fundamental to an understanding of the contemporary federal law of employment discrimination. Because of the rapid pace of change in this field, an unusually high proportion of the cited cases included were decided within the past several years. To serve the needs of law students, the book tracks the coverage of the most important issues canvassed in the principal employment discrimination casebooks.

Employment Discrimination: Examples & Explanations by Joel W. Friedman
Call Number: KF3464 .F738 2014
ISBN: 1454816104
Publication Date: 2013
A favorite among successful students, and often recommended by professors, the unique Examples & Explanations series gives you extremely clear introductions to concepts followed by realistic examples that mirror those presented in the classroom throughout the semester. Use at the beginning and midway through the semester to deepen your understanding through clear explanations, corresponding hypothetical fact patterns, and analysis. Then use to study for finals by reviewing the hypotheticals as well as the structure and reasoning behind the accompanying analysis.

---

8. For some research projects, you may need to review a secondary source that is available only in print. If so, read Section C.3, below, to learn how to find the print version.

Another type of legal research guide may be found in a **CALI lesson**. CALI, which stands for Center for Computer-Assisted Legal Instruction, has partnered with professors and law librarians to author online interactive tutorials. For most states, CALI has a tutorial covering the types of secondary materials available in the state and how to find these state-specific materials both online and in print. Most students have free access to all CALI lessons at www.cali.org. To find a lesson for your state, look for a lesson containing the name of your state and the phrase "secondary sources," "secondary resources," or something similar.

c. Legal Publishers' Websites

You can also identify titles of secondary sources by visiting the **websites of respected legal publishers**, such as Carolina Academic Press, the American Bar Association, Matthew Bender (LexisNexis), and Thomson Reuters (West). Legal publishers print single- and multi-volume books on substantially all areas of law, and their websites usually allow users to browse by practice area and limit by jurisdiction. To illustrate, Carolina Academic Press publishes a great legal research series for over thirty states. These books (such as *Michigan Legal Research*) identify all or virtually all secondary sources specific to the state.[9]

Upon learning the names of secondary sources from a publisher's website, you can, once again, jump onto Westlaw and Lexis Advance to determine whether an electronic version is available.

d. Legal Bibliographies

Another method to find secondary sources for your legal topic is to consult a **legal bibliography**, which contains a list of all or most sources covering the law of a specific jurisdiction. A leading bibliography for state law issues is *State Practice Materials: Annotated Bibliographies* (edited by Frank G. Houdek) and is available in print and in the HeinOnline database.[10] This bibliography lists many secondary sources covering the laws of each state and summarizes the content of the listed source. It is arranged alphabetically by state where each state is under a separate tab.

---

9. Each book also discusses the state's court system and the state's primary authorities and where to find them.

10. HeinOnline, like Westlaw and Lexis Advance, is available for free to students at most law schools. HeinOnline is an online research database containing, among other materials, over 2,500 legal journals, government documents, and international materials. HeinOnline provides images of books, law review articles, and other documents; the images are in PDF format exactly as they appear in the original print source. If a secondary source is not on Westlaw or Lexis Advance, it might be accessible through HeinOnline.

> ### Limitation of Online Catalogs
>
> A search of your law library's online catalog will yield only those print materials that are physically located in your law library; the online catalog will generally not indicate whether another law library has the print source on its shelves.

A highly respected legal bibliography for federal and state laws is the *Legal Information Buyer's Guide and Reference Manual* by Kendall F. Svengalis. This single-volume book lists many treatises, organizes them by over sixty topics, and explains their content in much greater detail than an online treatise finder or LibGuide. Although this book is not available online, your law library most likely owns a copy.

3. Two Methods to Find Secondary Sources in Print

Many readers of this book may not have a strong desire—or any desire—to research with print sources. Nonetheless, if other finding methods have proved unsuccessful, you need to know about the two excellent methods for locating secondary sources in print.

a. Online Library Catalogs

One excellent method to find secondary sources in print is to search a **law library's online catalog**. Your law school's library has an online catalog, but it may not be the only law library in your area. Your county or local courthouse may have a law library open to the public. With an online catalog, you can search a law library's collection by title and author; thus, once you know the name of a secondary source through one of the prior methods (*e.g.*, treatise finder or LibGuide), you can check whether a law library in your area has a print copy. And on most online catalogs, you can search the print collection by subject and keywords, which might help you identify additional secondary sources.

Suppose you need to review the book *Truck Accident Litigation* but cannot access it through any online database. You could locate this book in print by visiting your law school library's website and searching the online catalog by title. If the book is part of the library's collection, the results page will provide its call number. Make sure you retrieve the most recent edition of this book (2012), as the library also has the older edition (2006). **Figure 6.15** demonstrates this process.

Figure 6.15: Results from Online Library Catalog

b. Human Law Librarians

A second excellent—and seemingly obvious—method to find secondary sources in print is to enlist the help of the friendly **law librarians** at your school. They are a "living and breathing" treatise finder, legal research guide, legal bibliography, and online catalog—all wrapped in one person.

D. Navigating Within a Particular Secondary Source

Once you have found at least one secondary source on point, you need to find specific sections and pages within the source that address your client's legal issues. If you found a five-volume treatise, it is doubtful you would want to skim all five volumes in hopes of finding a few relevant pages. Three better options exist for navigating within a particular secondary source:

- Using an index (print and online);
- Reviewing a table of contents (print and online); and
- Performing keyword searches (online).

Keep in mind that each secondary source, such as an encyclopedia or treatise, probably has multiple sections that cover your issue; thus, you should not find and read just one section or just two pages within the source and stop. Rather, you should use the navigation tools stated above to locate other relevant sections and pages within the source.

1. Navigating Sources in Print

The two most helpful navigational tools in the print environment, and often in the electronic world, are **indexes** and **tables of contents**. These tools are the original search boxes!

An **index** is an alphabetical list of terms and topics that are discussed in the main volume or volumes of a particular secondary source. An index will direct you to the specific location in the source where the term or topic is addressed. For multi-volume books, the index is located in one or more separate volumes at the end of the set; for a single-volume book, the index is usually located at the back of the book. While reviewing an index, consider different terms that the indexer or author could have used. Assume your client was charged with driving while intoxicated and wants to challenge the breathalyzer test. To locate relevant sections within a secondary source, you should look up narrow and broad terms in the index, such as "breathalyzer," "field sobriety," "driving under the influence," "alcohol," "automobiles," and "vehicles."

In addition to using an index, you should **browse the table of contents** of a relevant secondary source. By browsing a table of contents at the beginning of a secondary source, you probably would locate sections and pages within the source that you did not find using an index. You should review a table of contents to understand the organizational structure of a source, to discover which topics are discussed in the source and their location, and to help you understand the relationship among the various topics.

> **Index vs. Table of Contents**
>
> For a single-volume book where the table of contents spans only a few pages, you should review the table of contents before using the index.

The table of contents in your torts casebook, for example, provides you with important information. It probably has a section heading for "intentional torts" and lists several torts under the heading, such as trespass to land and false imprisonment. Further, the table of contents of your casebook probably separates "negligence" from "strict liability," as well as having section headings that identify defenses to tort claims (*e.g.*, "assumption of risk"). As just demonstrated, a table of contents is very informative.

2. Navigating Sources Online

On Westlaw and Lexis Advance, many secondary sources have **indexes** and **tables of contents**. These navigation tools operate in a similar manner online as they do for print sources (see Section D.1). But using an index and table of contents online has a key advantage. You can quickly locate topics and terms with your internet browser's "Find" feature by pressing "Control" and the "F" key on a Chromebook or PC computer or pressing "Command" and the "F" key on a Mac.

Another method to locate relevant sections of a particular secondary source online is to **perform a keyword search of the text found in the headings** for each chapter, part, and section of the source. In other words, this type of search is limited to searching only the text found in the source's table of contents. To illustrate, say you want to search by keywords the headings of a Florida practice manual on personal injury law. With the treatise on your Westlaw or Lexis Advance screen, you would access the advanced search feature (next to the search box) and then type the keywords in the appropriate box. As shown in **Figure 6.16**, your search would return results only where your keywords appeared in the actual text of the headings for each chapter, each part, or each section; it would not return any results where the keywords appeared only in the main text of the treatise.

Searching just the text found in the headings of a secondary source has a major benefit: it reduces the number of irrelevant results, making it less likely you will be overwhelmed by the results. On the other hand, this searching method can give you a false negative. If you search with the wrong keywords, the results will not accurately reflect the number of relevant sections within a particular secondary source. You, therefore, should use this method in conjunction with other navigational tools.

Figure 6.16: Excerpt of Table of Contents of a Practice Manual on Westlaw

▢ PREFACE TO THE 2018-2019 EDITION
▢ Preliminary Materials
⊞ ▢ Chapter 1. Negligence: Basic Concepts and Duty
⊟ ▢ Chapter 2. The Standard of Care
⠀⠀⊞ ▢ Part I. Introduction to Basic Concepts
⠀⠀⊟ ▢ Part II. Establishing the Standard of Care
⠀⠀⠀⠀▢ § 2:2. Standard of care established by the courts
⠀⠀⠀⠀▢ § 2:3. Standard of care established by legislative enactment
⠀⠀⠀⠀▢ § 2:4. Standard of care established by contract
⠀⠀⠀⠀▢ § 2:5. Custom, industry standard, and defendant's rules of conduct
⠀⠀⊟ ▢ Part III. The Reasonable Person Standard
⠀⠀⠀⠀▢ § 2:6. The reasonable person
⠀⠀⠀⠀▢ § 2:7. Physical characteristics
⠀⠀⠀⠀▢ § 2:8. Mental capacity

Additionally, you can perform a **keyword search of the full text** of a secondary source. After retrieving a relevant secondary source on Westlaw or Lexis Advance, you would type the keywords in the main search box. In contrast to searching the text of headings, a full-text search of a secondary source usually produces numerous results, requiring you to review pages and pages of irrelevant sections. Nonetheless, a full-text search will help you locate relevant sections that were not found through the other navigational tools.[11]

After you perform a keyword search, you probably will find a few sections within the source addressing your issue. Once you do, you should also consult the source's table of contents to determine whether any surrounding sections are also relevant.

Recall the prior hypothetical based on Georgia law on whether a tenant may recover damages from a landlord after stepping on a hole and falling down. Recall, too, that you browsed the list of Georgia secondary sources on Westlaw and found four secondary sources. Now assume that you want to find relevant sections and pages from two of those sources: *Georgia Jurisprudence* (legal encyclopedia) and *Georgia Law of Torts* (treatise). As shown in **Figure 6.17**, if you used the three navigational tools discussed above, you would find the following information: multiple sections discussing your landlord issue, a summary of the relevant law, and citations to Georgia primary authorities.

---

11. Before performing keyword searches, you should review Chapter 9.

Figure 6.17: Navigating Georgia Secondary Sources on Westlaw

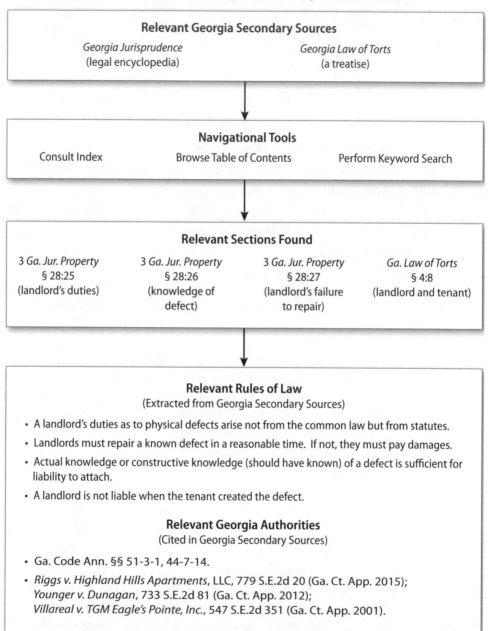

E. Updating Secondary Sources

A court or supervisor expects you to rely on current law. Similarly, when shopping online, you expect a company's website to be current. Imagine that you purchased a laptop online for in-store pickup, but when you arrived at the retailer, the employee told you that the laptop is unavailable and that the online database does not reflect current inventory. You would not be a happy shopper.

To find the most current law, you should rely on the most up-to-date secondary sources. An older edition of a source may cite primary authorities that no longer reflect current law, but the newest edition should discuss the most current law in the jurisdiction for the client's legal issues. Thus, for each secondary source relied on, you should determine whether you are reviewing the most current version available. Obtaining the most recent version of a source is called **updating the source**. Updates to a secondary source may include changes to the actual text or additional citations to newer statutes or cases.

Although the vast majority of secondary materials are updated, legal articles published in bar journals and law reviews (known as legal periodicals) are not updated. These articles reflect the law only as it stood at the time of publication. Thus, even if the law changes after publication, the articles will not be revised.

1. Updating in Print

Secondary sources in print are updated (*i.e.*, made current) in various ways. Hardbound sources, such as legal encyclopedias and treatises, are often updated with **pocket parts** in the back of the volumes. If available, a pocket part updates only the volume where it is found. For example, say you are reviewing section 50 of a legal encyclopedia on a landlord's common law duties. To determine whether that section has been revised and cites newer cases on the issue, you would turn to the back of the main volume and look for a pocket part, which is a paperback pamphlet in a "pocket." If you find a pocket part, at least one section of the main volume has been updated, but not necessarily your section 50. You must review the pocket part for any revision to section 50.

Another way hardbound secondary sources are updated is by a separate, freestanding **supplement**. These separate supplements are created when the size of a pocket part becomes too large to fit in the back of the volume. If available, the supplement will be shelved next to the main volume it updates or at the end of the set. But if a hardbound volume of a source has no pocket part and no supplement, the entire volume has not been updated since its publication date.

Softbound secondary sources, such as state-specific practice manuals, are usually not updated with pocket parts or separate supplements; instead, they are commonly updated only when a new edition is published. Check the copyright or publication date of these sources to determine their currency. When reviewing them in print, confirm that you have the most recent edition, as law libraries may keep the prior editions on the shelf.

2. Updating Online

Secondary sources found online are generally a reproduction of the most recent print edition. Publishers often do not update online versions more frequently than print versions. Nonetheless, because of the lag time between the publication of a pocket part or supplement and its shelving, for a limited period, the most recent update to a secondary source may be available only online. And some secondary materials are updated more frequently online, such as A.L.R. annotations.

F. Print Research: Four Reasons to Know It

You probably want to know why this book covers print research—what the younger generation might refer to as an obsolete and antiquated method of research. Before you designate this author as a "dinosaur" researcher, take five minutes and read about the four important reasons to know how to find and navigate secondary sources in print.

First, some secondary sources are not available in any online database, whether free or fee-based (are you shocked?). Although many secondary sources are available online, some sources like treatises, practice manuals, and legal articles are available only in print. For example, some bar journals published by state and local bar associations are available only in print.[12] In addition, the American Bar Association publishes many well-respected books on topics such as civil rights, criminal law, and tort law, but many of these book are not found online.

Second, knowing how to research with print sources will make you a more competent researcher on Westlaw and Lexis Advance. Substantially all secondary sources found in an online database are based on a print source. Thus, once you know how to use an index and browse a table of contents of a print source, you can easily replicate the process online.

Additionally, it is easier to understand the organizational scheme of a particular secondary source in print than online. To illustrate, if you walked in your law library and skimmed the spines of the many volumes of *American Jurisprudence 2d* (a national legal encyclopedia), you would notice that they are arranged in alphabetical order by topic, from "Abandoned, Lost, and Unclaimed Property," to "Negligence," to "Zoning and Planning." When you later jump online to research a negligence issue involving a landlord and see the citation "57A Am. Jur. 2d Negligence § 1," you would figure out that "Negligence" refers to the topic contained in Volume 57A. Because you previously noticed that the encyclopedia in print had many volumes covering many topics, you would consider whether topics other than "Negligence" exist for your negligence issue and would know to browse the list of topics on Westlaw or Lexis Advance. You would then find two more topics ("Landlord and Tenant" and "Torts") that may contain sections discussing your issue.

Third, many attorneys will expect you to know the basics of researching secondary materials in print. Accordingly to a recent survey by the American Bar Association,

---

12. Recall that legal articles in a bar journal often examine state laws, providing practical advice to attorneys.

about 77% of attorneys research with print materials "regularly" or "occasionally," and only 4.9% of attorneys never use print materials.[13] Here is one likely explanation for the survey results: Attorneys do not have access online to each important secondary source, especially given that the fee-based services are no longer "free" upon graduation. So even if your firm or organization subscribes to Westlaw or Lexis Advance, your employer's paid subscription plan may not provide access to certain state-specific secondary materials. For instance, if you were researching Arkansas law on recoverable damages and your Arkansas-based firm subscribed only to Lexis Advance, you could not retrieve online a leading Arkansas treatise on damages. But your law firm (or the local law library) probably would have a print version of that treatise, and your supervisor would expect you to know how to navigate the treatise and update it using pocket parts and supplements.

Fourth, you may surprise yourself and find you prefer secondary sources in print over their online counterparts. In a print source, the cited legal authorities are not hyperlinked like they are online; thus, you cannot "click on" each cited authority that seems relevant, a habit that often leads students into the research "black hole" on Westlaw and Lexis Advance. For that reason, law students have actually admitted their preference for print research to this author (albeit reluctantly).

G. Summary of Key Points

For **Step 2**, you should find and review at least one—but preferably two or three—**secondary sources** for every unfamiliar legal issue you must research. If you start with secondary sources instead of caselaw for your common law issue, you will save time by piggybacking on the legal work of experts on your issue. The wheel does not need to be invented again. Secondary sources will help you

- understand the law and how it applies to the client's factual situation,
- learn important legal terms of art, and
- identify citations to relevant primary authorities.

Of course, these benefits of secondary sources cannot be realized unless you know how to identify the names of relevant sources and how to retrieve the full text of each relevant source. Most students start researching secondary materials on Westlaw or Lexis Advance (or other online database) and browse by source or perform a keyword search or do both. But when those methods become overwhelming or underwhelming, you have other effective options to find secondary sources, including the following: (1) online treatise finders; (2) legal research guides; (3) websites of respected legal publishers; (4) legal bibliographies; (5) online catalogs of law libraries; and (6) humans called law librarians.

---

13. *See 2017 Legal Technology Survey Report*, at V-xi–xii, V-23 (ABA Legal Technology Resource Center). The survey respondents included attorneys at small, medium, and large law firms. *See id.*

After retrieving at least one relevant secondary source, you are ready to navigate within it to find the sections and pages that discuss the controlling law and cite primary authorities. For secondary materials found online or in print, you should consult the index and review the table of contents. When reviewing a source on Westlaw or Lexis Advance, you should also perform a keyword search of the headings in the table of contents or search the full text of the source.

You should not read in depth every secondary source you find. Initially, you should skim multiple sections of multiple secondary sources. For the sections and pages that are most relevant to your client's issue, read them carefully (maybe two or three times). And write down the citations to any primary authority that could be helpful.

For every secondary source relied on, you must confirm you have the most recent version. For a print source, this means you must update it by reviewing any pocket part or supplement. Recall that an older version may cite statutes or cases that no longer reflect current law.

The following two charts will help you identify and retrieve the best secondary sources for your legal issues. **Figure 6.18** summarizes the advantages and limitations of the secondary sources previously discussed, and **Figure 6.19** indicates the availability of these sources online and in print.

Figure 6.18: Comparison of Secondary Sources

Secondary Source	Number of Legal Topics	Depth of Discussion of Each Topic	Number of Cited Authorities for Each Topic	Updated
Legal Encyclopedias	Extensive	Limited	Few	At Least Annually
Model or Pattern Jury Instructions	Moderate	Limited	Few	Frequently (most states)
Treatises and Practice Manuals	Moderate	Moderate to Extensive	Few to Many	At Least Annually
American Law Reports (A.L.R.)	Moderate[1]	Extensive	Many	Online: Frequently Print: Annually
Law Reviews and Bar Journals	Extensive	Moderate to Extensive	Many	Not Updated

[1] Each A.L.R. annotation covers a specific legal issue.

Figure 6.19: Where to Retrieve Secondary Sources

Secondary Source	Westlaw and Lexis Advance (Fee-Based)	Casemaker and Fastcase (Free for Bar Members)[1]	Free Online Databases and Websites	Print
Legal Encyclopedias	Yes	No	No (one exception)[2]	Yes
Model or Pattern Jury Instructions	Yes	Yes (limited coverage)	Yes[3]	Yes
Treatises and Practice Manuals	Yes	Yes (limited coverage)	No	Yes
American Law Reports (A.L.R.)	Yes	No	No	Yes
Law Reviews and Bar Journals	Yes	Yes (limited coverage)	Yes[4]	Yes

[1] As explained in Chapter 5, Casemaker and Fastcase are available for free to members of certain state and local bar associations.

[2] The only free (and helpful) version of a legal encyclopedia is Wex, which is hosted by Cornell's Legal Information Institute. It is available at http://www.law.cornell.edu/wex.

[3] Some courts and bar associations post the state's model or pattern jury instructions on their websites, such as the State Bar of Arizona and the Supreme Court of Florida.

[4] These legal articles are widely available on free websites. For example, almost all law schools post recent editions of their law reviews or law journals on their websites. You can search the full text of legal articles on the internet by using Google Scholar or visiting the website of the American Bar Association's Legal Technology Resource Center.

H. Review Questions on Secondary Sources

At this point, you should have a basic understanding of secondary sources. To test your comprehension, answer the true-false and multiple-choice questions on this book's companion website, Core Knowledge. It will identify the correct answers and provide clear explanations for each question. The same questions are reproduced below.

1. A respected and reliable secondary source is the actual law.

   a. True

   b. False

2. You should start researching with secondary sources for each unfamiliar legal issue.

   a. True

   b. False

3. A legal encyclopedia usually discusses a single legal topic in great detail.

   a. True

   b. False

4. A treatise or practice manual usually provides a more detailed analysis of a legal topic than an encyclopedia.

   a. True

   b. False

5. An A.L.R. annotation covers a narrow, specific topic in depth and cites many primary authorities on the topic.

   a. True

   b. False

6. Identify the reason or reasons you should review secondary sources when researching an unfamiliar legal issue.

   a. Secondary sources summarize and explain the law.

   b. Secondary sources help researchers find primary authorities.

   c. Secondary sources inform a researcher of the terms of art used for an area of law.

   d. All of the above.

7. Aria wants to identify the names of several secondary sources on her breach of contract issue. What method or methods would help her locate these sources?

   a. Online treatise finder from the Harvard Law Library.

   b. LibGuide from a law library's website.

   c. Index to a national legal encyclopedia, such as *American Jurisprudence 2d*.

   d. Both A and B.

8. Jeremy knows the names of two treatises that discuss the liability of landlords for the criminal acts of third parties. What method should he use to locate these treatises in print in the law library at his school?

   a. LibGuide from a law library's website.

   b. Online catalog from the law library at his school.

   c. Online treatise finder from Georgetown Law Library.

   d. Legal bibliography.

9. How do publishers update (*i.e.*, make current) a hardbound volume of a secondary source, such as a volume of a state-specific legal encyclopedia?

   a. A publisher issues a pocket part or supplement.

   b. A publisher prints a new hardbound volume each year.

   c. A publisher only updates the volume online.

   d. A publisher docs not update hardbound volumes.

10. Charlie located *Nimmer on Copyright*, a well-respected treatise. He wants to find relevant sections in Volume 4 of the *print* version. How could he navigate this treatise?

    a. Consult a legal bibliography.

    b. Search on his law library's online catalog.

    c. Browse the table of contents at the beginning of the volume.

    d. Use an online LibGuide.

11. Hallie located a well-respected treatise, *Corbin on Contracts*, on Lexis Advance. She wants to find sections discussing whether punitive damages are recoverable for a breach of contract claim. How should she navigate this treatise?

    a. Perform a keyword search of only the text found in the headings for each part, chapter, and section of the treatise.

    b. Browse the table of contents.

    c. Use an online LibGuide.

    d. Both A and B.

I. Practice Researching with Secondary Sources

On this book's companion website, Core Knowledge, a few research assignments have been posted. The online assignments walk you through the steps for researching a common law issue on Westlaw and Lexis Advance, including finding and navigating secondary sources. Additionally, several exercises instruct you on using secondary sources in print. For each assignment, you will research the law to resolve legal issues for your hypothetical client.

Chapter 7

Step 3:
Research Cases by Topic

Step 1
(Research
Plan)

Step 2
(Secondary
Sources)

Step 3
(Cases
by
Topic)

Step 4
(Citators)

Step 5
(Keywords)

Step 6
(Expand)

Step 7
(Other States)

Step 8
(Validation)

In completing **Step 2**, you should have found and reviewed multiple sections of secondary sources on your legal issue. Accordingly, you should have a good overview of your area of law and have the citations for some relevant cases that were cited in those sources. But secondary sources do not usually cite all the necessary primary authorities to answer the client's question, especially when the question implicates multiple issues. The research journey, therefore, should move forward. For **Step 3** of the research process for a common law issue, you should look for cases by **topic** using a **caselaw classification system.**

To really appreciate the usefulness of a classification system (**Step 3**), you need to remember that books called reporters publish cases in chronological order, not by topic. If you need cases discussing breach of an employment contract and only had access to the print reporters for your jurisdiction, you would spend hours skimming the reported cases in hopes of finding a case involving contract law in the employment context. There is a much better solution: a classification system that organizes cases by topic.

This chapter discusses the two most popular and comprehensive classification systems: **West's Key Number System** and **LexisNexis Legal Topic Digest**. Both systems classify cases by topic, like a statutory code arranges statutes by topic. And both caselaw classification systems function as an index to cases found online and in reporters. Usually, these finding tools will help you locate relevant binding and highly persuasive cases that are legally and factually similar to the client's situation. As you complete this **Step 3**, do not forget your goal: finding and understanding the rules of law applicable to the client to predict the client's likelihood of success.

A. Finding Cases by Topic with West's Key Number System

The West Key Number System organizes cases by over 100,000 topics and subtopics and is available in print and on Westlaw. In print, this classification is often referred to as the West Digest System; on Westlaw, it is usually known as the Key Number System. Collectively, the print and online systems are called finding aids or finding tools because they help researchers find relevant authorities.

The Key Number System is essentially a topical index to cases published in reporters. Every federal and state case that a court designates "for publication" is published in a reporter that is a part of West's National Reporter System.[1] The Key Number System organizes those reported cases. It even classifies some unreported and unpublished cases for a few states such as Ohio and Texas. The Key Number System, however, does not contain the full text of cases. As explained next, it contains summaries of classified cases and provides citations to those cases.

1. Creation and Organization of the Key Number System

When a court publishes a decision, an attorney editor for Thomson Reuters (commonly known as West) reads the opinion and creates headnotes for the various legal issues from the opinion. The editors usually draft a one-sentence headnote, and they create a headnote for each issue, so a single case could have five or even twenty (or more) headnotes. A headnote may contain a concise sentence of a point of law or legal rule from the decision. For examples of these types of headnotes, review **Figure 7.1**, which shows headnotes from *Muela v. Gomez*, 343 S.W.3d 491 (Tex. App. 2011). Or a headnote may discuss how the court applied a rule to the facts in dispute. **Figure 7.2** shows an example of this type of headnote from *Labaj v. VanHouten*, 322 S.W.3d 416 (Tex. App. 2010).

Figure 7.1: Headnotes with Rules of Law

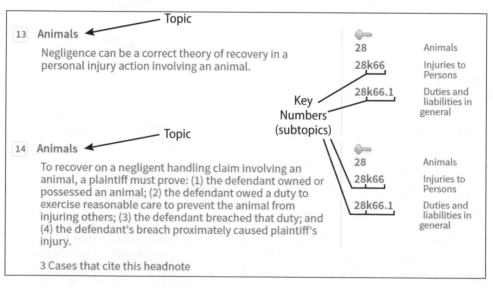

---

1. Chapter 3 explains the publication process for cases, including West's National Reporter System.

Figure 7.2: Headnote with Application of Rule to Facts

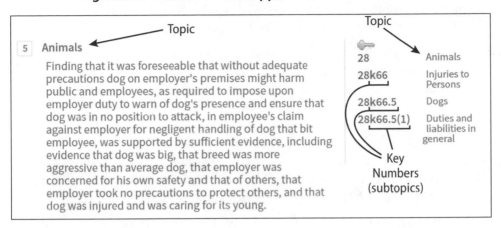

Every headnote summarizing a single issue from a case is "tagged" with a Topic and subtopic, and then placed into the West Key Number System, allowing future researchers to find the citation to the case. One headnote, therefore, will appear in two locations: in the Key Number System and at the beginning of the actual case. Again, only the headnotes, not the text of the opinion, are contained in the Key Number System. If one case has ten headnotes, then the headnotes and the citation to the case would appear in this finding aid ten times. In sum, the Key Number System is a collection of all headnotes from all cases published in all West reporters.

Each headnote is first assigned at least one Topic, which is the broadest classification in the Key Number System. This classification system divides the law into over 400 broad Topics, such as "Animals," "Constitutional Law," "Criminal Law," "Labor and Employment," "Property," and "Torts." The Topics are arranged in alphabetical order.

After a headnote is assigned a broad Topic, a West editor assigns it at least one Key Number that reflects the subtopic. For each Topic, the Key Numbers are listed in numerical order, and each Key Number represents a different subtopic. A Topic could have just 100 or over 4,000 Key Numbers, depending on the number of discreet legal issues for the Topic. The Topic "Animals," for instance, has over 100 Key Numbers, which means that West editors have divided this Topic into over 100 different subtopics. Because each headnote is first assigned a Topic, to locate a relevant Key Number (the subtopic), you must know the Topic. Key Number 100 under the Topic "Animals," for example, represents a different subtopic than Key Number 100 under the Topic "Contracts." In short, to find applicable cases with the Key Number System, you must know at least one relevant Topic and one relevant Key Number (subtopic) under that Topic.

An example from social media should help clarify the organization of West's System. On Twitter and Instagram, a user could tag one photograph with ten subject hashtags, making it available to other users through ten different links. Similarly, a West editor could "tag" ten headnotes from one case with one Topic but with ten different Key Numbers (the subtopics). If so, a researcher could locate the headnotes and corresponding case through ten different Key Number "links."

Revisit the headnote at **Figure 7.2** above to help you further understand how headnotes and their corresponding cases are classified in the Key Number System. That headnote is classified under the Topic "Animals," which is indicated in the left column in bold font and in the right column on the first line. The number "28" next to the Topic is not the Key Number; it means that "Animals" appears twenty-eighth in the alphabetical list of the 400+ Topics. In addition to being under the Topic "Animals," the headnote and case (*Labaj v. VanHouten*) are classified under Key Number 66.5(1) (duties and liabilities in general), which is indicated by the number immediately to the right of the little "k" in the right column on the last line.

An important feature of the Key Number System is that Topics and Key Numbers are the same throughout West's System in print and online on Westlaw. To illustrate, assume you are researching Florida law and the cases classified under the Topic "Negligence" and Key Number 344 (subtopic "Campfires, bonfires and cooking fires") are relevant. If you later need to research North Carolina law for the same issue, you would use the same Topic (Negligence) and same Key Number (344) to find cases from North Carolina courts. If necessary, you could also use the same Topic and Key Number to find federal cases on the issue of negligence and fires.

2. Four Steps for Using West's Digest System in Print

This section explains the four-step process to find cases with the West Digest System in print. By understanding the process in print, you will know how to navigate the Key Number System on Westlaw, which is based on print versions. For the print digest, you should follow these four steps:

1. Locate the correct digest set;
2. Find relevant Topics and Key Numbers;
3. Read the headnotes and cases and record case citations; and
4. Update and validate your research.

The following hypothetical will guide you through the four steps. Suppose your client is a municipality located in the State of Ohio. It wants to know whether it violated the Establishment Clause to the First Amendment by allowing a nativity scene on public grounds. The entire holiday display was funded in substantial part by private funds and included a few secular holiday objects.[2]

---

2. Although this hypothetical involves a constitutional law, and not common law, issue, the Key Number System is still useful. The meaning of the Establishment Clause is primarily derived from caselaw; similarly, the rules for a common law issue are derived from caselaw.

a. Locate the Correct Digest Set

The first step in researching with a print digest is to locate the correct digest set in your law library. West has created printed digest sets for federal courts, individual states, regions of the United States, individual courts, and combined jurisdictions. Of all the various print digest sets, attorneys most often use the *Federal Practice Digest* or the digest set covering the governing jurisdiction.

When researching a federal issue, you should start with the most recent series, *Federal Practice Digest 5th* (your library may no longer update the Fourth Series). This digest set contains all headnotes from the reported cases of the federal courts from 2003 to the present, including the United States Supreme Court, United States Courts of Appeals, and the United States District Courts. (For older cases, you should use the online version on Westlaw.) The *Federal Practice Digest* excludes headnotes from state court cases.

When researching a state issue, you should consult the digest covering the controlling jurisdiction. West publishes a state-specific digest for virtually every state. Each state digest contains headnotes and case citations not only from reported decisions of the state's appellate courts but also from cases originating from the federal courts located within the state. For instance, *West's Ohio Digest* contains headnotes from decisions by the Supreme Court of Ohio, Ohio Courts of Appeals (intermediate appellate courts), and United States District Courts located in Ohio. It also classifies headnotes from decisions by the United States Supreme Court and the Sixth Circuit Court of Appeals if the case originated from a federal district court located in Ohio.

As to the hypothetical, a dispute over the meaning of the Establishment Clause is a federal issue. Thus, you could start by visiting your law library and locating the many red volumes of the *Federal Practice Digest 5th*.

b. Find Relevant Topics and Key Numbers

The second step in navigating West's Digest System is to find relevant Topics and Key Numbers covering the issues being researched. By reviewing the headnotes under an on-point Key Number, you can find more applicable cases, because each headnote in a digest cites the case in which the headnote appears. The four common methods to identify helpful Topics and Key Numbers include the following:

- Reviewing headnotes from the "best" and "good" cases;
- Browsing the Key Number Outline for a Topic;
- Reviewing secondary sources; and
- Consulting the Descriptive-Word Index.

First, an excellent approach to find helpful Key Numbers is to review the headnotes from the **best** and **good** cases that you have previously found. The "best" and "good" cases include ones that are legally and factually similar to your client's situation, as well as cases with different facts but with the same legal issue. Retrieve these cases from Westlaw or a West reporter (not Lexis Advance), as only these cases have headnotes organized in the Key Number System. Skim the headnotes of these cases to find rules of law that deal directly with your issues. The headnotes with relevant rules will direct you to the Topics and Key Numbers that classify similar headnotes from similar cases. As a result, you would find additional helpful cases on your research issue.

For the Establishment Clause issue, assume you found the case of *Freedom from Religion Foundation, Inc. v. City of Warren*, 707 F.3d 686 (6th Cir. 2013), with headnotes addressing the constitutionality of nativity scenes on public property. As shown in **Figure 7.3**, the first and second headnotes from that case are classified under the Topic "Constitutional Law" and Key Numbers 1298 and 1378. With this information, you can quickly find other federal cases with similar legal issues and facts, including binding decisions from the United States Supreme Court and from the Sixth Circuit Court of Appeals (which hears appeals from district courts located in Ohio).

In the library, once you have located the red volumes for the *Federal Practice Digest 5th*, you would scan the spines to find the Topic "Constitutional Law." (Recall

Figure 7.3: Print Reporter: Headnotes from Case of *Freedom from Religion Foundation*

1. Constitutional Law ☞1298

The Establishment Clause prohibits government from favoring one religion over another or from favoring religion over irreligion or irreligion over religion. U.S.C.A. Const.Amend. 1.

2. Constitutional Law ☞1378
Municipal Corporations ☞717

Winter holiday display in atrium of city's civic center with secular and religious symbols including a lighted tree, reindeer, snowmen, a "Winter Welcome" sign, a mailbox for Santa, and nativity scene did not violate the Establishment Clause prohibition against endorsement or religion; display did not advance any one religion. U.S.C.A. Const.Amend. 1.

that Topics are arranged in alphabetical order.) Then you would retrieve Volume 103 and find the pages where Key Numbers 1298 and 1378 start. (Remember that Key Numbers are in numerical order under each Topic.) All the headnotes from the reported federal cases under Key Number 1378 deal with the specific issue of nativity scenes on public property, and the citations for the cases containing the listed headnotes are provided. **Figure 7.4** depicts some headnotes and case citations listed under that Key Number.

Figure 7.4: Headnotes for Topic "Constitutional Law" and Key Number 1378

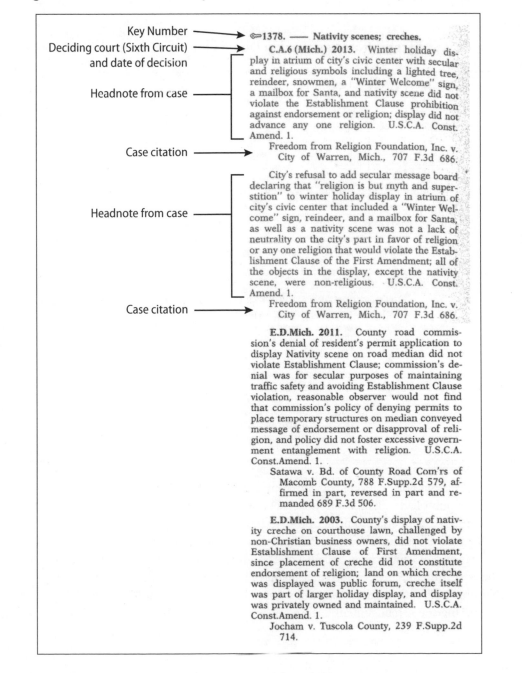

When you know at least one relevant Topic and Key Number, another effective method to discover classified headnotes and cases is to review the **Key Number Outline** for the Topic. This outline is located at the beginning of each Topic and functions as a table of contents for the Topic by providing a list of *all* Key Numbers and subtopics under that Topic. If you pursued the outline for the Topic "Constitutional Law," you would see several relevant Key Numbers that lead to additional relevant cases on your Establishment Clause issue. As shown in **Figure 7.5**, the pertinent subtopics include Key Number 1294 (establishment of religion), Key Number 1374 (government property, in general), and Key Number 1377 (holiday and seasonal displays).

Figure 7.5: Excerpt from Key Number Outline for Topic "Constitutional Law"

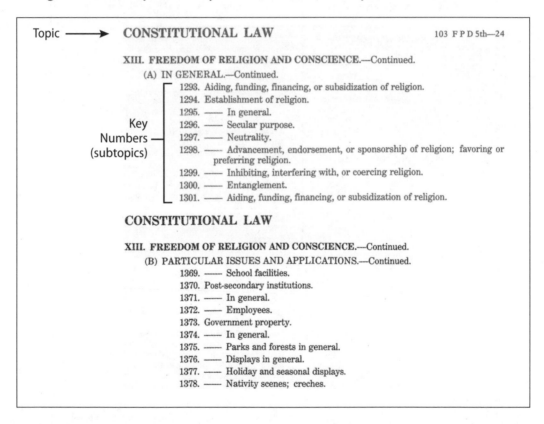

A third method to locate relevant Topics and Key Numbers is to review **secondary sources** published by Thomson Reuters (West), such as a treatise or legal encyclopedia. These sources, whether in print or on Westlaw, may provide Topics and Key Numbers that you did not locate through the prior two methods. **Figure 7.6** is an excerpt from one section of *American Jurisprudence 2d* addressing the establishment of religion by the government. This section directs you to the Topic "Constitutional Law" and Key Numbers 1295 through 1301, where you would find case citations and headnotes discussing the Establishment Clause.

Figure 7.6: Excerpt from 16A *Am. Jur. 2d*, Constitutional Law, § 436

16A Am. Jur. 2d Constitutional Law § 436

American Jurisprudence, Second Edition | August 2018 Update
Constitutional Law
George Blum, J.D., James Buchwalter, J.D., Paul M. Coltoff, J.D., Jefferson James Davis, J.D.,
Laura Hunter Dietz, J.D., Romualdo P. Eclavea, J.D., Tracy Farrell, J.D., J.S., Richard Link, J.D.,
Lucas Martin, J.D., Thomas Muskas, J.D., Jeffrey J. Shampo, J.D., Eric C. Surette, J.D., Susan L.
Thomas, and Eleanor L. Grossman, J.D., Glenda K. Harnad, and Anne E. Melley, J.D., LL.M. of
the staff of the National Legal Research Group, Inc.

IX. Fundamental Rights and Privileges
C. Specific Fundamental Rights
1. First Amendment Rights
b. Religious Freedom
(2) "Establishment of Religion"

§ 436. Generally

Topic Summary | Correlation Table | References

West's Key Number Digest

- West's Key Number Digest, <u>Constitutional Law</u> ⌖ <u>1295</u> to <u>1301</u>

A fourth method to find relevant Topics and Key Numbers is to use the **Descriptive-Word Index** located at the end of every digest set. This index is an excellent tool to find Topics and Key Numbers when you do not know at least one relevant Key Number and have no access to Westlaw.

The Descriptive-Word Index contains a list of alphabetical terms that a researcher may use when looking for relevant headnotes and cases that are classified in West's Digest System. Even if a researcher looks up the wrong term, the index will cross-reference the right index term for the legal issue. To illustrate, if you looked up the term "intentional infliction of emotional distress," the Descriptive-Word Index would direct you to the term "damages." You would then look up the term "damages" in the index, which would inform you that cases addressing a claim for intentional infliction are classified under the Topic "Damages." If you had attempted to guess the correct Topic, you probably would have looked under the Topic "Torts." Although a logical choice, it would have been incorrect.

c. Read the Classified Headnotes and Cases

The third step in researching with a print digest is somewhat obvious: review all the pertinent headnotes under every relevant Key Number. For each headnote with a rule or other point that seems to apply to the client's circumstances, record the

> ### Never Cite to Headnotes
>
> Although headnotes help researchers find relevant cases, you should never quote or cite to a headnote in any legal document. Judges do not draft headnotes; instead, editors of Thomas Reuters (West) and LexisNexis create headnotes. If a headnote misrepresents the law from a case and you rely solely on the headnote in a court document, you—not the drafting editor—could face an ethical complaint.

citation of the corresponding case. Then retrieve and read the potentially helpful cases to determine whether they have legal issues and facts similar to your client's situation. And remember to focus on rules from judicial decisions that bind your court; if necessary, review decisions that are highly or moderately persuasive on your court.

As to the Establishment Clause hypothetical, you should review the rules of law from the cases and headnotes classified under all Key Numbers previously mentioned. In under twenty minutes, you would learn that the Sixth Circuit Court of Appeals and district courts within that circuit have ruled that the Establishment Clause does not demand strict separation between religion and the government and have upheld the constitutionality of various nativity scenes placed on public grounds.

d. Update and Validate Your Research

For the fourth—and final—step in researching with a print digest, you need to update the research by reviewing pocket parts, supplements, and any interim pamphlets. The hardbound volumes of a digest set are updated and made current with paperback pocket parts located in the back of each volume (usually published annually). If cases were decided after the publication of the main volume, their headnotes and citations would be published in the pocket part. When a pocket part becomes too large, Thomson Reuters (West) prints a separate softbound supplement, which would be located next to the hardbound volume it updates. Additionally, West updates an entire digest set with an interim pamphlet covering cases decided after the publication date of the pocket parts.

Recall that Volume 103 of the *Federal Practice Digest 5th* contains the case citations and headnotes classified under Key Number 1378 (nativity scenes; creches). To find cases that were decided after the publication of Volume 103 and classified under the same Key Number, locate the pocket part at the end of that volume. As of this textbook's publication date, the most recent pocket part was published in 2017 and classifies only one case under Key Number 1378, as shown in **Figure 7.7**.

3. Navigating the Key Number System on Westlaw

On Westlaw, the Key Number System is substantially the same as West's Digest in print; the Key Number System online organizes cases and headnotes by the same

Figure 7.7: Excerpt from Pocket Part of Volume 103

> ⟅⟆1378. —— **Nativity scenes; creches.**
> **W.D.Ark. 2015.** Record left no room for doubt
> that county judge's purpose in signing resolution
> providing that county was to lease county court-
> house property in order to display nativity scene
> was predominantly religious, rather than secular,
> in violation of the Establishment Clause; judge
> denied other requests to install banner near the
> display that carried secular messages, and lease
> was entered for fundamentally religious purpose
> of displaying nativity scene. U.S.C.A. Const.
> Amend. 1.—American Humanist Association v.
> Baxter County, Arkansas, 143 F.Supp.3d 816.
>   Secular humanist association, which brought
> suit against county alleging violation of the Estab-
> lishment Clause based on county's nativity dis-
> play on county courthouse property, was entitled
> to declaratory relief, nominal damages in amount
> of one dollar for violations of their First Amend-
> ment rights, and injunctive relief for having ob-
> tained success on merits because association
> showed that it suffered irreparable harm, that
> harm suffered exceeded any injury an injunction
> might have inflicted on the other parties, and that
> the public had an enormous interest in seeing its
> government comply with the First Amendment.
> U.S.C.A. Const.Amend. 1; 28 U.S.C.A. § 2201.—
> Id.

Topics and same Key Numbers (the subtopics) as the print digests. Accordingly, the three finding methods previously discussed—reviewing headnotes from the "best" and "good" cases, browsing the Key Number Outline, and consulting a secondary source—should be used when looking for Topics and Key Numbers on Westlaw.

To illustrate, return to the hypothetical on whether the client violated the Establishment Clause by allowing a nativity scene on public grounds. Recall you found a pertinent case, *Freedom from Religion Foundation, Inc. v. City of Warren*. By reviewing the first and second headnotes, you would learn that they have been classified under the Topic "Constitutional Law" and Key Numbers 1298 and 1378 (see **Figure 7.8**). You could then jump on Westlaw and find multiple headnotes under both Key Numbers. Each headnote in the online Key Number System links to the case in which the headnote appears.

On Westlaw, you could follow the steps listed below to locate Key Number 1298 (advancement, endorsement, or sponsorship of religion) and Key Number 1378 (nativity scenes). **Figure 7.9** illustrates these steps with four screen captures.

1. From the home page, click "Key Numbers" to view the list of over 400 Topics.

2. Click the Topic "Constitutional Law" to view the Key Numbers (subtopics) under that Topic.

3. Scroll down to the heading "Freedom of Religion and Conscience" and select the "+" icon to view the Key Numbers under that heading.

4. To see the relevant headnotes, click the hyperlinked Key Numbers 1298 and 1378.

Although the Key Number Systems online and in print are similar, there are two primary differences, making them fraternal, not identical, "twins." First, the online version is updated much more frequently than print digests. Immediately after West editors draft headnotes for a new judicial decision, the case and its headnotes are classified and available to view on Westlaw, whereas the same headnotes would not appear in an interim pamphlet or pocket part until the next printing date.

Figure 7.8: Westlaw: Headnotes from Case of *Freedom from Religion Foundation*

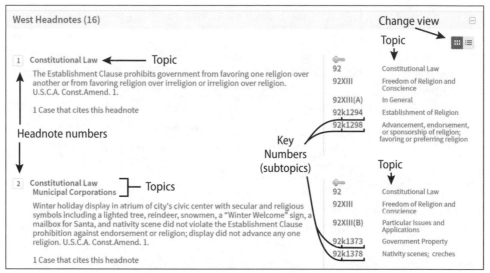

Figure 7.9: Westlaw: Navigating the Key Number System

Figure 7.9: *Continued*

☐ 83 COMMERCE	☐ 228 JUDGMENT
☐ 83H COMMODITY FUTURES TRADING REGULATION	☐ 229 JUDICIAL SALES
☐ 83T COMMON INTEREST COMMUNITIES	☐ 230 JURY
	☐ 231 JUSTICES OF THE PEACE
☐ 84 COMMON LANDS	☐ 231E KIDNAPPING
☐ 85 COMMON LAW	☐ 231H LABOR AND EMPLOYMENT
☐ 89 COMPROMISE AND SETTLEMENT	☐ 233 LANDLORD AND TENANT
☐ 90 CONFUSION OF GOODS	☐ 234 LARCENY
☐ 91 CONSPIRACY	☐ 237 LIBEL AND SLANDER
☐ 92 CONSTITUTIONAL LAW	☐ 238 LICENSES
☐ 93 CONTEMPT	☐ 239 LIENS
☐ 95 CONTRACTS	☐ 240 LIFE ESTATES
	☐ 241 LIMITATION OF ACTIONS

☐ ☐ ☞ **1294** Establishment of religion

   ☐ ☞ **1295** —In general

   ☐ ☞ **1296** —Secular purpose

   ☐ ☞ **1297** —Neutrality

   ☐ ☞ **1298** —Advancement, endorsement, or sponsorship of religion;

   ☐ ☞ **1299** —Inhibiting, interfering with, or coercing religion

   ☐ ☞ **1300** —Entanglement

   ☐ ☞ **1301** —Aiding, funding, financing, or subsidization of religion

☐ ☐ ☞ **1302** Free exercise of religion

☐ ☐ **(B)** PARTICULAR ISSUES AND APPLICATIONS, k1310-k1429

   ☐ ☞ **1310** In general

   ☐ ☞ **1311** Indians in general

   ☐ ☞ **1312** Aiding, funding, financing, or subsidization of religion

   ☐ ☞ **1313** Government meetings and proceedings

   ☐ ☞ **1318** Government seals, insignia, emblems, logos, or mottos

   ☐ ☞ **1319** Labor and employment

   ☐ ☞ **1322** Public officials; judges

Figure 7.9: *Continued*

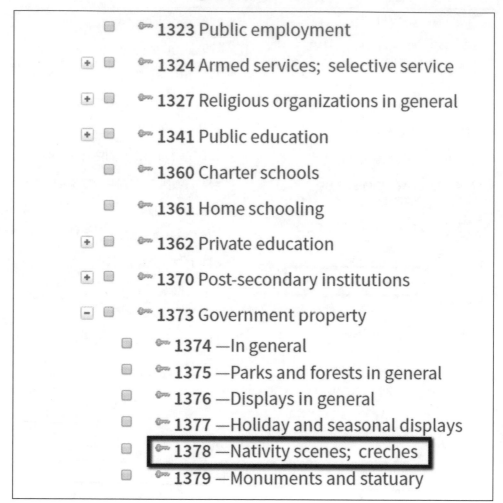

Second, the coverage of cases in the Key Number System online is not limited by date or jurisdiction, but print digest sets include headnotes only from cases for a certain

Figure 7.10: Comparison of Key Number System in Print and Online

Benefits/Limitations	Westlaw (Online)	Digest (Print)
Perform keyword searches of the text of classified headnotes	Yes	No
Updates each day	Yes	No
Sort headnotes by date (*e.g.*, newest cases listed first)	Yes	No
Outline for each Topic	Yes	Yes
Coverage limited by date of cases	No	Yes
Coverage limited by jurisdiction	No	Yes
Limit results to headnotes from specific courts	Yes	No
Consult the Descriptive-Word Index	No	Yes

period and only from a specific jurisdiction or court. The Fifth Series of the *Federal Practice Digest*, for instance, only covers federal cases from 2003 to the present.

Figure 7.10 summarizes important similarities and differences of the Key Number System in print and on Westlaw.

B. Finding Cases by Topic on Lexis Advance

On Lexis Advance, you can also research cases online by topic. The caselaw classification system on Lexis Advance has several names, including LexisNexis Legal Topic Hierarchy, LexisNexis Headnotes and Topics, and LexisNexis Legal Topic Digest. The Legal Topic Digest collects headnotes and cases that have been arranged by topic.

Although West's and Lexis's classification systems are similar, there are several differences. The LexisNexis Legal Topic Digest is available only online and is not based on print reporters, unlike West's system. Further, the classification system on Lexis has fewer subtopics than its competitor's system. The Lexis system has around 30,000 subtopics, but West's system has over 100,000 subtopics. Last, you will not find West's Topics and Key Numbers on Lexis or other research services; the Key Number System is exclusive to Thomson Reuters.

1. Creation and Organization of the LexisNexis Legal Topic Digest

The headnotes classified on Lexis Advance are created and assigned topics in a similar manner as headnotes in West's Key Number System. The attorney editors for Lexis analyze federal and state cases and create one or more headnotes based on the rules of law and legal issues in the decision. A case with five distinct issues would have five headnotes. Each headnote of a case is then assigned one or more topics, just like one photograph on social media can be assigned multiple subject hashtags. As a result, you could find the same case through the LexisNexis Legal Topic Digest using different topics. For example, if a case has one headnote classified under the topic "defamation" and another headnote tagged with the topic "elements of assault," you could locate that case under both topics.

The headnotes on Lexis differ from those in West's system in one important respect. Lexis editors create headnotes by quoting language directly from the judicial opinion, whereas West editors paraphrase a court's language and editorialize rules from cases.

2. Methods for Finding Cases on Lexis Advance

Once you have identified one or more relevant topics in the LexisNexis Legal Topic Digest, you can locate rules of law and cases related to the client's situation. You can locate topics and helpful cases in two primary ways: (1) reviewing headnotes from the **best** and **good** cases; and (2) using the **Browse Topics** feature.

a. Best and Good Case Method

An easy method to find relevant topics on Lexis Advance is to review the headnotes from the **best** and **good cases** that you have already found. Headnotes from these cases provide three paths for finding additional cases that are relevant.

One path is to **identify the topic** where each relevant headnote has been classified. The headnotes of a case on Lexis Advance are located near the top of the decision, and the assigned topics are listed immediately above the text of each headnote. As shown in **Figure 7.11**, each line above an individual headnote represents a different topical classification; the first headnote is classified under two topics, and the second headnote is classified under one topic. If you click on a hyperlinked topic and then

**Figure 7.11: Headnotes from *Harder v. Edwards*, 174 So. 3d 524
(Fla. Dist. Ct. App. 2015)**

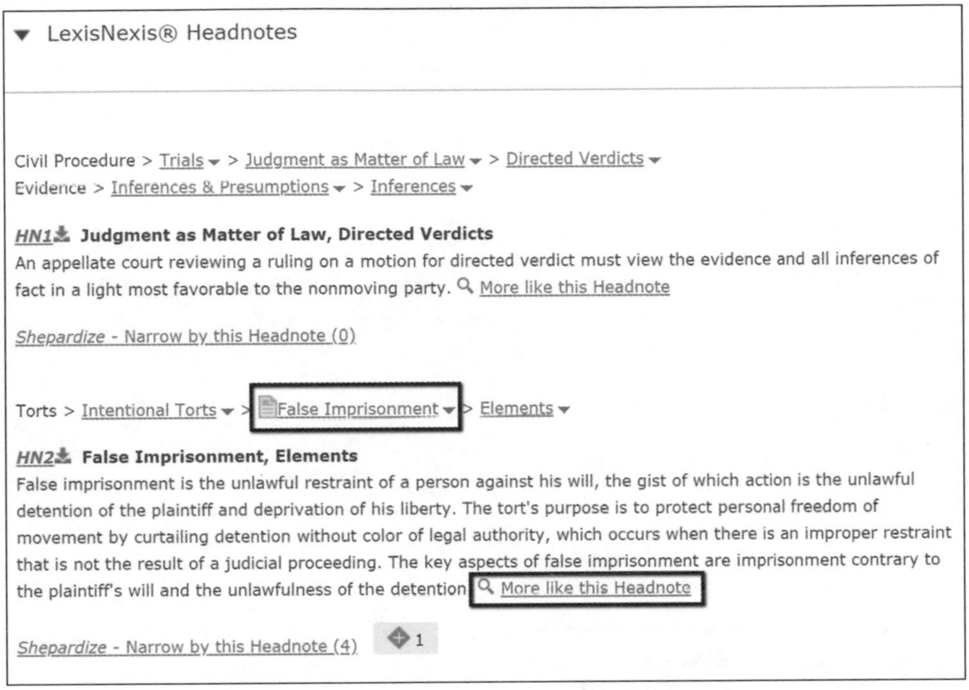

select "Get Documents," you would retrieve a list of cases with at least one headnote categorized under that topic in the Legal Topic Digest. Some listed cases should apply to your legal issue. Because many topics in the Legal Topic Digest are broad, clicking a topic from a headnote often leads to numerous results. In the left column, multiple filtering options are available. You can filter and narrow the results by jurisdiction, court, date, and keywords. At a minimum, you should limit the results to cases from the controlling jurisdiction.[3]

A second path is to use headnotes to discover **Topic Summaries** that apply to the client's issue, which would lead to helpful cases. In the second headnote in **Figure 7.11**, there is a small icon next to the topic "False Imprisonment." Clicking that icon would retrieve a Topic Summary report. Although a report is not available for every

---

3. For a detailed discussion on how to filter results, review Chapter 8 (citators) and Chapter 9 (keyword searching).

Figure 7.12: Topic Summary for False Imprisonment

📄**Topic Summary: False Imprisonment**

Practice Area: Torts
Jurisdiction: U.S. Federal
Context:
Torts > Intentional Torts > **False Imprisonment**

Definitions (1)

1. **False imprisonment** is the unlawful restraining of a person's liberty or freedom of movement. Padlo v. Vg's Food Ctr., 2005 U.S. Dist. LEXIS 37454

Seminal Cases (10)

1. Weyant v. Okst, 101 F.3d 845
2. Wallace v. Kato, 549 U.S. 384
3. Cameron v. Fogarty, 806 F.2d 380

View more

Elements of (1)

1. The essential elements of a false imprisonment claim are: (1) willful detention; (2) without consent; and (3) without authority of law. Ewans v. Wells Fargo Bank, N.A., 389 Fed. Appx. 383

Figure 7.13: Results Page for "More Like This Headnote" Feature

1. ◆Harder v. Edwards ⬡

   Court of Appeal of Florida, Fourth District │ Aug 26, 2015 │ 174 So. 3d 524

   Overview: A judgment against a store and its employee on plaintiff's false imprisonment claim was reversed, because their cooperation with a detective's investigation amounted to neither actual detention nor active instigation of plaintiff's arrest.

   HN2 - False imprisonment is the **unlawful restraint** of a person against **his will**, the **gist** of which action is the **unlawful detention** of the plaintiff and **deprivation** of his **liberty**. The **tort's** purpose is to protect personal **freedom of movement** by **curtailing detention** without **color** of **legal authority**, which occurs when there is an **improper restraint** that is not the result of a judicial proceeding. The **key aspects** of **false imprisonment** are **imprisonment** contrary to the plaintiff's will and the **unlawfulness** of the **detention.** - More Like This Headnote

   HN3 - To state a cause of action for **false imprisonment**, the plaintiff must establish four elements: (1) the **unlawful detention** and **deprivation** of liberty of a person (2) against that person's will (3) without **legal authority** or **color** of authority and (4) which is unreasonable and unwarranted under the circumstances. - More Like This Headnote

   HN4 - With regard to the type of conduct that will subject a defendant to liability for **false imprisonment**, the Supreme Court of Florida has written that to be liable in an action for **false imprisonment**, one must have personally and actively participated therein, directly or by indirect procurement. The concept of "indirect procurement" is not precise and arguably could cover a large swath of citizen contact with the police. However, the Florida Supreme Court has narrowed the scope of the "indirect procurement" phrase in Johnson v. Weiner and has held that where a citizen provides information to law enforcement, without more, such action does not constitute **false imprisonment**. Even if the private citizen makes an honest, good faith mistake in reporting an incident, the mere fact that his communication to an officer may have caused the victim's arrest does not make him liable when he did not in fact request any **detention.** - More Like This Headnote

2. ▲James v. City of Wilkes-Barre Wright Twp.

   United States District Court for the Middle District of Pennsylvania │ Jun 10, 2011 │ 2011 U.S. Dist. LEXIS 90674

topic, Lexis has over 6,000 Topic Summary reports. Each report summarizes and defines a legal topic, identifies a few secondary sources on the topic, and lists seminal cases on the topic. The headnotes from the seminal cases, even if they are from outside your jurisdiction, should take you to relevant cases in the controlling jurisdiction through the topical classifications. An excerpt from a Topic Summary on false imprisonment is shown in **Figure 7.12**.

A third path to find applicable cases is to use the **More Like This Headnote** feature for each headnote that identifies a good rule of law. Review the second headnote on false imprisonment in **Figure 7.11** above. If you click "More Like This Headnote" (at end of the headnote), you would retrieve a list of cases with headnotes containing similar language as your headnote; the results are generated by performing a Google-like search using the words in the headnote as the search terms. The results page displays the actual text of each headnote containing the similar terms, and it highlights the terms (see **Figure 7.13**).

b. Browse Topics Method

A second method to find relevant topics—and helpful cases—on Lexis Advance is through its Browse Topics feature. This feature is similar to browsing the outline for a Topic on West's Key Number System. On the home page of Lexis Advance, you would view the list of topics by clicking the "Browse" tab at the top of the screen and then selecting "Topics" from the drop-down menu. After clicking through the hierarchy of topics, you can retrieve all cases that have at least one headnote classified under a specific topic.

For instance, suppose you need to research whether courts award punitive damages for a breach of contract claim. To locate cases on that issue, you would click through the following hierarchy:

"Browse" tab → "Topics" → "Contract Law"
→ "Remedies" → "Damages"
→ "Punitive Damages" (the final, most specific topic in hierarchy)
→ "Get Documents."

Lexis Advance would return a list of cases addressing contract law and punitive damages. Unlike the Key Number System on Westlaw, Lexis does not provide a list of just the headnotes classified under "Punitive Damages." To view those headnotes, you need to retrieve the full text of a case by clicking the case name from the results list and then locate the headnotes tagged with the topic "Punitive Damages."

C. Other Caselaw Classification Systems

Although the most robust and powerful systems, West's Key Number System and the LexisNexis Legal Topic Digest do not monopolize the market on classification systems for cases. Other digests classify cases, including ones published by commercial entities and bar associations. For instance, Casemaker is an online research service available for free to members of some state and local bar associations, and its digest classifies federal and state cases into different areas of law. The Ohio State Bar Association maintains a digest called the *OSBA Report* that summarizes Ohio cases and categorizes them into one or more practice areas. Further, LexisNexis publishes specialized case-finding tools, such as *Florida Family Law Case Summaries* (organizes Florida caselaw on family law matters) and *Virginia Criminal Law Case Finder* (organizes Virginia caselaw on criminal and traffic matters).

In short, do not assume that West's system or the LexisNexis Legal Topic Digest are the only classification systems applicable to your research. You should always check whether another case-finding tool is available for the governing jurisdiction. As technology advances, other research platforms may offer new ways to research cases by topic.

D. Summary of Key Points

You should research cases by topic at this **Step 3**, especially for an unfamiliar common law issue. The most comprehensive systems that classify cases by topic are **West's Key Number System** (on Westlaw and in print) and the **LexisNexis Legal Topic Digest** (on Lexis Advance only). The building blocks of both classification systems are headnotes. Headnotes are usually one-sentence summaries found at the beginning of cases. A headnote may summarize a rule of law from a case or identify how the court applied an existing rule to its facts. Headnotes are "tagged" with at least one Key Number (West) or one topic (Lexis), allowing researchers to locate other cases containing headnotes classified under the same Key Number or topic.

By using either classification system and scanning just the concise headnotes of cases, you can find relevant judicial decisions and can eliminate irrelevant cases. Unless reading cases is your favorite hobby, you will appreciate the time saved by not having to analyze the full text of every irrelevant case, freeing up time for more exciting adventures outside the legal world. Thus, at some point in the research process, you should complete **Step 3** and harness the power of the West or Lexis classification system. But do not rely exclusively on the text of any headnote; review the language of every case you plan to cite in a legal document.

As set forth in **Figure 7.14**, there are several options to find Key Numbers on Westlaw and topics on Lexis Advance. Once you know the Key Numbers and topics assigned to headnotes that address the client's legal issue, you can find relevant cases.

As you complete this **Step 3**, stay focused on the ultimate goal: reaching a reliable answer on the client's legal question. For this endeavor, all authorities are not equal. Judicial decisions that bind your court and that are legally and factually similar to the client's situation would be the "best" cases, and decisions that are highly or moderately persuasive on your court and that involve similar legal issues would be "good" cases. These "best" and "good" cases fall in rows A and B in the "Best Authority" and

**Figure 7.14: Finding Methods for Cases on
Westlaw and Lexis Advance**

Finding Methods for Key Numbers (Westlaw) and Topics (Lexis)	West's Key Number System	LexisNexis Legal Topic Digest
Review headnotes from the "best" and "good" cases	Yes	Yes
Browse the Key Number Outline for a Topic	Yes	No
Browse Topics feature	No	Yes
Review secondary sources	Yes[1]	No
Examine headnotes in cases listed in a Topic Summary	No	Yes
Use the "More Like This Headnote" feature	No	Yes

[1] Only secondary sources published by Thomson Reuters (West) identify Key Numbers.

"Good Authority" columns in **Table 2** in Appendix B. In short, the rules, holdings, and reasoning from cases falling within those two rows and two columns would be the most helpful in resolving your issue.

E. Review Questions on Classification Systems

At this point, you should have a basic understanding of researching cases by topic. To test your comprehension, answer the true-false and multiple-choice questions on this book's companion website, Core Knowledge. It will identify the correct answers and provide clear explanations for each question. The same questions are reproduced below.

1. The headnotes in the classification system on Lexis Advance contain direct quotations from the cases.

   a. True

   b. False

2. The headnotes in West's Key Number System contain direct quotations from the cases.

   a. True

   b. False

3. The Key Number System on Westlaw organizes statutes by topic.

   a. True

   b. False

4. Each headnote of a case published in a reporter by Thomson Reuters (West) is assigned at least one Topic and one Key Number.

   a. True

   b. False

5. West's Key Number System and the LexisNexis Legal Topic Digest are the only available classification systems for cases.

   a. True

   b. False

6. What is the difference between West's Key Number System and a West reporter?

   a. A reporter is arranged by topic, but the Key Number System is arranged in chronological order.

   b. A reporter is arranged in chronological order, but the Key Number System is arranged by topic.

   c. A reporter helps a researcher locate cases, and the Key Number System contains the actual cases.

   d. The Key Number System is a primary source, but a reporter is a secondary source.

7. The *Federal Practice Digest* contains headnotes from which courts?

   a. Only from the United States Supreme Court.

   b. Only from United States Courts of Appeals.

   c. Only from United States District Courts.

   d. All three courts listed above.

8. Which features of West's Key Number System are available online on Westlaw but not in a print digest?

   a. Searching the text of all classified headnotes by keywords.

   b. Sorting headnotes under a Key Number by date.

   c. Updating each day.

   d. All of the above.

9. Identify which method is available on both Westlaw and Lexis Advance to find relevant Key Numbers (Westlaw) and topics (Lexis).

   a. Browse the Key Number Outline for a Topic.

   b. Review secondary sources.

   c. Review headnotes from the "best" and "good" cases.

   d. Use the "More Like This Headnote" feature.

10. *West's Florida Digest* contains headnotes from which of the following courts?

  a. Only the Supreme Court of Florida and Florida intermediate appellate courts.

  b. Only the Supreme Court of Florida.

  c. The Supreme Court of Florida, Florida intermediate appellate courts, and United States District Courts located in Florida.

  d. All federal courts.

F. Practice Researching with Classification Systems

On this book's companion website, Core Knowledge, a few research assignments have been posted. The online assignments walk you through the steps for researching a common law issue on Westlaw and Lexis Advance, including how to navigate West's Key Number System and the LexisNexis Legal Topic Digest. Additionally, several exercises instruct you on using the West Digest in print. For each assignment, you will research the law to resolve legal issues for your hypothetical client.

Step 1
(Research
Plan)

Step 2
(Secondary
Sources)

Step 3
(Cases
by
Topic)

Chapter 8

Step 4:
Use a Reliable Citator to Find
Relevant Cases and to Confirm
Their Validity

By this point in the research process for your unfamiliar common law issue, you should have created a research plan (**Step 1**, Chapter 5), reviewed at least one helpful secondary source (**Step 2**, Chapter 6), and researched with West's Key Number System or LexisNexis Legal Topic Digest (**Step 3**, Chapter 7). Through those three steps, you should have found some binding or at least persuasive cases that will help you accurately answer your client's legal question. But your research journey should continue with an **online citator** at **Step 4**.

Even if you have already found cases on point, as a beginner researcher, you do not know whether you have found the universe of relevant cases for your unfamiliar issue. Simply put, you do not know what you do not know. For example, if most of the relevant cases are not designated "for publication" (that is, not printed in a reporter), then you probably would not find them with West's Key Number System. Recall that West's System does not classify headnotes from unpublished cases (few exceptions exist). To further illustrate, an exception to the law may apply to your client's situation, but the courts may not have identified the exception in the cases you already found. Last, you can craft stronger arguments as you find more authorities with relevant rules.

For this **Step 4**, you should use an **online citator**. In a nutshell, an online citator, or citation service, is a fancy word for a research tool that informs a legal researcher which primary and secondary authorities have cited a particular legal authority (*e.g.*, a case or statute). A citator also identifies which authorities agree or disagree with the cited legal authority. This chapter focuses on using citators for cases for common law issues, but later chapters discuss citators for other legal authorities.

The original citator was *Shepard's Citations in Print* and was later purchased by LexisNexis and made available online. The print version is cumbersome and not updated as frequently as the online counterpart; in fact, few attorneys use *Shepard's Citations in Print*. To the delight of law students, most professors do not teach print citators and instead teach only online citators.

The two most popular and reliable online citators are **Shepard's** on Lexis Advance and **KeyCite** on Westlaw. Indeed, for many years, both citators have garnished the most respect from attorneys and judges. The alternative online citators, such as BCite on Bloomberg Law, Authority Check on Fastcase, and CaseCheck+ on Casemaker, are not as comprehensive and have not demonstrated their reliability. Thus, this chapter focuses on Shepard's (Lexis) and KeyCite (Westlaw).

A. Three Reasons to Use Citators

At this point of your research for a common law issue (**Step 4**), you should use an online citator—particularly Shepard's or KeyCite—for three purposes:

- Finding additional relevant cases;
- Confirming the validity of your cases and determining whether the rules of law in them remain good law; and
- Understanding the persuasive value of your cases.

When using citators for these three reasons, do not forget your goal: resolving your client's legal questions with reliable answers.

Although using a citator at this **Step 4** is often a good approach, your legal issue may demand that you travel a different research path. No single research process or path applies to every assignment. The goal of these eight research steps is to shine a light on your research path, directing you through the process to keep you on track and to help you avoid the research "black hole." You may need to swap this **Step 4** with other steps or may need to return to this **Step 4** more than once. For instance, if you discover a exception to the law when using a citator (**Step 4**) and the exception could relieve your client of liability, you should return to secondary sources for insight about the exception (**Step 2**). Or if a supervisor asks you only to determine whether any court has recently cited a leading decision from the state's supreme court, you would jump to this **Step 4** and use a citator. The process of legal research is not linear.

With those alternative research paths in mind, you are ready to learn about the three reasons to use a citator, such as Shepard's and KeyCite.

B. Finding Relevant Cases with Shepard's and KeyCite

At **Step 4**, you can use a citation service to find additional cases that are legally on point and factually similar to your client's situation. These additional cases should shed further light on the law supporting and opposing your client's position. And to the extent a citation service identifies the same cases you found through other research steps, it may indicate that you have found the universe of relevant cases.

Both Shepard's in Lexis Advance and KeyCite in Westlaw provide reports listing each *subsequent* case that has cited your case.[1] So if the *Smith v. Jones* case was cited

---

1. Occasionally, a subsequent case may not be included because of a technical problem.

once (or more) by ten other courts, the Shepard's or KeyCite report would identify all ten later cases (referred to as the "citing cases"). Citators, therefore, educate you on what you did not previously know—whether newer relevant cases exist—and thus alleviate at least some fear that you have missed important authorities.

Initially at this **Step 4**, you should use Shepard's or KeyCite for each case with legal issues and facts similar to your client's circumstances. (These cases fall within the "Best Authority" column in **Table 2** in Appendix B.) Under this approach, the citator report should include relevant cases but exclude some irrelevant cases. For instance, suppose you found one highly relevant case on your issue of whether a neighbor's dog showed "vicious" propensities prior to attacking your client. If you Shepardized or KeyCited your relevant case, many citing cases listed on the report should involve courts addressing the viciousness issue because courts often cite and rely on prior cases with similar legal issues and facts.

Triggering a Shepard's or KeyCite report for a case is simple. On Lexis Advance, while the full text of your case is displayed, click "Shepardize this document" in the right column, and select the "Citing Decisions" tab in the left column on the next screen. On Westlaw, while viewing your case, click the "Citing References" tab near the top of the screen, and then select "Cases."

A Shepard's or KeyCite report may contain hundreds (or thousands) of citing cases. If so, the results need to be reduced to a manageable number. Both citators have built-in filtering tools that can save researchers time without sacrificing accuracy. When used appropriately, the filtering tools on Westlaw and Lexis Advance help you weed out *irrelevant* cases from a citator report, while minimizing the likelihood of eliminating *relevant* results.

The following hypothetical will illustrate how to filter the results on a citator report. Suppose your client plans to argue that the noncompetition clause in her employment agreement is unreasonable and unenforceable under Ohio law because it covers too large of geographic area. She also plans to challenge the nonsolicitation clause prohibiting her from contacting former customers. Assume you found a leading case from the Supreme Court of Ohio, *Rogers v. Runfola & Associates, Inc.*, 565 N.E.2d 540 (Ohio 1991), and you Shepardized and KeyCited that case. As shown in the citator reports in **Figures 8.1** and **8.2**, more than 120 cases cite *Rogers*. If you are bored on a rainy day, you could read all citing decisions to find the "needle in the haystack." Or you could use the citator filters to reduce the more than 120 results to a reasonable number.

As explained next, the following four filters are effective tools to exclude irrelevant results from a Shepard's or KeyCite report:

- Jurisdiction and court;
- Depth of treatment and discussion;
- Legal issue and headnotes; and
- Keywords.

Figure 8.1: Shepard's Report for *Rogers v. Runfola & Assocs., Inc.*

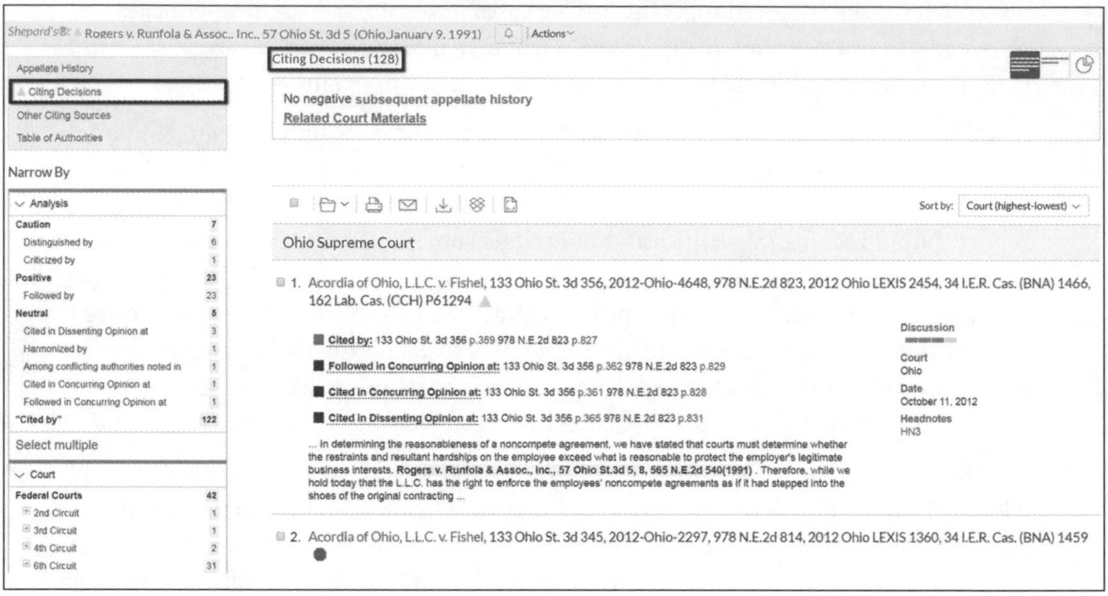

Figure 8.2: KeyCite Report for *Rogers v. Runfola & Assocs., Inc.*

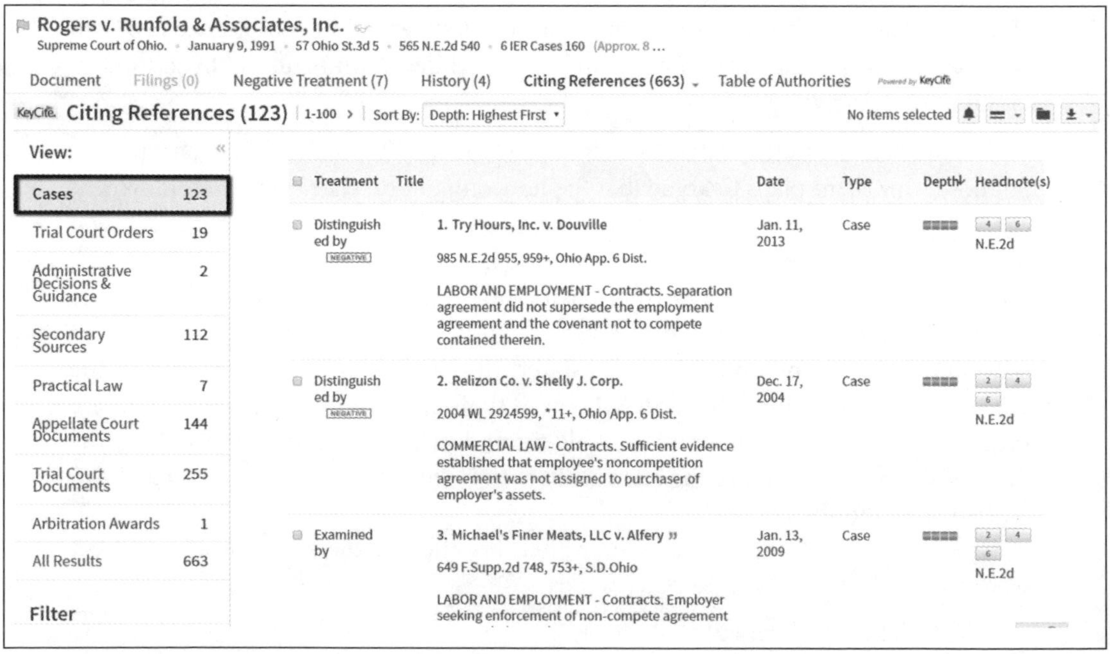

Saving Time with Editorial Summaries and Headnotes

As you find cases with a citator, remember to scan the editorial summaries and headnotes that appear before the text of the opinion (see Chapter 3). Many times, an editorial summary identifies the legal question in dispute and identifies the facts the court relied on in resolving the dispute. Headnotes summarize rules of law from a case. Thus, by reviewing these editorial enhancements, you often can determine whether a case applies to the client's situation. These enhancements also may provide new insights about a case.

But you should never cite to an editorial summary or headnote in a legal document. The editors of Thomas Reuters (West) and LexisNexis, not the deciding court, draft these enhancements.

---

1. Filtering by Jurisdiction and Court

In the left column of a citator report, you can filter the results by jurisdiction and specific courts, as shown in **Figures 8.3** and **8.4**. Continuing with the Shepard's and KeyCite reports for the *Rogers* case, you should initially eliminate nonbinding decisions from the reports and limit the results to binding cases, such as decisions by the Supreme Court of Ohio. The Ohio Supreme Court is the final decision-maker on the validity of your client's noncompetition agreement under Ohio law. But if the binding cases do not lead to a reliable answer, you should review nonbinding decisions from the controlling jurisdiction (Ohio), including cases by the United States Court of Appeals for the Sixth Circuit and the federal district courts located in Ohio.

2. Filtering by Depth of Treatment and Discussion

You can also filter the citing results by "depth of treatment" on a KeyCite report or by depth of "discussion" on a Shepard's report. (This filter is located in the left column of each citator report.) Both filters limit citing results using essentially the same criteria. As shown in **Figures 8.5** and **8.6**, the number of horizontal bars represents the level of treatment or discussion of your case contained in the citing cases. A citing case with four horizontal bars, for instance, means it has analyzed your case in great detail. On Lexis Advance, if you filter the report for *Rogers* by three or more bars, you would limit the results to eleven citing cases (see **Figure 8.5**). That filter should eliminate cases that cite *Rogers* only once or that have minimal, if any, discussion of *Rogers*.

Figure 8.3: Shepard's (Lexis): Filtering by Jurisdiction and Court

Narrow By	
> Analysis	
∨ Court	
Federal Courts	42
⊞ 2nd Circuit	1
⊞ 3rd Circuit	1
⊞ 4th Circuit	2
⊟ 6th Circuit	31
⊞ 6th Circuit - Court of Appeals	5
⊞ 6th Circuit - U.S. District Courts	24
⊞ 6th Circuit - U.S. Bankruptcy Courts	2
⊞ 7th Circuit	4
⊞ 9th Circuit	3
Select multiple	
State Courts	86
⊞ Connecticut	1
⊞ Idaho	1
⊟ Ohio	83
Ohio Supreme Court	4
⊞ Ohio Court of Appeals	68
Ohio Court of Common Pleas	2
Other Ohio Decisions	9
⊞ Tennessee	1
Select multiple	

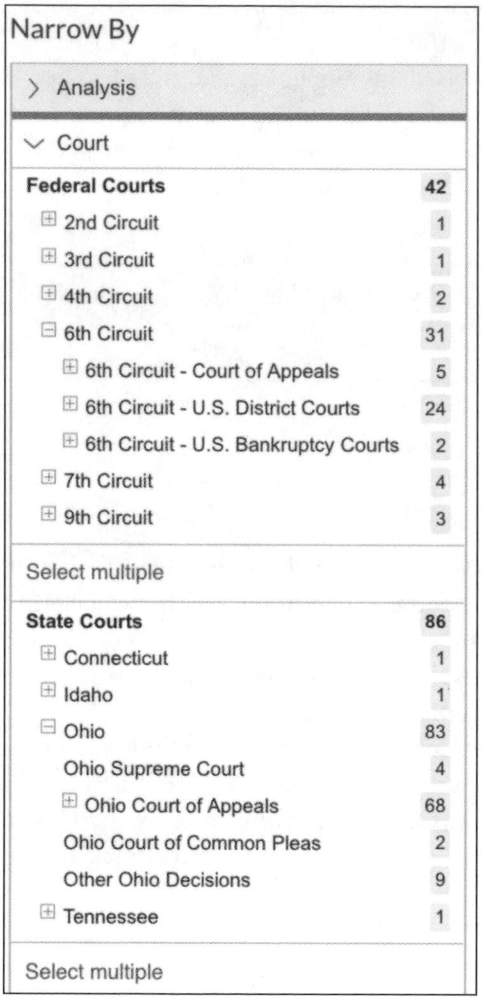

Figure 8.4: KeyCite (Westlaw): Filtering by Jurisdiction and Court

Filter	
⬤ Select multiple	
Search within results	
🔍	
Jurisdiction	—
Narrow Jurisdiction	
⊟ ☐ Federal	47
⊟ ☐ Courts Of Appeals	6
⊞ ☐ Sixth Circuit Ct. App.	5
⊞ ☐ Seventh Circuit Ct. App.	1
⊞ ☐ District Courts	40
⊞ ☐ Bankruptcy Courts	1
⊟ ☐ State	76
⊞ ☐ Connecticut	1
⊞ ☐ Idaho	1
⊟ ☐ Ohio	73
☐ Ohio	4
☐ Ohio App. 1 Dist.	3
☐ Ohio App. 10 Dist.	14
☐ Ohio App. 11 Dist.	3

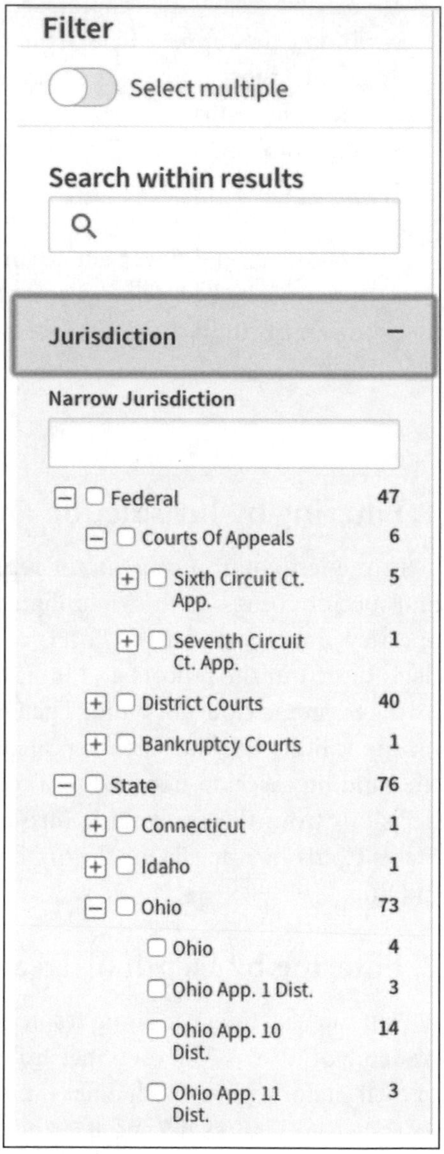

On Westlaw, by filtering by three or more bars, you would see twenty-two citing cases (see **Figure 8.6**).

3. Filtering by Legal Issue and Headnotes

The results on a Shepard's or KeyCite report can also be filtered by legal issues and headnotes. As to the report for *Rogers*, you can limit the cases citing *Rogers* to those involving legal issues that are similar to your client's situation. In **Figures 8.5** and **8.6**, the "headnotes" filters refer to the headnotes from the Shepardized or KeyCited case (*i.e.*, the *Rogers* case). Assume you know that headnote 3 of *Rogers* directly relates to the client's issue. If you click the "HN3" filter for *Rogers* from the Shepard's report (**Figure 8.5**), the only results in the report would be the cases citing *Rogers* that have at least one headnote classified under the same topic as headnote 3 of *Rogers*.

Figure 8.5: Shepard's (Lexis): Filtering by Discussion and Headnotes

Figure 8.6: KeyCite (Westlaw): Filtering by Depth of Treatment and Headnotes

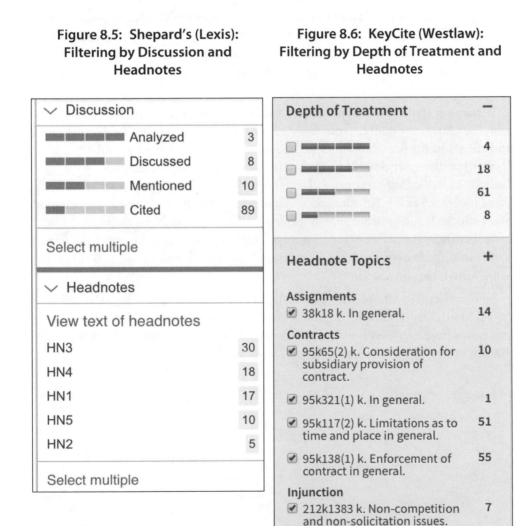

Many of the citing cases should help you determine the enforceability of the client's noncompetition agreement.

For both citators, you can also find cases citing *Rogers* with analogous issues through another method. On Lexis Advance, if you retrieve the full text of *Rogers*, you could scroll down to headnote 3 and click on "Shepardize — Narrow by this Headnote" (see **Figure 8.7**) to access the same Shepard's report discussed in the prior paragraph. On Westlaw, you could retrieve *Rogers*, locate headnote 4 of *Rogers*, and then click the link "51 Cases that cite this headnote" to obtain a KeyCite report (see **Figure 8.8**); it would identify the cases citing *Rogers* that have at least one headnote classified under the same Topic and Key Numbers as headnote 4 of *Rogers*.

4. Filtering by Keywords

You can filter Shepard's and KeyCite reports by keywords. After Shepardizing or KeyCiting an important case, you could limit the citing cases by performing a keyword search called a terms and connectors (Boolean) search.[2] A Boolean search directs a database to return only the results that match the words and criteria you specify.

Returning to the Ohio hypothetical, you need cases involving agreements prohibiting a former employee (your client) from soliciting or contacting the customers and clients of the previous employer. To filter by keywords, you would KeyCite or Shepardize *Rogers* and could limit the citing cases only to the ones where the term "solicit" or "soliciting" appears within ten words of the term "customer" or "client" (see **Figures 8.9** and **8.10**). But those search terms should not be your sole method of searching. If you searched within the cases citing *Rogers* only for the terms "solicit" or "soliciting," the citator report would exclude relevant cases in which the agreements in dispute used the term "contacting" customers instead of the term "soliciting" (the term you used).

Before filtering a citator report by keywords, you should read Chapter 9 and then return to this **Step 4**. Chapter 9 discusses in detail different types of keyword searches and how to use them properly and efficiently. That chapter will help you minimize the risk of excluding relevant cases from a citator report.

---

2. This book uses the phrase "keyword searching" broadly to include two types of electronic word searching: natural language searching (think Google) and terms and connectors (Boolean) searching.

Figure 8.7: Lexis Advance: Headnote 3 of Rogers

Business & Corporate Compliance > ... > Contracts Law ▾ > Types of Contracts ▾ > 📄
Covenants ▾
Labor & Employment Law > ... > Conditions & Terms ▾ >
Trade Secrets & Unfair Competition ▾ > 📄Noncompetition & Nondisclosure Agreements ▾

HN3⬇ Types of Contracts, Covenants

A covenant restraining an employee from competing with his former employer upon termination of employment is reasonable if the restraint is no greater than is required for the protection of the employer, does not impose undue hardship on the employee, and is not injurious to the public. 🔍 More like this Headnote

Shepardize - Narrow by this Headnote (30)   ◆ 5

Figure 8.8: Westlaw: Headnote 4 of Rogers

4	Contracts	🔑	
	Covenants not to compete in employment contracts imposed restraints and resultant hardships on employees which exceeded that which was reasonable to protect employer's legitimate business interests, where employees were prohibited from engaging in court reporting or public stenography in certain county for two years, and were also restricted, for a lifetime, from soliciting or diverting any of employer's clients.	95	Contracts
		95I	Requisites and Validity
		95I(F)	Legality of Object and of Consideration
		95k115	Restraint of Trade or Competition in Trade
	51 Cases that cite this headnote	95k117	General or Partial Restraint
		95k117(2)	Limitations as to time and place in general

Sorting Results on a Citator Report

When using a citator, make sure you know how Lexis Advance and Westlaw are sorting the results. Depending on your settings, they may sort the citing cases by court, date, or depth of discussion. Accordingly, a binding case or the newest citing case may not be listed in the first few results on the report. You can easily change the sorting method by clicking on the drop-down menu near the top of the Shepard's or KeyCite report.

Figure 8.9: Shepard's (Lexis): Filtering by Keywords

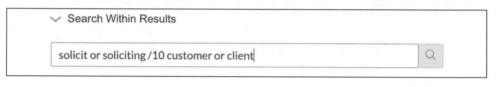

Figure 8.10: KeyCite (Westlaw): Filtering by Keywords

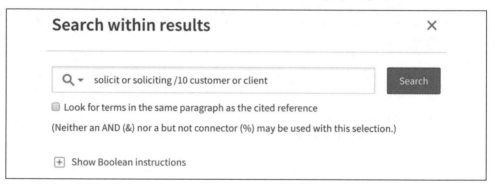

C. Confirming the Validity of Cases with Shepard's and KeyCite

At **Step 4,** in addition to finding helpful cases, you must use citators to check the validity of the cases you plan to rely on in crafting your arguments. The law is not static. A court's holding reflects the law at the time of the decision, but the law could change immediately or gradually, even law stated by a court of last resort. If you rely on a decision in a motion that no longer reflects current law, you will have an unpleasant conversation with your judge and client.

A case could become "bad" law in three ways:

- **Same Litigation:** A case could be reversed on appeal in the same litigation, such as when one party loses at the trial court but appeals to and wins at the intermediate appellate court.

- **Different Litigation:** A decision could be overruled in a different, subsequent litigation. An example is when the United States Supreme Court overruled its repugnant *Plessy v. Ferguson* decision years later in *Brown v. Board of Education.*

- **Enacted Laws:** A case could be superseded by a statute or administrative regulation.

The citators Shepard's and KeyCite are the most comprehensive and reliable tools available to determine whether a case remains good law or has become bad law. Both citators indicate the "treatment" of one case by future cases, whether positive, negative, or neutral, and the treatment is represented by colorful graphical signals. The signals inform a researcher whether a case has been reversed, overruled, disapproved, criticized, questioned, distinguished, followed, or simply cited by another court.

On both Lexis Advance and Westlaw, the citation services automatically run in the background; no other step is necessary to trigger the treatment signal. If a case has negative treatment (*e.g.*, it has been overruled), a signal would appear next to the case name. Thus, if you retrieve an overruled case by entering a citation in the search box or by clicking a hyperlinked case name from a secondary source, a signal would appear next to the case name. Treatment signals also appear next to the names of cases in a list of search results. Every case, however, is not tagged with a signal. If a case lacks positive or negative treatment, no signal would be generated.

On Westlaw, KeyCite may tag a case with a red, yellow, or blue-striped flag. These signals inform you to proceed with caution and carefully review the decisions on which the negative treatment is based. A case with a red flag on Westlaw *usually* means that the case is no longer good law for at least one rule of law or one legal issue. And a case with a yellow flag *usually* means the case remains good law but has negative treatment from at least one court for at least one legal issue. A later court may have limited the holding of the prior case to a particular factual circumstance or may have factually distinguished the prior decision.

Westlaw's new platform, Westlaw Edge, has a new citator feature called **KeyCite Overruling Risk**. It tags cases that may have been implicitly, but not expressly, overruled by a subsequent court. Powered by artificial intelligence, Westlaw Edge indicates with an orange signal that a case may be invalid, even though no court has expressly held or stated that the prior case is no longer good law. To illustrate, a case may be implicitly overruled when it has relied on a prior case and that prior case has been expressly overruled or invalidated. This scenario is depicted in **Figure 8.11.**

Because a KeyCite signal provides only a snippet of information, you must review the authority on which the negative treatment is based. After retrieving a "tagged" case on Westlaw, click the "Negative Treatment" tab near the top of the document to view the cases from different litigations that have negatively referenced the

Figure 8.11: Graph Explaining KeyCite Overruling Risk

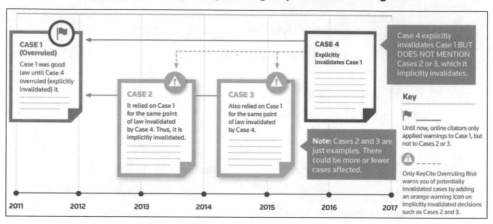

KeyCited case. (Only one case may be listed.) You should also determine whether a higher court in the same litigation has criticized or reversed your case. You can view the direct history of a case by clicking the "History" tab near the top of the screen.

The negative treatment signals used for cases on Westlaw have the meanings set forth in **Figure 8.12**.[3]

On Lexis Advance, although the actual signals indicating negative treatment differ from those on Westlaw, they provide the same warning: proceed with caution. To show negative treatment, Shepard's (Lexis) tags a case with a red, orange, or yellow signal. If you see a red stop sign next to a case name, the case probably is bad law

Figure 8.12: Negative Treatment Signals on Westlaw

KeyCite Signal	Meaning of Signal
Red flag	The case is no longer good law for at least one rule or legal issue.
Orange triangle with an exclamation point	The case may have been implicitly, but not expressly, overruled.
Yellow flag	The case has received negative treatment, but it has not been reversed or overruled by a court or superseded by a statute.
Blue-striped flag	The case has been appealed to a federal circuit court or to the U.S. Supreme Court.

---

3. This figure has been adapted from Mary G. Algero et al., *Federal Legal Research* 218, 227 (2014).

Figure 8.13: Negative Treatment Signals on Lexis Advance

Shepard's Signal	Meaning of Signal
Red stop sign	The case is no longer good law for at least one rule or legal issue.
Orange "Q"	The continuing validity of the case has been questioned by a court.
Yellow triangle	The case may have received negative treatment; it may have been distinguished, limited, or criticized by a court.

for at least one legal issue. A case tagged with an orange "Q" or a yellow triangle *usually* means the case remains good law but has negative treatment from one or more courts. A more recent decision, for example, may have attacked or questioned the reasoning of the prior case.

Again, you must review all judicial decisions that have treated your case in a negative manner to determine its validity. Like a KeyCite report, a Shepard's report on Lexis Advance identifies all negative treatment, including subsequent decisions that have overruled, criticized, or distinguished the Shepardized case. To view a full Shepard's report, retrieve the case that has been tagged with a negative treatment signal and click "Shepardize this document" in the right column. You should then select the "Citing Decisions" tab in the left column of the next screen (if not already selected). Under the "Analysis" heading in the left column, the report indicates the number of courts that have negatively referenced your case. Review those decisions. To see the direct history of your case, select the "Appellate History" tab in the left column.

You can view negative treatment without having to trigger a full Shepard's report. Lexis Advance provides two options to quickly determine the number of judicial decisions (if any) that have negatively referenced your case. First, after retrieving the full text of a case, a Shepard's preview box appears in the right column. Second, after performing a keyword search in any caselaw database, a Shepard's case card displays in the right column next to each result.[4] Both the Shepard's preview box and the Shepard's case card identify the number of citing decisions for each negative treatment signal. For instance, if three courts have criticized your case, you would see the number "3" next to the treatment phrase "caution." Clicking the "caution" phrase in the Shepard's preview box or case card would take you directly to those three cases.

With Shepard's, you can quickly determine which authority had the strongest influence on the negative treatment signal. After retrieving a case, click the "Reason for Shepard's Signal" link in the right column. Shepard's will display the passage from the subsequent case that the Lexis editors selected as having the strongest influence on the Shepard's signal.

---

4. A Shepard's case card does not appear for every case listed in the search results.

The negative treatment signals used for cases on Lexis Advance have the meanings set forth in **Figure 8.13**.[5]

You should not ignore or discount a case simply because it has a red or yellow signal, because the case may still be good law for your legal issue. To illustrate, suppose you must research Georgia law to determine the enforceability of your client's non-competition agreement, and you found on Westlaw the relevant binding case shown below, *Holsapple v. Smith*. Upon noticing that KeyCite tagged *Holsapple* with a red flag, you clicked the "Negative Treatment" tab and learned that the Supreme Court of Georgia (court of last resort) has "disapproved" of *Holsapple* (see **Figure 8.14**). If you took the path of least resistance and relied solely on the red flag, you would have excluded *Holsapple*, an important case. If you read the actual Supreme Court decision, however, you would learn that the court disapproved only the part of *Holsapple* that applied to a defamation claim, an unrelated issue.

Knowing the difference between binding and nonbinding authorities is vital in deciding whether you can ignore or discount any negative treatment of your case by a later court. (For a refresher on binding and nonbinding authorities, review Chapter 2.) Suppose you found a federal district court case in your jurisdiction

Figure 8.14: KeyCite Report for *Holsapple v. Smith*

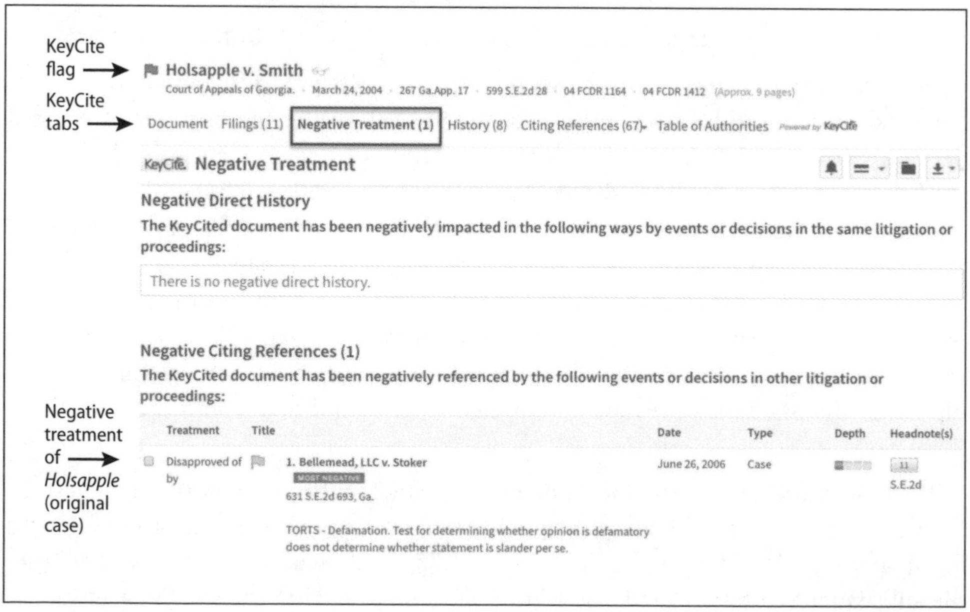

---

5. This figure has been adapted from Algero, *supra* note 3, at 227.

(nonbinding) with reasoning that you plan to rely on in arguing that your Georgia court should invalidate the client's noncompetition agreement, but further assume that Shepard's and KeyCite indicate that the reasoning of the federal case has been criticized. If the Supreme Court of Georgia has criticized the federal case, you probably should not base an argument on the federal case. If, however, the Supreme Court of Montana is the only court that has attacked the federal case, you could rely on the federal decision because your Georgia court is not required to follow out-of-state cases.

In addition to not relying on the *existence* of a negative treatment signal (*e.g.*, a red or yellow signal), you should not rely on the *absence* of one on Shepard's or KeyCite in determining the validity of a case. Although both citators are highly accurate, they are imperfect. A case may not be tagged with a red flag or red stop sign, even though a rule from the case has been overruled.

In sum, do not use the existence or absence of a Shepard's or KeyCite signal as substitutes for effective research skills or good legal analysis. You should look for negative treatment signals throughout the research process and especially for cases you plan to cite in any legal document. If you rely on a case that has been overruled, your judge will not excuse your mistake, even if you could respond this way: "Your Honor, I Shepardized this case, and it was not tagged with a red stop sign or a yellow triangle."

D. Understanding the Persuasive Value of a Case with Shepard's and KeyCite

A third reason to use citators is to help you evaluate the quality of your research. The number of citing cases on a Shepard's or KeyCite report may provide insight into the persuasive value of your case. If courts have cited your case numerous times without any negative treatment, the case probably contains solid reasoning. In contrast, if your case is twenty years old and has never been cited, the case could be poorly reasoned or could not reflect current law. Whatever the situation, the number of citing cases should be a starting point in evaluating your cases and not a substitute for good legal analysis.

Another way to understand the persuasive value of your cases is to view the direct history of a case, which is how the case worked its way through the court system in the same litigation. By using a citator to follow the path of a case through the courts, you will know whether your case has been affirmed or reversed in whole or in part, whether your case has been remanded to the trial court for further proceedings, or whether your case is pending on appeal (KeyCite only).

Both Shepard's and KeyCite reports provide the prior and subsequent history of a case in the same litigation. For example, say a party filed a complaint in the United States District Court for the Middle District of Florida, and the District Court granted defendant's motion to dismiss a defamation claim in a published decision and one year later granted defendant's motion for summary judgment on the breach of contract claim in a separate published decision. The plaintiff appealed summary judgment, and the Eleventh Circuit Court of Appeals reversed the grant of summary judgment. Further assume that the United States Supreme Court agreed to hear the appeal (a very unlikely scenario) and affirmed the Eleventh Circuit decision. If a researcher viewed the direct history report for the Eleventh Circuit decision, it would identify both prior decisions by the District Court (one dismissing defamation claim and one dismissing breach claim), would identify the Eleventh Circuit decision reversing summary judgment and remanding the case to the District Court, and would identify the subsequent decision by the Supreme Court.

To conclude, a citator may inform a researcher of the persuasive value of the cases he or she plans to cite in a memorandum, motion, or brief.

E. Limitations of Citators

Despite the reliability of Shepard's and KeyCite, these citators have limitations. It is possible, for example, that a case is no longer good law for at least one legal issue, even though no red or yellow signal is generated. **Figure 8.15** summarizes several of their limitations and identifies methods to circumvent each limitation.

F. Summary of Key Points

By **Step 4** of the research process for your client's common law issue, you need to use an online citator. You should use a citator for three primary reasons:

1. Finding additional relevant cases to help resolve the client's legal question;

2. Confirming you are relying only on good law—meaning, cases reflecting current law; and

3. Evaluating the persuasive value of your cases.

As discussed in later chapters, you could also use citators to find secondary sources (Chapter 10), and you should use KeyCite or Shepard's to re-confirm the validity of each authority you plan to cite in a legal document (Chapter 12).

The most comprehensive citators are Shepard's on Lexis Advance and KeyCite on Westlaw. They are reliable and offer the most features (*e.g.*, many filtering options). If a court has discussed a prior case negatively, Shepard's and KeyCite will tag the case with a red, orange, or yellow signal (absent rare exceptions).

A few cost-effective research platforms have online citators. Of those platforms, the more effective citators are available on **Casemaker** and **Fastcase.**[6] The online citators on Casemaker (CaseCheck) and Fastcase (Authority Check) identify subse-

---

6. Many state and local bar associations provide their members with access to either Casemaker or Fastcase (see Chapter 5).

Figure 8.15: Limitations of Shepard's and KeyCite and Possible Solutions

Limitations	Possible Solutions
Future Cases: Citators identify only later citing cases and exclude cases decided before the date of your case.	Find prior cases through other methods: • Review the cases cited by relevant cases. • Review secondary sources (Step 2). • Research cases by topic with a caselaw classification system (Step 3). • Perform keyword searches in a caselaw database (Step 5).
Negative Treatment Signals: Your case may be bad law, even though it is not tagged with a red, orange, or yellow signal.	Confirm the validity of your case using other methods: • Carefully read decisions that have cited your case. • Review secondary sources that have cited your case. • Review the table of authorities to determine whether your case has cited and relied on an earlier case that is no longer good law.
Negative Treatment Signals: Your case may be good law as it applies to your client's facts, even though it is tagged with a red, orange, or yellow signal.	Carefully read each case on which the negative treatment is based.
Statutes and Cases: If a statute abrogates a case, Shepard's and KeyCite will not show the negative treatment of the Shepardized or KeyCited case unless a later court expressly identifies the conflict.	Complete the research steps for statutory issues (Part III) to find all relevant statutes for your issue.
Filters: By filtering the citing cases, such as by headnote or depth of discussion, you may exclude relevant citing results.	Avoid excluding relevant results with these options: • Review each citing case listed on a citator report (not feasible if have numerous results). • Complete other research steps, including finding cases cited in secondary sources (Step 2) and researching cases by topic with a caselaw classification system (Step 3).

quent decisions that have cited your case. CaseCheck and Authority Check, however, do not usually identify as many citing cases as Lexis and Westlaw because the coverage of cases on the cost-effective platforms is more limited. Further, the citation services on Casemaker and Fastcase indicate only negative treatment for cases, not positive treatment. Known as CaseCheck+ and Bad Law Bot, these citators *may* identify when a court has overruled or reversed a prior case. The reliability of these citators pales

Figure 8.16: Key Features of Shepard's, KeyCite, and Other Citators

Citator Features	Shepard's (Lexis Advance)	KeyCite (Westlaw)	Casemaker and Fastcase[1]
Includes federal and state cases	Yes	Yes	Yes
Includes select unpublished cases	Yes	Yes	No[2]
Updates within 24 hours	Yes	Yes	No
Filters citing cases by negative treatment	Yes	Yes	Yes
Filters citing cases by jurisdiction and court level	Yes	Yes	Yes (limited)
Filters citing cases by depth of discussion and legal issues (headnotes)	Yes	Yes	No
Identifies which citing cases directly quote your case	No	Yes[3]	No
Indicates negative treatment of your case with colored signals	Yes	Yes	Yes[4]
Indicates positive treatment of your case	Yes	Yes	No
Provides direct history of a case in the same litigation	Yes	Yes	Yes (limited jurisdictions)
Indicates when a federal case is pending on appeal	No	Yes	No
Confirms validity of cases with 100% accuracy	No	No	No

[1] As explained in Chapter 5, members of various state and local bar associations have access to Casemaker and Fastcase as a benefit of membership.

[2] On cost-effective platforms like Casemaker and Fastcase, you cannot use a citator to find authorities that have cited an unpublished case and cannot confirm the validity of an unpublished decision.

[3] In the list of citing cases, look for green quotation marks next to a case name.

[4] Bad Law Bot (Fastcase) tags cases with negative treatment with red flags, and CaseCheck+ (Casemaker) uses a red thumbs down signal to reflect bad law.

in comparison to Shepard's and KeyCite; thus, do not use CaseCheck+ and Bad Law Bot as a complete replacement for Shepard's or KeyCite.

Review **Figure 8.16** for a summary of the key features of Shepard's and KeyCite. **Figure 8.16** also addresses the citator features on Casemaker and Fastcase.

G. Review Questions on Citators

At this point, you should have a basic understanding of citators. To test your comprehension, answer the true-false and multiple-choice questions on this book's companion website, Core Knowledge. It will identify the correct answers and provide clear explanations for each question. The same questions are reproduced below.

1. The citator Shepard's is available on Lexis Advance, and the citator KeyCite is available on Westlaw.

    a. True

    b. False

2. The citators Shepard's and KeyCite provide a list of *prior* cases that have cited your case.

    a. True

    b. False

3. The citators Shepard's and KeyCite always identify when a case is no longer good law.

    a. True

    b. False

4. You should Shepardize or KeyCite a relevant case for which of the following reason(s)?

    a. To confirm it remains good law.

    b. To find additional cases involving similar legal issues and facts.

    c. Both A and B.

    d. None of the above.

5. You found a relevant case on Lexis Advance for your negligence issue, but Shepard's has tagged it with a red stop sign. You then retrieved the same case on Westlaw, which tagged it with a red flag. Should you rely on the case in your memorandum to your boss?

    a. It depends. The case may still be good law on your negligence issue.

    b. No, because the case is no longer good law for every legal issue it discusses.

    c. Yes, because the red signals on Shepard's and KeyCite are usually inaccurate.

    d. None of the above.

6. Annie wants to find recent decisions from the Supreme Court of Florida that have discussed in detail a leading case decided in 1999, which is directly on point to her client's situation. The 1999 case has been cited over 100 times. What is an effective and quick approach?

   a. She should Shepardize or KeyCite the 1999 case and then filter the results by keywords.

   b. She should Shepardize or KeyCite the 1999 case and view its direct history.

   c. She should Shepardize or KeyCite the 1999 case and then filter the results to just Florida Supreme Court cases and to citing cases with three or four horizontal bars.

   d. She should review a secondary source discussing the 1999 case.

7. Identify how a reported decision by the Georgia Court of Appeals (intermediate appellate court) can become bad law.

   a. On appeal, the decision could be reversed by the Supreme Court of Georgia (court of last resort).

   b. The decision could be reversed by the Supreme Court of Georgia ten years later in a different lawsuit.

   c. The decision could be superseded by a statute.

   d. All of the above.

8. As a summer associate, Zoey has a new research project on a common law claim of fraud under Texas law, an unfamiliar issue. What steps should she take to research this issue?

   a. She should initially perform a keyword search in a database of all Texas cases (Step 5) and then review secondary sources (Step 2).

   b. After reviewing secondary sources on fraud (Step 2), she could skip Step 3 (caselaw classification system) and instead jump to Step 4 and use the citator KeyCite or Shepard's to find additional relevant cases, especially if she finds on-point cases in those sources and the application of law to the client's situation is straightforward.

   c. After reviewing secondary sources on fraud (Step 2), she should move directly to Step 3 (caselaw classification system) because the research process is always linear.

   d. She should start researching with secondary sources (Step 2) and skip all other research steps if she finds a few on-point cases in those sources.

H. Practice Researching with Citators

On this book's companion website, Core Knowledge, a few research assignments have been posted. The online assignments walk you through the steps for researching a common law issue on Westlaw and Lexis Advance, including using the citators Shepard's (Lexis) and KeyCite (Westlaw). For each assignment, you will research the law to resolve legal issues for your hypothetical client.

Chapter 9

Step 5:
Perform Keyword Searches in the Relevant Caselaw Databases

Step 1
(Research
Plan)

Step 2
(Secondary
Sources)

Step 3
(Cases
by
Topic)

Step 4
(Citators)

Step 5
(Keywords)

Step 6
(Expand)

Step 7
(Other States)

Step 8
(Validation)

If you have followed the prior four research steps for your common law issue, you would have found some relevant, binding cases (if any exist) and would have an idea about your client's likelihood of success on the disputed issue. Nonetheless, when researching unfamiliar legal issues, beginner researchers—and even seasoned attorneys—cannot follow just one or two steps and be confident that they have located all on-point cases. The research process requires multiple approaches, especially when researching new areas of law. So your research journey should move to the next step.

Step 5 of the process is the step you have been waiting and looking for since Chapter 1. For **Step 5** of the process, you should perform **keyword searches** in the relevant caselaw databases. Although you are familiar with searching by keywords on Google, Bing, and other internet search engines, you should rarely start a legal research project with this method. Your experience with Google-type searching will not translate into successful keyword searching for legal issues.

Once you are ready to keyword search, you must decide which caselaw database to search. One common method is to search in the narrowest database likely to provide relevant cases and, if necessary, expand to a larger database. You could limit initial keyword searches to decisions from binding courts; if those decisions do not provide a reliable answer, you would expand the search to nonbinding cases. To illustrate, for a common law issue in Georgia trial court, if the cases from the binding Georgia courts are insufficient, you would then keyword search cases from the federal courts encompassing Georgia, which include the Eleventh Circuit Court of Appeals and all three district courts located in Georgia. (Review **Table 1** in Appendix A to refresh your memory on binding and nonbinding authorities.)

You usually should not skip the step of performing keyword searches for two primary reasons. First, by keyword searching one or more caselaw databases, you will confirm whether you have found the universe of relevant cases. If you see the same cases you previously found from the prior steps, then you probably could stop researching the issue. Second, keyword searching is an excellent tool to find cases with the same or similar legal issues and facts as your client's situation.

The following warning from the prior chapters is worth repeating: every project does not require a researcher to move through the eight research steps systematically, because the research process is not linear. Thus, the first time you run a keyword search in a caselaw database does not always have to be at **Step 5**. For instance, if your supervisor asked you to identify the basic elements of a common law claim for intentional infliction of emotional distress as stated by the Supreme Court of Florida, you could skip the prior research steps and run a keyword search in the database for that specific court. Or say your boss wants to know when a supervisor's conduct is "outrageous" in the employment context and wants specific examples from Florida courts. After reviewing at least one Florida secondary source (**Step 2**), you could jump to this **Step 5** and perform a keyword search of Florida caselaw, which could help you find either the leading case or a few cases where courts determined a supervisor's conduct was and was not outrageous. After the initial keyword search, however, you should move back to **Step 3** (caselaw classification system) and **Step 4** (citators) to find additional relevant cases.

A. Introduction to Keyword Searching

This book uses the term **keyword searching** to include two types of electronic word searching: **natural language searching** (think Google) and **terms and connectors (Boolean) searching**. Keywords are the individual words and phrases that represent and relate to your client's legal issues and legally relevant facts. Once you understand basic legal concepts and have identified some keywords, you can jump online and run keyword searches. You can search the full text of cases in an online database or search only a specific field or segment of a case like the headnotes or editorial summaries.

One difficult aspect of keyword searching is balancing breadth with precision. A keyword search that is too broad will yield too many results; a search that is too narrow will yield too few results. Another difficulty, especially early in the process, is deciding which keywords to use. Different judges describe the same law or concept in their opinions with different words, so a researcher must brainstorm and search with various keywords to avoid excluding important authority.

Before keyword searching, therefore, you must identify the facts relevant to your client's situation. Recall from Chapter 1 that you should start by answering questions such as *who* are the parties (*e.g.*, what is the legal relationship?); *what* is the wrongful conduct and injury and *what* are the claims and defenses; *where* did the conduct and injury take place; *when* did the conduct and injury occur; and *why* a party wants to sue or is being sued. When answering those questions, review secondary sources in determining the additional issues and sub-issues that arise from the law and the client's situation. You should also identify synonyms for your initial keywords to have alternative words to use for searching. The ultimate goal, of course, is to search with the right keywords to find relevant cases.

To illustrate how to develop a list of keywords, suppose you represent a client who was bitten by the defendant's German Shepherd. The client and defendant have been neighbors and friends for many years. On the day of the incident, the client entered the neighbor's property to mow his yard when the neighbor's German Shepherd attacked him. Immediately before the attack, the client threw a few small rocks at the dog because it would not leave the yard. Although the neighbor was nearby and saw his dog running toward your client, the neighbor did not stop the dog, claiming that it showed no signs of aggression. Your boss has asked you to research Ohio law and determine the likelihood of success on a claim for negligence against the neighbor.

In answering the *who*, *what*, and *where* questions, you remember a few concepts about negligence and the reasonable person standard from your torts course and identify the following keywords and related concepts:

Questions	Initial Keywords	Similar Concepts (Additional Keywords)
Who — plaintiff (client)	Injured party Neighbor	Guest Visitor Friend
Who — defendant (neighbor)	Property owner	Landowner Homeowner
What — injury-causing thing or person	Dog German Shepherd	Pet Companion animal
What — claims and defenses	Negligence Breach of duty of care Contributory negligence Comparative negligence	Reasonable person Negligent conduct
What — type of injury	Dog bite Dog attack Personal injury	Nip
Where — location of conduct & injury	Dog owner's property Homeowner's property	Residence Dwelling Premise Private property

You then read a state-specific treatise on tort law and identify the new sub-issues and keywords listed in the chart below.

New Sub-Issues	Additional Keywords
Did the client assume the risk of being attacked?	Assumption of risk Implied assumption Express assumption
Could the neighbor have prevented the attack?	Last clear chance
Has the dog previously harmed any other person?	Aggressive Dangerous Vicious Viciousness

As a result of this multiple-step process, you are now armed with many relevant keywords and thus ready to search online by keywords.

B. Two Keyword Search Options on Westlaw and Lexis Advance

On Westlaw and Lexis Advance, a researcher can perform keyword searches using a natural language search or terms and connectors search. You usually should search with both methods as each method has advantages and disadvantages, depending on the law, the client's legal questions, and the client's facts. The next sections explain each search method and identify tips to help you strike the right balance between retrieving too many results and too few results.

1. Natural Language Searches

The most popular type of keyword searching is a **natural language search**. Internet search engines like Google and Bing employ this type of searching. Put simply, natural language searching involves sophisticated search algorithms to identify relevant results. The algorithms attempt to anticipate the intent of the searcher and returns results based on that intent. Google's multiple algorithms, for instance, search billions of websites and weigh many factors in deciding which results are relevant and worthy of appearing on the first page of results, including the reliability of a website, the age of a website, and how often and where the search terms appear on a website (*e.g.*, title or heading of a page).

Westlaw and Lexis Advance have borrowed from Google's playbook, allowing researchers to have a similar experience as they have when searching the internet. By default, when you search on Westlaw or Lexis Advance, you are running a natural language search. If you type search terms into the big blue box (Westlaw) or big red box (Lexis Advance) on the home pages, you will automatically search using the proprietary algorithms on Lexis and Westlaw.

Research providers refer to their search algorithms with various names. Lexis Advance refers to its searching capability as a **natural language search**, but Westlaw describes its capability as a **plain language** or **natural language search**. Regardless of their technical name, the goal of each provider's algorithm is to translate a researcher's keywords into relevant cases and other documents that appear near the top of your result list.

Although Westlaw and Lexis Advance do not use the same algorithms, their algorithms weigh similar factors in returning cases or other documents that the providers consider relevant. They include the following factors:

- Number of times a case or document has been cited and the recency of the citations;
- Number of times the search terms appear in a case or document;
- The date of a case or document;
- How other users have interacted (if at all) with a case or document that was returned in prior searches;
- Proximity of the search terms to each other in a case or document; and
- Whether the search terms appear in the editorial enhancements.

Although students (and this author) rely on Google's algorithms for "everyday" research, you should not rely solely on natural language searching for legal research. You will retrieve different results on Westlaw and Lexis Advance, even when using the same keywords. Indeed, the algorithms for both providers will be under- and over-inclusive; some relevant cases will be excluded from the results (at least the top results), and some irrelevant cases will be included.

To illustrate, say your client was attacked by a neighbor's dog, and before the attack, the dog previously bit one other person. You need to research whether the dog was "vicious" to prove a negligence claim. If you performed a natural language search on Westlaw and Lexis Advance in the Ohio caselaw database, the appellate case with the same legal issue and very similar facts probably would *not* appear in the top ten results.[1] The searches also returned irrelevant cases in the top ten results.

The empirical study by Professor Susan Nevelow Mart exemplifies the danger of relying too heavily on natural language searching.[2] In her study, Professor Mart evaluated the top ten results after running fifty different searches in caselaw databases on Westlaw, Lexis Advance, and four other online providers. On average, 67 percent of

---

1. This author performed several natural language searches, including the following: "dog bite negligence vicious," "dog bite viciousness," and "dog bite vicious." On Lexis Advance, however, when the word "claim" was added next to "negligence," the on-point case appeared in the top ten results.

2. *See* Susan Nevelow Mart, *The Algorithm as a Human Artifact: Implications for Legal [Re]Search*, 109 LAW LIBR. J. 387, 412–16 (2017).

the cases returned on Westlaw were relevant and 57 percent were relevant on Lexis Advance. Do not miss this important fact: those percentages represent the relevant cases listed in the *top ten* results based on searches for fifty different issues. In other words, 33 and 43 percent of the cases listed in the top ten results on Westlaw and Lexis Advance, respectively, were not relevant.

Here is a key takeaway from the study: natural language searching does not replace human thinking — at least not yet.

2. Terms and Connectors (Boolean) Searches

Unlike a natural language search, a **terms and connectors search**, or **Boolean search**, is precise and places control in the hands of the researcher, not the computer. When you search using terms and connectors, the database will return only the results that match the words and criteria you specify. For instance, if you perform this search in a caselaw database, *dog AND bite AND vicious*, only cases with all three words (anywhere in the case) would be returned; if a judge used the term "pet" instead of "dog" in a judicial opinion, it would be excluded from the results.

There are a few basic things you must know before running a Boolean search on Westlaw or Lexis Advance. This search method has at least two components: the **terms** and the **connectors** (also called Boolean operators). The **terms** are your keywords or phrases, and the **connectors** identify the relationship between the keywords or phrases. Examples of connectors include *and, or, but not, /s* (sentence connector), and */n* (numerical connector). Connectors are not case sensitive on Westlaw and Lexis Advance but may be on other databases. In addition to having **terms** and **connectors**, a Boolean search may include **characters** such as quotation marks and parentheses, and **symbols** like the an exclamation point (!) and asterisk (*). To retrieve the most relevant results, you should craft multiple **search strings** with various combinations of keywords, connectors, characters, and symbols.

Suppose your boss asked you to research a negligence claim and the duty of care a corporate landlord has to protect its tenants from the criminal acts of others. Here are a few sample search strings listed in order of breadth.

Example #1: (landlord and negligen!) or (landlord and duty and crim!)

Example #2: landlord /50 duty /50 crim!

Example #3: landlord /50 (duty /25 crim! /25 third /25 party)

The first example will retrieve the most cases. The database will return cases containing the word *landlord* **and** words with the root *negligen* (negligence, negligent, negligently). Because the search string in the first example includes the *or* connector, the database will also retrieve cases with the words *landlord* **and** *duty* **and** words with the root *crim* (crime and crimes and criminal), even if a case does not contain the root *negligen*. Cases containing just one of the terms in either parenthetical (such as the word *landlord*) would be excluded from the results because both parentheticals contain the *and* connector.

The second example will retrieve fewer cases than the first search and should produce fewer irrelevant results. The */50* proximity connector in the second example forces the database to return only the cases in which all three terms appear within 50 words of each other. That search string will retrieve cases dealing with the duty of landlords as to criminal acts — cases that should help you answer the legal question. And by using a proximity connector in the second example, your results should exclude irrelevant cases, such as ones involving a landlord's duty to repair the rental property or the duty to provide a sanitary premises.

The third example will retrieve the fewest cases and produce the fewest irrelevant results. The database will return cases that match the following criteria: the words *duty* and *third* and *party* and the root *crim* appear within twenty-five words of each other, and that combination appears within fifty words of *landlord*. The retrieved cases should address the duty of landlords relating to criminal acts of third parties (*e.g.*, guests of tenants) — the precise issue being researched. In short, including proximity connectors in search strings often reduce the number of irrelevant results.

To add one more layer of complication, you also need to consider the order in which Westlaw and Lexis Advance process a search string, which is determined by the type of connector. If all connectors are the same, the order will be processed from left to right. When using different connectors, the processing order can become quite complicated. You, however, can control the processing order by using parentheses. If a search string contains parentheses, the contents of the parentheses are processed first, and if the search string has multiple sets of parentheses, the parentheses are processed from left to right. To illustrate, in Example #3 above, Westlaw and Lexis Advance will process "landlord" last because it is outside the parentheses.

Figure 9.1 identifies the common connectors and symbols that you should use. Remember that connectors are not case sensitive on Westlaw and Lexis Advance. Both providers also have a template to help researchers craft effective Boolean searches. You can access the template by clicking on the advanced search link next to the global search box.

This chapter has scratched the surface on how to craft effective search strings for a Boolean search. You will become more proficient with practice—and with patience. When your search strings are producing too many or too few results, seek help. The support and help pages for Westlaw and Lexis Advance (and other online services) identify all the available connectors and symbols, as well as providing example search strings with various combinations of keywords, connectors, and symbols. Additionally, law librarians have created research guides (often called LibGuides) that provide tons of tips and techniques for Boolean searching. You can find these guides posted on library websites with a search like this:

terms and connectors search legal research LibGuide

Figure 9.1: Connectors and Symbols for Boolean Searching

Connector or Symbol Westlaw and Lexis Advance	What It Does	Example Search Strings
and &	Finds cases or documents with all terms and phrases	**dog AND bite AND negligence** ~ results will include all three terms
or	Finds cases or documents with any of the terms or phrases	**dog OR bite** ~ results will include "dog" or "bite" or both terms
but not and not	Finds cases or documents without the term or phrase	**dog AND negligence BUT NOT landlord** ~ results will include "dog" and "negligence" but will exclude documents with any mention of "landlord"
" " (quotation marks)	Finds cases or documents with the exact term or phrase	**"dog bite" OR "negligence claim"** ~ results will include "dog bite" or "negligence claim" or both phrases
/n (proximity connector)	Finds cases or documents with terms or phrases that appear within a certain number of words of each other in any order	**dog /15 bite /15 negligence** ~ results will include only documents in which all three terms appear within fifteen words of each other in any order (*e.g.*, "negligence" could appear before or after "dog")
/s (proximity connector)	Finds cases or documents with terms or phrases that appear within the same sentence in any order	**dog /s bite /s negligence** ~ results will include only documents in which all three terms appear in the same sentence
ATLEASTn (must use with term enclosed in parentheses)	Finds cases or documents with terms or phrases that appear at least a certain number of times	**ATLEAST2(negligence) AND ATLEAST3("dog bite")** ~ results will include only documents in which "negligence" appears at least twice and "dog bite" appears at least three times
! (root expander)	Finds all variations at the end of a root term, regardless of the number of characters appearing after the symbol	**negligen!** ~ results will include "negligence" and "negligent" and "negligently"
* (wildcard) (universal character)	Finds variations within a term	**wom*n** ~ results will include "woman" and "women"
( ) (parentheses)	Changes the order a search string is processed where terms inside parentheses are processed first (from left to right)	**negligence /50 (dog /5 bite)** ~ the database will first process "(dog /5 bite)" and then process "negligence"

C. Mechanics of Performing Keyword Searches on Westlaw and Lexis Advance

You are almost ready to perform keyword searches online. As you run various searches, keep in mind these important points from the prior sections of this chapter:

- Before running a search, develop a list of terms that relate to the client's issue by answering the *who, what, when,* and *where* questions.

- A natural language search is similar to a Google-type search.

- A terms and connectors (Boolean) search allows you to specify the relationship between words so that the database returns only the cases and documents that match the stated criteria.

- A natural language search usually returns more results than many Boolean searches, especially when compared to a Boolean search string containing proximity connectors or terms in quotation marks.

1. Selecting a Caselaw Database

Before running a keyword search on Westlaw or Lexis, consider which database would lead you to the most helpful primary authorities. When you initially log into Westlaw or Lexis Advance, the global search box is prominently displayed on the screen. You might have an impulse to enter keywords into the search box. If you did, you would search all legal authorities contained in their databases.[3] There is a more thoughtful approach: search in the narrowest database that is likely to lead to relevant judicial decisions.

For instance, imagine you must research Ohio common law to determine the enforceability of a noncompetition agreement against a physician. You have two good options in selecting the appropriate database. You could search within the database for state and federal cases from Ohio (the controlling jurisdiction), which would include cases from the Ohio Supreme Court, Ohio intermediate appellate courts, federal district courts located in Ohio, and the United States Court of Appeals for the Sixth Circuit. Or you could select the more narrow database containing Ohio cases that bind your court, as long as you remember to search for persuasive cases from federal courts if the binding cases fail to provide a reliable answer to the client's question. Initially, do not research cases from outside Ohio — they may conflict with the binding cases that you have not yet found. (Researching out-of-state cases is discussed in Chapter 11.)

---

3. If preferred, you can narrow your results on Westlaw and Lexis with post-search filters.

Figure 9.2: Drop-Down Menu from Search Box on Westlaw

Ohio cases

Suggestions	Content Pages
Cases	Ohio State Cases
Statutes	Ohio State & Federal Cases
	Ohio Federal Cases
	Ohio Court of Appeals Cases
Secondary Sources	Ohio Trial Court Cases
Other	

All state & federal

Figure 9.3: Drop-Down Menu from Search Box on Lexis Advance

Lexis Advance®

Advanced Search | Tips | Get a Doc Assistance

Ohio cases   Search: Everything

Sources	All OH Federal & State Cases
	All OH State Cases
	OH Courts of Appeals Cases from 1913
	OH Lower Courts - Trial Orders
	OH Supreme Court Cases from 1821

South Dakota

Figure 9.4: Natural Language Search on Westlaw

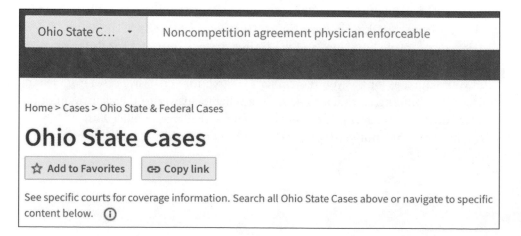

Ohio State C... ▾   Noncompetition agreement physician enforceable

Home > Cases > Ohio State & Federal Cases

Ohio State Cases

☆ Add to Favorites   ⊂⊃ Copy link

See specific courts for coverage information. Search all Ohio State Cases above or navigate to specific content below. ⓘ

Figure 9.5: Boolean Search on Lexis Advance

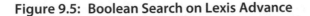

noncompetition /25 physician /25 enforce!

◉ Search all sources on this page ○ Select sources to search

All Ohio State Cases, Combined

OH Supreme Court Cases from 1821 | ⓘ

OH Courts of Appeals Cases from 1913 | ⓘ

The process for selecting a caselaw database on Westlaw and Lexis Advance is almost identical. On the home pages of both platforms, you can type the name of a state and the word "cases," and the drop-down menus display some caselaw databases for that state. See **Figures 9.2** and **9.3**. You can also locate a particular caselaw database using the following method on Westlaw or Lexis:

1. From the home page, view a list of all states by selecting the "State Materials" tab on Westlaw or the "State" tab on Lexis.

2. Click the name of your state.

3. Under the heading "Cases," click the link for the caselaw database to be searched (*e.g.*, "All Ohio State & Federal Cases" or "All Ohio State Cases").

Upon accessing a relevant database, you are ready to run keyword searches on Westlaw and Lexis Advance. Assume you are looking for Ohio cases dealing with the enforceability of noncompetition agreements against physicians. You could perform a natural language search by entering keywords into the global search box, as shown in **Figure 9.4**. A Boolean search with proximity connectors could also be performed, as demonstrated in **Figure 9.5**.

2. Searching by Fields or Segments

By default, both research platforms search the full text of cases in the selected database. When you perform a natural language or Boolean search using the global search box, Lexis and Westlaw search every part of a case, including enhancements like headnotes.

Figure 9.6: Segments on Lexis Advance for Cases

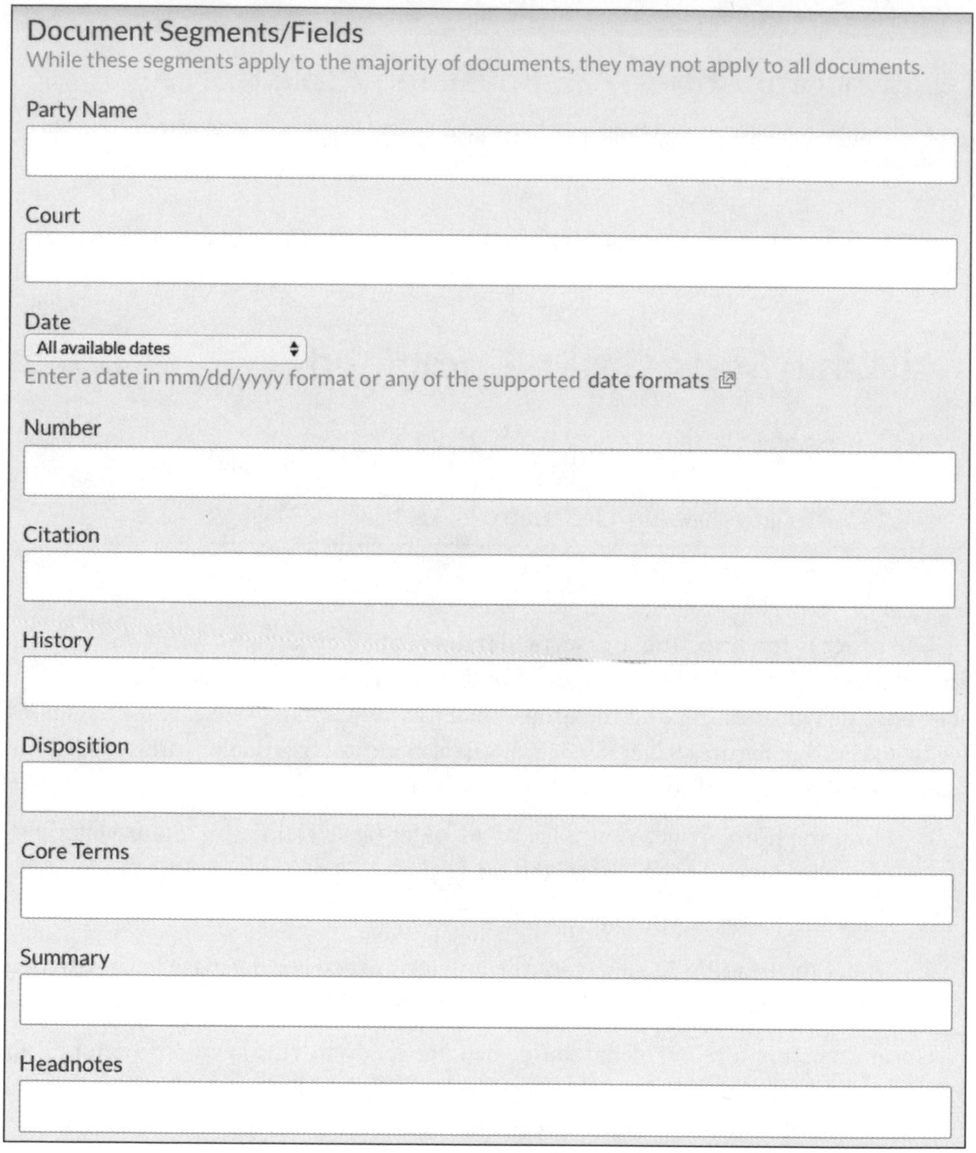

Document Segments/Fields

While these segments apply to the majority of documents, they may not apply to all documents.

Party Name

Court

Date

| All available dates ⬍ |

Enter a date in mm/dd/yyyy format or any of the supported date formats 🗗

Number

Citation

History

Disposition

Core Terms

Summary

Headnotes

But a keyword search can be limited to specific fields or segments of cases. As explained in Chapter 3, Westlaw and Lexis break down each case in their databases into fields or segments, such as case summary or synopsis (collectively, "editorial summaries"), headnotes, and opinion. The summary and headnotes from a particular case may identify three important pieces of information about the case: the legal issues, key facts, and rules of law. A Boolean search of just the text of the editorial summaries and headnotes, therefore, is a great approach to find cases that deal directly with the client's legal issue and to weed out irrelevant cases from the results list. Because this search method is narrow in scope, do not rely on it exclusively.

Figure 9.7: Fields on Westlaw for Cases

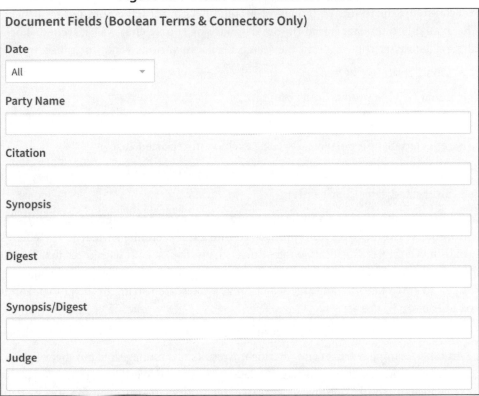

Returning to the hypothetical on the client's noncompetition agreement, you can use the advanced search template on Westlaw or Lexis to search fields or segments of Ohio cases. On either platform, after selecting an Ohio caselaw database, click the "advanced" link next to the global search box to view the template. To limit a Boolean search to the case summary on Lexis, you would enter the search string into the segment "Summary" (see **Figure 9.6**). To search just the headnotes on Westlaw, you would type the search string into the field "Digest" (see **Figure 9.7**). Assume you used the following Boolean search string in the segment "Summary" and the field "Digest":

(noncompet! or non-compet!) and (physician or doctor)

If those keywords appear in either segment or field of an Ohio case, the case probably has at issue a noncompetition agreement involving physicians (or other professional).

3. Filtering and Sorting Search Results

Westlaw and Lexis Advance offer many options to filter and limit the list of results after executing a natural language or Boolean search. Take advantage of these filtering options, especially when searching the full text (versus a field or segment) of judicial decisions. Filtering search results helps reduce the number of irrelevant authorities in the results, saving you precious time.

After running a keyword search in the database for the controlling jurisdiction, you can refine the results with the post-search filters in the left column of the screen. The available filters are based on the database or source that was searched. For a caselaw database, you can limit the search results in various ways, including by

- jurisdiction (*e.g.*, Ohio),

- court (*e.g.*, Supreme Court of Ohio),

- date (*e.g.*, cases decided after 2015),

- reported or unreported cases (*e.g.*, exclude unreported cases),

- topic or legal issue (*e.g.*, Key Numbers on Westlaw), and

- most cited cases (Lexis only).

In addition, both Westlaw and Lexis provide a filter to narrow the search results by additional keywords—a great approach to find cases factually similar to the client's situation. To trigger this filter, enter your terms in the "search within results" box in the left column. That search box defaults to running a Boolean, not natural language, search. To run a natural language search, revise the search string in the global search box at the top of the screen.

Figures 9.8 and **9.9** display the filtering options on Lexis and Westlaw, respectively.

After performing searches and filtering the results to a manageable number of cases, consider how the results are sorted. By default, Lexis and Westlaw sort search results by relevance, but other options are available. On both platforms, you can sort by date of decision and highest to lowest court level. And Westlaw allows a researcher to sort by frequency of keywords and cases that have been the most cited by later decisions.

4. Sample Path for Keyword Searching

To further understand the post-search filters, revisit the hypothetical above where you have been asked to research Ohio common law to determine whether your client, a victim of a dog bite, would prevail on a claim for negligence against the neighbor. Suppose you completed **Step 1** through **Step 4** of the common law research process, but you still need cases to determine whether the neighbor's German Shepard showed "vicious" propensities prior to attacking your client. **Figure 9.10** sets forth some steps you could follow on Westlaw and Lexis Advance in researching the viciousness issue, but it is not the *only* effective process for searching by keywords.

Again, the steps identified in **Figure 9.10** represent just *one* effective path for performing natural language and Boolean searches. Other approaches should lead to relevant cases.

Figure 9.8: Post-Search Filtering Options for Cases on Lexis

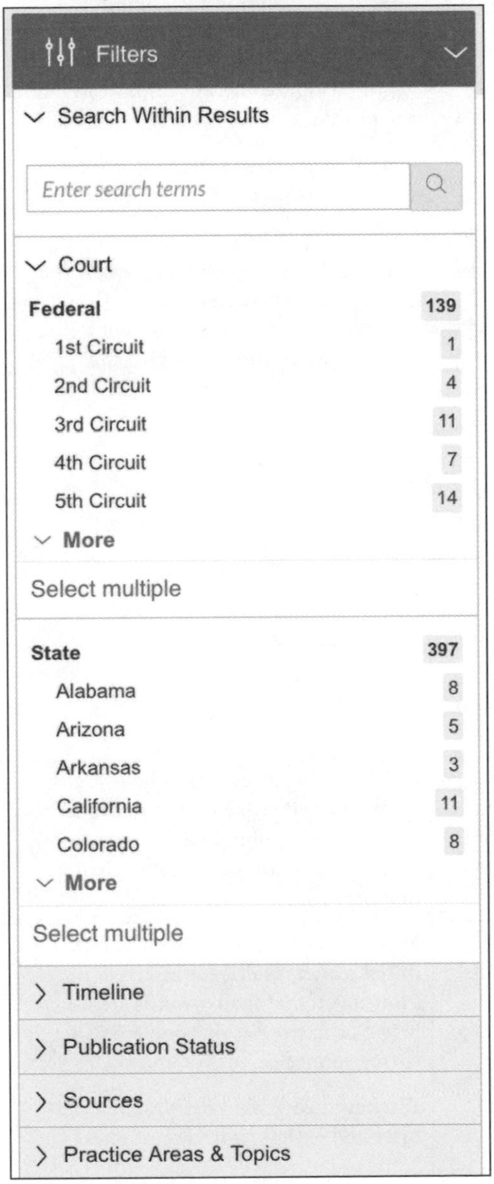

⇵ Filters	⌄

⌄ Search Within Results

Enter search terms 🔍

⌄ Court

Federal	139
1st Circuit	1
2nd Circuit	4
3rd Circuit	11
4th Circuit	7
5th Circuit	14
⌄ **More**	

Select multiple

State	397
Alabama	8
Arizona	5
Arkansas	3
California	11
Colorado	8
⌄ **More**	

Select multiple

> Timeline

> Publication Status

> Sources

> Practice Areas & Topics

Figure 9.9: Post-Search Filtering Options for Cases on Westlaw

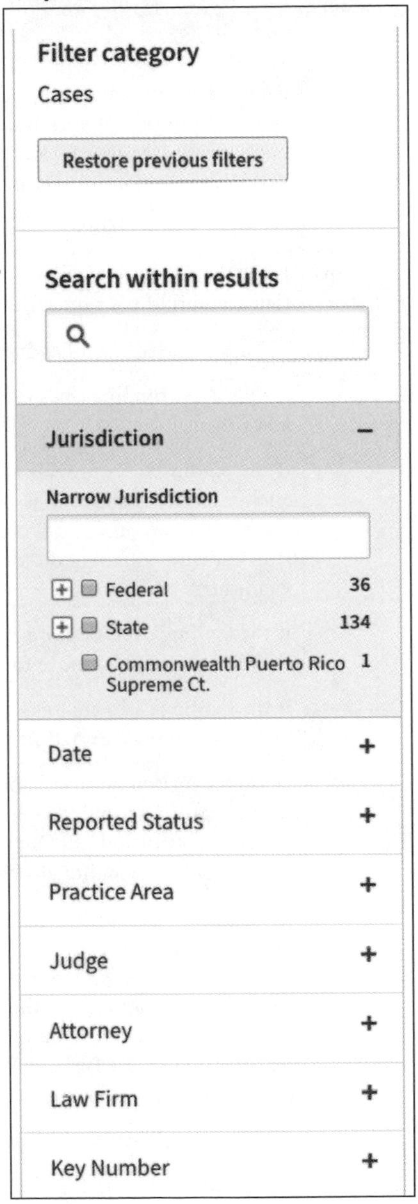

Filter category

Cases

[Restore previous filters]

Search within results

🔍

Jurisdiction —

Narrow Jurisdiction

⊞ ☐ Federal	36
⊞ ☐ State	134
☐ Commonwealth Puerto Rico Supreme Ct.	1

Date	+
Reported Status	+
Practice Area	+
Judge	+
Attorney	+
Law Firm	+
Key Number	+

Figure 9.10: Sample Research Process for Keyword Searching

Action	Process for Keyword Searching	Reasons for Each Action
Action 1	On Westlaw or Lexis Advance, select the database for all Ohio state and federal cases. Search the full text of cases with a natural language search by typing these keywords into the global search box: animal bite negligence	Initial keyword search should be broad to avoid excluding relevant results early in the process. A natural language search often returns more results than a Boolean search.
Action 2	Filter the results to binding Ohio cases (left column of your screen).	You should first find binding cases. If a conflict exists between a binding and nonbinding case, your court will follow the binding authority, making the nonbinding case useless.
	Then, do one of the following: If only a few binding cases exist, review all of them. If the binding cases provide a reliable answer on the viciousness issue and they are recent decisions, you probably can stop keyword searching on the viciousness issue. If the binding cases do *not* provide a reliable answer, then move to **Action 3**. If the binding cases are too numerous to review, then move to **Action 4**.	
Action 3	Undo the jurisdiction/court filter (left column) from **Action 2**, so that your search results include all Ohio state and federal cases, as you initially had in **Action 1**.	If the binding cases do not help you determine whether the dog was vicious, you need to find nonbinding, persuasive cases. Some authority is better than none.
	Filter the search results by entering keywords into the "search within results" box. (That box appears in the left column after performing a natural language search at **Action 1**.) Perform Boolean searches with different search strings: negligen! /50 vicious! vicious! /50 (dog or animal or pet) (negligen! and vicious!) /50 (dog or animal or pet) (dog or animal or pet) /50 (bit or bite or bitten)	Multiple searches are necessary. The initial search results, for instance, may inform you that the keywords are too broad or narrow or that you are using the wrong connector. You have two goals: retrieving relevant cases and excluding irrelevant ones. The root expander (!) tells the database to find all variations of the root term, such as *viciously* and *viciousness*.
	If the returned cases provide a reliable answer or are the same ones you found from the prior research steps, you probably can stop keyword searching on the viciousness issue.	

Figure 9.10: *Continued*

Action	Process for Keyword Searching	Reasons for Each Action
Action 4	Limit your search of binding cases to a particular field or segment, such as the case summary or headnotes. Click the "advanced" search link near the global search box to access the search template. Then perform Boolean searches by entering keywords in the proper document field or segment, such as this search string: negligen! and (dog or animal or pet) and (vicious! or dangerous or propensity)	Because your full text search of cases at **Action 2** returned too many results, you need to reduce the number of irrelevant results. Limiting a search by document field (Westlaw) or segment (Lexis) is a good option. If your search terms (*e.g.*, vicious) appear in the editorial summaries or headnotes, the viciousness issue will likely be in dispute in the returned cases.
	Then, do one of the following: If the returned cases provide a reliable answer or are the same ones you found from the prior research steps, you probably can stop keyword searching on the viciousness issue. If the returned cases are too few and fail to provide a reliable answer, then move to **Action 5**.	
Action 5	Complete **Action 1** again using different search strings. Then filter the search results by entering keywords into the "search within results" box. Perform Boolean searches with different search strings: (dog or animal or pet) /25 (vicious! or danger! or agressive!) (dog or animal or pet) /50 (human or person or people or individual) /50 (bit! or attack! or nick! or mouth!)	Limiting a search by field or segment of cases (**Action 4**) could return too few results. You might exclude relevant cases in which your keywords are not mentioned in the editorial summaries or headnotes but are mentioned only in a court's actual opinion. Remember to use multiple search strings to strike the right balance between retrieving relevant cases and excluding irrelevant ones. Boolean searching is precise, so account for synonyms in a search string. For instance, a court may refer to a dog as an "animal" or "pet."
	If the returned cases provide a reliable answer or are the same ones you found from the prior research steps, you probably can stop keyword searching on the viciousness issue.	

D. Summary of Key Points

When researching an unfamiliar common law issue, performing keyword searches should not be your go-to method. You should complete **Step 1** through **Step 4** for most assignments involving a new area of law. If you jump to keyword searching (**Step 5**) and skip the prior steps, you will not know the legal terms and concepts applying to the client's legal question and facts and thus not know which keywords to use. If that shot-in-the-dark approach proved successful, your research skills (and this book) would not be needed; clients would not pay you over $100 an hour for something they could have accomplished in a few minutes.

Performing keyword searches will not "magically" retrieve all relevant cases, even when searching on the sophisticated platforms of Westlaw and Lexis. With natural language and Boolean searching, it is easy to retrieve an unmanageable number of results and to exclude relevant cases from your results. Thus, you should run multiple keyword searches with various search strings for each disputed issue to have any degree of confidence that your results accurately reflect the existence or absence of cases on your issue.

As a beginner researcher, you will encounter various setbacks and frustrations while keyword searching. **Figure 9.11** identifies some obstacles you may encounter and identifies potential paths around them.

E. Review Questions on Keyword Searching

At this point, you should know how to perform basic keyword searches. To test your comprehension, answer the true-false and multiple-choice questions on this book's companion website, Core Knowledge. It will identify the correct answers and provide clear explanations for each question. The same questions are reproduced below.

1. As used throughout this chapter (and book), keyword searching includes a natural language search and a terms and connectors (Boolean) search.

    a. True

    b. False

2. Westlaw and Lexis Advance process a natural language search and a Boolean search in the same manner.

    a. True

    b. False

3. A natural language search is usually more precise and exact than a Boolean search.

    a. True

    b. False

Figure 9.11: Keyword Searching: Roadblocks and Solutions

Potential Roadblocks with Keyword Searching	Potential Solutions
You are retrieving too many cases.	Confirm that you are searching the proper caselaw database.
	Perform terms and connectors (Boolean) searches; do not rely solely on natural language searches.
	Instead of searching the full text of cases, limit your search by field or segment, such as overview/synopsis/summary, digest, or headnote.
	Filter results to binding and recent cases.
	Your search strings may have the following errors: • Using the *or* connector (broad) instead of the *and* connector (narrower). • Not using a proximity connector to limit results (*e.g.*, /n, /s, /p). • Not using the *ATLEASTn* connector.
	Revist secondary sources to learn how to narrow your issue and keywords.
You are retrieving too few cases.	Confirm that you are searching the proper caselaw database.
	Use both natural language and Boolean searches.
	Include synonyms and separate them with the *or* connector in your search strings. • Example: landlord or lessor or innkeeper
	Search for related concepts, not just the client's exact situation. • Example: Your issue is whether client-coach's conduct toward his player was "outrageous." Searches should include all situations involving special relationships, such as the employer-employee relationship.
	Your search strings may have the following errors: • Using quotation marks for phrases instead of proximity connectors. • Using proximity connectors of unrelated terms/concepts instead of the *and* connector. • Not using the root expander (!) to pick up variations of words.
	Revist secondary sources to learn about additional legal terms that could be included in your keyword searches.
You cannot find cases analyzing a specific legal phrase or contractual term that applies directly to your client's dispute.	When precision is important, use a Boolean search instead of a natural language search. • Example: You need a case addressing a noncompetition agreement against a surgeon with a geographic reach of several miles. You could use this Boolean search: (noncompet! or non-compet! or covenant) /50 (agreement or contract or employment) /50 (physician or doctor or surgeon or practitioner or hospitalist) /25 (miles or kilometers)

4. For a Boolean search on Westlaw and Lexis Advance, a researcher may connect terms in a search string with *and, /s,* or */n.*

    a. True

    b. False

5. On Westlaw and Lexis Advance, you can filter the search results by jurisdiction, court, date, and reported or unreported cases.

    a. True

    b. False

6. After selecting the proper caselaw database, you enter the following search string in the global search box: employment /2 agreement. What cases will be returned?

    a. Only cases in which "employment" and "agreement" appear within two words of each other, regardless of the order.

    b. Cases in which "employment" and "agreement" appear anywhere in the cases.

    c. Cases in which "employment" or "agreement" appear anywhere in the cases.

    d. None of the above.

7. You want to find cases with all and any variations of the phrase "contributory negligence." What search string should you use?

    a. "contributory negligence"

    b. contributory /3 negligence

    c. contribut! /3 negligen!

    d. contributory and negligence

8. You want to find only the cases in which the exact phrase "scope of employ-ment" appears ten or more times anywhere in the cases. What search string should you use?

    a. "scope of employment"

    b. scope /10 employment

    c. atleast10(scope) and atleast10(employment)

    d. atleast10("scope of employment")

9. You plan to run a keyword search on Westlaw to find only the cases that mention the word "outrageous" and mention both phrases "intentional infliction" and "emotional distress" anywhere in the cases. Which of the following searches should you perform?

   a. Boolean Search: outrageous or ("intentional infliction" and "emotional distress")

   b. Boolean Search: outrageous and ("intentional infliction" and "emotional distress")

   c. Boolean Search: outrageous /s "intentional infliction" /s "emotional distress"

   d. Natural Language Search: outrageous intentional infliction emotional distress

10. You have been keyword searching caselaw for your client's common law negligence issue but are consistently retrieving over 100 results. What steps could you take to reduce the number of irrelevant results?

    a. Filter results to binding and recent cases.

    b. Limit your search by field or segment of cases, such as overview or headnote.

    c. In your search strings, use the *and* connector instead of the *or* connector and use a proximity connector (*e.g.*, */s* or */p*) to limit results.

    d. All of the above.

F. Practice Performing Keyword Searches

On this book's companion website, Core Knowledge, a few research assignments have been posted. The online assignments walk you through the steps for researching a common law issue on Westlaw and Lexis Advance, including performing natural language and terms and connectors (Boolean) searches. For each assignment, you will research the law to resolve legal issues for your hypothetical client.

Chapter 10

Step 6:
Expand Your Research Within the Controlling Jurisdiction, If Necessary

Step 1
(Research Plan)

Step 2
(Secondary Sources)

Step 3
(Cases by Topic)

Step 4
(Citators)

Step 5
(Keywords)

Step 6
(Expand)

Step 7
(Other States)

Step 8
(Validation)

If you have spent hours and hours researching your common law issue but have only a few or no relevant cases, then your next action plan depends on the reason for your predicament. If you skipped any of the prior five research steps, do not admit it to your professor and "secretly" complete them now for each separate legal issue in dispute. On the other hand, if you followed all five steps and still lack sufficient authority, then you are ready for **Step 6**. Remember the goal is to find legal authority to resolve your client's issue; without supporting authority, any conclusion you state in a memorandum or court document would reflect only your opinion and would be discounted by your supervisor or the deciding court.

For **Step 6**, you should expand your research but stay focused on finding state and federal cases from the controlling jurisdiction. Do not search for cases outside your jurisdiction until you have completed this **Step 6** and still cannot confidently predict your client's likelihood of success. To illustrate, suppose a Georgia trial court will decide a negligence claim under Georgia law. The decisions from the controlling jurisdiction would include the Supreme Court of Georgia, Georgia Court of Appeals, the United States Court of Appeals for the Eleventh Circuit, and the three federal district courts located in Georgia. Your trial court must follow the rulings from the higher state courts, and it probably would treat the federal cases as highly to moderately persuasive authority.

The next sections identify multiple research methods that should lead you to additional relevant cases—if they exist—to help answer your legal questions. While you do not have to complete each method, consider each option before moving to **Step 7** in the next chapter. But if you have found sufficient cases providing a reliable conclusion on each disputed issue, you should skip **Step 6** and **Step 7** and jump to **Step 8**.

A. Return to Step 2 (Secondary Sources)

One option is to revisit **Step 2** and find and read more **secondary sources** on your topic. As explained in Chapter 6, secondary sources explain and analyze the law, identify important legal terms and concepts, and provide citations to relevant authorities. Again, most of these sources are drafted by legal experts in their fields. It is not an insult to your intelligence to rely on the hard work of others; it is what smart researchers do. Your corporate client will not be impressed for billing it for hours of research that could have been completed in minutes with a secondary source.

You could be missing helpful cases for reasons that could be remedied by revisiting secondary sources. You could have a misunderstanding of the law and how it applies to your client's factual situation. Or you could be keyword searching with the wrong terms; performing many keyword searches with the wrong terms will not produce relevant results, just like searching on Amazon.com with the phrase "Samsung Galaxy" will not return results for the iPhone. Or you might be too narrowly focused on your legal issue. For instance, say you are researching whether the client can recover an unusual type of damages for a claim of false imprisonment (an intentional tort), but no cases exist. A secondary source may inform you that courts in your jurisdiction have allowed recovery for that unusual damage for other intentional torts such as conversion and fraud. You could then rely on those cases to support the client's argument.

As to finding helpful secondary sources, Chapter 6 sets forth various methods to locate secondary materials. There is another good option: use a **citator** like KeyCite on Westlaw or Shepard's on Lexis Advance. When you have at least one relevant case, you can use a citator to quickly locate secondary sources addressing your legal issue. Chapter 8 explains how to use citators to find cases, but citation services also identify citing secondary sources. Both Shepard's and KeyCite provide reports listing secondary sources that have cited your case at least once.

Using a citator to research secondary sources has one notable drawback: each citator identifies only those secondary sources contained in the research provider's online databases. The databases on Westlaw and Lexis Advance contain different secondary materials, and the coverage varies based on the jurisdiction. If possible, use both citation services to find secondary sources.

B. Review a Restatement of Law

A second method to locate relevant cases in the controlling jurisdiction is to rely on the *Restatements of Law*, a respected secondary source on the common law. The *Restatements of Law* are published in three series, and each *Restatement* covers a separate topic, including agency, contract, employment law, judgements, property, and tort law. They are drafted by judges, attorneys, and law professors from the American Law Institute (a private organization); and many courts rely on the *Restatements*. The highly-respected and most cited series include the *Restatement (Second) of Contracts* and *Restatement (Second) of Torts*.

Each section of a *Restatement* "restates" and synthesizes the law in the *majority* of jurisdictions, but remember that your jurisdiction may follow a different rule. (Some sections, however, do not reflect the majority rule and instead state what the drafters think the law ought to be.) In addition to providing a concise statement of the law, each section of a *Restatement* includes detailed commentary from the drafters and illustrations on how the rule should apply to various factual circumstances.

An example from the *Restatement (Second) of Torts* will help you understand the structure and usefulness of a *Restatement*. Although this *Restatement* has many sections addressing a claim for defamation, assume only section 559 of Chapter 24 applies to your client. In **Figure 10.1**, the text in bold font is the concisely-stated rule defining a defamatory communication in the majority of jurisdictions, and the official comments by the drafters, which further explain a defamatory communication, are immediately under that rule. The illustrations within the official comments for section 559 show some circumstances in which a communication is and is not defamatory; they highlight that whether a statement is defamatory depends on the beliefs of the hearers of the statement (**Figure 10.1**).

You might be asking yourself, "How do I find relevant cases after I find an applicable section of a *Restatement*?" Because many courts cite the *Restatements of Law* (unlike most other secondary sources), you can use a citator like Shepard's or KeyCite to find relevant cases.

Assume that section 559 on a defamatory communication applies to your client's situation. You should retrieve it on Lexis Advance or Westlaw, Shepardize or KeyCite the section, and limit your citing results to cases from the controlling jurisdiction. You may find cases in the controlling jurisdiction that you did not find using the prior five research steps, and these newly-discovered cases may provide newly-discovered law that applies to the disputed issue. Even if this process reveals only one case with one rule (*e.g.*, "a statement must defame another in the eyes of a majority in the community"), it was worth your time. As the number of rules and authorities increases, the strength of your arguments in an office memorandum, motion, and brief also increases.

C. Return to Step 4 (Citators) and Step 5 (Keyword Searching)

Another option to uncover relevant cases that you previously did not find is to repeat **Step 4** (citators) and **Step 5** (keyword searching) on Westlaw or Lexis Advance. While completing those steps, you probably applied various filters to screen out cases from your results that you expected to be unhelpful. By using filters, however, you could have accidently excluded helpful state and federal cases from the controlling jurisdiction. Now, you should revisit **Step 4** (citators) and **Step 5** (keyword searching) and either use no filter or use different filters.

Figure 10.1: Excerpt from Section 559 of *Restatement (Second) of Torts*

§ 559 Defamatory Communication Defined

Comment:
Reporter's Note
Case Citations - by Jurisdiction

A communication is defamatory if it tends so to harm the reputation of another as to lower him in the estimation of the community or to deter third persons from associating or dealing with him.

Comment:

a. The word "communication" is used to denote the fact that one person has brought an idea to the perception of another. As to the distinction between a "communication" and a "publication," see § 577.

b. Types of disparagement. Communications are often defamatory because they tend to expose another to hatred, ridicule or contempt. A defamatory communication may tend to disparage another by reflecting unfavorably upon his personal morality or integrity or it may consist of imputations which, while not affecting another's personal reputation, tend to discredit his financial standing in the community, and this is so whether or not the other is engaged in business or industry. As to ridicule, see § 566, Comment *d.*

c. Social aversion. A communication may be defamatory of another although it has no tendency to affect adversely the other's personal or financial reputation. Thus the imputation of certain physical and mental attributes such as disease or insanity are defamatory because they tend to deter third persons from associating with the person so characterized. Although these imputations reflect upon neither the personal nor business character of the other they are nevertheless defamatory under the rule stated in this Section.

Illustrations:

1. A advertises in a newspaper that B, a nurse, uses and recommends to her patients the use of a certain brand of whiskey for medicinal purposes. If a substantial number of respectable persons in the community regard this use of whiskey as discreditable, A has defamed B.

2. A writes in a letter to B that C is a member of the Ku Klux Klan. B lives in a community in which a substantial number of the citizens regard this organization as a discreditable one. A has defamed C.

3. A, a member of a gang of hoodlums, writes to B, a fellow bandit, that C, a member of the gang, has reformed and is no longer to be trusted with the loot of the gang. A has not defamed B.

For instance, assume you completed all the prior research steps (Steps 1 through 5) and have found very few relevant cases. Suppose at **Step 4** (citators), you Shepardized the *Smith v. Jones* case, received twenty results, and then filtered by depth of discussion and reviewed only the handful of citing cases with three or more horizontal bars. At this **Step 6**, you could re-Shepardize *Smith* on Lexis and remove the depth of discussion filter and review all citing cases that you failed to read at **Step 4** (citators).

This process may lead you to more relevant rules from the citing cases, making your conclusion on the client's issue more reliable.

You may have to return to **Step 4** (citators) and **Step 5** (keyword searching) and focus on finding cases that you may have previously ignored. For instance, you could research cases that have not been designated "for publication" in a reporter. State appellate courts issue unpublished decisions, as do federal circuit courts (intermediate appellate courts) and federal district courts (trial courts). Many unpublished decisions are available in electronic format on Westlaw and Lexis Advance.[1] Although unpublished cases are usually not binding, they may be necessary to resolve your legal issue, especially if you have not found sufficient authority through the prior research steps. Some authority—even an unpublished decision—is better than none. Before citing unpublished cases, however, check the rules of your court on citing these decisions.

One method to locate unpublished decisions is to use two citators: Shepard's on Lexis Advance and KeyCite on Westlaw. These platforms provide different coverage of unpublished cases, so a KeyCite and Shepard's report for the same relevant case may not return the same unpublished decisions. (A citator identifies only the citing cases contained in the respective database.) Thus, a Shepard's report for a relevant case may list one or more unpublished cases that a KeyCite report did not identify.

When the prior methods to find helpful unpublished cases in the controlling jurisdiction have failed, you have another option: **Google Scholar**. As explained in Chapter 5, Google Scholar is a free service for everybody with internet access. In addition to published cases, its database contains some unpublished decisions from state and federal courts. Google Scholar, therefore, might lead you to relevant unpublished decisions that are not available on Westlaw and Lexis Advance.

One way to find unpublished decisions is through Google Scholar's citation service. You can access the citation service by keyword searching with Google's powerful algorithm in the caselaw databases for the controlling jurisdiction and then clicking "cited by" underneath each case that is relevant to your issue (see **Figure 10.2**). You also can access its citator by clicking "how cited" after retrieving a case on Google Scholar. The citation service will return any subsequent unpublished decision that has cited a published case, as long as the unpublished decision is part of Google Scholar's database. The citation service, however, does not work for unpublished decisions. As shown in **Figure 10.3**, the "cited by" link disappears for unpublished decisions.

---

1. Unpublished and unreported cases are discussed in more detail in Chapter 3.

Figure 10.2: Google Scholar's "Cited By" Feature for Published Cases

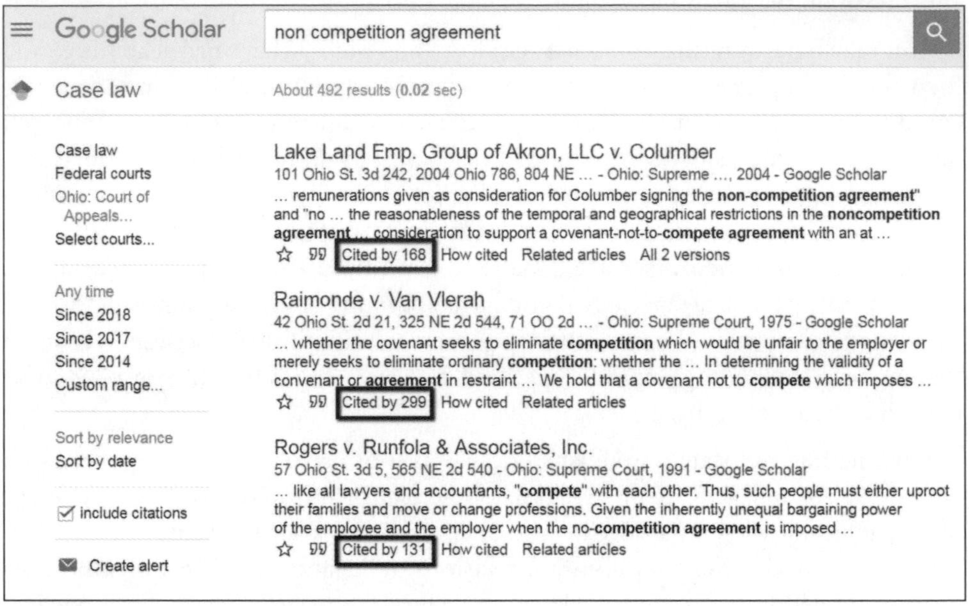

Figure 10.3: Google Scholar's "Cited By" Feature for Unpublished Cases

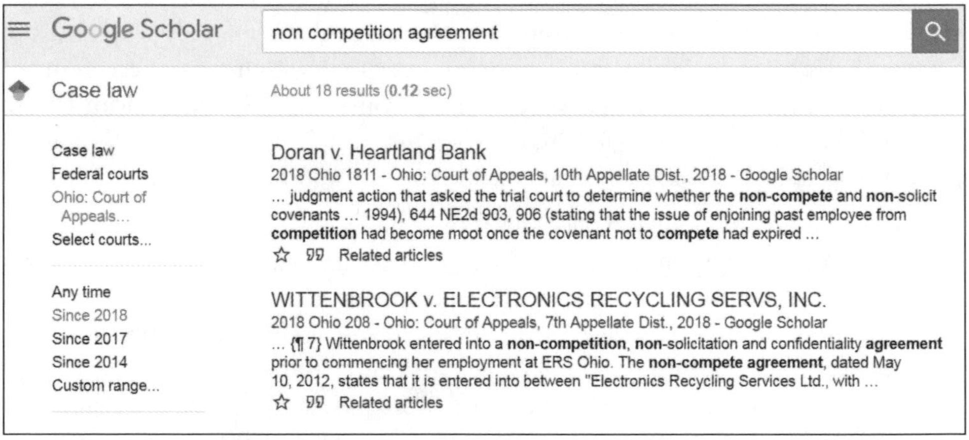

D. Summary of Key Points

For many projects, you do not need to complete **Step 6** because you would have found sufficient cases for your client's legal issue by completing the prior research steps. Once you determine that **Step 6** is necessary, however, stay focused on finding cases by courts in the controlling jurisdiction, which includes state and federal courts located in the state where the deciding court is situated. In addition to those cases being more persuasive than cases by courts outside your jurisdiction, courts in the controlling jurisdiction are more likely to discuss the state law applying to your legal issue.

You have learned about several methods to expand your research at **Step 6** for a common law issue. They include (1) finding more secondary sources on your issue through a citator (Shepard's or KeyCite), (2) reviewing a *Restatement of Law* and then using a citator to research additional cases, and (3) repeating **Step 4** (citators) and **Step 5** (keyword searching) to find relevant cases. If those methods fail to uncover sufficient authority, you should move to **Step 7**.

Wherever you are in the research process, remember your primary goal: reaching a reliable conclusion on whether your client prevails on a disputed legal issue or whether the client may move forward with a proposed transaction.

E. Review Questions on Expanding Research

At this point, you should know when and how to expand your research in the controlling jurisdiction. To test your comprehension, answer the true-false and multiple-choice questions on this book's companion website, Core Knowledge. It will identify the correct answers and provide clear explanations for each question. The same questions are reproduced below.

1. At Step 6, you should focus on finding cases from courts outside the controlling jurisdiction.

   a. True

   b. False

2. At Step 6, you should focus on finding cases from state and federal courts in the controlling jurisdiction.

   a. True

   b. False

3. A researcher can use KeyCite and Shepard's to find unpublished (unreported) decisions.

   a. True

   b. False

4. Anna Kate has been unable to find helpful published cases, so she plans to research unpublished decisions from courts in the controlling jurisdiction. She should use which of the following online research service(s)?

   a. Lexis Advance

   b. Westlaw

   c. Google Scholar

   d. All of the above

5. Johnny found section 465 of *Restatement (Second) of Torts*, and it applies to his client's common law negligence issue. Johnny wants a list of all cases from the controlling jurisdiction where that section has been cited. What should Johnny do to minimize irrelevant cases from the list of results?

    a. Perform a keyword search in the caselaw database for the controlling jurisdiction with this search string: (Restatement /5 Torts) and 465 and negligence

    b. Perform a keyword search in the caselaw database for the controlling jurisdiction with this search string: (Restatement /5 Torts) or (section /5 465)

    c. Retrieve section 465 on Lexis Advance or Westlaw, Shepardize or KeyCite that section, and then filter the results.

    d. None of the above.

F. Practice Expanding Your Research

On this book's companion website, Core Knowledge, a few research assignments have been posted. The online assignments walk you through the steps for researching a common law issue on Westlaw and Lexis Advance, including expanding your research within the governing jurisdiction. For each assignment, you will research the law to resolve legal issues for your hypothetical client.

Step 1
(Research
Plan)

Step 2
(Secondary
Sources)

Step 3
(Cases
by
Topic)

Chapter 11

Step 7:
Research Cases from Outside the
Controlling Jurisdiction,
If Necessary

You probably cannot believe that there is another research step to complete for your common law issue that once upon a time seemed simple. But if you lack sufficient legal authority for your client's issue, you cannot predict with a high level of confidence how your court will resolve the issue. You should consider continuing the research journey to find cases from outside your jurisdiction. As previously stated, some supporting authority is better than none.

You should consider completing this **Step 7** in two main circumstances.

First, you should research caselaw from outside the controlling jurisdiction when you have exhausted the cases in your jurisdiction and still lack legal rules governing your client's situation. (Remember, courts in the "controlling jurisdiction" include all state and federal courts geographically located in the same state of the deciding court.) To illustrate, say you must research whether your state recognizes a common law claim of retaliation for your client, an employee who was discharged after consulting an attorney about the employer's shady practices on workers' compensation. If no court in the controlling jurisdiction has addressed this legal question, you could research cases from other jurisdictions that have recognized this retaliation claim and then rely on those out-of-state cases in arguing that your jurisdiction should do likewise.

Second, when you cannot find any case in the controlling jurisdiction involving facts similar to your client's situation, you should research out-of-state cases. Absent a binding case addressing the governing law, your court would be influenced by decisions from other jurisdictions. Indeed, your court would likely rely heavily on out-of-state decisions from courts in states sharing similar common law rules and from courts in neighboring jurisdictions (unless the states' laws conflict).

The good news is that you can skip this **Step 7** for many research assignments. By following the prior six research steps, you will find all necessary cases for many projects. Indeed, you will often know that you have found the universe of available cases in the controlling jurisdiction when you research with different

Step 4
(Citators)

Step 5
(Keywords)

Step 6
(Expand)

Step 7
(Other States)

Step 8
(Validation)

methods, sources, and finding tools and they all yield the same authority. It is only when those prior steps fail to yield relevant cases in your jurisdiction that you should consider completing **Step 7**. But before researching out-of-state cases, you should consult with your professor or supervisor.

A. Return to Step 2 (Secondary Sources) and Review the American Law Reports to Find Out-of-State Cases

To find cases from outside the controlling jurisdiction, you should research with the *American Law Reports* (A.L.R.s). As explained in Chapter 6, an A.L.R. annotation analyzes a specific topic in detail and cites many cases from many jurisdictions that have addressed the topic, and it may even cite cases from your jurisdiction. The beginning of each annotation contains an outline of the topics addressed and a list of all cases cited in the annotation, organized by jurisdiction.

If an A.L.R. annotation covers your legal issue, you should review the annotation. Because each annotation cites many cases and covers a narrow topic, you probably will find at least one case legally and factually on point. For instance, suppose your client's dog attacked another person in Mississippi, and the client wants to argue that the victim assumed the risk by attempting to straddle and hug the dog. Suppose you found a relevant annotation, "Intentional Provocation, Contributory or Comparative Negligence, or Assumption of Risk as Defense to Action for Injury by Dog." Even though you would not find Mississippi cases on point in the annotation, you would find short summaries of several cases from other jurisdictions where courts addressed when straddling or hugging a dog constitutes an assumption of risk. Of course, make sure that no cases with similar facts exist from your jurisdiction and that the law announced in any out-of-state case does not conflict with the governing law of Mississippi.

B. Return to Step 3 (Cases by Topic) to Find Out-of-State Cases

To find cases from outside the controlling jurisdiction, you should consider returning to **Step 3** where you learned to research with the two most comprehensive caselaw classification systems: West's Key Number System and LexisNexis Legal Topic Digest. Recall that both systems organize cases by topic and subtopics. Further recall that West's Key Numbers and the topics in Lexis Advance are the same across all jurisdictions. Once you learn the mechanics of each system, therefore, you can use it to find cases from any jurisdiction.

Because it has over 100,000 topical classifications, the Key Number System on Westlaw is a great method to quickly locate out-of-state cases on your issue in a matter of minutes. Suppose you have been asked to research Arkansas law on whether a landlord has a duty to protect tenants from criminal acts of others when the landlord

**Figure 11.1: Headnote 2 from *Hall v. Rental Mgmt., Inc.*,
913 S.W.2d 293 (Ark. 1996)**

2	**Landlord and Tenant**	**233**	Landlord and Tenant
	As general rule, landlord does not owe duty to protect tenant from criminal acts.	**233V**	Enjoyment and Use of Premises
		233V(J)	Liability for Dangerous or Defective Conditions
	9 Cases that cite this headnote	**233V(J)2**	Existence of Duty of Care
		233k1221	Landlord's Duty
		233k1231	Protection against acts of third persons
			(Formerly 233k164(1))

knows that violent crimes have recently taken place near its apartment complex. Further assume that you could not find an Arkansas case involving similar facts but found one articulating the general rule that landlords have no duty to protect tenants. You could then retrieve the Arkansas case on Westlaw and use the headnotes to locate factually similar cases from other jurisdictions.

As shown in **Figure 11.1**, the second headnote from the Arkansas case is classified under the Topic "Landlord and Tenants" and Key Number 1231 (protection against acts of third persons). If you click on that Key Number and then select a neighboring jurisdiction such as Texas, you would retrieve citations to Texas cases with at least one headnote categorized under Key Number 1231 and containing a point of law relating to landlords and criminal acts of others. In fact, as shown in **Figure 11.2**, this method would lead you to a factually similar case involving prior crimes near a landlord's rental property.

C. Return to Step 4 (Citators) to Find Out-of-State Cases

Another method to research caselaw from out-of-state is to return to another prior research step (**Step 4**) and use an online citator. To refresh your memory, an online citator, or citation service, provides a list of all subsequent cases that have cited your case. Shepard's on Lexis Advance and KeyCite on Westlaw are the most respected and comprehensive citators (see Chapter 8).

Although you may feel like the lead character in the movie *Groundhog Day* (who relived the same day multiple times) given that this author has asked you multiple times to "relive" your prior research steps, at this **Step 7**, you will use a citator for a different purpose. You were previously focused on finding cases from *your* jurisdiction, but now your goal is to find relevant cases from *outside* your jurisdiction. You should Shepardize or KeyCite relevant cases from the controlling jurisdiction to determine whether courts in other jurisdictions have cited them. If out-of-state cases have cited a relevant decision from your jurisdiction, those cases probably addressed an issue applicable to your client's situation.

Figure 11.2: Excerpt of Headnotes for Key Number 1231

Search k1231 —Protection against acts of third persons   ▾   Texas   🔍

☐   **14. Texas Real Estate Holdings, Inc. v. Quach**
Court of Appeals of Texas, Houston (1st Dist.). · October 31, 2002 · 95 S.W.3d 395

Headnote: When the general danger of risk of injury on landlord's property is the risk of injury from criminal activity, the evidence must reveal specific previous crimes on or near the premises in order to establish foreseeability to support finding that the landlord provided negligent security.

> **Document Preview:** REAL PROPERTY - Landlord and Tenant. Landlords could not have foreseen violent carjacking that occurred in their parking lot.

☐   **15. Texas Real Estate Holdings, Inc. v. Quach**
Court of Appeals of Texas, Houston (1st Dist.). · October 31, 2002 · 95 S.W.3d 395

Headnote: For a landowner to foresee criminal conduct on property, there must be evidence that other crimes have occurred on the property or in its immediate vicinity for purposes of suit against the landlord for providing negligent security; criminal activity occurring farther from the landowner's property bears less relevance because crime rates may be expected to vary significantly within a large geographic area.
2 Cases that cite this legal issue

> **Document Preview:** REAL PROPERTY - Landlord and Tenant. Landlords could not have foreseen violent carjacking that occurred in their parking lot.

D. Use a Citator for a Restatement of Law

Additionally, you can Shepardize or KeyCite relevant sections of a *Restatement of Law* to determine how courts in other jurisdictions have interpreted those sections and the official comments. Chapter 10 (**Step 6**) discusses using a citator for a *Restatement* to find cases from the controlling jurisdiction. You should complete that step again, focusing on out-of-state cases.

Before digging too deep into out-of-state cases, you should determine whether courts in your jurisdiction have adopted or approved of the sections or official comments of a *Restatement* that cover the client's legal issue. If a relevant section or comment has been adopted in a binding case, it would essentially reflect the governing law, and the out-of-state courts' interpretation of the section or comment would be persuasive authority. On the other hand, if courts in your jurisdiction have rejected a section or comment, your court would likely disregard the interpretations of the section or comment by other courts.

E. Summary of Key Points

You will not need to complete this **Step 7** for many research assignments, such as when the authority you have found provides a reliable conclusion on the client's legal question. But when you are unsure of the client's likelihood of success, the methods discussed in this chapter will help you find relevant out-of-state cases for a common law issue.

F. Review Questions for Out-of-State Research

At this point, you should have a basic understanding of researching out-of-state cases. To test your comprehension, answer the true-false questions on this book's companion website, Core Knowledge. It will identify the correct answers and provide clear explanations for each question. The same questions are reproduced below.

1. For an unfamiliar legal issue, a researcher should always complete Step 7 and find out-of-state cases.

    a. True

    b. False

2. Each annotation in the *American Law Reports* covers a specific topic and cites cases from various jurisdictions.

    a. True

    b. False

3. West's Key Numbers and the topics in Lexis Advance are the same across all jurisdictions.

    a. True

    b. False

4. If you KeyCite a section of a *Restatement of Law*, you would retrieve a list of other secondary sources that have cited the section but not a list of cases that have cited the section.

    a. True

    b. False

5. You will often know that you have found the universe of available cases in the controlling jurisdiction when you research with different methods, sources, and finding tools, and they all yield the same authority.

    a. True

    b. False

G. Practice Researching Out-of-State Cases

On this book's companion website, Core Knowledge, a few research assignments have been posted. The online assignments walk you through the steps for researching a common law issue on Westlaw and Lexis Advance, including finding out-of-state cases. For each assignment, you will research the law to resolve legal issues for your hypothetical client.

Step 1
(Research Plan)

Step 2
(Secondary Sources)

Step 3
(Cases by Topic)

Step 4
(Citators)

Step 5
(Keywords)

Step 6
(Expand)

Step 7
(Other States)

Step 8
(Validation)

Chapter 12

Step 8:
Use a Reliable Citator to
Re-Confirm the Validity of
Each Relevant Case

You may have felt that the research process has moved at a snail's pace. But you have arrived at the final step for researching a common law issue. By this **Step 8**, you should have found the relevant cases addressing the client's legal issue. For the final task, you must re-confirm that every rule of law or other proposition from every relevant case is still valid. Relying on "bad" law invites ethical complaints and malpractice lawsuits.

As explained in depth in Chapter 8, the citators Shepard's on Lexis Advance and KeyCite on Westlaw are the most reliable tools available to determine whether a case remains good law or has become bad law. These citators indicate that a case has negative treatment by tagging it with a red, yellow, or orange signal.[1] Both Shepard's and KeyCite inform you whether a judicial decision no longer reflects current law in the following circumstances:

- The case was reversed on appeal in the same litigation;

- The case was overruled in a different, subsequent litigation; or

- The case was superseded by a statute or administrative regulation (but the later case must identify the conflict).

Although you have been checking the validity of cases throughout the prior research steps, you should complete this task again. It is possible that a valid case you found early in your research process is no longer valid. Basing a legal analysis or legal conclusion on a rule or case that is invalid violates ethical rules. Indeed, a court suspended an attorney's license, in part, because the lawyer had not "Shepardized the cases he relied on regarding the statute of limitations before

---

1. Westlaw's new platform, Westlaw Edge, tags some cases with an orange triangle with an exclamation point (see Chapter 8). Its new feature, KeyCite Overruling Risk, informs researchers that a case may have been implicitly overruled by a subsequent court.

filing the claim."[2] Thus, before submitting a legal document to your court, supervisor, opponent, or client, you must use KeyCite or Shepard's for every cited case.

---

2. *Idaho State Bar v. Tway*, 919 P.2d 323, 325, 328 (Idaho 1996).

Part III

Ten Steps for Researching Statutory Issues

Introduction: What You Should Know About Researching Statutes

This Part III sets forth ten steps that students and attorneys should complete when researching an unfamiliar issue governed by one or more **statutes**. By following these research steps, you will find the relevant legal authorities that will lead you to a reliable answer to your client's legal question.

As explained in Chapter 4, a **statute** is a fancy word for a law enacted by a legislative body, such as Congress or a state's legislature. Statutes may be classified as either criminal or civil, and they usually prohibit, require, or authorize conduct. To illustrate, one statute may prohibit texting while driving a vehicle; another statute may require a father to support and protect his child; and another statute may authorize an employer to drug test its employees. In addition to regulating conduct, statutes grant rights to individuals, establish penalties for crimes, and provide remedies for civil wrongs.

Once you determine a statute applies to your client's situation or reasonably believe that one could apply, you should follow the ten research steps discussed in the following ten chapters. These steps are summarized below.

Step 1: Create a Research Plan (Chapter 13)

Step 2: Research Every Unfamiliar Legal Issue with Secondary Sources (Chapter 14)

Step 3: Find All Relevant Statutes (Chapter 15)

Step 4: Confirm the Validity of Each Relevant Statute, Determine Each Statute's Effective Date, and Identify All Amendments (Chapter 16)

Step 5: Read All Relevant Statutes Critically (Chapter 17)

Step 6: Research and Update Administrative Regulations, and Find Cases That Have Interpreted Them (Chapter 18)

> **Step 7: Research Cases from the Controlling Jurisdiction That Have Interpreted Relevant Statutes** (Chapter 19)
>
> **Step 8: Research the Legislative History of Relevant Statutes, If Necessary** (Chapter 20)
>
> **Step 9: Research Comparable Statutes and Cases from Other Jurisdictions, If Necessary** (Chapter 21)
>
> **Step 10: Use a Reliable Citator to Re-Confirm the Validity of Each Relevant Authority** (Chapter 22)

Although ten steps may seem excessive (you may have had the same reaction to the prior eight steps), a statutory issue often involves various types of laws. In addition to researching statutes, you need to research administrative regulations that a governmental agency may have adopted pursuant to statutory authority (**Step 6**, Chapter 18). You must also research cases interpreting each relevant statute (**Step 7**, Chapter 19). The cases will illustrate how courts have applied your statutory language to different factual circumstances, increasing the reliability of your conclusion on the client's legal issue.

The ten research steps are an excellent approach to maximize the probability that you will find *all* relevant statutes and other pertinent authorities. Recall that federal and state statutes bind individuals, entities, and courts. By failing to uncover an applicable statute, you probably would violate your ethical duty to provide competent representation to clients. And your failure to find a relevant statute could result in losing the lawsuit — and any chance of repeat business from the client. For example, if you rely only on judicial decisions but your opponent relies on a favorable statute that has superseded the prior decisions, your court would follow the statute and rule against your client. But do not fear. By following these research steps, you should have a substantial degree of certainty that you have found all statutes that apply to your client's situation.

Further, the ten steps remind you of the importance of finding each relevant statute *before* spending hours reading judicial decisions. Suppose your client was charged with burglary in the first degree for stealing computers from a Honda Accord the victim used as his home, and suppose that the burglary statute prohibited "entering another's dwelling with the intent to commit a theft." Further assume that the statute originally defined a "dwelling" as a "physical building," that two cases interpreted the original definition, and that after both cases were decided, the statutory definition was amended to expand "dwelling" to include "motor vehicles." If you jumped to **Step 7** to research caselaw (and skipped the research step on updating statutes), you would not know about the binding, statutory amendment. Consequently, you probably would rely on both cases interpreting the original definition limiting "dwelling" to a "physical building" and would incorrectly conclude that the client's Honda Accord is not a "dwelling."

As with common law issues, the process for researching a statutory issue is not linear; thus, you may need to skip research steps or move through the steps in a different order in light of the law, the client's situation, the number of legal authorities on point, and the scope of your project. Say your boss, an expert on unfair competition, provided your state's unfair competition statute to you, asking you to research only cases decided in the past year defining the phrase "unfair and deceptive trade practice." If you have researched this issue previously, you could jump to **Step 7** (finding cases) and focus on recent cases interpreting the unfair competition statute. If any concept or term from a case is confusing, however, you could move back to **Step 2** (secondary sources) for insight.

To summarize, you do not need to complete each research step for every statutory issue, as long as you have considered each step along the research journey. These ten steps are intended to help you find the universe of relevant legal authorities and, more importantly, reach a reliable conclusion on the client's legal question. But do not use the research steps as a substitute for good legal analysis.

Chapter 13

Step 1:
Create a Research Plan

Step 2
(Secondary
Sources)

Step 3
(Find
Statutes)

The first of the ten steps in researching a new and unfamiliar statutory issue is to develop a research plan. By drafting a research plan for a statutory issue— or any legal issue, for that matter—you minimize the chance of feeling over- whelmed with the research project and maximize the likelihood of staying on the right research path. Remember to update your research plan throughout the process, such as identifying newly-discovered legal issues and documenting the authorities you have found.

Step 4
(Update
Statutes)

Step 5
(Read
Statutes)

A. Comparison of Research Plans for Common Law and Statutory Issues

For your statutory issue, you should essentially follow the research plan set forth in Chapter 5, which discusses the various parts to a good plan for a common law issue. You should also complete the Research Action Plan Form in Appendix C to stay organized during the research process.

The key difference between a research plan for a common law and statutory issue is that cases are not the sole binding authorities. In addition to decisions from higher courts, the court deciding the client's legal issue is bound by all rel- evant statutes. Courts must interpret and apply the statutes in dispute as written; they cannot add language to, or subtract words from, the statute, even if they conclude that the statute is unfair. And if a conflict exists between a statute and judicial opinion, the statute prevails. Further, an administrative regulation adopted through the formal rulemaking process binds a court.[1] A regulation has the same force of law as a statute.

There is another difference between common law and statutory issues that should be a part of the research plan. Although a federal court addressing state law is not bound by decisions from all state courts (see Chapter 2), a federal court is bound by a relevant state statute. And even though a state court addressing federal law is

---

1. The rulemaking process for regulations is discussed in Chapter 18.

not bound by decisions from all federal courts, a state court is bound by a relevant federal statute.

Although complicated, do not avoid taking time — and brain power — to determine what authorities bind your court. Ignoring the problem does not eliminate it, just like ignoring credit card debt does not extinguish it. A better approach would be to review **Table 1** (Binding vs. Nonbinding Cases) in Appendix A and **Table 2** (Choosing the Best Authority) in Appendix B. **Table 1** will help you distinguish between binding and nonbinding authorities, and **Table 2** will help you differentiate between highly relevant and slightly relevant authorities. See Chapter 5 (research plan for common law issues).

With your initial research plan in hand, you should move to the next research step of finding and analyzing secondary authorities.

B. Review Questions on Research Plans

At this point, you should know how to create a research plan for a statutory issue. To test your comprehension, answer the true-false questions on this book's companion website, Core Knowledge. It will identify the correct answers and provide clear explanations for each question. The same questions are reproduced below.

1. You should create a research plan for a statutory issue in a similar manner as you would for a common law issue.

    a. True

    b. False

2. You should consult **Table 1** (Binding vs. Nonbinding Cases) in Appendix A to determine which authorities are binding on the court that will decide your client's legal dispute.

    a. True

    b. False

3. Judicial decisions are the sole binding authorities when a statute applies to a client's situation.

    a. True

    b. False

4. A court must interpret and apply a statute as written.

    a. True

    b. False

5. A state court may ignore a state statute that it determines is unfair to a party.

    a. True

    b. False

C. Practice Completing a Research Plan

On this book's companion website, Core Knowledge, a few research assignments have been posted. The online assignments walk you through the steps for researching a statutory issue on Westlaw and Lexis Advance, including how to develop research plans. For each assignment, you will research the law to resolve legal issues for your hypothetical client.

Chapter 14

Step 2:
Research Every Unfamiliar Legal Issue with Secondary Sources

Step 1
(Research Plan)

Step 2
(Secondary Sources)

Step 3
(Find Statutes)

Step 4
(Update Statutes)

Step 5
(Read Statutes)

Step 6
(Find Regulations)

Step 7
(Find Cases)

Step 8
(Legislative History)

Step 9
(Other States)

Step 10
(Validation)

You have arrived at **Step 2** for researching statutory issues. The second step for re-searching issues governed by at least one federal or state statute is to review secondary sources. It is especially important that you find and review secondary materials for unfamiliar statutory issues because they are often more complicated than common law issues.

By this point in the book, you probably have reviewed the prior chapters on secondary sources, researched with secondary materials for a common law issue, and heard your professor explain the importance of these materials. Thus, you will be spared another lengthy discussion on secondary sources in this chapter. Instead, this chapter provides a few "friendly" reminders about secondary sources.

As explained in Chapter 6, you should find and review secondary sources for three primary reasons:

- Secondary sources summarize and explain federal and state statutes, adminis-trative regulations, and judicial decisions;
- They identify important legal terms for an area of law; and
- They cite federal and state statutes, administrative regulations, and judicial decisions.

In that chapter, you also learned about five common types of secondary materials, including legal encyclopedias, state jury instructions, treatises and practice manuals, *American Law Reports* (A.L.R.), and legal articles. To identify relevant secondary sources like treatises, you can jump on Westlaw or Lexis Advance and browse by source or perform keyword searches. But you can locate relevant sources in print or online using six other methods, such as an online treatise finder or an online legal research guide. In addition, you can use a citator to locate helpful secondary sources. Both Shepard's on Lexis Advance and KeyCite on Westlaw provide reports listing sec-ondary sources that have cited a particular statute or case.

Additionally, in Chapter 6, you learned to navigate within a particular secondary source to find the sections and pages that discuss the controlling law and cite primary authorities. The navigational tools include consulting the index, reviewing the table of contents, and performing keyword searches.

Last, in Chapter 6, you learned the importance of updating secondary sources. An outdated secondary source may provide rules of law that have been changed or superseded. A current secondary source, however, should cite the most recent primary authorities that reflect current law.

With your "walk down memory lane" completed, you are ready to learn three additional secondary materials that are helpful for statutory issues. While researching and reviewing secondary materials, remember your final destination: finding relevant primary authorities and obtaining a reliable answer to your client's legal question.

A. Effective Types of Secondary Sources for Statutory Issues

The five categories of secondary sources that were discussed in Chapter 6 are great sources to consult when researching a client's issue governed by a statute. In addition to those sources, you should consider researching with the sources discussed next.

1. Jury Instructions for Statutes

For federal and state statutes, there are two types of jury instructions: (1) **pattern or model instructions**, and (2) **non-pattern instructions**.

Federal trial courts (called district courts) often rely on **pattern jury instructions** to instruct jurors on federal statutes during trials.[1] Pattern jury instructions address frequently-litigated civil and criminal issues, summarize the elements and defenses for federal statutes, and cite federal statutes and cases interpreting the statutes. Most pattern jury instructions are drafted by committees appointed by United States Courts of Appeals, such as the Sixth Circuit Court of Appeals. These committees work under the supervision of the appointing circuit courts and are commonly comprised of lawyers, judges, and academics.

You should review pattern jury instructions drafted by court-appointed committees. First, these jury instructions usually restate the law accurately. In fact, federal circuit courts encourage their trial courts to use model or pattern jury instructions.[2] Second, because these jury instructions are intended to maximize jury comprehension, they simplify federal laws, making them understandable to novice researchers. Third, many pattern jury instructions include the committee's commentary that explains the statute and cases on which the instruction is based.

---

1. A few federal courts use the term "model" instead of "pattern" for their jury instructions.

2. *See, e.g., United States v. Cornelison*, 717 F.3d 623, 628 (8th Cir. 2013) (explaining that the Eighth Circuit's model jury instructions are not binding but are "helpful suggestions to assist the district courts").

Review Multiple Jury Instructions

Almost every federal circuit court has model or pattern jury instructions covering civil and criminal statutes. But the extent of coverage varies by circuit. For example, the Sixth Circuit's pattern criminal jury instructions do not discuss bank robbery, but other pattern instructions cover that crime. Thus, you should review the jury instructions from more than one circuit court.

As to state statutes, recall that most states have **model or pattern jury instructions** that are drafted by a committee appointed by the state's bar association or the state's court of last resort. Revisit Chapter 6 for a refresher on those types of instructions.

Non-pattern jury instructions may help you understand the law governing your client's issue. These instructions concisely state the elements and defenses for claims brought under both federal and state statutes. Many of the non-pattern jury instructions published by the American Bar Association and commercial entities cover specific subjects. You could find a set of non-pattern instructions on a range of subjects, including automobile actions, employment law, real estate, and torts.

You can locate pattern and non-pattern jury instructions in print and online. Given their availability on Westlaw, Lexis Advance, and free websites, you can usually find at least one set of jury instructions that applies to your legal issue.

The jury instructions in **Figure 14.1** set forth the elements for the crime of bank robbery.

2. Continuing Legal Education Materials

Lawyers in almost every state must attend continuing legal education (CLE) courses to maintain their licenses to practice law. CLE courses are offered by law schools, national associations (*e.g.*, American Bar Association), private organizations (*e.g.*, National Business Institute), state bar associations (*e.g.*, State Bar of Texas), and local bar associations (*e.g.*, Cincinnati Bar Association). These programs are taught by attorneys, judges, and professors.

Almost all CLE programs include written materials. These **CLE materials** provide practical tips for attorneys on specific practice areas and often discuss new developments for federal and state laws. CLE materials cover a range of legal issues, from the basic ("Personal Injury 101"), to the complex ("Advanced Copyright Issues"). They also address newly-enacted or amended statutes having an important impact on individuals or businesses. In short, reviewing CLE materials is a great way to stay current on the constant changes in the law.

216 PART III · STATUTORY ISSUES

Figure 14.1: Fifth Circuit's Pattern Criminal Jury Instructions

---

SUBSTANTIVE OFFENSE INSTRUCTIONS 2.80A

2.80A

BANK ROBBERY
18 U.S.C. §§ 2113(a) and (d)

Title 18, United States Code, Sections 2113(a) and 2113(d), make it a crime for anyone to take from a person [the presence of someone] by force and violence [by intimidation] any money [property] in the possession of a federally insured bank [credit union] [savings and loan association], and in the process of so doing to assault any person [put in jeopardy the life of any person] by the use of a dangerous weapon or device.

For you to find the defendant guilty of this crime, you must be convinced that the government has proved each of the following beyond a reasonable doubt:

First: That the defendant intentionally took from the person [the presence of another] money [property];

Second: That the money [property] belonged to or was in the possession of a federally insured bank, credit union, or savings and loan association at the time of the taking;

Third: That the defendant took the money [property] by means of force and violence [by means of intimidation]; and

Fourth: That the defendant assaulted some person [put in jeopardy the life of some person] by the use of a dangerous weapon or device, while engaged in taking the money [property].

After the completion of a CLE program, the written materials are often available in electronic format. Although Westlaw and Lexis Advance do not have large collections of CLE materials, these materials are usually available for purchase on the website of the CLE provider.

Figure 14.2 is an excerpt from CLE materials addressing changes to the Texas Trade Secrets Act.

Figure 14.2: Excerpt from CLE Materials from State Bar of Texas

II. TEXAS LEGISLATURE ENACTS NEW AMENDMENTS
TO THE TEXAS UNIFORM TRADE SECRETS ACT

Since the passage of TUTSA in 2013, two significant events occurred. First, in May 2016, Congress passed the Defend Trade Secrets Act (DTSA), an amendment to the Economic Espionage Act of 1996, 18 U.S.C. §§ 1831-36. DTSA is a federal law that creates a civil cause of action for misappropriation of trade secrets. Like TUTSA, DTSA is largely based on the Uniform Trade Secrets Act; however, there were some minor differences that could result in non-uniform application of trade secret law in Texas. Second, the Texas Supreme Court decided *In re M-I*, L.L.C., 505 S.W.3d 569 (Tex. 2016), which held that even in trade-secret misappropriation cases, there is a presumption that a party is allowed to participate and assist in the defense and that this presumption can only be overcome if the trial court balances certain factors.

In the 2017 Legislative Session, House Bill 1995 was introduced to address these new developments. The bill passed unanimously in the House and Senate and was one of the earliest bills signed into law by Governor Greg Abbott. House Bill 1995 amended TUTSA to make some of its provisions coextensive with DTSA to eliminate confusion and to avoid possible forum shopping between state and federal courts. In particular, the amendment makes several changes to the definitions found in TUTSA. For example, the amendment modifies the definition of "trade secret" and includes additional illustrative examples. It also adds new definitions for "clear and convincing" evidence and for "willful and malicious" misappropriation. In addition, the amendment preserves the common law rule that an employee cannot be enjoined from using general knowledge, skill, and experience that the employee acquires during employment. Finally, the amendment codifies the Texas Supreme

3. Looseleaf Services

Looseleaf services (sometimes called topical services) are excellent secondary sources for federal and state areas of law that are heavily legislated or regulated, including environmental law, immigration law, and labor law. A looseleaf covers one area of law in great depth; thus, they have been designated "mini-libraries" and "one-stop shops." For a specific area of law, most looseleaf services print the text of relevant statutes and administrative regulations, provide citations to cases interpreting the statutes and regulations, and include commentary explaining the law.

Looseleafs have traditionally been published in three-ring binders that are updated by inserting or removing loose pages (thus their name). The major publishers include Bloomberg BNA, Commerce Clearing House (Wolters Kluwer), and Matthew Bender (LexisNexis).

When researching an area of law that is heavily legislated or regulated, you should find and review at least one **looseleaf service**. Some looseleafs are available only in print, but many are accessible online on Westlaw and Lexis Advance. Because looseleafs can be complicated to find and navigate, you should consult your friendly law librarian for assistance. You should also review the CALI lesson titled "Print Looseleafs, E-Looseleafs, and Subject Specific Resource Centers."

Figure 14.3 is an excerpt from a looseleaf service in print titled *Estate, Tax, and Personal Financial Planning*.

Figure 14.3: Excerpt from Looseleaf Service by Thomson Reuters

---

§ 32:46   Distributions from Qualified Plans

The Code generally recognizes four types of qualified plans,[15] all of which are funded principally by the employer:[16]

1. pension plans;
2. profit sharing plans;
3. stock bonus plans; and
4. annuity plans.

Additionally, many individuals may establish an Individual Retirement Account (IRA),[17] although the tax advantages may be reduced for certain individuals.[18] Self-employed individuals may establish IRAs with larger tax-deductible contributions, called Self-Employed Pensions (SEPs)[19] or Keogh plans.[20] All of these are designed to provide retirement benefits to the participants or the participant's beneficiary. Distributions generally are included in the gross income of the recipient.[21] This is because the benefits were excluded from gross income when used to fund the plan.[22]

---

[12]Reg. § 1.661(a)-2(f)
[13]I.R.C. § 643(e).
  See § 32:43.
[14]I.R.C. § 643(e)(1).
  See § 32:41.

[Section 32:46]

[15]I.R.C. § 401 et seq.
[16]See ch 5 for a discussion of qualified plans.
[17]I.R.C. §§ 408 and 219. The availability of the IRA has been substantially

restricted by TRA 1986.
  See ch 5 for further discussion.
[18]I.R.C. § 219(g).
  The availability of the IRA deduction is phased out for individuals who are active participants in an employer provided retirement plan when adjusted gross income arises above a certain level.
  For a discussion of these rules, see ch 5.
[19]I.R.C. § 408(k), (j).
[20]I.R.C. § 401.

©2018 Thomson Reuters, Rel. 2, 5/2018   32-47

B. Summary of Key Points

Like for common law issues, at this **Step 2**, you should find and review several secondary sources when embarking on your research journey for a statutory issue. To avoid "nagging" you, this author will not remind you again of the numerous benefits—and zero risks—associated with using secondary materials. If you were offered an investment with high rewards and no risks, you would seize the opportunity. Do the same thing with secondary sources.

Figure 14.4 summarizes the features of the three types of secondary materials just discussed, and **Figure 14.5** indicates the availability of these sources online and in print.

Figure 14.4: Comparison of Secondary Sources

Secondary Source	Number of Legal Topics	Depth of Discussion of Each Topic	Number of Cited Authorities for Each Topic	Updated
Pattern and Non-Pattern Jury Instructions	Moderate	Limited to Moderate	Few to Many	Varies by Federal Court and by Publisher
Continuing Legal Education (CLE) Materials	Moderate	Moderate to Extensive	Few to Many	Not Updated
Looseleaf Services	Moderate	Extensive	Many	Frequently[1]

[1] Some looseleafs, whether in print or online, are updated weekly.

Figure 14.5: Where to Retrieve Secondary Sources

Secondary Source	Westlaw and Lexis Advance (Fee-Based)	Casemaker and Fastcase (Free for Bar Members)[1]	Free Online Databases and Websites	Print
Pattern and Non-Pattern Jury Instructions	Yes	Yes (limited coverage)	Yes[2]	Yes
Continuing Legal Education (CLE) Materials	Yes (limited coverage)	Yes (limited coverage)	Yes (limited availability)[3]	Yes
Looseleaf Services	Yes	No	No	Yes

[1] As explained in Chapter 5, Casemaker and Fastcase are available for free to members of certain state and local bar associations.

[2] The pattern jury instructions that federal trial courts commonly rely on are available online for free. Almost every United States Court of Appeals and many United States District Courts post pattern jury instructions on their websites. As for the pattern jury instructions for state statutes, they are often posted on the websites of state bar associations, state supreme courts, and administrative offices of state courts.

[3] Occasionally, CLE providers make CLE materials available on their websites for free.

C. Review Questions on Secondary Sources

At this point, you should have a basic understanding of secondary sources. To test your comprehension, answer the true-false and multiple-choice questions on this book's companion website, Core Knowledge. It will identify the correct answers and provide clear explanations for each question. The same questions are reproduced below.

1. Many United States Courts of Appeals (*e.g.*, the Sixth Circuit Court of Appeals) have appointed committees to draft pattern jury instructions for federal statutes.

    a. True

    b. False

2. CLE courses and the accompanying CLE materials usually cover common law, not statutory, issues.

    a. True

    b. False

3. Pattern and non-pattern jury instructions are never updated to reflect changes to the law.

    a. True

    b. False

4. Looseleaf services are great secondary sources for areas of law that are heavily legislated or regulated, such as immigration law.

    a. True

    b. False

5. Lisa, a law student, must research a complex federal statute. Why should Lisa review at least one set of pattern jury instructions drafted by a court-appointed committee?

    a. These jury instructions usually restate the law accurately.

    b. These jury instructions help novice researchers understand complex federal laws.

    c. These instructions often include the committee's commentary that explains the statute and cases on which the instruction is based.

    d. All of the above.

6. Tim needs to research the Americans with Disabilities Act, a federal statute. He has already created a research plan for this unfamiliar issue. What should be his next research step?

   a. Use a citator (KeyCite or Shepard's) to find cases interpreting the Americans with Disabilities Act.

   b. Use West's Key Number System to find cases interpreting the Americans with Disabilities Act.

   c. Find and review a treatise or other secondary source discussing the Americans with Disabilities Act.

   d. Perform keyword searches in a relevant caselaw database.

D. Practice Researching with Secondary Sources

On this book's companion website, Core Knowledge, a few research assignments have been posted. The online assignments walk you through the steps for researching a statutory issue on Westlaw and Lexis Advance, including finding and navigating secondary sources. For each assignment, you will research the law to resolve legal issues for your hypothetical client.

Step 1
(Research
Plan)

Step 2
(Secondary
Sources)

Step 3
(Find
Statutes)

Step 4
(Update
Statutes)

Step 5
(Read
Statutes)

Step 6
(Find
Regulations)

Step 7
(Find Cases)

Step 8
(Legislative
History)

Step 9
(Other States)

Step 10
(Validation)

Chapter 15

Step 3:
Find All Relevant Statutes

In the prior chapter, you were reminded of the importance of researching with secondary sources and how to find and navigate these sources. By following the prior **Step 2** and reviewing a few secondary sources on a statutory issue, you should know whether the client's legal question is governed by federal or state statutes (or both). You should have also found some statutes and cases that apply to your client's situation. But secondary sources rarely discuss the law in sufficient detail or provide all the necessary legal authorities to help you resolve a client's statutory issues. The research journey must continue.

For this **Step 3**, you should use an **annotated code** for the controlling jurisdiction to find all statutes that apply to your client's situation, including statutory definitions. An annotated code, as explained in Chapter 4, organizes statutes currently in force by topic and includes references to primary and secondary authorities. Annotated codes are available in print and online for all federal and state statutes.

When enacted laws apply to the client's situation, you should not focus on researching cases early in the research process. Instead, concentrate your efforts on finding the relevant statutes. Recall that courts must interpret and apply every statute as written. When a conflict exists between a statute and case, the statute controls (assuming the statute is constitutional). You must not base any legal argument on a case—even a case from the court of last resort—that directly conflicts with a valid statute.

The following scenario illustrates the importance of finding applicable statutes as soon as possible. Assume that your client, a neurosurgeon, wants to know whether the noncompetition agreement with his practice group is enforceable. The agreement prohibits your client-neurosurgeon from working for a competitor for one year. Further assume that two authorities in your jurisdiction are applicable:

- A **case** where the state supreme court held that noncompetition agreements for *physicians* that last for one year are enforceable.
- A **state statute** declaring that noncompetition agreements for *neurosurgeons* that last for one year are *not* enforceable.

223

If you ignore this book's advice and start the research process by looking for cases (**Step 7**), you would find the supreme court decision enforcing a one-year agreement against a physician. You might stop researching and advise your client of the bad news that her agreement is enforceable. If you failed to research whether a statute exists that protects neurosurgeons from noncompetition agreements, you would believe that the only relevant authority was the supreme court decision. That belief would be wrong. On the other hand, if you followed the research methods set forth in this chapter, you would have found the statute on neurosurgeons and could then deliver the good news that the agreement is unenforceable against your client.

When to Review Judicial Opinions

If you see cases cited in secondary sources and they interpret a relevant statute, you should not pretend they do not exist. You may read those cases to gain insight into the meaning of the statute, and you should add them to your research plan. But do not spend the bulk of your time researching and analyzing cases until later in the research process (**Step 7**).

The quickest method to find a statute is to know its citation. Every statute is published in a print code and made available online. Thus, if you know a statutory citation is "Ga. Code Ann. § 10-1-393," you could retrieve it on Westlaw and Lexis Advance by typing that citation in the global search box. You could also find the statute in a law library by locating the volume of the code containing Title 10 and turning to the correct section.

For most assignments, you will not have a citation to all the relevant statutes. But do not distress: this chapter on **Step 3** will walk you through how to find all statutes, including statutory definitions, that apply to your client's situation. After following the methods set forth below, you should have confidence that you have found all relevant statutes to accurately answer your client's legal question.

As you find relevant statutes, you need to complete some additional tasks to comply with your ethical duties to research accurately and to provide competent representation to your client. You must determine whether every statute that you plan to cite in a legal document is still good law. By checking the validity of statutes as you find them, you will not inadvertently rely on a statute that has been repealed or ruled unconstitutional. You must also check the effective date of each potentially relevant statute— the date on which a statute becomes enforceable. The next chapter explains in detail the process for confirming the validity of statutes and for checking effective dates. Read this chapter and the following one together. Although both chapters will not solve the world's problems, they will help you find the right authority to resolve your client's problem.

A. Types of Statutes to Research

When faced with a statutory issue, you often need to find not one but multiple statutes. Initially, you should research all statutes that prohibit, require, or authorize the conduct in dispute. If a consumer has alleged that your client, a retailer, has deceptively advertised, you must find the statute prohibiting false advertising to consumers. Or if your client has been sued for unlawful employment discrimination, you must find not only the statute prohibiting the alleged discrimination but also any statute that may authorize the employer's conduct (*e.g.*, a statute permitting discrimination when it directly corresponds to a job qualification).

After finding the statutes that prohibit, require, or authorize the disputed conduct, you need to determine whether related statutes exist. Recall that one legislative bill often proposes multiple laws on the same subject matter; and these related laws, upon enactment, are usually placed under the same topical heading in a code. These related statutes are collectively known as a statutory scheme (or act). For instance, Congress has enacted a statutory scheme known as the Americans with Disabilities Act (ADA). The ADA contains over twenty code sections pertaining to legal protections for individuals with disabilities, and these sections are codified under the same title and chapter. The ADA includes a statute prohibiting discrimination "on the basis of disability," as well as a statutory definition that specifically describes a "disability."[1]

Because most statutes are not enacted in isolation, more than one statute may apply to your client's situation. Thus, you must research statutes that are part of the same statutory scheme, including the following:

- Purpose of a statutory scheme or act (*e.g.*, protecting consumers);

- Exceptions or defenses to a prohibition or requirement (*e.g.*, exempting newspapers from liability for printing deceptive advertisements);

- Proper party to bring a lawsuit or charge (*e.g.*, private party? government?);

- Remedies, penalties, and other consequences for violations (*e.g.*, punitive damages); and

- Statutory definitions that explain the meaning of the terms used throughout a statutory scheme or act (*e.g.*, defining "consumer" to mean a "natural person," not a corporation).

In short, you should determine whether multiple statutes have been enacted that apply to your client's situation. Keep this principle in mind as you consult codes to research federal and state statutes.

---

1. 42 U.S.C.A. §§ 12102, 12112 (Westlaw through P.L. 115-253).

> ### Importance of Finding Statutory Definitions
>
> You must carefully research statutory definitions. If Congress or a state legislature has defined any term used throughout a statutory scheme or act, your court will—indeed must—rely on the statutory definitions. Not even the United States Supreme Court may ignore or rewrite statutory definitions.
>
> In addition, how a legislature defines a term may determine your client's civil liability or a criminal defendant's innocence. Suppose the prosecuting attorney in your office has tasked you with researching whether a potential defendant can be charged with burglary for stealing money from an automobile. The state's burglary statute prohibits "entering another's dwelling with the intent to commit a theft." If the statutory definition excludes "automobiles" from the term "dwelling," the defendant could not be charged with burglary.

B. Advantages of Researching with Annotated Codes

As explained in Chapter 4, federal and state statutes are compiled and arranged by topic in codes. These codified statutes can be found in official and unofficial codes, as well as annotated and unannotated codes. Official and unofficial codes for the same jurisdiction contain the same statutes (with very rare exceptions). The same is true for annotated and unannotated codes for the same jurisdiction.

Most attorneys and judges research federal and state statutes with **annotated codes**. You should do likewise for two key reasons. First, all annotated codes contain annotations—an invaluable research tool. Annotations are enhancements added by editors, not legislatures, and they include references to primary and secondary authorities that address the codified statutes. To illustrate, assume you consulted an annotated code to retrieve a Texas statute (Tex. Penal Code § 37.02) prohibiting perjury. In the annotations, you would find short descriptions of cases that have applied the perjury statute to various factual situations. You would also find citations to practice guides and treatises that explain the perjury statute.

Second, many annotated codes are updated more frequently than unannotated codes. Annotated codes are usually published by private companies that have a financial incentive to keep their codes up-to-date. Unannotated codes, however are often published by government entities that are slower to update their codes.

This chapter, therefore, focuses on researching with annotated codes. If federal statutes apply to your client's situation, consult either of the following annotated codes: the *United States Code Annotated* (U.S.C.A.) published by Thomson Reuters and available on Westlaw or the *United States Code Service* (U.S.C.S.) published by LexisNexis and available on Lexis Advance.[2] If state statutes apply, use an annotated code for your jurisdiction. Almost all annotated codes for state statutes are published by private companies,[3] and they are available in print and on Westlaw and Lexis Advance.

In the following sections of this chapter, you will learn how to locate all relevant statutes in an annotated code in print and online. In Chapter 19, you will learn how to research cases using the annotations that accompany each relevant code section (statute).

C. Methods for Researching Federal and State Statutes in Print

The process for researching both federal and state statutes in a print annotated code is very similar. Thus, this section walks you through only the process of print research for federal statutes.

You should research statutes in print using these four methods:

1. Consulting an index;

2. Browsing the table of contents;

3. Reviewing annotations for cross-referenced statutes; and

4. Consulting the popular name table.

Through the following hypothetical, you will learn to use these four methods with the *United States Code Annotated* (U.S.C.A.) and the *United States Code Service* (U.S.C.S.). Suppose you represent an employer covered by the Americans with Disabilities Act (ADA). The former employee has threatened a lawsuit, alleging that the employer discriminated against her on the basis of her disability. The employee alleges that the employer engaged in intentional discrimination when it failed to provide a reasonable accommodation despite its knowledge of the employee's disability. Your supervisor has tasked you to research the ADA to determine whether the employer will likely be held liable and the amount of potential damages.

1. Consult an Index

Both annotated federal codes, the U.S.C.A. (Thomson Reuters) and the U.S.C.S. (LexisNexis), have a **General Index** spanning multiple volumes.[4] These indexes contain an alphabetical list of subject headings that help researchers locate relevant statutes. Using key terms, the General Index will direct you to the relevant titles and sections of the code that apply to your client's situation.

---

2. As explained in Chapter 4, both the U.S.C.A. and U.S.C.S. are unofficial codes.

3. A few states (*e.g.*, Colorado and Oregon) have annotated codes that are published by, or under the direction of, the government.

4. Each volume of these codes has a specific index for the title or titles contained in the volume.

Returning to the ADA hypothetical, assume that you read two treatises discussing the requirements under the ADA. Further assume that you found the citation to the statute requiring a covered employer to provide a "reasonable accommodation" to an employee "with a disability" (42 U.S.C.A. § 12112). The General Index will help you locate additional provisions of the ADA that may apply to your client's situation.

If you looked up the term "Americans with Disabilities Act" in the General Index (2018) for the U.S.C.S., you would see the heading "Employment" and a list of code sections that apply in the employment context (see **Figure 15.1**). And under the heading "Employment," you would also see multiple sub-headings like "Discrimination" and "Enforcement" (see **Figure 15.1**). Those sub-headings direct you to sections 12111 (definitions) and 12117 (enforcement), two sections that appear relevant and that you may not have located in the two treatises you previously reviewed. You know from **Figure 15.1** that both sections are codified under Title 42 of the U.S.C.S. ("Public Health and Welfare") based on the number "42" appearing immediately before each section number. (If the General Index included "et seq." next to a listed section, it would be directing you to the statute listed and the sections that follow it.)

2. Browse the Table of Contents

Another effective method to locate relevant statutes is to browse the **table of contents**. Each volume of the U.S.C.S. (LexisNexis) and U.S.C.A. (Thomas Reuters)—and of every other code—has a table of contents.

Browsing the table of contents helps you understand the organizational structure of a code, informing you whether the code is divided into chapters, parts, articles, or other divisions. It also helps you understand the relationship between your codified statute and the ones surrounding it. To illustrate, suppose you pick up the volume of the U.S.C.A. containing Chapter 126 of Title 42, which codifies the ADA. A glance of the table of contents would inform you that Title 42 is divided into more than 150 chapters. And as shown in **Figure 15.2**, a careful review of the table of contents would inform you of the following information:

- Chapter 126 is divided into Subchapters I and II;
- The sections codified under Subchapter I apply in the employment context;
- The sections codified under Subchapter II apply to public services (*e.g.*, public transportation); and
- The section requiring a "reasonable accommodation" (§ 12112), which is the codified statute relevant to your client-employer, is surrounded by multiple related sections.

Further, by browsing the table of contents of a code, you probably would locate statutes that you did not find in a secondary source or through an index. Because a statutory scheme or act usually contains multiple related statutes, these statutes are often codified together. Thus, scanning the sections surrounding your codified statute often alerts you to additional statutes. You may find statutes setting forth exceptions

Figure 15.1: Excerpt from General Index for the U.S.C.S.

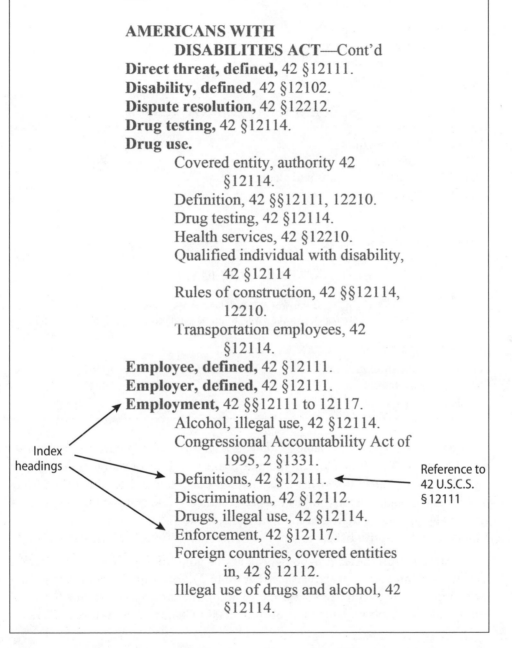

and defenses to a prohibition or requirement and statutes providing for certain remedies or penalties for a violation.

Figure 15.2: Table of Contents for Chapter 126 of Title 42 of U.S.C.A.

CHAPTER 126—EQUAL OPPORTUNITY FOR INDIVIDUALS WITH DISABILITIES

Sec.
12101.   Findings and purpose.
12102.   Definition of disability.
12103.   Additional definitions.

SUBCHAPTER I—EMPLOYMENT
12111.   Definitions.
12112.   Discrimination.
12113.   Defenses.
12114.   Illegal use of drugs and alcohol.
12115.   Posting notices.
12116.   Regulations.
12117.   Enforcement.
12118 to 12130.   Reserved.

SUBCHAPTER II—PUBLIC SERVICES

PART A—PROHIBITION AGAINST DISCRIMINATION AND
OTHER GENERALLY APPLICABLE PROVISIONS

12131.   Definitions.
12132.   Discrimination.
12133.   Enforcement.
12134.   Regulations.

Importantly, browsing the table of contents is an excellent approach to locate statutory definitions. You should look in multiple places in a code for statutory definitions, including immediately under the title, chapter, part, and article where the statute prohibiting or requiring the conduct has been codified.[5] Note that statutory definitions are not always under a topical heading called "definitions"; they may be placed under a much less descriptive heading, such as "General Provisions" or "In General."

Continuing with the ADA hypothetical, at this point of the research process, you have located three relevant statutes (see **Figure 15.3**), including the statute requiring a covered employer to make a "reasonable accommodation" in certain situations. You should scroll through the table of contents for Chapter 126 of the U.S.C.A. (or

---

5. You might find relevant definitions at the beginning of a code. For instance, Title 1 of the U.S.C.A. and U.S.C.S. has several definitions that apply throughout the code.

U.S.C.S.) to determine whether any surrounding codified statutes need to be reviewed. As shown in **Figure 15.2**, the table of contents would lead you to several *additional* statutes that could affect your client's liability under the ADA, including two sections containing definitions (§ 12102 and § 12103). After reviewing the definition of a "disability" (§ 12102), you might realize that your client-employer has a plausible argument that the reasonable accommodation requirement (§ 12112) was not triggered because the employee never had a "disability" as defined by the ADA (§ 12102).

In sum, the table of contents would have revealed the additional relevant statutes listed in **Figure 15.3**.

Figure 15.3: Relevant Sections of the ADA

Sections Found Through Secondary Sources and the General Index	Sections Found by Browsing the Table of Contents
§ 12112 (requiring a "reasonable accommodation" for employees with a "disability")	§ 12102 (defining a "disability")
§ 12111 (defining a "reasonable accommodation")	§ 12103 (additional definitions)
§ 12117 (providing remedies for a violation of the ADA)	§ 12101 (explaining the purpose of the ADA)
	§ 12113 (setting forth several defenses)

3. Review Annotations for Cross-Referenced Statutes

A third method to find relevant statutes in print is to scan the **annotations** added by Thomson Reuters (U.S.C.A.) and LexisNexis (U.S.C.S.). The annotations, which appear under the text of each code section, may cross reference statutes addressing similar topics. The cross-referenced statutes should be related to the codified statute and could even be directly on point to your legal issue.

As to the ADA hypothetical, you should review the annotations for *each* section of the code that applies to your client's legal questions. If you reviewed the annotations in the U.S.C.A. and U.S.C.S. for section 12112 (which requires a "reasonable accommodation"), you would see the editors have referenced section 1981a of Title 42— a statute you did not find through the prior research methods. See **Figure 15.4**. That relevant section authorizes enhanced damages (*e.g.*, punitive damages) for "intentional discrimination," which the client's employee has alleged.

4. Consult a Popular Name Table

A fourth helpful tool to research statutes in print is the **Popular Name Table**. When proposing new laws on the same subject, known as an "Act," Congress often gives the Act an official short name. A few examples include the "Cable Television Consumer Protection and Competition Act of 1992" and the "Immigration Act of 1990." And

Figure 15.4: Cross References from the U.S.C.A.

HISTORICAL AND STATUTORY NOTES

Revision Notes and Legislative Reports
1990   Acts. House Report No.
101-485(Parts I-IV), House Conference
Report No. 101-596, and Statement by
President see 1990 U.S. Code Cong. and
Adm. News, p. 267.

1991   Acts. House Report No.
102-40(Parts I and II), Interpretive Memorandum, and Statement by President,
see 1991 U.S. Code Cong. and Adm.
News, p. 549

Amendments
2008 Amendments. Subsec. (a).
Pub.L. 110-325, § 5(a)(1), struck out
"with a disability because of the disability
of such individual" and inserted "on the
basis of disability" following "qualified
individual".

 Subsec. (b). Pub.L. 110-325, § 5(a)(2),
struck out "discriminate" and inserted
"discriminate against a qualified individual on the basis of disability".

1991 Amendments. Subsec. (c).
Pub.L. 102-166, § 109(b)(2), added subsec. (c) and redesignated former subsec.
(c) as (d).
 Subsec. (d). Pub.L. 102-166,
§ 109(b)(2), redesignated former subsec.
(c) as (d).

Effective and Applicability Provisions
2008 Acts. Pub.L. 110-325 and the
amendments made by such Act shall take
effect on Jan 1, 2009, see Pub.L.
110-325, § 8, set out as an Effective and
Applicability Provisions note under 29
U.S.C.A. § 705.

1991 Acts. Amendment by Pub.L.
102-166 not to apply to conduct occurring before November 21, 1991, see section 109(c) of Pub.L. 102-166, set out as
a note under section 2000e of this title.

1990 Acts. Section effective 24 months
after July 26, 1990, see section 108 of
Pub.L. 101-336, set out as a note under
section 12111 of this title.

CROSS REFERENCES

Congressional accountability and extension of rights and protections, see 2 USCA
        § 1311.
Damages in cases of intentional discrimination in employment, see 42 USCA
        § 1981a.

---

through time, many federal statutes become known by a "popular" name, such as
the "Blue Sky Laws" (for securities laws).

If you know the short or popular name of an Act, you should consult the Popular
Name Table, which is shelved near the General Indexes of the U.S.C.A. (Thomson
Reuters) and U.S.C.S. (LexisNexis). This Table will inform you of the title and section
numbers where the Act has been codified.[6] The Popular Name Table is especially

---

6. The Popular Name Table does not always identify *all* code sections. For example, the Popular
Name Table of the U.S.C.S. does not indicate that part of the ADA has been codified under Title 47.

helpful when an Act has been codified under more than one title or chapter. In that circumstance, it helps you determine whether you have missed a relevant statute.

Suppose you looked up the term "Americans with Disabilities Act" in the Popular Name Table of the U.S.C.A. It identifies the section numbers contained in the public law (also known as a session law) and shows where each section has been compiled in the U.S.C.A. (see **Figure 15.5**). The Popular Name Table indicates that the ADA has been codified under Title 42 of the federal code in over fifty different sections (see **Figure 15.5**). It also shows that a small part of the ADA has been codified under Title 47. You may not have located that "hidden" provision using the other finding methods.

5. Summary of Hypothetical on the Americans with Disabilities Act

You have been researching the ADA to determine your client-employer's potential liability under the Act. By using the research methods discussed above, you have found six different statutes addressing the client's potential legal issues. These statutes include the purpose of the ADA (§ 12101), the reasonable accommodation requirement (§ 12112), definitions (§§ 12102, 12103, 12111), and remedies (§§ 12117, 1981a). Next, you should confirm the validity of each potentially relevant statute and should carefully review the language of each statute.[7]

D. Methods for Researching Federal and State Statutes on Westlaw and Lexis Advance

Of course, you can research federal and state statutes online. Although print codes are easy to navigate, the codes on Westlaw and Lexis Advance have three distinct advantages over print codes. First, online codes provide hyperlinks to secondary and primary authorities. Second, they are more current than their print counterparts (see Chapter 4). Third, online codes provide an additional method to find relevant statutes — namely, keyword searching.

An almost identical version of both the *United States Code Annotated* (U.S.C.A.) and *United States Code Service* (U.S.C.S.) is available on Westlaw and Lexis Advance, respectively. And annotated codes for every state (and the District of Columbia) are available on both Westlaw and Lexis Advance. Additionally, the research tools previously discussed — **indexes, tables of contents, annotations, and popular name tables** — are available on these online research services.

---

7. Chapter 16 explains the process for validating and updating statutes, and Chapter 17 provides guidance on reading statutes critically.

Figure 15.5: Excerpt of Popular Name Table for the U.S.C.A.

POPULAR NAME TABLE

American War Mothers Incorporation Act—Continued
> *This Public Law enacted no currently effective sections. For sections*
> *affected by this law, see Act Feb. 24, 1925, ch. 308 in the USCA-TABLES*
> *database and the enacting credit set out below.*
> **Enacting law:**
> Feb 24, 1925, ch. 308, 43 Stat. 966 (See 36 § 22501 et seq.)
> **Amending laws:**
> Sept. 26, 1942, ch 563, 56 Stat. 758 (36 § 97)
> June 26, 1953, ch. 152, 67 Stat. 81 (36 §§ 97, 98)
> Apr. 2, 1974, Pub.L., 93-267, 88 Stat. 85 (36 § 97)

Americans with Disabilities Act
> See Americans with Disabilities Act of 1990

Americans with Disabilities Act of 1990 (Americans with Disabilities Act)
(ADA)
> Pub L. 101-336, July 26, 1990, 104 Stat. 327
> Short title, see 42 USCA § 12101 note
> **Current USCA classifications:**

Section of Pub. L. 101-336	USCA Classifications
2	42 USCA § 12101
3	42 USCA § 12102
4	42 USCA § 12103
101	42 USCA § 12111
102	42 USCA § 12112
103	42 USCA § 12113
104	42 USCA § 12114
105	42 USCA § 12115
106	42 USCA § 12116
107	42 USCA § 12117
201	42 USCA § 12131
202	42 USCA § 12132
203	42 USCA § 12133
204	42 USCA § 12134
221	42 USCA § 12141
222	42 USCA § 12142
223	42 USCA § 12143
224	42 USCA § 12144
225	42 USCA § 12145
226	42 USCA § 12146
227	42 USCA § 12147
228	42 USCA § 12148
229	42 USCA § 12149
230	42 USCA § 12150
241	42 USCA § 12161
242	42 USCA § 12162
243	42 USCA § 12163
244	42 USCA § 12164
245	42 USCA § 12165
301	42 USCA § 12181
302	42 USCA § 12182
303	42 USCA § 12183
304	42 USCA § 12184
305	42 USCA § 12185
306	42 USCA § 12186
307	42 USCA § 12187
308	42 USCA § 12188
309	42 USCA § 12189

1. Consult an Electronic Index and Table of Contents

Westlaw and Lexis Advance provide **electronic indexes** to their federal and state codes. Both research services have an electronic version of the *General Index* to the U.S.C.A. (Westlaw) and U.S.C.S. (Lexis Advance). As to state statutes, Westlaw has indexes for all state codes, but Lexis Advance has these tools only for some states.[8] You can quickly access an index by typing its full or partial name in the global search box on either home page (*e.g.*, "United States Code Index" or "California Codes Index").[9]

Like federal and state codes in print, each online code has an **electronic table of contents**. The table of contents of an online code is an invaluable research tool. Use it. And use it often.

A code's table of contents will often lead you to relevant statutes that you did not locate through other methods. To illustrate, assume that your client has been sued by consumers for violating the Texas Deceptive Trade Practices-Consumer Protection Act. After reading a Texas legal encyclopedia, you found the statute setting forth the general prohibition against "deceptive acts or practices" (Tex. Bus. & Com. Code Ann. §17.46). If you retrieved that statute on Westlaw or Lexis Advance and then clicked on "table of contents," you would find multiple related statutes that could apply to the client's circumstance. The text of each section heading will inform you which statutory sections you should click on to review. As indicated in **Figure 15.6**, you should review all statutes dealing with construction of the Act, waivers, exemptions and defenses, definitions, and remedies.

2. Review Annotations and Consult an Electronic Popular Name Table

All federal and state codes on Westlaw and Lexis Advance include **annotations** that may cross reference related statutes. On Westlaw, these annotations are located under the tab "Context & Analysis"; on Lexis Advance, however, they are located under the statutory text.

Additionally, **popular name tables** are available online. Both Westlaw and Lexis Advance have an electronic version of the *Popular Name Table* for the U.S.C.A. and U.S.C.S, respectively. Regarding state statutes, Westlaw has popular name tables for all state codes, but Lexis Advance has these tools only for some states. You can retrieve a popular name table by typing its full or partial name in the global search box on either home page (*e.g.*, "United States Code Popular Name Table").

---

8. If you want access to an index, you could use a code in print. Every print code includes an index.

9. On Westlaw, while viewing the full table of contents of a code, a link to the code's index will appear in the right column.

Figure 15.6: Excerpt of Table of Contents on Westlaw

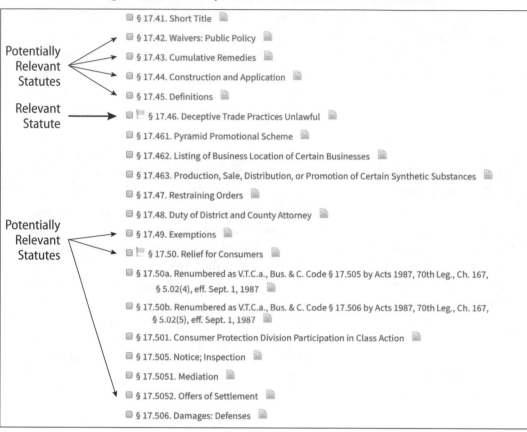

3. Perform Keyword Searches

At this **Step 3**, you should also research statutes by searching the full text of a federal or state code on Westlaw and Lexis Advance.[10] As explained earlier in Chapter 9, there are two types of keyword searches: **natural language searches** and **terms and connectors (Boolean) searches.** You should use both types of searches when researching statutes online.

A **natural language search** on Westlaw and Lexis Advance is similar to a Google search in that a user enters keywords into an online database, the database finds results that match the keywords, and the database organizes the results based on numerous factors. When performing a natural language search on Westlaw or Lexis, the results on the top of the list should be the most relevant to your client's legal issue. But the best legal authority is not always listed in the top results because of the complexity of the law and the countless number of fact patterns (see Chapter 9).

---

10. You could also use KeyCite on Westlaw or Shepard's on Lexis Advance to identify statutes that have cited another statute. These citators may reveal a relevant statute that you did not find through another method.

That is actually good news. You do not want a machine to replace a human researcher—namely, you.

A **terms and connectors search**, however, is much more precise than a natural language search; the online database will return only the results that match the exact words and criteria you specify.[11] A terms and connectors search (also called Boolean searching) places more control in your hands. You can require your search results to contain an exact phrase, all your search terms, or just one term, and you can exclude certain terms. To illustrate its precision, imagine you need to determine whether your client must obey traffic laws when riding her horse on a public road. Imagine, also, that you searched the statutory database for your jurisdiction with this search string:

vehicle /15 riding /15 horse

Both Westlaw and Lexis Advance would return only the statutes in which all three keywords appear within fifteen words of each other (in any order). Even if a relevant statute did exist, it would not appear on your results list if the legislature used the generic term "animal" instead of "horse" or used the term "driving" instead of "riding."

Performing a keyword search for federal and state statutes is similar to searching for cases. The initial step is to limit your search to the correct online database. For federal statutes, you would select the database for the *United States Code Service* on Lexis Advance or the *United States Code Annotated* on Westlaw. For state statutes, you would select the database containing the code for the controlling jurisdiction.

On Westlaw, here is one approach to run a keyword search in a state code:

1. From the home page, select the "State Materials" tab to view a list of all states.

2. Click the name of your state.

3. Under the heading "Statutes & Court Rules," select the link to the code for the controlling jurisdiction.

4. Enter the search terms into the global search box near the top of the screen, or click "Advanced" (next to search box) to access the guided search template.

On Lexis Advance, you can perform a keyword search in a state code using this method:

1. From the home page, select the "State" tab to view a list of all states.

2. Click the name of your state.

3. Under the heading "Statutes & Legislation," select the link to the code for your jurisdiction. The relevant database may include the term "statutes" or "laws" in its name instead of "code."

4. Enter the search terms into the global search box near the top of the screen, or click "Advanced Search" (next to search box) to access a guided search template.

---

11. You should review Chapter 9 for a good refresher on constructing terms and connectors searches and how to maneuver around potential obstacles. That chapter contains a chart that identifies the most helpful connectors and symbols, as well as providing specific examples.

Pitfalls of Searching for Statutes by Keywords

Researching statutes with keyword searches—either Boolean or natural language—can be more difficult than researching cases with this method.

First, after searching by keywords, the statutes listed in the results may be over-inclusive. For example, imagine you are researching whether the client, a consumer, may bring a state claim against a retailer for deceptive advertising, and suppose you ran a keyword search on Lexis Advance, finding one statute prohibiting deceptive advertising. If a different statute authorized only the government, not a private party, to bring a lawsuit and that statute was not listed in your search results, you would not discover this limitation and could incorrectly determine that your client has a viable claim.

Second, statutes may contain very precise language. If you use the wrong search terms, your search results may exclude relevant statutes—even when performing natural language searches. To illustrate, some state statutes regulate motorized devices like Segways, but they call these devices "electric personal assistive mobility devices." Without knowledge of that term of art, you probably would not locate the relevant statute through a keyword search.

Although running a keyword search is often not the best place to start researching a common law issue, you could research a statutory issue with this method immediately after you have created a research plan (**Step 1**) and read secondary sources (**Step 2**). But using a keyword search cannot be your sole method to locate relevant statutes; you must supplement keyword searching with other finding tools. Indeed, if you rely exclusively on keyword searching, you may miss relevant statutes and not know it until opposing counsel—or worse, your judge—points out your omission.

For some research projects, performing a full-text search of an entire federal or state code could result in hundreds or thousands of documents. No doubt, many of those search results would be irrelevant to your client's legal issues. When encountering that obstacle, it is time to limit your keyword searches. As with cases, you can limit a keyword search on Westlaw and Lexis Advance to specific fields or segments of a code.

a. Limit a Keyword Search to the Statutory Text

One option to limit your search results to a reasonable number is to keyword search only within the **statutory text** contained in the code for the controlling jurisdiction. When running a keyword search in a database for a particular code, the default on Lexis Advance and Westlaw is to search not only the statutory text but also the annotations. These annotations include case annotations, which are summaries of judicial decisions that have interpreted and applied the codified statutes (see Chapter 4).[12] Thus, a keyword search of an annotated code, by default, will search all the summaries of cases.

---

12. The case annotations on Westlaw are called "Notes of Decisions" but known as "Case Notes" on Lexis Advance.

Because all the case annotations are searched by default, some keyword searches will yield statutes where the search terms appear only in the case annotations, making it difficult to find the relevant statutes among the "sea" of irrelevant results. You can avoid that problem on Lexis Advance and Westlaw and retrieve only those results where your search terms appear within the statutory text. Indeed, Lexis and Westlaw provide templates to limit searches to specific fields or segments of federal and state codes.[13]

On Westlaw, you can search just the statutory text by following these steps:

1. From the home page, click the tab "Content Type" and select "Statutes & Court Rules."

2. For federal statutes, select the U.S.C.A. link. For state statutes, click the name of your state.

3. Click the "Advanced" link next to the search box near the top of your screen.

4. Enter search terms into the field "Statutory Text."

The available fields for searching codes on Westlaw are displayed in **Figure 15.7.**

Figure 15.7: Available Fields for Codes on Westlaw

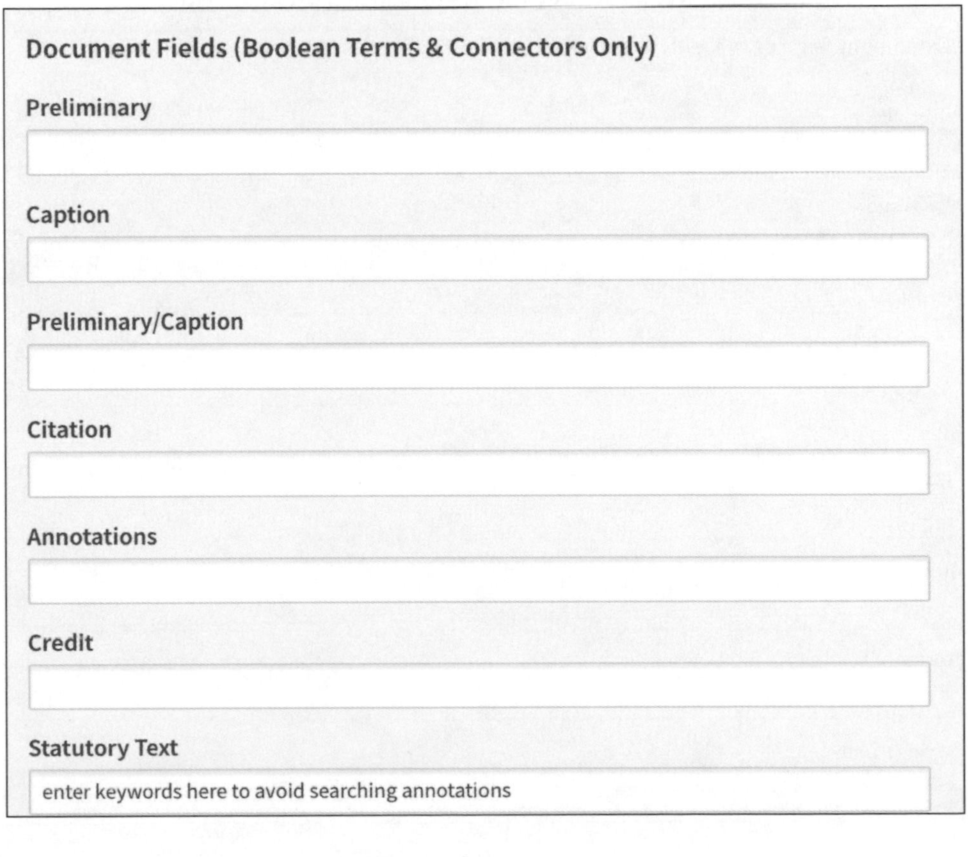

Document Fields (Boolean Terms & Connectors Only)

Preliminary

Caption

Preliminary/Caption

Citation

Annotations

Credit

Statutory Text

enter keywords here to avoid searching annotations

---

13. Westlaw also has databases for unannotated codes for many jurisdictions, so you could search the statutory text by selecting the unannotated code for your state. While viewing the full table of contents of a code, a link to the unannotated database will appear in the right column.

Searching just the statutory text of codes on Lexis Advance involves a similar process.

1. From the home page, click the tab "Content Type" and select "Statutes & Legislation."

2. For federal statutes, select "federal" and then click the U.S.C.S. link. For state statutes, click the name of your state and then select the code for your jurisdiction.

3. Click the "Advanced Search" link next to the search box near the top of your screen.

4. Enter search terms into the segment "Unannotated" or "Text."

Figure 15.8 shows the available segments for searching codes on Lexis.

Figure 15.8: Available Segments for Codes on Lexis Advance

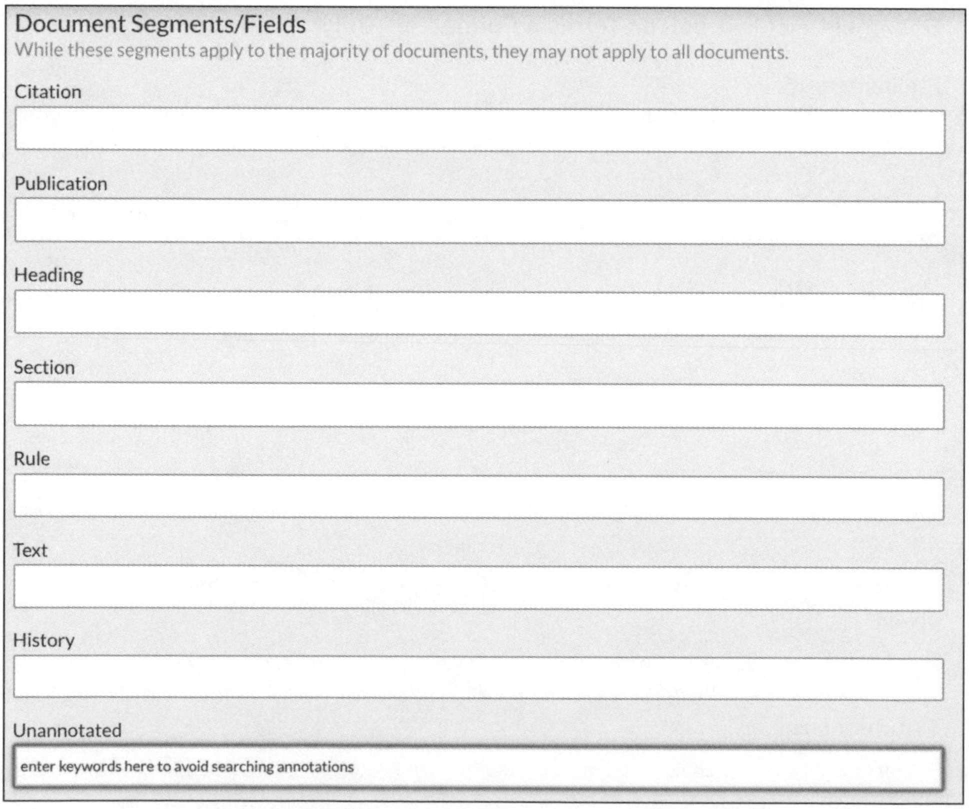

Document Segments/Fields
While these segments apply to the majority of documents, they may not apply to all documents.

Citation

Publication

Heading

Section

Rule

Text

History

Unannotated

enter keywords here to avoid searching annotations

b. Limit a Keyword Search to the Table of Contents

A second option to reduce irrelevant results is to limit a keyword search to the table of contents of a code. When performing this type of search, your results would include only the statutes where your keywords appear in the headings of a code, such as the title or section. So a search of the table of contents in **Figure 15.9** would be limited to the words next to each title, chapter, article, and section number. Searching the table of contents would not return statutes where your keywords appear only in the statute itself (and not a heading).

Figure 15.9: Excerpt of Table of Content of *Official Code of Georgia Annotated* on Lexis Advance

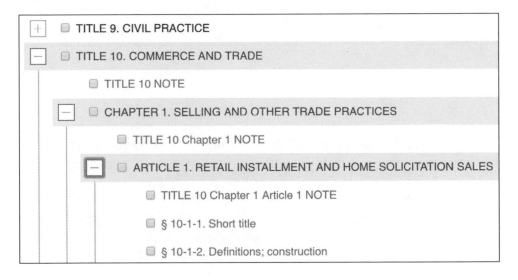

On Lexis Advance, you can search the text of a table of contents with a few clicks. With a federal or state code on your screen, you could click "Table of Contents (TOC) only," and then enter keywords into the search box (see **Figure 15.10**). In addition, while viewing the table of contents of a code, you could click "Advanced Search" (near the search box) and type your search terms into the segment "Heading" or "Section."

On Westlaw, while viewing the table of contents of a code, you could click "Advance" and enter keywords in the field "Preliminary/Caption" (see **Figure 15.11**).

Figure 15.10: Searching the Table of Contents of a Code on Lexis Advance

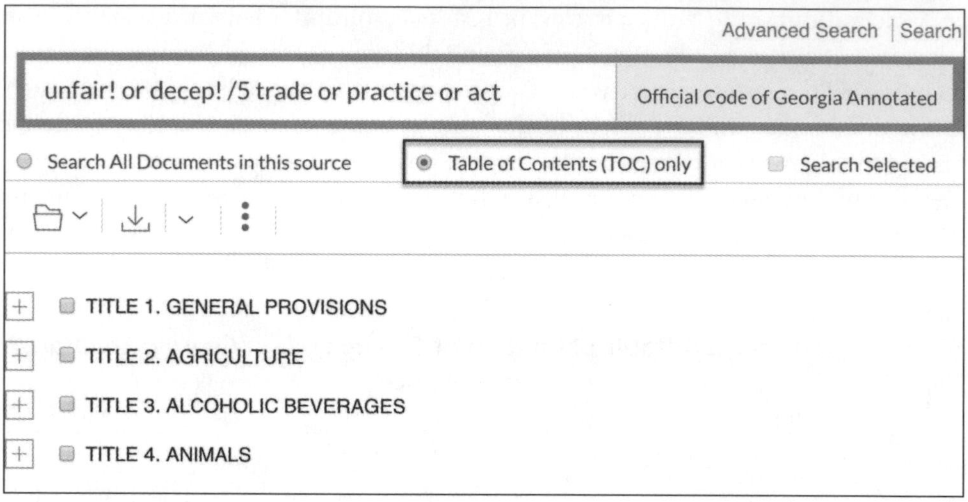

	Advanced Search │ Search
unfair! or decep! /5 trade or practice or act	Official Code of Georgia Annotated

○ Search All Documents in this source   ◉ Table of Contents (TOC) only   ☐ Search Selected

📁⌄ ⤓⌄ ⋮

[+] ☐ TITLE 1. GENERAL PROVISIONS

[+] ☐ TITLE 2. AGRICULTURE

[+] ☐ TITLE 3. ALCOHOLIC BEVERAGES

[+] ☐ TITLE 4. ANIMALS

Figure 15.11: Searching the Table of Contents of a Code on Westlaw

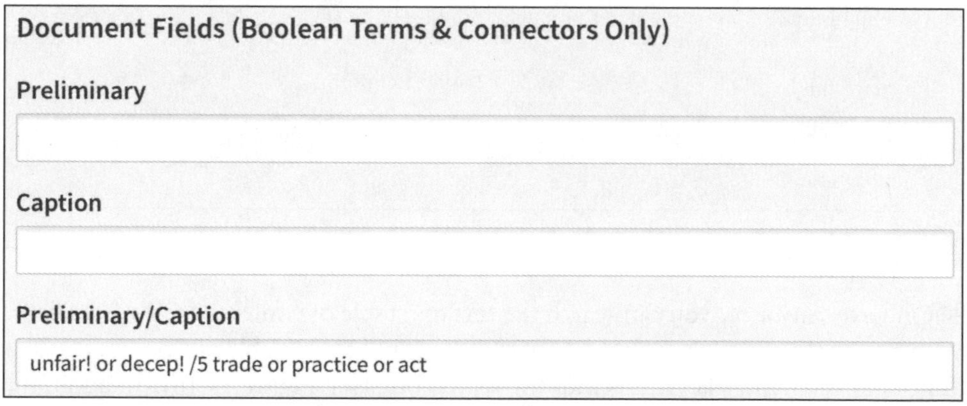

Document Fields (Boolean Terms & Connectors Only)

Preliminary

Caption

Preliminary/Caption

unfair! or decep! /5 trade or practice or act

When searching by field or segment, keep in mind two points. Westlaw and Lexis Advance automatically run a terms and connectors, not a natural language, search; thus, you need to carefully construct your search strings. Additionally, after clicking on the advanced search link, review the visual in the right column. It matches the name of a field or segment with the part of the code that would be searched.

E. Researching Federal and State Statutes on Cost-Effective Online Platforms

While Lexis Advance and Westlaw are the most comprehensive legal research services, there are other reputable cost-effective options to research statutes. The entire *United States Code* is available on the public websites of the **House of Representatives' Office of the Law Revision Counsel**[14] and **Cornell Law School's Legal Information Institute.**[15] Both websites are updated frequently with newly-enacted laws. You can browse the table of contents of the federal code, consult a popular name table, and perform keyword searches.

For researching federal and state statutes, two other good alternatives exist: **Casemaker** and **Fastcase.** Many state and local bar associations provide their members with access to either Casemaker or Fastcase. These research platforms have online databases for the federal code and the codes for all fifty states (and District of Columbia). Casemaker and Fastcase offer basic browsing and searching features, including searching with terms and connectors. Although both platforms regularly update the codes for most states, Fastcase sometimes has a state code that does not include many enacted laws from the current legislative session. As explained in the next chapter, you must always check the currency of a code, especially codes found on free and low-cost databases.

The cost-effective platforms just discussed have some important limitations. For instance, almost all codes in their online databases—including the federal code—do not include annotations. Thus, when viewing an individual code section, you will not find summaries of cases that have interpreted the codified statute. Additionally, these research platforms do not offer all the tools for finding statutes (*e.g.*, indexes) that Lexis and Westlaw provide.

F. Locating Secondary Sources for Statutes

As discussed in Chapter 14, you should start researching a statutory issue with secondary sources. They explain the law and usually cite at least one statute pertinent to the client's legal issue. (Chapter 6 sets forth eight methods for locating helpful secondary sources, such as legal encyclopedias and treatises.) After finding additional statutes through the previously-discussed methods, you may have new questions about some statutes. You may not understand the meaning of a specific word or phrase in the statute. Or you may be unable to determine whether the newly-found statutes even

---

14. The Office of the Law Revision Counsel compiles the *United States Code.* The code is available at http://uscode.house.gov.

15. You can access this site at https://www.law.cornell.edu.

apply to the client's situation. In either scenario, you have two good options to find relevant secondary sources.

One option is to scan the annotations contained in the annotated code in print or online. The annotations often include citations to secondary sources that discuss the codified statutes. For instance, assume you plan to review secondary materials to know when an employer is subject to punitive damages for "intentional discrimination" under 42 U.S.C. § 1981a. In the print versions of the *United States Code Annotated* (Thomson Reuters) and *United States Code Service* (LexisNexis), you would pick up the volume for Title 42 and turn to section 1981a. You would then review the annotations after the text of this code section and would find law review articles and treatises that discuss section 1981a and damages for intentional discrimination. On Lexis Advance, the annotations with citations to secondary materials are also located after the statutory text. On Westlaw, while viewing section 1981a, you would click the "Context & Analysis" tab (near the top of the document).

Another option for locating secondary sources is to use the citator Shepard's (Lexis Advance) or KeyCite (Westlaw). For example, imagine you need more clarification on the definition of a disability under the Americans with Disabilities Act. You could retrieve 42 U.S.C.S. § 12102 (which defines "disability") on Lexis Advance and then click the "Shepardize this document" link in the right column. Or you could retrieve this code section on Westlaw, click the tab "Citing References," and then select "Secondary Sources." The Shepard's and KeyCite reports will provide hyperlinked citations to secondary sources that discuss this code section.

G. Researching with Print Codes: Three Reasons to Know It

Although all federal and state codes are available online, you should know how to research codified statutes in print. You should understand print research for statutes for several reasons.

First, by understanding the process for researching with print codes, you will be a more effective researcher on Westlaw and Lexis Advance. The codes online are a reproduction of the print source. Thus, the methods used to find relevant statutes in a print code also apply to a code found in those online databases.

Second, many attorneys and judges research statutes in print, especially state statutes. In fact, your employer likely has a print code for the statutes covering your jurisdiction. If so, you must know how to navigate the many volumes of the code to locate relevant statutes. You do not want to be faced with this question from your boss: "Why did you spend $1,000 researching statutes online when our office has the state code in print?"

Third, after placing their hands on a print code, many students and attorneys quickly realize its ease of use and other benefits. (That is no exaggeration.) The organizational scheme of a federal or state code is fairly easy to grasp with a print code, such as understanding how a code is divided into title, chapters, parts, and sections. Additionally, a print code often makes it easier to understand how one code section relates to surrounding sections.

H. Summary of Key Points

For this **Step 3** of the process for researching a statutory issue, you should focus on finding all relevant statutes; most of your time should not be spent researching and reading cases—at least not yet.

Because Congress and state legislatures often enact bills containing multiple, related laws, one statute usually will not provide a reliable answer to your client's question. Thus, you should not stop researching statutes after you have found just one statute prohibiting, requiring, or permitting the conduct at issue. You must also look for these statutory provisions: definitions, exceptions and defenses, the proper plaintiff to bring a lawsuit for a violation, remedies and penalties for a violation, and other related statutes. Remember that all applicable statutes are binding on your court.

The best type of code for researching federal and state statutes is an annotated code. An annotated code provides not only the actual statutes but also citations to secondary and primary authorities. When researching statutes with an annotated code on Westlaw or Lexis Advance or in print, you should use these four methods:

- Consulting the index (if available online);
- Browsing the table of contents and reviewing all surrounding sections;
- Reviewing the annotations for any cross-referenced statutes; and
- Consulting a popular name table (if available online).

When researching on Westlaw or Lexis, you should also perform keyword searches in the online code for your jurisdiction. Two types of keyword searches are available: (1) a natural language search, and (2) a terms and connectors (Boolean) search. But if full-text searching leads to an unmanageable number of results, you could search only the statutory text (which excludes annotations) or search the code's table of contents.

A multi-method approach will maximize the likelihood of finding the universe of statutes that apply to your client's situation. Further, you should use multiple research methods to comply with your ethical obligations to be a competent attorney and to act with "reasonable diligence" in representing clients.[16] **Figure 15.12** describes the various research methods and tools that you should use on Westlaw and Lexis Advance. It also identifies the benefits of each method and tool.

---

16. *See Idaho State Bar v. Tway*, 919 P.2d 323, 327 (Idaho 1996) (concluding that attorney did not act with reasonable diligence based on, in part, failing to perform adequate legal research).

Figure 15.12: Methods for Finding Statutes Online

Search Method or Finding Tool	Benefits
Search the full text of a code with natural language searches.	Retrieves many results, minimizing the possibility of excluding relevant statutes early in the research.
	Good method to find at least one relevant statute listed in top ten search results (if using effective search terms).
Search the full text of a code with terms and connectors (Boolean) searches.	Retrieves fewer results than a natural language search (if using effective search terms).
	Targeted method to find statutory definitions that are codified in multiple parts of a code (*e.g.*, under different chapters or articles) or that are codified under the heading "general provisions" or "in general."
	Targeted method to find statutes setting forth remedies and penalties for a violation.
Limit keyword searching to the statutory text and table of contents of a code.	Reduces number of irrelevant results (if using effective search terms).
	Targeted method to find statutory definitions and statutes setting forth remedies and penalties for a violation.
Browse the table of contents, and consult the index and popular name table (if available).	Helps confirm whether you have found the universe of relevant statutes.
	Finds statutes related to the one that prohibits, requires, or authorizes the conduct in dispute.
	Finds statutes that are codified in multiple parts of a code (*e.g.*, under different titles).
Review the annotations for cross-referenced statutes.	Helps confirm whether you have found the universe of relevant statutes.
	Finds statutes that are codified in multiple parts of a code (*e.g.*, under different titles).

I. Review Questions on Researching Statutes

At this point, you should have a basic understanding of researching statutes. To test your comprehension, answer the true-false and multiple-choice questions on this book's companion website, Core Knowledge. It will identify the correct answers and provide clear explanations for each question. The same questions are reproduced below.

1. If a statute and supreme court decision directly conflict, the statute would control.

   a. True

   b. False

2. After you have found one statute prohibiting the conduct in dispute, you should stop researching statutes.

   a. True

   b. False

3. When researching a statutory issue, you should look for statutory definitions.

   a. True

   b. False

4. When researching with a print code, you should consult the index, browse the table of contents, review the annotations for cross-referenced statutes, and consult the popular name table.

   a. True

   b. False

5. When researching with a code on Westlaw or Lexis Advance, the only type of keyword search you should perform is a natural language search.

   a. True

   b. False

6. Dylan has been researching Texas law and found one relevant statute that prohibits businesses from engaging in unfair competition. What other statutes should he research?

   a. Statutes defining the terms used in the statute prohibiting unfair competition.

   b. Statutes setting forth remedies and penalties for a violation of the unfair competition statute.

   c. Statutes identifying who may bring a lawsuit against a business that competes unfairly.

   d. All of the above.

7. On Lexis Advance, Cruise is researching federal statutes. After selecting the database for the U.S.C.S., he clicked on the advanced search link and entered his search terms into the segment "unannotated" or "text." What part of the U.S.C.S. will be searched?

   a. The text of each statute and the case annotations will be searched.

   b. The text of each statute will be searched but not the case annotations.

   c. Only the table of contents will be searched.

   d. None of the above.

8. You need to determine whether any Ohio statute requires a tenant to keep a rental property safe or sanitary. On Westlaw and Lexis Advance, which of the following terms and connectors search would return the most number of results?

    a. tenant /50 sanitary

    b. tenant /50 safe

    c. tenant /50 (safe or sanitary)

    d. tenant /25 (safe or sanitary)

9. After you have performed keyword searches on Westlaw or Lexis Advance, what should you do to find relevant statutes?

    a. Browse the table of contents.

    b. Consult the index (if available).

    c. Review the annotations for any cross-referenced statutes.

    d. All of the above.

10. Anne must research federal statutes relating to employment discrimination. Identify why she should consult an index and browse the table of contents of the relevant code.

    a. To find statutes related to the one that prohibits, requires, or authorizes the conduct in dispute.

    b. To find statutes that are codified in multiple parts of a code (*e.g.*, under various titles or chapters).

    c. Both A and B.

    d. To find cases that interpret the relevant statutes.

J. Practice Researching Statutes

On this book's companion website, Core Knowledge, a few research assignments have been posted. The online assignments walk you through the steps for researching a statutory issue on Westlaw and Lexis Advance, including finding statutes with the methods discussed in this chapter. For each assignment, you will research the law to resolve legal issues for your hypothetical client.

Step 1
(Research
Plan)

Step 2
(Secondary
Sources)

Step 3
(Find
Statutes)

Step 4
(Update
Statutes)

Step 5
(Read
Statutes)

Step 6
(Find
Regulations)

Step 7
(Find Cases)

Step 8
(Legislative
History)

Step 9
(Other States)

Step 10
(Validation)

Chapter 16

Step 4:
Confirm the Validity of Each Relevant Statute, Determine Each Statute's Effective Date, and Identify All Amendments

You have arrived at **Step 4**. Through the prior steps for your unfamiliar statutory issue, you should have created a research plan (**Step 1**, Chapter 13), reviewed two or more secondary sources (**Step 2**, Chapter 14), and researched statutes in your jurisdiction using multiple methods (**Step 3**, Chapter 15). As a result, you should have found all the statutes that apply or could apply to your client's situation.

But you should not actively research cases—yet. Because statutory language controls over any conflicting judicial decision, stay focused on researching and understanding all relevant statutes. To the extent you have found relevant cases cited in secondary sources, you should have recorded their citations. You could skim a few cases now, as long as you remember to re-assess their relevance after completing this **Step 4**.

For this **Step 4**, you must **update** all statutes that you intend to rely on in answering your client's legal question. Updating statutes is the process of determining whether they are still **valid**. Of course, you should not build a legal argument for your client based on a statute that no longer reflects the law of the land. A statute could become invalid by legislative or judicial action in four circumstances:

- A legislature repealed the entire statute;
- A legislature amended the statute, repealing part of it;
- A court held that a state statute was preempted in whole or in part by federal law; or
- A court declared the statute unconstitutional in whole or in part.

249

Updating also means **checking the effective date** of each relevant statute, including each amendment. This process will inform you whether statutes you have found were in effect at the time of the conduct, transaction, or event in dispute. Generally, newly-enacted statutes do not apply retroactively to previous conduct. To illustrate, a relevant statute you retrieve online may be effective now, but the legislature may have recently amended the statute and added a new requirement to recover damages. If the client's conduct occurred *before* the amendment took effect, the original version of the statute, not the amended version on your computer screen, would probably apply to the client's situation.

At **Step 4**, in addition to updating statutes, you must determine the **language of every amendment** to each relevant codified statute. By knowing what words were added or deleted by an amendment, you will learn two important things.

First, you will know whether the amendment applies to your client's legal issue. The amendment could have added a prohibition to a relevant statute or deleted language that is irrelevant to the client's issue.

Second, you will know that cases decided *before* the amendment would have interpreted different statutory language than cases decided *after* the amendment. Thus, if an amendment added or deleted language from a statute and the addition or deletion directly applies to your client, you must research cases interpreting the amended language. For instance, imagine that a statute defined "vehicles" to include only "vehicles weighing over 3,000 pounds," but was later amended to expand that definition to include "all self-propelled vehicles." If the amendment applies to your client, you must find cases construing the expanded definition. If, however, you relied only on the cases interpreting the original definition, you would probably provide the wrong advice to your client, subjecting you to an ethical violation or legal malpractice — neither option would be good for future business.

A. Westlaw and Lexis Advance: Updating Statutes

Although print codes are easier to navigate than online codes, the same is not true for updating statutes. The most accurate, current, and easiest method to update each relevant statute is to use Westlaw or Lexis Advance.

1. Use KeyCite or Shepard's to Confirm the Validity of Each Statute

You can determine the validity of a statute by using the citator KeyCite on Westlaw or the citator Shepard's on Lexis Advance.[1] (You should review Chapter 8, for a refresher on citators.) As with cases, both citators "tag" statutes with colorful signals to indicate negative treatment.[2] The negative treatment may be a result of an action by a legislature or court. A red, yellow, or orange signal could mean the statute has been repealed by a newly-enacted statute or has been declared unconstitutional or preempted by federal law.[3] Or a negative treatment signal may indicate that the statute could be repealed or amended by a pending legislative bill. When you see any of those signals, you need to further investigate the statute's validity.

Westlaw and Lexis Advance use different signals to indicate negative treatment, and their signals have different meanings. The signals used for statutes on Westlaw and Lexis Advance have the meanings set forth in **Figures 16.1** and **16.2**, respectively.[4]

Figure 16.1: Negative Treatment Signals for KeyCite on Westlaw

KeyCite Signal	Meaning of Signal
Red flag	Negative treatment based on legislative or judicial action.
	The statute has been amended, repealed, or superseded by a subsequent enacted law in whole or in part.
	The statute has been held unconstitutional or preempted in whole or in part.
Yellow flag	Negative treatment based on legislative or judicial action.
	The statute has been limited on constitutional or preemption grounds, has been renumbered or transferred, or may be affected by a pending legislative bill.
	A prior version of the statute has received negative treatment by a court.

---

1. In Chapter 19, you will learn how to use KeyCite and Shepard's to find cases that discuss applicable statutes.

2. The negative treatment signals for cases are listed in Chapter 8.

3. Even after a statute has been ruled unconstitutional or preempted, it may remain in a code.

4. Both figures have been adapted from Mary G. Algero et al., *Federal Legal Research* 218, 227 (2014).

Figure 16.2: Negative Treatment Signals for Shepard's on Lexis Advance

Shepard's Signal	Meaning of Signal
Red exclamation point	Negative treatment based on legislative or judicial action.
	The statute has been superseded or repealed by a subsequent enacted law in whole or in part.
	The statute has been declared unconstitutional or preempted in whole or in part.
Orange "Q"	The validity of the statute has been questioned by a court.
Yellow triangle (inverted)	The statute may be affected by a pending legislative bill.

The process of using a citator to confirm the validity of a statute differs on Westlaw and Lexis Advance.

On Westlaw, when you retrieve a statute that has negative treatment, a red or yellow flag automatically appears next to the section number (see **Figure 16.3**). If the statute lacks negative treatment, no signal would appear. The most negative treatment phrase for your statute is automatically displayed next to the flag near the top of the document, and the statute or case on which the most negative treatment is based is listed. As demonstrated in **Figure 16.3**, the most negative treatment phrase is "unconstitutional or preempted," and that treatment is based on the *Cooper v. State* case. You must read the *Cooper* case carefully. The Georgia statute may be invalid in whole, but it may be invalid only for an issue unrelated to your client's situation.

In addition to the case or statute on which the most negative treatment is based, the validity of your statute may have been affected by other primary authorities. With your statute on your Westlaw screen, click the "History" tab at the top of the document (**Figure 16.3**) and then select "Validity." (Or you could click the red or yellow flag

Figure 16.3: KeyCite Report for Ga. Code Ann. § 40-5-55

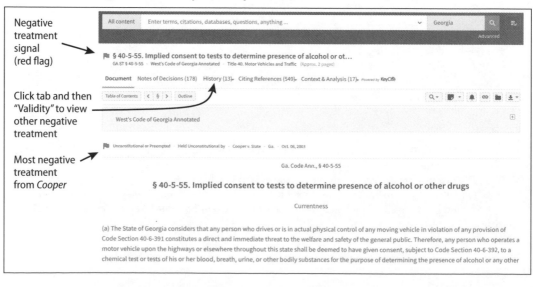

next to the section number of the statute.) The KeyCite report displays authority that could affect your statute's validity. Read each listed authority.

On Lexis Advance, you can see whether your statute is still in force and has any negative treatment by retrieving the statute and viewing the Shepard's preview box in the right column of your screen. If the retrieved statute has any negative treatment, a red exclamation point, orange Q, or yellow triangle (inverted) automatically appears in the preview box (see **Figure 16.4**). Once alerted to negative treatment, you should trigger a full Shepard's report by clicking "Shepardize this document" in the right column. The treatment signal on a full report displays next to the section number at the top of your screen (see **Figure 16.5**).

Figure 16.4: Shepard's Preview for Ga. Code Ann. § 40-5-55

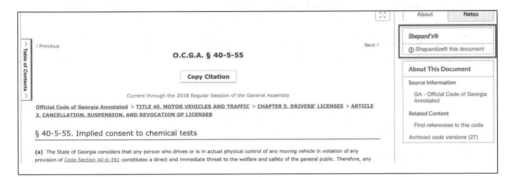

Figure 16.5: Shepard's Report for Ga. Code Ann. § 40-5-55

Figure 16.6: Shepard's Report for Cal. Rev. & Tax Code § 7094

Shepard's® Comprehensive Report: ❶ Cal. Rev. & Tax. Code sec. 7094   🔔   Actions⌄

History	Citing Decisions
Citing Decisions	
❶ Other Citing Sources	▽ **Pending Legislation**
	Subsection reports by specific court citation

You need to check two places on a Shepard's report to find the authority on which the negative treatment is based. The first place to look is under the "warning" heading in the left column. As shown in **Figure 16.5**, you would click "unconstitutional in part by" to display the case or cases that have declared the statute unconstitutional. The second place to look is under "Citing Decisions" near the top center of the document. If a newly-enacted law or pending legislative bill could affect your statute, a link to that authority would appear. For instance, if you clicked "Pending Legislation" in **Figure 16.6**, Lexis Advance would retrieve the bill that could amend the California statute that you just Shepardized. Again, read all authority that could negatively impact your statute.

In sum, both KeyCite and Shepard's reports display the following information on the validity of a statute, if applicable:

- Cases that have negatively impacted the validity of the current or prior version of your statute;

- Pending legislative bills that may negatively affect your statute; and

- Enacted laws that have repealed your statute in whole or part.

2. Check the Effective Date for Each Relevant Statute, and Review the Text of Amendments

The next step is to check the **effective dates** of applicable statutes and to review **relevant amendments**. Specifically, you should check the effective date of each potentially relevant statute, determine whether any relevant statute has been amended, and identify and review the language of each relevant amendment.

After a legislative bill becomes law and is codified in a federal or state code, the text of the statute does not always remain static. Indeed, Congress or a state legislature may enact new laws that amend and change the language of existing codified statutes. Amendments may expand or limit existing statutes. For instance, the Georgia General Assembly enacted the Gift Card Integrity Act, which amended section 10-1-393 of the *Official Code of Georgia Annotated*. The amending Act expanded that code section, making certain practices related to gift cards to be unlawful. If your client was sued

---

Date of Enactment vs. Effective Date

The date on which a legislative bill becomes law is its date of enactment, but the date that a law becomes enforceable is its effective date. The two dates are often different. For instance, Congress enacted the Americans with Disabilities Act in 1990 (date of enactment), but some prohibitions and requirements did not take effect until two years later (effective date).

---

for a practice related to gift cards, you must determine the amendment's effective date to ultimately decide whether the amendment is enforceable against your client.

a. Editorial Summaries

One quick method to identify a statute's **effective date** and the **text of an amendment** is to review the editorial summaries on Lexis Advance and Westlaw. In these summaries, the publisher or compiler of a code expressly states when each statute and amendment took effect or will take effect. These summaries also provide a short description of what each amendment added to, or deleted from, a code section (statute).[5]

The editorial summaries are easy to locate. After retrieving a statute on Lexis Advance, scroll to the end of the statutory text and look under the heading "Notes" or "Commentary." On Westlaw, while viewing a statute, click the "History" tab near the top of the document, and then select "Editor's and Revisor's Notes."

Review the editorial summaries from Lexis and Westlaw in **Figures 16.7** and **16.8**, respectively. These summaries identify the following information on effective dates and amendments for an Alabama statute (Ala. Code § 13A-11-231) defining service and therapy dogs:

- This code section (statute) became effective on July 1, 2016;

- The amendment to this code section became effective on August 1, 2017; and

- The amendment added one sentence to existing subsection (4), added a new subsection (5), and renumbered the original subsection (5) as (6).

The information on effective dates and amendments is important. For example, if your client's conduct occurred in 2018, then you know the version of the dog service statute on your Lexis Advance or Westlaw screen would be the exact version that was in effect at all relevant times.

---

5. Editorial summaries, however, do not always contain information on effective dates and amendments.

Figure 16.7: Editorial Summary on Lexis Advance for Ala. Code § 13A-11-231

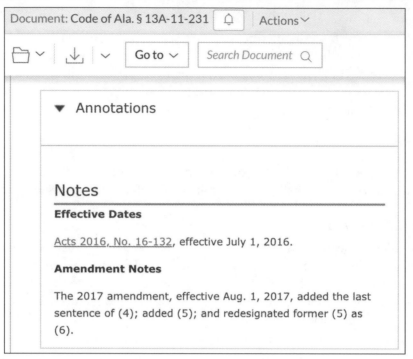

Figure 16.8: Editorial Summary on Westlaw for Ala. Code § 13A-11-231

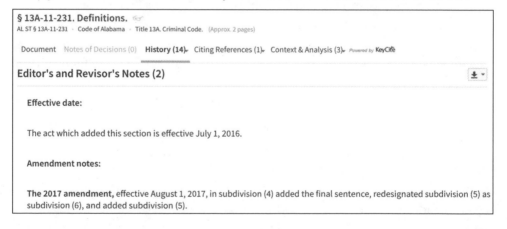

b. History Notes or Credits

When the editorial summaries do not provide the necessary information on **effective dates** and **amendments**, you have another option: review the **history notes** or **source credits** that accompany a section of a code. These notes or credits appear after the text of each code section. On Lexis Advance, they are under the heading "History"; on Westlaw, they are under the heading "Credits."

When the history notes or credits identify the effective date of a code section, the date should be indicated with the abbreviation "eff." To illustrate, the traffic law shown in **Figure 16.9** became effective on May 29, 2003.

Figure 16.9: Source Credits on Westlaw for Ga. Code Ann. § 40-6-320

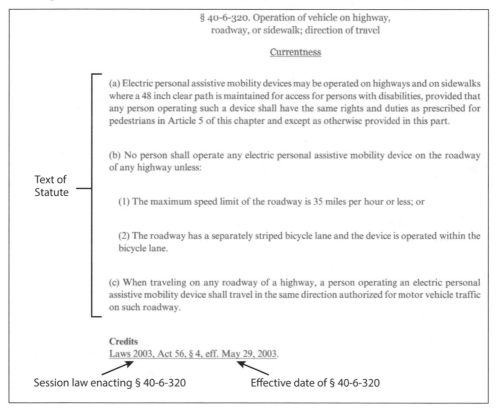

Unfortunately, the history notes on Lexis and the credits on Westlaw do not always include effective dates. Sometimes, they provide only the date of enactment for the original statute and subsequent amendments. If a date in the history notes or credits is not accompanied by "eff." or "effective," the listed date may reflect just the date of enactment. The history notes for the federal statute in **Figure 16.10** identify the date of enactment (July 26, 1990) for the original statute but not its effective date.

Through the history notes or credits, you can also find the **language of each amendment.** They often provide hyperlinked citations to the public laws or session laws that enacted or amended the code section.[6] Both Lexis Advance and Westlaw provide

---

6. Recall that Chapter 4 explains public laws and sessions laws. In short, every law Congress approves is assigned a public law number in the order of passage. As to state legislatures, all the enacted laws for a particular session are compiled and arranged in chronological order based on the date of enactment. These laws are known as session laws.

Figure 16.10: History Notes on Lexis Advance for 42 U.S.C.S. § 12112

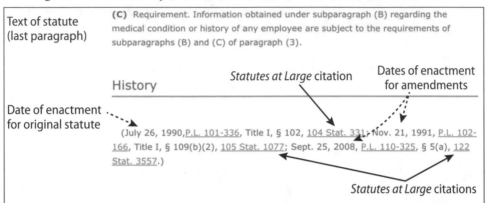

the full text of many public laws and session laws. To compare the language of the current statute that you are viewing on your screen to a prior version, you would click on the hyperlinked citation in the history notes or credits. For many amendments (but not all), both research services will visually depict what language an amendment added or deleted. The additions may be highlighted in color, and the deleted text may contain a strike-through.

Returning to the Alabama statute on service dogs (Ala. Code § 13A-11-231), suppose you need to review the language of the session law enacting the 2017 amendment. To display the full text of that session law (Alabama Laws Act No. 2017-412), you would retrieve the statute on Lexis or Westlaw, scroll down to the history notes or credits, and click "Acts 2017, No. 17-412" on Lexis or click "Act 2017-412" on Westlaw. See **Figures 16.11** and **16.12**. The language added to subsections (4) and (5) is highlighted in green on Lexis and in blue on Westlaw. See **Figures 16.13** and **16.14**.

Figure 16.11: History Notes on Lexis Advance for Ala. Code § 13A-11-231

(5) THERAPY DOG. A trained emotional support dog that has been tested and registered by a nonprofit national therapy dog organization that sets standards and requirements for the health, welfare, task work, and oversight of therapy dogs and their handlers. The term therapy dog includes a dog trained to visit and provide emotional support to children, the sick and disabled, the aged, and victims in the court system. A registered therapy dog is trained for public access to facilities including, but not limited to, libraries, nursing homes, hospitals, schools, hospice, courthouse facilities, funeral homes, disaster areas, and homes where visits are needed to aid in health care and emotional support. A registered therapy dog is covered under this article from the time the dog leaves its home until the time it returns while in the performance of its duties as defined herein. The handler of a registered therapy dog shall be a member in good standing of a national therapy dog organization and be clearly identified with an organization and have authorized credentials.

(6) VALUE. The value of the service dog to the service dog user as demonstrated by any of the following elements:

    a. Cost of the service dog.

    b. Replacement and training or retraining expenses for the service dog and the user.

    c. Veterinary and other medical and boarding expenses for the service dog during a period of treatment for injury.

    d. Lost wages or income incurred by the service dog user during any period the user is without the services of the service dog.

    e. Any additional expenses incurred by the service dog user directly because of the loss of the use of the service dog.

History

Acts 2016, No. 16-132, § 2, July 1, 2016; Acts 2017, No. 17-412, § 1, Aug. 1, 2017.

Figure 16.12: Credits on Westlaw for Ala. Code § 13A-11-231

(5) THERAPY DOG. A trained emotional support dog that has been tested and registered by a nonprofit national therapy dog organization that sets standards and requirements for the health, welfare, task work, and oversight of therapy dogs and their handlers. The term therapy dog includes a dog trained to visit and provide emotional support to children, the sick and disabled, the aged, and victims in the court system. A registered therapy dog is trained for public access in facilities including, but not limited to, libraries, nursing homes, hospitals, schools, hospice, courthouse facilities, funeral homes, disaster areas, and homes where visits are needed to aid in health care and emotional support. A registered therapy dog is covered under this article from the time the dog leaves its home until the time it returns while in the performance of its duties as defined herein. The handler of a registered therapy dog shall be a member in good standing of a national therapy dog organization and be clearly identified with an organization and have authorized credentials.

(6) VALUE. The value of the service dog to the service dog user as demonstrated by any of the following elements:

a. Cost of the service dog.

b. Replacement and training or retraining expenses for the service dog and the user.

c. Veterinary and other medical and boarding expenses for the service dog during a period of treatment for injury.

d. Lost wages or income incurred by the service dog user during any period the user is without the services of the service dog.

e. Any additional expenses incurred by the service dog user directly because of the loss of the use of the service dog.

Credits

(Act 2016-132, p. 312, § 2; Act 2017-412, § 1.)

Figure 16.13: Depiction on Lexis Advance of Language Added to Ala. Code § 13A-11-231 by a 2017 Session Law

Text

BE IT ENACTED BY THE LEGISLATURE OF ALABAMA:

(Next) **Section 1.** Section 2 of Act 2016-132 of the 2016 Regular Session, now appearing as Section 13A-11-231 of the Code of Alabama 1975, is amended to read as follows:

§ 13A-11-231.

For the purposes of this article, the following terms have the following meanings:

"**(1) HARASS.** To engage in any conduct directed toward a service dog or handler that is likely to impede or interfere with the performance of a service dog in its duties or places the health and safety of the service dog or its handler in jeopardy. Such conduct includes actions which distract, obstruct, or intimidate the service dog, such as taunting, teasing, or striking.

"**(2) INJURY.** Physical or emotional injury to the service dog.

"**(3) NOTICE.** An actual verbal or other communication warning that the behavior of the person or the dog of the person is harassing toward the performance of a service dog in its duty or endangering the health and safety of the service dog.

"**(4) SERVICE DOG.** A dog that has been individually trained for the purpose of assisting or accommodating a physician-diagnosed physical or mental disability or medical condition of a person as that term is used in the federal Americans with Disabilities Act. Service dogs include, but are not limited to, guide or leader dogs for persons who are blind; dogs that assist persons with physical disabilities by providing balance support, pulling a wheelchair, or performing other tasks; dogs that provide hearing assistance by alerting individuals who are deaf to specific sounds; and dogs who alert persons to an impending potential medical crisis. The term includes a therapy dog.

"**(5) THERAPY DOG.** A trained emotional support dog that has been tested and registered by a nonprofit national therapy dog organization that sets standards and requirements for the health, welfare, task work, and oversight of therapy dogs and their handlers. The term therapy dog includes a dog trained to visit and provide emotional support to children, the sick and disabled, the aged, and victims in the court system. A registered therapy dog is trained for public access in facilities including, but not limited to, libraries, nursing homes, hospitals, schools, hospice, courthouse facilities, funeral homes, disaster areas, and homes where visits are needed to aid in health care and emotional support. A registered therapy dog is covered under this article from the time the dog leaves its home until the time it returns while in the performance of its duties as defined herein. The handler of a registered therapy dog shall be a member in good standing of a national therapy dog organization and be clearly identified with an organization and have authorized credentials.

Figure 16.14: Depiction on Westlaw of Language Added to Ala. Code § 13A-11-231 by a 2017 Session Law

BE IT ENACTED BY THE LEGISLATURE OF ALABAMA:

Section 1. Section 2 of Act 2016–132 of the 2016 Regular Session, now appearing as Section 13A–11–231 of the Code of Alabama 1975, is amended to read as follows:

<< AL ST § 13A–11–231 >>

"§ 13A–11–231.

"For the purposes of this article, the following terms have the following meanings:

"(1) HARASS. To engage in any conduct directed toward a service dog or handler that is likely to impede or interfere with the performance of a service dog in its duties or places the health and safety of the service dog or its handler in jeopardy. Such conduct includes actions which distract, obstruct, or intimidate the service dog, such as taunting, teasing, or striking.

"(2) INJURY. Physical or emotional injury to the service dog.

"(3) NOTICE. An actual verbal or other communication warning that the behavior of the person or the dog of the person is harassing toward the performance of a service dog in its duty or endangering the health and safety of the service dog.

"(4) SERVICE DOG. A dog that has been individually trained for the purpose of assisting or accommodating a physician-diagnosed physical or mental disability or medical condition of a person as that term is used in the federal Americans with Disabilities Act. Service dogs include, but are not limited to, guide or leader dogs for persons who are blind; dogs that assist persons with physical disabilities by providing balance support, pulling a wheelchair, or performing other tasks; dogs that provide hearing assistance by alerting individuals who are deaf to specific sounds; and dogs who alert persons to an impending potential medical crisis. The term includes a therapy dog.

"(5) THERAPY DOG. A trained emotional support dog that has been tested and registered by a nonprofit national therapy dog organization that sets standards and requirements for the health, welfare, task work, and oversight of therapy dogs and their handlers. The term therapy dog includes a dog trained to visit and provide emotional support to children, the sick and disabled, the aged, and victims in the court system. A registered therapy dog is trained for public access in facilities including, but not limited to, libraries, nursing homes, hospitals, schools, hospice, courthouse facilities, funeral homes, disaster areas, and homes where visits are needed to aid in health care and emotional support. A registered therapy dog is covered under this article from the time the dog leaves its home until the time it returns while in the performance of its duties as defined herein. The handler of a registered therapy dog shall be a member in good standing of a national therapy dog organization and be clearly identified with an organization and have authorized credentials.

Westlaw Edge has a new feature, **Statutes Compare**, that simplifies the process to identify language of amendments. While viewing a statute, click the "Compare Versions" button near the top of the screen or click the "History" tab and then select "Versions" (see **Figure 16.15**). Westlaw Edge will then depict how the text of a statute has changed by highlighting added language and showing deleted text with strikethroughs. Statutes Compare, however, is not available for all amendments in all state codes (at least not currently).

With this feature on Westlaw Edge, you are not limited to comparing a current version with a prior one; you can compare any two versions of a statute. For example, imagine a relevant statute was amended three times: once in 2015, once in 2016, and once in 2018. You can compare the original statute with the 2015 amendment or compare the changes between the 2015 and 2016 amendments.

Figure 16.15: Statute Compare Feature on Westlaw Edge

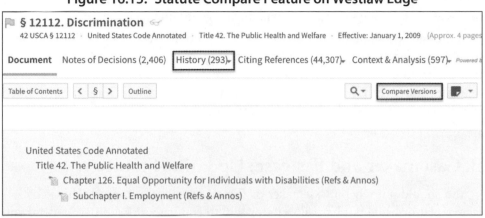

3. Check the Currency of the Online Code

Last, you should check whether any new laws have been enacted since the last time the code on Westlaw or Lexis Advance has been updated. In other words, you should look for public laws and session laws that have not yet been codified but could apply to your client's legal question.[7] Although the codes on both research services are frequently updated,[8] newly-enacted laws are not incorporated into a code immediately. After a bill has been approved, it may take weeks—or even months—to be incorporated into a code.

Each federal and state code on Westlaw and Lexis Advance provides currency information. On Westlaw, scroll to the end of the statutory text; on Lexis Advance, you need to look immediately above the statutory text for currency information.

For federal statutes, the online database identifies the last public law number that has been codified. For instance, Westlaw or Lexis may state the code is "current through P.L. 115-223," which means the code includes the 223rd law enacted in the 115th Congress. Any public law passed after the 223rd law would be excluded from the code. Thus, you should determine whether any subsequent public law (*e.g.*, Pub. L. No. 115-225) applies to your client's situation. You can quickly do that by visiting Congress.gov. This website lists all public laws passed by the current Congress and provides the actual text of each law. You should scan the list and read any public law that appears relevant.

For state codes, the terminology for currency information depends on a few factors, such as the name of a state legislature and how a state numbers its session laws. The databases on Westlaw and Lexis Advance may provide that the code is current through "the 2018 legislative session," "the 110th General Assembly," or "Act 2018-579." To locate any session law enacted since the code was last updated, you can visit

---

7. In most situations, KeyCite and Shepard's identify an uncodified law that affects your statute.

8. The most current code for federal statutes is on the website of the Office of the Law Revision Counsel of the House of Representatives. It is available to the public at http://uscode.house.gov.

a government website for the controlling jurisdiction. Often, session laws are available on the website of the secretary of state for the governing jurisdiction.

Although you should check the currency of an online code, you will rarely need to find an enacted law that has not been included in a federal or state code. Substantially all statutes apply prospectively, not retroactively—meaning, a statute rarely regulates conduct that occurred *before* its date of enactment. Thus, an uncodified statute usually does not apply to your client's previous conduct.[9]

B. Casemaker and Fastcase: Updating Statutes

You should not rely on Casemaker or Fastcase to update statutes. These cost-effective platforms do not have any citator tool to confirm the validity of federal and state *statutes*; their citators (CaseCheck+ and Bad Law Bot) show negative subsequent treatment only for *cases*. Casemaker and Fastcase do not "tag" statutes with any negative treatment signal, even if a statute is no longer good law. Thus, you would have to read—or at least skim—every case that cites a controlling statute to determine whether a court has struck down the statute as unconstitutional or on other grounds. Further, checking the effective dates of statutes may be difficult. Although the history notes on Casemaker and Fastcase sometimes include effective dates, their online codes do not contain editorial summaries.

Instead of relying on a cost-effective platform, you should update statutes using Westlaw or Lexis Advance. Keep in mind that a county law library or court library in your area may provide public access to either fee-based service.

C. Print Code: Updating Statutes

Updating statutes in print is more complicated and prone to errors than updating them on Lexis Advance or Westlaw. Thus, when possible, you should update statutes online, not in print. (That advice may bring you great joy.) This section provides a basic overview of the updating process in print. If updating statutes in print is necessary, seek help from a friendly law librarian.

The first step for updating federal and state statutes in print is to confirm the validity of each relevant statute. You should check each statute's validity with an annotated code for your jurisdiction, such as one published by Thomson Reuters or LexisNexis. You need to determine whether your statutes have been repealed in whole or in part by subsequent legislation. For example, assume you consulted the main volume of the annotated code for your jurisdiction and found a statute holding land-

---

9. Sometimes, however, a newly-enacted law applies retroactively. For instance, a statute that reduces prison sentences or penalties may apply retroactively to prior crimes. In addition, you would need to find new laws when advising a client on actions it plans to take in the future.

Updating Statutes with Citators

In the commentary or notes part of an annotated code in print, the publisher or compiler of the code may not cite a case that has invalidated a statute in whole or part. But you are not "up the creek without a paddle." You already know the solution to that predicament: KeyCite or Shepard's. Those citators will identify all cases that have negatively impacted the validity of your statute. Use them.

---

lords liable for injuries caused by their tenants' dogs. If the main volume was published in 2015 but your state legislature repealed the dog-bite statute in 2018, the repeal would not be reflected in that volume.

To locate newly-enacted statutes and amendments, you should consult the pocket parts (or supplements) for the annotated code. Pocket parts are inserted into the back of a hardbound volume of a code set, covering the period between the publication date of the volume and the pocket part. Each pocket part updates only the volume where it is found. Thus, if relevant statutes are codified in two different hardbound volumes, you need to check the pocket parts in both volumes.[10]

Next, you need to update the pocket parts. For many annotated codes, pocket parts are issued annually, so new laws may have been enacted since the publication date of a pocket part. (The publication date is listed on its cover.) For laws enacted during that period, you should look for any separate, softbound supplement that may be shelved next to the volume it updates or located at the end of the annotated code set. These supplements may include interim pamphlets and pamphlets known as an "advance legislative service." These supplements will inform you of any newly-enacted laws that affect your statute. You may need to consult more than one supplement.

In addition to consulting pocket parts and other supplements, you should check the validity of a statute by reviewing any commentary or notes by the publisher or compiler of the print code. This commentary would be located after the text of each statute you found in a hardbound volume or pocket part. The commentary may identify judicial decisions that have ruled the statute unconstitutional or preempted by federal law. If so, read the cited cases carefully to determine their applicability to your client's situation.

After updating each statute, you need to check the effective dates of each statute and amendment. As with online codes, you will locate this information in the history notes and in the commentary or notes part of a print code. The history notes, like

---

10. When pocket parts become too large, the publisher will issue a softbound supplement that should be shelved next to the hardbound volume it updates.

the commentary, appear after the text of each codified statute. These notes identify the date of enactment for the original statute and every amendment (if any) and provide citations to the public laws or session laws that enacted the codified statute. The commentary usually identifies when each statute and amendment became effective and enforceable.

D. Summary of Key Points

For every statute that applies or could apply to your client's situation, you should complete this **Step 4**. This step involves several parts. You must update all relevant statutes. To update, you should check the validity of each relevant statute, as well as checking the effective date of each statute and amendment and determining the currency of a code. Updating statutes should be done on Lexis Advance or Westlaw and not in print. And if any statute has been amended, you should review the language of the amendment to determine which words have been added or deleted.

Figure 16.16 summarizes the process for completing the various parts of this **Step 4** on Lexis Advance and Westlaw, and it identifies the important information that each part reveals.

E. Review Questions on Updating Statutes

At this point, you should know how to update relevant statutes. To test your comprehension, answer the true-false and multiple-choice questions on this book's companion website, Core Knowledge. It will identify the correct answers and provide clear explanations for each question. The same questions are reproduced below.

1. If a statute and state supreme court decision directly conflict, the statute would control.

    a. True

    b. False

2. The date on which a legislative bill becomes law is always its effective date.

    a. True

    b. False

3. The date on which a law becomes enforceable is its date of enactment.

    a. True

    b. False

4. A statutory code on Lexis Advance or Westlaw may not include a newly-enacted law.

    a. True

    b. False

Figure 16.16: Step 4 of the Research Process in a Nutshell

Action	Importance of Action	Process on Lexis Advance and Westlaw
1. Check validity of each relevant statute.	Determine whether • a legislature has repealed a relevant statute in whole or part; and • a court has declared a relevant statute to be preempted or unconstitutional in whole or part.	Look for a negative treatment signal next to the code section. On Shepard's (Lexis Advance), look for a red exclamation point, orange Q, or a yellow triangle. On KeyCite (Westlaw), look for a red or yellow flag.
2. Check effective date of each relevant statute and amendment.	Determine whether • any relevant statute or amendment became effective before or after the conduct or transaction in dispute occurred; and • the original statute or amended version applies to the client's situation.	1. Review the history notes or source credits after the text of each code section (statute). On Lexis Advance, after the statutory text, look under the heading "History." On Westlaw, after the statutory text, look under the heading "Credits."
		2. Review the editorial summaries for each code section. On Lexis Advance, after the statutory text, look under the heading "Notes" or "Commentary." On Westlaw, after retrieving a statute, click the "History" tab and then select "Editor's and Revisor's Notes."
3. Review the language of each amendment to a relevant statute.	Determine whether • any amendment applies to your client's situation; and • the cases you have found are interpreting the original statute or amended version.	1. Review the editorial summaries for each code section.
		2. Compare the current statute to a prior version. Locate the history notes on Lexis Advance or the source credits on Westlaw, and click on the public law or session law that is hyperlinked. On Westlaw, while viewing a statute, click the "Compare Versions" button.
4. Check the currency of a code.	Determine whether any new laws have been enacted since the code has been updated.	Review the currency information above the statutory text (Lexis Advance) or after the statutory text (Westlaw).

5. One method to identify the language of an amendment is to review the editorial summaries for a code section.

   a. True

   b. False

6. A court may invalidate a state statute in which of the following ways?

   a. A court could hold that the statute was preempted in whole or part by federal law.

   b. A court could declare the statute unconstitutional in whole or part.

   c. A court could amend the language of the statute.

   d. Both A and B.

7. Congress or a state legislature may invalidate a statute in which of the following ways?

   a. A legislature could repeal the entire statute.

   b. A legislature could amend the statute, repealing only part of it.

   c. A legislature could declare the statute to be unconstitutional.

   d. Both A and B.

8. Julie found a statute favoring her client, but Shepard's has tagged the statute with a red exclamation point. Should Julie develop an argument for her client based on the statute?

   a. No, because the statute is no longer valid for all aspects of the client's situation.

   b. Yes, because Julie should ignore negative treatment signals.

   c. It depends. The statute may still be valid as to one aspect of her client's situation.

   d. None of the above.

F. Practice Updating Statutes

On this book's companion website, Core Knowledge, a few research assignments have been posted. The online assignments walk you through the steps for researching a statutory issue on Westlaw and Lexis Advance, including validating statutes and checking their effective dates. For each assignment, you will research the law to resolve legal issues for your hypothetical client.

Step 1
(Research
Plan)

Step 2
(Secondary
Sources)

Step 3
(Find
Statutes)

Step 4
(Update
Statutes)

Step 5
(Read
Statutes)

Step 6
(Find
Regulations)

Step 7
(Find Cases)

Step 8
(Legislative
History)

Step 9
(Other States)

Step 10
(Validation)

Chapter 17

Step 5:
Read All Relevant Statutes
Critically

You are almost ready to start diving into researching cases that interpret and apply relevant statutes. But you are not there yet. By completing the prior **Step 4**, you should know whether each relevant statute remains valid. You should also know the effective date of each statute and any amendment, as well as what language was changed by an amendment.

At this **Step 5,** you should critically analyze the words of each statute that applies or could apply to your client's situation. Of course, during the process of finding relevant statutes, you should have at least skimmed them to determine whether they apply—if at all—to your client's situation. For this **Step 5**, however, you must pause researching and carefully read each statute at the macro- and micro-levels. For each relevant statute, you need to consider (1) the full context, and (2) the plain meaning of the words as written.[1]

A. Consider a Statute's Context

You first need to get **context** for each statute you have identified as potentially relevant. The table of contents of a code provides important context. It helps you understand how your statute fits into the larger statutory scheme.

Recall that legislatures often approve bills containing multiple laws related to the same subject matter. These related statutes are collectively known as a statutory scheme (or act) and are usually codified together in a code. The Ohio legislature, for example, has enacted a statutory scheme (the Ohio Consumer Sales Practices Act) to protect consumers against unlawful sales practices, such

---

1. A full discussion of statutory interpretation is outside the scope of this book. For an excellent discussion of statutory analysis, review the book by Christine Coughlin, Joan Malmud Rocklin & Sandy Patrick, *A Lawyer Writers: A Practical Guide to Legal Analysis* 35–43, 193–209 (3d ed. 2018). This chapter is based in substantial part on that legal writing book.

as deceptive advertising. As part of this statutory scheme, there are eighteen separate statutes that are codified together under the same chapter of the *Ohio Revised Code*.[2]

Suppose you have found one statute, Ohio Rev. Code § 1345.02, comprising part of the Ohio Consumer Sales Practices Act, and it prohibits "suppliers" from engaging in unfair or deceptive practices involving a "consumer transaction." By browsing the table of contents and viewing the code section that appears before your statute, you would see section 1345.01 with the heading "definitions" (see **Figure 17.1**). If you reviewed those statutory definitions, you would find definitions for "supplier" and "consumer transaction." These definitions will assist you in determining whether the prohibition against unfair or deceptive practices applies to your client. Additionally, skimming the table of contents would alert you to other related statutes. As shown in **Figure 17.1**, they include

- a code section prohibiting unconscionable practices (§ 1345.03),
- a separate section setting forth remedies to injured consumers (§ 1345.09), and
- a separate section limiting damages for consumers who reject a supplier's attempt to cure a violation (§ 1345.092).

In short, a code's table of contents provides you with important context.

Figure 17.1: Excerpt of Table of Contents from *Ohio Revised Code Annotated*

1345.01 Definitions

1345.02 Unfair or Deceptive Acts or Practices

1345.021 Disclosure of Ethanol Content of Gasoline Not Required

1345.03 Unconscionable Acts or Practices

1345.031 Residential Mortgages

1345.032 Solicitation of Certain Deeds

1345.04 Jurisdiction of Common Pleas, Municipal and County Courts

1345.05 Duties and Powers of Attorney General; Petition for Adoption, Amendment, or Repeal of Rules

1345.06 Investigations; Powers of Attorney General

1345.07 Action for Declaratory Judgment or Injunction by Attorney General; Appointment of Master or Receiver; Limitation of Action; Termination of Enforcement Proceedings; Civil Penalty

1345.08 Complaints as to Suppliers Subject to Other Administrative Supervision

1345.09 Consumer's Relief; Intervention by Attorney General; Attorney's Fee

1345.091 Claims Against Mortgage Loan Purchasers or Assignees

1345.092 Cure Offers

1345.10 Final Judgment as Prima-Facie Evidence; Consumer Precluded from Later Class Action; Limitation of Action

1345.11 Limitations on Liabilities; Appointment of Receiver; Effect of Violations on Licenses

1345.12 Application of Laws

1345.13 Effect on Other Remedies

---

2. *See* Ohio Rev. Code Ann. §§ 1345.01–.13 (West, Westlaw through File 105 of the 132nd General Assemb.).

Figure 17.2: Excerpt from Ohio Rev. Code § 1345.02

(A) No supplier shall commit an unfair or deceptive act or practice in connection with a consumer transaction. Such an unfair or deceptive act or practice by a supplier violates this section whether it occurs before, during, or after the transaction.

(B) Without limiting the scope of division (A) of this section, the act or practice of a supplier in representing any of the following is deceptive:

(1) That the subject of a consumer transaction has sponsorship, approval, performance characteristics, accessories, uses, or benefits that it does not have;

…

(10) That a consumer transaction involves or does not involve a warranty, a disclaimer of warranties or other rights, remedies, or obligations if the representation is false.

Further, you should get context by reading the entire statute. Do not stop reading your statute after locating just one relevant sub-section. Review the excerpt of the Ohio statute in **Figure 17.2**. Sub-section (A) sets forth the general rule prohibiting a supplier from committing "an unfair or deceptive act or practice." If you stopped at that sub-section, however, you would have missed the list of deceptive acts and practices in sub-section (B). Additionally, when reading a statute, consider how the sub-sections are tabulated. The tabulation of the statute in **Figure 17.2** makes clear that all ten examples under sub-section (B), which are indented and numbered (1) through (10), are considered to be "deceptive" acts or practices.

B. Examine a Statute's Plain Meaning

After consider context, you should analyze each statute's **plain meaning**.[3] This means to read the words and phrases as written and give them their ordinary meaning. Indeed, the United States Supreme Court and the state supreme courts agree that the starting point for determining legislative intent is the actual text of a statute.[4]

---

3. Most of the discussion on a statute's plain meaning is based on Coughlin, Rocklin & Patrick, *supra* note 1, at 35–43, 193–209.

4. *See, e.g., Lamie v. U.S. Tr.*, 540 U.S. 526, 527 (2004) (explaining that the "starting point in discerning congressional intent is the existing statutory text"); *People v. Scott*, 324 P.3d 827, 829 (Cal. 2014) ("We begin by examining the statute's words, giving them a plain and commonsense meaning."); *People v. Pabon*, 65 N.E.3d 688, 691 (N.Y. 2016) ("It is well established that since the clearest indicator of legislative intent is the statutory text, the starting point in any case of interpretation must always be the language itself, giving effect to the plain meaning thereof.").

A careful reading of each relevant statute will reveal important information, including the following:

- Who or what is covered by the statute (*e.g.*, landlord, employer, consumer, retailer, companion animals);

- The type of conduct prohibited, required, or authorized (*e.g.*, false advertising);

- Whether conduct must occur at a certain location or situation for the statute to apply (*e.g.*, homeowner's property, federal land);

- Existence of elements, factors, or both; and

- Criminal penalties or civil remedies for a violation.

In addition, when analyzing a statute's plain meaning, you must pay attention to punctuation marks and find all the "red flag" words. The red flag words restrict or expand the reach of a statute and include the words "and," "or," "shall," "must," and similar words. You must carefully look for these words. **Figure 17.3** lists common red flag words and their meanings. The list is not exhaustive.

Figure 17.3: Red Flag Words*

Red Flag Words	Common Meanings
And	Requires all elements that it joins to be present for a standard to be met, or requires all factors that it joins to be considered.
Or Either	Only one of the elements it joins must be present for a standard to be met, or only one of the factors that it joins must be considered.
Unless Except If ... then	Creates an exception to the standard.
Shall Must	Requires conduct.
Shall not May not Must not	Prohibits conduct.
Provided that	Creates a condition, an exception, or adds an additional requirement.

* Figure 17.3 has been taken in substantial part from Coughlin, Rocklin & Patrick, *supra* note 1, at 42, and reproduced with permission of the authors.

Figure 17.4: Excerpt from Ala. Code § 13A-7-41

(a) A person commits the crime of arson in the first degree if he intentionally damages a building by starting **or** maintaining a fire **or** causing an explosion, **and** when:
   (1) Another person is present in such building at the time, **and**
   (2) The actor knows that fact, **or** the circumstances are such as to render the presence of a person therein a reasonable possibility.

Figure 17.5: Diagram of Section 13A-7-41

A person commits the crime of arson in the first degree if he intentionally damages a building by
   starting or maintaining
   a fire or causing an explosion
   and when
      (1) Another person is present in such building at the time,
      and
      (2) The actor knows
         that fact
         or
         the circumstances are such as to render the presence of a person therein
         a reasonable possibility.

Once the red flags have been identified, you can diagram the statute for a deeper understanding. Review the arson statute in **Figure 17.4** where the red flag words are in bold font. This statute's requirements are visually depicted in **Figure 17.5**.

C. Summary of Key Points

Every word of an applicable statute matters to your client's situation. Courts must follow statutory language and cannot amend or disregard language they dislike. Thus, at this **Step 5**, you must read each potentially relevant statute critically.

Initially, you should read a statute in light of its context. Review the table of contents to locate surrounding, related statutes. While viewing a statute, you should also consider its tabulation. For instance, if a statute has two sub-subsections indented and placed underneath a sub-section (A), the two sub-subsections are related to sub-section (A).

To read a statute carefully, you must also analyze its plain meaning. This means to read a statute at the sentence and word levels. You should have a laser-like focus on punctuation marks and all red flag words. If a statute sets forth four requirements and joins them with an "and," all four are necessary to prove a violation. But if those requirements were joined with an "or," proof of any one requirement would prove a violation.

After you have a good understanding of the meaning of each statute, you are ready for the next step: researching and analyzing cases that interpret and apply relevant statutes.

D. Review Questions on Reading Statutes

At this point, you should have a basic understanding of reading statutes carefully. To test your comprehension, answer the true-false and multiple-choice questions on this book's companion website, Core Knowledge. It will identify the correct answers and provide clear explanations for each question. The same questions are reproduced below.

1. At Step 5 of the process for researching a statutory issue, you should read potentially relevant statutes critically.

   a. True

   b. False

2. Browsing a table of contents and viewing the code sections that appear before and after a relevant statute provide important context.

   a. True

   b. False

3. When reading a statute, you should ignore how the sub-sections are tabulated.

   a. True

   b. False

4. A careful reading of a statute reveals what information?

   a. Who or what is covered by the statute

   b. What conduct is prohibited or required

   c. Existence of elements, factors, or both

   d. All of the above

5. Identify common red flag words contained in statutes.

   a. Shall

   b. May

   c. Except

   d. All of the above

E. Practice Reading Statutes

On this book's companion website, Core Knowledge, a few research assignments have been posted. The online assignments walk you through the steps for researching a statutory issue on Westlaw and Lexis Advance, including reading statutes critically. For each assignment, you will research the law to resolve legal issues for your hypothetical client.

Step 1
(Research Plan)

Step 2
(Secondary Sources)

Step 3
(Find Statutes)

Step 4
(Update Statutes)

Step 5
(Read Statutes)

Step 6
(Find Regulations)

Step 7
(Find Cases)

Step 8
(Legislative History)

Step 9
(Other States)

Step 10
(Validation)

Chapter 18

Step 6: Research and Update Administrative Regulations, and Find Cases That Have Interpreted Them

In addition to researching statutes, you need to research administrative rules and regulations at this **Step 6**. Federal and state agencies may adopt rules that govern individuals and entities. When a regulation has been adopted through the formal rulemaking process, it has the same force of law as a statute, making it binding on courts. Thus, you should look for applicable regulations in the controlling jurisdiction before spending hours researching cases. You should then determine whether each relevant regulation is still good law. Last, you should research cases that interpret pertinent statutes and regulations.

A. Federal Regulations: Overview and Forms of Publication

Administrative law is an area of law that encompasses rules and regulations from the executive branch. As discussed in Chapter 1, the executive branch includes many federal administrative agencies, such as the Department of Transportation (DOT), Internal Revenue Service (IRS), and Food and Drug Administration (FDA). These agencies promulgate and adopt laws called **rules** and **regulations**.[1] These regulations tend to be more detailed than statutes. For example, the FDA adopted this regulation on food labeling: "Ingredients required to be declared on the label or labeling of a food ... shall be listed by common or usual name in descending order of predominance by weight on either the principal display panel or the information panel."[2]

To adopt regulations that are enforceable, the agency must have the legal authority to do so. Congress or the President may delegate rulemaking authority to an administrative agency. A federal agency often adopts regulations based on

---

1. "Regulation and rule have the same meaning." 1 C.F.R. § 1.1 (2018).
2. 21 C.F.R. § 101.4.

a federal statute, which is known as an "enabling statute" or "authorizing statute." Every regulation adopted under the authority of an enabling statute is enforceable against state or local governments, individuals, and businesses.

Even when an agency has been delegated authority to adopt rules and regulations, the agency cannot adopt a regulation and make it effective immediately. The agency must comply with the Administrative Procedure Act,[3] as discussed next.

1. Federal Register

Under the Administrative Procedure Act, every proposed regulation and rule must be published and made available for public comments. Any person or business may submit comments in support of or against the proposed rule, and they may suggest changes. The issuing agency must consider the comments, but is not required to follow them. After providing time for public comments, the agency may approve the rule as proposed, amend it, or reject it entirely.

Figure 18.1: Excerpt from Page 32221 of Volume 83 of the *Federal Register*

83 FR 32221-01, 2018 WL 3377360(F.R.)
PROPOSED RULES
DEPARTMENT OF HEALTH AND HUMAN SERVICES
Food and Drug Administration
21 CFR Part 101
[Docket No. FDA-2011-F-0171]
RIN 0910-AH83

Food Labeling: Calorie Labeling of Articles of Food Sold
From Certain Vending Machines; Front of Package Type Size

Thursday, July 12, 2018

AGENCY: Food and Drug Administration, HHS.

*32221 ACTION: Proposed rule.

SUMMARY: The Food and Drug Administration (FDA, the Agency, or we) proposes to revise the type size labeling requirements for front of package (FOP) calorie declarations for packaged food sold from glass front vending machines. We are taking this action in response to requests from the vending and packaged foods industries to reduce the regulatory burden and increase flexibility, while continuing to provide calorie declarations for certain articles of food sold from vending machines.

DATES: Submit either electronic or written comments on the proposed rule by September 25, 2018. Please note that late, untimely filed comments will not be considered.

---

3. 5 U.S.C. § 500 *et seq.*

The text of each proposed rule and each final rule must be published in the *Federal Register*. Publication in this official source is necessary to make a rule and regulation legally binding. (The *Federal Register* also publishes notices of federal agencies and executive orders.) The *Federal Register* is issued daily, Monday through Friday, and is available at www.govinfo.gov, where it is updated each weekday. **Figure 18.1** shows a proposed rule in the *Federal Register*.

2. Code of Federal Regulations

After a final regulation has been adopted and published in the *Federal Register*, it is published in the *Code of Federal Regulations* (C.F.R.). The C.F.R. contains all regulations of federal agencies and departments that are currently in force. It organizes regulations by topic, like the *United States Code* (U.S.C.) organizes statutes topically. The C.F.R. is divided into 50 broad titles, such as "Animals and Animal Products" (Title 9) and "Food

Figure 18.2: Table of Contents of Title 21 of the C.F.R.

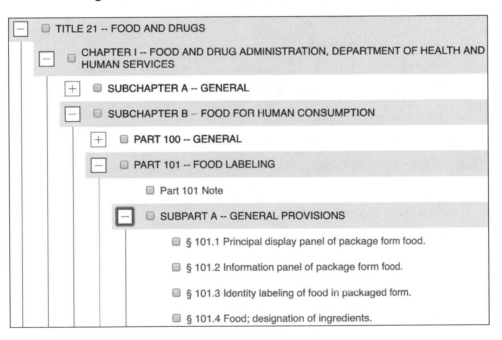

and Drugs" (Title 21). Each title is further divided into chapters, parts, and sections (see **Figure 18.2**). Like statutes in the U.S.C., the smallest break down is the section.

A citation to a regulation is similar to one for a statute. In the following regulatory citation, 21 C.F.R. § 101.56, "21" is the title, "101" is the part, and ".56" is the section, although most attorneys would refer to "101.56" as the section number. Chapters are not identified in a C.F.R. citation.

B. Federal Regulations: Researching on Westlaw and Lexis Advance

The *Code of Federal Regulations* (C.F.R.) compiles final federal regulations and organizes them topically. Thus, this part of the chapter discusses how to find regulations in the C.F.R.

Researching administrative regulations is often more tedious and complex than researching statutes. To start, you should learn as much as possible about the administrative agency that has adopted regulations on the client's legal issue. Secondary sources, such as respected treatises and practice manuals, explain the inner-workings of various federal agencies. Another good source is the *United States Government Manual* (www.usgovernmentmanual.gov), which addresses an agency's core functions and often includes an organizational chart. Last, the websites for many agencies identify their organizational structure, purpose, and enforcement mechanisms.

With background information on the pertinent agency, you are ready to research federal regulations. There are six effective methods to find regulations on Westlaw and Lexis Advance:

1. Review secondary sources;

2. Review the annotations in a statutory code for related regulations;

3. Use the citator KeyCite or Shepard's;

4. Consult an index to the C.F.R.;

5. Browse the table of contents of the online C.F.R.; and

6. Perform keyword searches in the C.F.R. database.

1. Review Secondary Sources

Lexis Advance and Westlaw include extensive coverage of secondary sources.[4] These sources should inform you whether regulations apply to the client's legal issue. Secondary materials should also cite administrative regulations and summarize their meaning. As explained in Chapter 14 (secondary sources), **looseleaf services** provide comprehensive coverage on heavily regulated areas of law, including environmental law, health care, and labor law. Many looseleafs compile and publish the text of federal regulations for a particular subject, making looseleafs an invaluable time-saving tool.

---

4. Recall that Chapter 2 sets forth various methods for finding and navigating secondary sources in print and online.

2. Review Annotations in a Statutory Code

A second method to find relevant federal regulations is to consult the annotations in the *United States Code Annotated* (U.S.C.A.) on Westlaw or the *United States Code Service* (U.S.C.S.) on Lexis Advance. To find citations to regulations in either statutory code, you need to first locate relevant codified statutes by completing **Step 3** (see Chapter 15). A relevant statute includes the enabling statute that delegated rulemaking authority to the agency. It also includes the statute that prohibits or requires the conduct in dispute.

After retrieving a codified statute, scan the annotations (*i.e.*, editorial enhancements) to see if related regulations are cross-referenced. The regulatory annotations are located in different places on Westlaw and Lexis Advance. When viewing a statute on Westlaw, click the "Context & Analysis" tab near the top of the screen. On Lexis Advance, the regulatory annotations are located after the statutory text, and they are more extensive on Lexis than Westlaw.

3. Use Shepard's or KeyCite

Another method to research administrative regulations is to use a comprehensive citator like Shepard's (Lexis Advance) or KeyCite (Westlaw). You could start with the enabling statute. Because the C.F.R. contains citations to enabling statutes, a citator report for an enabling statute identifies regulations citing that statute.

To illustrate, suppose you must research whether any regulations exist that define a "disability" as the term is used in the Americans with Disabilities Act (ADA). You could begin by retrieving 42 U.S.C. § 12116, a provision of the ADA that authorized the Equal Employment Opportunity Commission (EEOC) to "issue regulations." You would then Shepardize or KeyCite that enabling statute. Both citator reports would list all regulations that cite the enabling statute, including two regulations that define a "disability" in depth.

4. Consult an Electronic Index

A fourth method to find federal regulations is to consult an electronic index. As with federal statutory codes, Westlaw and Lexis Advance provide indexes for navigating the C.F.R. online. You can look up the name of the federal agency regulating the conduct in dispute (*e.g.*, EEOC) or terms related to the topic (*e.g.*, "employment"). Both indexes will direct you to specific locations in the C.F.R. where regulations on your topic have been codified. Note that the index on Westlaw is more detailed than the one on Lexis.

To retrieve the index, enter the full or abbreviated name of the C.F.R. in the global search box on either home page (*e.g.*, "C.F.R. Index"). Further, Westlaw provides a link to the index in the right column while viewing the full table of contents of the C.F.R.

5. Browse the Table of Contents

Further, browsing the C.F.R.'s table of contents may lead to relevant regulations. On Westlaw or Lexis, you can browse the 50 titles and the subdivisions under each title. Because pertinent regulations may be located under multiple titles, this approach should be used in conjunction with the previously-discussed methods.

6. Perform Keyword Searches

A final method to locate administrative regulations is to search the full text of the C.F.R. on Westlaw or Lexis Advance. Recall that two types of keyword searches are available: natural language searches and terms and connectors (Boolean) searches.[5] You can limit a keyword search to particular fields or segments by accessing the C.F.R. database and selecting the "advanced" link next to the global search box. Performing keyword searches should not be the sole method used, especially given the complexity of researching regulations.

C. Federal Regulations: Updating on Westlaw and Lexis Advance

As with statutes, you must update your administrative law research. You must confirm the validity of each regulation and check the effective date. An excellent method to confirm whether each relevant regulation is still good law is to use Shepard's (Lexis Advance) or KeyCite (Westlaw). These citators "tag" regulations (and statutes) with red or yellow signals to indicate negative treatment. A red signal could mean the regulation has been repealed or held unconstitutional or preempted in whole or in part. KeyCite (but not Shepard's) also indicates when a pending proposed rule would amend or repeal an existing regulation.[6]

In addition to confirming the validity of pertinent regulations, you must check the currency of the version of the *Code of Federal Regulations* (C.F.R.) that you are using. That is, you need to determine whether any recent regulations have been formally adopted but not yet codified in the C.F.R. The C.F.R. in print is updated slowly; thus, do not rely on the print version for updating regulations. The entire C.F.R. set of over 200 volumes is updated with new regulations only once per year. Titles are revised on the following quarterly cycle:

- Titles 1–16 are revised as of January 1;
- Titles 17–27 are revised as of April 1;
- Titles 28–41 are revised as of July 1; and
- Titles 42–50 are revised as of October 1.

---

5. For a detailed discussion of keyword searching, return to Chapter 9.
6. For a refresher on validating statutes using citators, revisit Chapter 16.

Names of Compilations for State Rules

To identify the official title of the source containing a state's administrative rules, you can review Table T1 in *The Bluebook* or Appendix 1 in the *ALWD Guide*. Almost every compilation of state rules includes the phrase "administrative code" in its title.

In contrast, the C.F.R. databases on Lexis Advance and Westlaw are usually current within one week—meaning, newly-adopted regulations are added to their databases within roughly one week after adoption. To locate currency information on Lexis, look immediately above the text of the regulation. On Westlaw, the currency data is located at the end of the regulatory text.

D. State Regulations

The agencies comprising the executive branch at the state level also propose and adopt rules and regulations (often known as "rules"). The administrative law systems of most states are similar to the federal system. Like Congress, state legislatures can delegate rulemaking authority to state agencies. And similar to federal agencies, most state agencies must seek public comments on proposed rules before they can become enforceable. In addition, most states have codes that compile state administrative rules. The *Florida Administrative Code*, for example, publishes rules by Florida executive agencies. In short, the knowledge you have about researching federal regulations is transferable to state rules.

Nonetheless, the rulemaking and research processes for state rules in your jurisdiction may have important differences. To illustrate, many state agencies publish proposed rules in a monthly or weekly "bulletin," where federal agencies publish them daily in the *Federal Register*. You should review a book or online guide on researching your jurisdiction's rules as soon as you know that state rules govern the client's situation. Carolina Academic Press publishes books for over thirty states that explain how to research each state's rules. Additionally, a law library in your state may have created an online research guide. The following searches on the internet should produce relevant results:

> [name of your state] researching administrative rules LibGuide
>
> [name of your state] administrative law research

E. Finding Cases Interpreting Regulations

After finding relevant statutes and regulations, you should research cases that interpret and apply both laws. The methods and processes for finding these interpretive cases on regulations and statutes overlap. Sometimes you should research interpretive cases on a relevant statute before researching them on regulations, but other situations may require finding interpretive cases on a pertinent regulation sooner. Thus, you should read this part of the chapter in conjunction with the next chapter, which discusses in detail how to find cases that interpret and apply statutes.

There are several effective methods to find cases interpreting federal regulations and state rules, including the following:

1. Reviewing the case annotations in an administrative code;

2. Using the citators of KeyCite or Shepard's; and

3. Performing keyword searches in a caselaw database.

First, you should review the case annotations in an administrative code. These annotations include summaries of *select* cases that have cited a particular regulation and provide citations to those cases. The *Code of Federal Regulations* (C.F.R.) on Westlaw and Lexis Advance contains case annotations for many federal regulations. Although more sparse, some online administrative codes for state rules also contain case annotations. Keep in mind that case annotations are not available for every federal regulation or every state rule, even when an annotated code is available.

The case annotations for federal regulations and state rules are located in different places on Westlaw and Lexis. Westlaw refers to these case summaries as "Notes of Decisions." While viewing a regulation or rule, click that tab near the top of the document to see the summaries. Lexis Advance, however, refers to case summaries as "Case Notes," which are located after the text of a regulation or rule.

Second, you should use the citation services of Shepard's (Lexis) or KeyCite (Westlaw) to find cases that discuss relevant regulations and rules. For federal regulations, both citator reports identify cases that have cited your regulation at least once. Nonetheless, KeyCite and Shepard's do not provide coverage for all state administrative codes.

Retrieving a citator report for regulations is fairly straightforward. On Lexis Advance, click "Shepardize this document" (right column) when viewing a regulation and then select "Citing Decisions" (left column). On Westlaw, while viewing a regulation, click the "Citing References" tab (near the top) and then select "Cases."

Third, you should perform keyword searches within the caselaw database for the controlling jurisdiction. After selecting the appropriate caselaw database, you would enter the keywords into the global search box on Lexis Advance or Westlaw.[7] Your search string should include, at a minimum, the code section number for the relevant federal regulation or state rule.

---

7. For a helpful discussion of how to perform keyword searches, review Chapter 9 (keyword searching), and Chapter 15 (finding statutes).

F. Summary of Key Points

A federal regulation or state rule that has been authorized and properly adopted has the same force of law as a statute. Thus, if regulations apply to the client's situation, you must find and analyze them. You can research federal regulations on Lexis Advance and Westlaw using these methods:

1. Reviewing secondary sources, such as looseleaf services;

2. Scanning the annotations in a statutory code for cross-referenced regulations;

3. Using the citator KeyCite or Shepard's;

4. Consulting an electronic index to the *Code of Federal Regulations* (C.F.R.);

5. Browsing the table of contents of the online C.F.R.; and

6. Performing keyword searches in a C.F.R. database.

After finding all relevant regulations, you need to confirm their validity and update them. You should answer the following questions:

• Has a court invalidated your regulation?

• Has your regulation been repealed or superseded by a subsequent statute or regulation?

• Is a legislative bill or proposed rule pending that would affect your regulation?

• When was the C.F.R. database last updated to include newly-enacted regulations?

Although Westlaw and Lexis Advance are the most comprehensive platforms to research regulations, a free alternative is available. The federal government maintains a website (www.ecfr.gov) with an unofficial version of the C.F.R.: the **e-CFR** (Electronic Code of Federal Regulations). You can find federal regulations by browsing the table of contents or performing keyword searches. The e-CFR updates frequently; newly-adopted regulations are added to the e-CFR database within one or two days.

This chapter has simplified the process of researching regulations and interpretive cases. Before jumping into the "sea" of administrative law research, you should gain a deeper understanding of this area of law. Several options are available. You could complete these two CALI lessons: "Rulemaking: Federal Register and CFR" and "Researching Federal Administrative Regulations." You could also review the administrative law research guide and watch the related videos on Georgetown Law Library's website. Several good resources are available on the website of The Law Librarians' Society of Washington, D.C.

G. Review Questions on Administrative Regulations

At this point, you should have a basic understanding of administrative regulations and rules. To test your comprehension, answer the true-false and multiple-choice questions on this book's companion website, Core Knowledge. It will identify the correct answers and provide clear explanations for each question. The same questions are reproduced below.

1. To adopt enforceable regulations, a federal agency, such as the Internal Revenue Service, must have been delegated rulemaking authority.

    a. True

    b. False

2. The *Federal Register* compiles and organizes final regulations by topic.

    a. True

    b. False

3. The *Code of Federal Regulations* compiles proposed regulations that have not been adopted.

    a. True

    b. False

4. Which of the following methods would be effective to find federal regulations on Westlaw and Lexis Advance?

    a. Review the annotations in the *United States Code Annotated* (U.S.C.A.) or the *United States Code Service* (U.S.C.S.) to locate cross-referenced regulations.

    b. Shepardize or KeyCite an enabling statute.

    c. Both A and B.

    d. Only B.

5. Identify at least one method to find cases that have interpreted a federal regulation.

    a. Review the case annotations in the *Federal Register* on Westlaw or Lexis Advance.

    b. Review the case annotations in the *Code of Federal Regulations* (C.F.R.) on Westlaw or Lexis Advance.

    c. Consult an electronic index to the C.F.R. on Westlaw or Lexis Advance.

    d. All of the above.

H. Practice Researching and Updating Administrative Regulations

On this book's companion website, Core Knowledge, a few research assignments have been posted. The online assignments walk you through the steps for researching a statutory issue on Westlaw and Lexis Advance, including researching administrative regulations and rules. For each assignment, you will research the law to resolve legal issues for your hypothetical client.

Step 1
(Research
Plan)

Step 2
(Secondary
Sources)

Step 3
(Find
Statutes)

Step 4
(Update
Statutes)

Step 5
(Read
Statutes)

Step 6
(Find
Regulations)

Step 7
(Find Cases)

Step 8
(Legislative
History)

Step 9
(Other States)

Step 10
(Validation)

Chapter 19

Step 7:
Research Cases from the
Controlling Jurisdiction That
Have Interpreted Relevant Statutes

Congratulations for arriving at this **Step 7** on finding relevant cases. Even though you have read each statute critically, you may not have a definitive answer to your client's legal question. Any preliminary answer at this point of the research process should be qualified with "likely" or "probably." For a more reliable answer, you need to research and review cases from your jurisdiction that have interpreted and applied the controlling statutes. Finding these interpretive cases is vital for several reasons.

First, in applying a statute to your client's situation, your court will rely not only on the statutory language at issue but also on judicial decisions. Thus, you need to know how courts have resolved disputes involving your statute. Ideally, you should find binding or highly persuasive cases in which the legal issues and facts are similar to your client's circumstances.

Second, if a word or phrase of a relevant statute is ambiguous or vague on its face, court decisions will provide clarity.[1] Congress and state legislatures write statutes to apply to many different circumstances, but they cannot predict all future situations that could arise. Additionally, legislatures may include ambiguous or vague language in a statute as part of a political compromise. Either way, you must find cases discussing the controlling statutes.

To illustrate, imagine that you found a relevant statute prohibiting retailers like your client from engaging in "unfair practices." Is it "unfair" for a retailer to price gouge consumers after a natural disaster? Or suppose you located a statute that prohibits speeding while driving a "vehicle." Does "vehicle" include golf carts? Without cases or other statutes defining "unfair" and "vehicle," it would be difficult to determine their applicability to your client.

---

1. An ambiguous term or phrase is one that could be interpreted in two or more ways. A vague term or phrase, such as "reasonable," could have several meanings based on the context.

Third, you should research cases even when the meaning of a statute seems clear on its face. Although seemingly clear, the statute may be unclear as applied to your client's situation. Assume your client received a ticket for speeding in a school zone, and assume the statute requires a "properly marked school zone" to trigger the reduced speed limit. If the road sign that displayed the hours of the reduced speed limit was difficult to read, how the phrase "properly marked school zone" applies to the client's ticket would be unclear. You, therefore, would need to find cases interpreting that phrase.

The Research Process Is Not Linear

For some projects, you can eliminate one or more of the ten research steps for statutory issues. For other assignments, you can complete the research steps in a different order and may have to repeat the same step. To illustrate, suppose you browse the table of contents of a state code and find an additional relevant statute (**Step 3**). If the statute is difficult to understand, you could return to **Step 2** and locate secondary sources (*e.g.*, treatises and practice manuals) that explain the meaning of the statute and that cite relevant cases.

You are now ready to dive into judicial decisions. The next sections set forth three effective methods to research cases that interpret and apply relevant statutes. They include the following:

1. Reviewing the case annotations in a statutory code;

2. Using a citator like KeyCite or Shepard's; and

3. Performing keyword searches in a caselaw database.

A. Review Case Annotations

After examining secondary sources, you should continue your quest for cases with an annotated statutory code for the controlling jurisdiction. Recall that the publisher or compiler of an annotated code enhances it with research tools called **annotations**. These annotations are available for codes in print and on Lexis Advance and Westlaw.

Every annotated code contains citations to court decisions addressing the statutes, as explained in Chapter 4 (codes) and Chapter 15 (finding statutes). These **case annotations** include summaries of judicial decisions that have interpreted and applied the codified statutes. A summary, like a headnote from a case, may identify a rule of law or may indicate how the court applied the statute to the facts before it. The case annotations are organized by topic, making it easy to locate cases dealing with the client's legal issue.

Warnings on Case Annotations

Although useful for researching, you should not cite or rely solely on the case annotations. The annotations, or enhancements, are not the law because commercial editors, not the legislatures, draft them. So after tracking down relevant rules of law from the case annotations, you must retrieve and review the actual opinions of the cited cases.

Additionally, the case annotations in almost all codes are not exhaustive. There is a good probability that all relevant cases are not listed in the annotations. Reviewing case annotations, therefore, should not be the sole method to find interpretive cases.

Case annotations are attached to individual code sections (statutes). Thus, to view these annotations, you need to locate a relevant statute and then scan the case annotations that follow the text of the code section. Some statutes have many case annotations, and other code sections have little to none. But when case annotations are available for a relevant statute, they are a researcher's "friend." You should consult them often, just like you do your human friends.

1. Annotated Statutory Codes in Print

Finding case annotations in federal and state codes involves similar processes. This section, therefore, discusses only federal codes in print.

The two federal codes with case annotations are the *United States Code Annotated* (U.S.C.A.) published by Thomson Reuters and the *United States Code Service* (U.S.C.S.) published by LexisNexis. The case annotations in both federal codes are drafted by different editors; therefore, the annotations contain different cases and different summaries. Further, the U.S.C.A. (Thomas Reuters) contains more case annotations than the U.S.C.S. (LexisNexis). Last, the summaries in the U.S.C.A. are the headnotes from the cited cases, but that is not necessarily true for the summaries in the U.S.C.S.

Finding case annotations for a statute is fairly straightforward (unlike most other aspects of legal research!). In the U.S.C.A. (Thomas Reuters), the case annotations follow the statutory language and are under the heading "Notes of Decisions"; in the U.S.C.S. (LexisNexis), they are under the heading "Interpretative Notes and Decisions."

To illustrate this process, suppose an employee had a back injury, and you need to determine whether the employee had a disability under the Americans with Disabilities Act (ADA). In Title 42 of the U.S.C.A., you found the definition of a "disability" in section 12102. To find cases interpreting that statutory definition, you would pick up the volume for Title 42 of the U.S.C.A. and turn to section 12102 (see **Figure 19.1**). Following the statutory language, there are thousands of case annotations. Do not fret. The annotations are organized topically and are preceded by an outline of the topics covered, so you can locate the cases dealing with your specific issue. As shown in **Figure 19.1**, the summaries of cases under the heading "back or neck condition" will help you determine which back conditions fall within the definition of a "disability."

Figure 19.1: Case Annotations for 42 U.S.C.A. § 12102

---

121. Back or neck condition

Psychiatric ward nurse, who used a cane as a result of spinal stenosis and hip replacement, had a disability, as required to establish prima facie case of discrimination under the ADA against hospital, where her spinal stenosis and hip replacement impaired her ability to walk, which qualified as a major life activity, she could only walk short distances without her cane, and she suffered from gait dysfunction.   United States Equal Employment Opportunity Commission v. St. Joseph's Hospital, Inc., C.A.11 (Fla.) 2016, 842 F.3d 1333.   Civil Rights ☞ 1218(3)

Affidavit of former employee's treating physician was sufficient to demonstrate that former employee was disabled at the time of his termination, as required for former employee to establish a prima facie case of employment discrimination under the ADA on a motion for summary judgment; treating physician stated in his affidavit that former employee's disc herniation problems and resulting pain, which had existed for years and were serious enough to require surgery, substantially and permanently limited the former employee's ability to walk, bend, sleep, and lift more than ten pounds.   Mazzeo v. Color Resolutions Intern., LLC, C.A.11 (Fla.) 2014, 746 F.3d 1264.   Federal Civil Procedure ☞ 2497.1

Former employee, a registered nurse, was not significantly restricted in performing a class of jobs because of her back injury and lifting limitations, as required to establish that she was substantially limited in major life activity of working, so as to be disabled under ADA; employer itself had available nursing positions, including patient care nursing positions, for which all of the duties fell within her physical abilities.   Squibb v. Memorial Medical Center, C.A.7 (Ill.) 2007, 497 F.3d 775.   Civil Rights ☞ 1218(3)

---

2. Annotated Statutory Codes on Lexis Advance and Westlaw

Case annotations are also contained in online codes. Case annotations are called "Notes of Decisions" on Westlaw but known as "Case Notes" on Lexis Advance. Like print codes, the case annotations online are organized topically. For many states, Westlaw and Lexis have competing annotated state codes. When possible, you should examine the case annotations on both research services because they usually do not reference the same authorities.

The following hypothetical will demonstrate the simple process of finding and navigating the case annotations on Westlaw and Lexis Advance. Imagine that your client resides in Minnesota and her dog attacked a neighbor after the neighbor threw a stick at the animal. Assume the only relevant statute is Minn. Stat. Ann. § 347.22, which provides in part: "If a dog, without provocation, attacks or injures any person … the owner of the dog is liable in damages." Because "provocation" is a defense that could relieve the client of liability, you need to determine whether the neighbor provoked the animal. If no statutory definition exists, you need to research how Minnesota courts have defined "provocation," the term in dispute.

On Westlaw, you would follow these steps to locate the Notes of Decisions on the provocation issue.

1. Retrieve Minn. Stat. Ann. § 347.22;

2. Click the "Notes of Decisions" tab near the top of the document;

3. In the outline of topics covered, look for the heading "provocation" and click on it; and

4. Scan the summaries for the cases that have explained the meaning of "provocation" in the dog-bite statute.

As shown in **Figure 19.2**, you would find multiple rules of law from the Minnesota cases listed in the annotations.

On Westlaw, another method to research interpretive cases is to use the Notes of Decisions as an access point into West's Key Number System.[2] After the case citations

Figure 19.2: Notes of Decisions (Westlaw) for Minn. Stat. Ann. § 347.22

---

2. For a reminder on using West's Key Number System, return to Chapter 7.

in the Notes of Decisions, Westlaw often provides the topic and Key Number where the summary has been classified. (Remember that most case summaries on Westlaw are the actual headnotes from the cited cases.) You would click the Key Number to enter the Key Number System and retrieve a list of headnotes with rules on your statute. For example, the first case summary in **Figure 19.2** cites *Engquist v. Loyas* and identifies the topic "Animals" and Key Number "66.5(5)." If you clicked that Key Number, you would retrieve headnotes from, and citations to, Minnesota cases that discuss the meaning of "provocation" — the term at issue. Through this method, you may find additional cases that interpret your statute and involve similar facts.[3]

Finding case annotations on Lexis Advance is somewhat different. You would do the following to locate summaries of cases on the provocation issue:

1. Retrieve Minn. Stat. Ann. § 347.22;

2. Scroll to the end of the statutory text;

3. Under "Case Notes," review the outline and click the arrow next to the heading "Torts: Strict Liability: Harm Caused by Animals: Defenses"; and

4. Review the summaries on the meaning of "provocation."

Figure 19.3 identifies the Case Notes that you would find.

Figure 19.3: Case Notes (Lexis) for Minn. Stat. Ann. § 347.22

347.22 DAMAGES, OWNER LIABLE

If a dog, without provocation, attacks or injures any person who is acting peaceably in any place where the person may lawfully be, the owner of the dog is liable in damages to the person so attacked or injured to the full amount of the injury sustained. The term "owner" includes any person harboring or keeping a dog but the owner shall be primarily liable. The term "dog" includes both male and female of the canine species.

---

3. The Key Number System will not always lead to additional cases. For some code sections, the Notes of Decisions contain all the headnotes from cases that have cited the section.

Figure 19.3: *Continued*

History
_____

1951 c 315 s 1; 1980 c 347 s 1; 1986 c 444.

▼ Annotations

LexisNexis® Notes
_____

Case Notes
_____
⚓ **Civil Procedure: Summary Judgment: Standards: General Overview**
⚓ **Civil Procedure: Summary Judgment: Standards: Appropriateness**
⚓ **Civil Procedure: Trials: Jury Trials: Jury Instructions: General Overview**
⚓ **Civil Procedure: Trials: Jury Trials: Province of Court & Jury**
⚓ **Governments: Local Governments: Claims By & Against**
⚓ **Governments: Local Governments: Employees & Officials**
⚓ **Torts: Negligence: Causation: Proximate Cause: Foreseeability**
⚓ **Torts: Negligence: Defenses: Comparative Negligence: Types**
⚓ **Torts: Negligence: Duty: Animal Owners: General Overview**
⚓ **Torts: Negligence: Duty: Animal Owners: Statutory Duties**
⚓ **Torts: Negligence: Proof: Violations of Law: General Overview**
⚓ **Torts: Public Entity Liability: Excessive Force**
⚓ **Torts: Public Entity Liability: Immunity: General Overview**
⚓ **Torts: Public Entity Liability: Liability: General Overview**
⚓ **Torts: Strict Liability: Harm Caused by Animals: General Overview**
⚓ **Torts: Strict Liability: Harm Caused by Animals: Defenses**
⚓ **Torts: Strict Liability: Harm Caused by Animals: Statutory Liability**

Figure 19.3: *Continued*

Torts: Strict Liability: Harm Caused by Animals: Defenses

In a dog-bite case, the district court erred in instructing the jury that "provoke" meant to engage in an act that excited, stimulated, irritated, aroused, induced, or enraged because, to support a finding of provocation, the evidence had to show that the conduct was not inadvertent or that there was a voluntary act involving an apparent hazard of provocation. Permitting the jury to find provocation where the child acted to "stimulate" or "excite" the dog, without more, was improper; moreover, the district court's definition of "provoke" improperly permitted the jury to determine that any deliberate act that caused a dog to react violently, for whatever reason, could constitute provocation. Engquist v. Loyas, 787 N.W.2d 220, 2010 Minn. App. LEXIS 125,14 No. 34 Minn. Lawyer 9 (2010), affirmed by, modified by 803 N.W.2d 400, 2011 Minn. LEXIS 562,15 No. (2011).

Example of an instruction that accurately reflects Minnesota law on the defense of provocation is as follows: A person provokes a dog when, by voluntary conduct, and not by inadvertence, the person invites or induces injury. Mere physical contact with a dog, or conduct that results in stimulating a dog, does not constitute provocation unless the danger of injury is apparent when the person acts to invite or induce injury. Engquist v. Loyas, 787 N.W.2d 220, 2010 Minn. App. LEXIS 125,14 No. 34 Minn. Lawyer 9 (2010), affirmed by, modified by 803 N.W.2d 400, 2011 Minn. LEXIS 562,15 No. (2011).

In order for a jury to find provocation under Minnesota's dog-bite statute, Minn. Stat. § 347.22 (2008), the evidence must show that plaintiff's allegedly provocative conduct was not inadvertent or that there was a voluntary act involving an apparent hazard of provocation. Permitting the jury to find provocation where appellant acted to "stimulate" or "excite" the dog, without more, is improper. Engquist v. Loyas, 787 N.W.2d 220, 2010 Minn. App. LEXIS 125,14 No. 34 Minn. Lawyer 9 (2010), affirmed by, modified by 803 N.W.2d 400, 2011 Minn. LEXIS 562,15 No. (2011).

Summaries of cases that have interpreted § 347.22

Citation to Minnesota appellate case

3. Statutory Codes on Casemaker and Fastcase

Substantially all codes on Casemaker and Fastcase—including the federal code—do not have case annotations.[4] These platforms have annotated codes only for a small fraction of states, such as Colorado and Connecticut. The annotations are extracted from the official codes published by an office of the legislative branch. But the case annotations in a few official codes (*e.g.*, *Oregon Revised Statutes* and *Wisconsin Statutes*) are not always available on both Casemaker and Fastcase, even when the annotations are available to the public on a legislature's website.

Fastcase claims to have case annotations for all codes. But its annotations are unlike the ones you will find on Westlaw and Lexis Advance. Fastcase's annotations are computer generated, do not summarize judicial decisions, and are not organized topically. The annotations provide a short excerpt from the actual citing case where the statute was mentioned, as shown in **Figure 19.4** for the Minnesota dog-bite statute.

4. As mentioned in Chapter 5, Casemaker and Fastcase are online research services that are available as a benefit to members of state and local bar associations.

State Trial Court Opinions

More recently, Lexis Advance and Westlaw have been adding an increasing number of state trial court decisions to their caselaw databases. The decisions of state trial courts are almost always excluded from the case annotations but appear on a KeyCite or Shepard's report for a statute (when available). That is another reason you should not rely only on the annotations. Although these decisions do not bind other courts, you may need to cite them when more persuasive authority is unavailable. Citing one case interpreting your statute—even a trial court decision—is better than citing none.

Figure 19.4: Fastcase's Annotations for Minn. Stat. § 347.22

Authority Check   ✕

Cooper v. Beaver (Minn. App., 2018)
⚑ 🖶 ☆ Case Law | Oct 21, 2018

...Judge; and Jesson, Judge. UNPUBLISHED OPINION WORKE, Judge   Appellant claims that the district court erred by denying his motion for judgment as a matter of law (JMOL), arguing that respondent is liable under the dog-owner liability Page 2 statute, **Minn. Stat. § 347.22** (2016), because appellant was injured when he fell off his bicycle after being frightened by respondent's dogs. We affirm. FACTS   Respondent Christopher Beaver and Lester Michaels are neighbors. Behind their homes is a walking and...

Oldenhof v. Hansen (Minn. App., 2018)
⚑ 🖶 ☆ Case Law | Jun 17, 2018

...acting peaceably in any place where the person may lawfully be, the owner of the dog is liable in damages to the person so attacked or injured to the full amount of the injury sustained. The term "owner" includes any person harboring or keeping a dog but the owner shall be primarily liable. . . . **Minn. Stat. § 347.22 (2016)** (emphasis added); see also 1951 Minn. Laws ch. 315, § 1, at 413-14. In short, a dog's owner is, as a general rule, strictly liable to a person who has been attacked or injured by the dog. Engquist v. Loyas, 803 N.W.2d

B. Use a Reliable Citator Like KeyCite (Westlaw) or Shepard's (Lexis) to Find Cases

You should also use a citator when researching interpretive cases. At **Step 4**, you should have used KeyCite or Shepard's to confirm the validity of each relevant statute. But at this **Step 7**, the purpose of cite checking a statute is to find cases that have interpreted your statute and that you did not locate in secondary sources and the case annotations. To find citing cases on Westlaw, while viewing a statute, click the "Citing References" tab and then select "Cases." On Lexis Advance, click "Shepardize this document" when viewing a statute and then select "Citing Decisions."

Unlike case annotations, KeyCite and Shepard's provide an exhaustive list of citing cases. Both citators will return every case that has cited a controlling statute at least once.[5] All the citing cases, however, will not always be relevant to your client's legal issue. Both KeyCite and Shepard's have filtering tools to reduce the number of irrelevant results from a citator report. Simply put, these filters will save you time. You should review Chapter 8 for a good refresher on how the filtering tools for these citators work.

Westlaw and Lexis Advance have different options to filter the list of cases that have cited your statute. On Westlaw, you can filter the citing cases by jurisdiction and court (*e.g.*, Supreme Court of Minnesota), Notes of Decisions Topics (*i.e.*, legal issue), and keywords. In addition, you can exclude from a KeyCite report all cases referenced in the Notes of Decisions, thus avoiding having to see the same cases twice.

On Lexis Advance, you can filter a Shepard's report by jurisdiction and court and by keywords. You can also limit the results to cases that cite a specific subsection of your statute. (This filter is triggered by clicking the link "Subsection reports by specific court citation.") Thus, if only subsection (a) of your statute is in dispute, you can view only those cases citing that particular subsection.[6]

Figures 19.5 and **19.6** show the filtering options on Lexis Advance and Westlaw, respectively.

---

5. On rare occasions, a KeyCite or Shepard's report may exclude a relevant case. For instance, if your statute has been renumbered in the code, a citator may not retrieve cases that cite only the original section number.

6. Do not rely solely on this filtering option, as it may be under-inclusive. A court may discuss language from a particular subsection of a statute but not expressly cite the subsection. In that circumstance, this filter would exclude the case from the citator report.

Figure 19.5: Filtering Options for a Shepard's Report

Figure 19.6: Filtering Options for a KeyCite Report

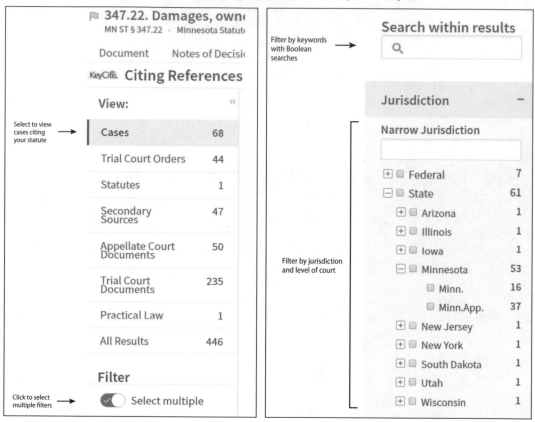

In addition to KeyCiting or Sheparding the relevant statute, you could locate interpretive cases by running a KeyCite or Shepard's report for the relevant cases you have already found.[7] This method may lead you to newer cases addressing the same topic because of how courts resolve statutory disputes. When faced with a statutory issue, courts cite not only the controlling statutes but also prior judicial decisions that have interpreted the disputed statutory language. Courts often cite decisions involving similar issues and facts (if they exist) to support their conclusions on the meaning of a statute. (Remember that under *stare decisis*, courts generally resolve similar disputes in a similar manner and treat parties in like circumstances the same.) KeyCiting or Shepardizing the cases that have applied your statutory language, therefore, will probably return helpful cases.

To illustrate this case-finding method, return to the hypothetical above (Section A.2). The client's dog attacked a neighbor after the neighbor threw a stick at the animal, and the parties dispute the meaning of the term "provocation" in the Minnesota statute (§ 347.22). Now, assume you found a 2010 decision from the court of appeals holding that the injured party provoked the dog by attempting to sit on it. Subsequent cases that have addressed the "provocation" issue may have cited the 2010 decision to support their holdings and reasoning. To locate these relevant cases, you should Shepardize or KeyCite the 2010 decision and initially filter the citator report to cases mentioning the Minnesota statute by entering the code section (347.22) in the "search within results" box in the left column. The results should exclude the cases that cite the 2010 decision for an unrelated issue (e.g., personal jurisdiction) and may include more recent cases involving similar legal issues and facts, such as cases in which the injured parties threw something at the animals prior to the attacks.

Casemaker and Fastcase also have basic citators that retrieve cases that cite a particular code section (statute). Casemaker refers to its citator feature as "Annotator," and Fastcase calls its service "Authority Check." On Casemaker, while viewing a statute, click "Annotator" near the top of the screen. On Fastcase, with a relevant statute on your screen, click the flag icon near the top of the document. Both citator reports provide a list of citing cases.

---

7. When thousands of cases have cited a relevant statute, you should consider this method. KeyCiting or Shepardizing the cases that have interpreted the exact statutory terms applicable to the client's situation may eliminate decisions that have cited your statute for an unrelated issue.

The citator features on Casemaker and Fastcase have two primary limitations. First, they are not as comprehensive as KeyCite or Shepard's. Because the caselaw databases on Lexis and Westlaw are more extensive, their citation services usually return more citing cases than Casemaker and Fastcase. Second, Fastcase and Casemaker do not offer as many filtering options as the fee-based citators.

Confirming the Validity of Interpretive Cases

As with cases addressing common law issues, you must confirm the validity of cases that interpret and apply statutes. As Chapter 8 discusses, citators "tag" cases with colorful signals to show negative treatment from a later court, including when a case is no longer good law for at least one rule of law. Use citators as you find relevant interpretive cases. Do not base a legal argument on "bad" authority; it tarnishes your professional reputation — and may subject you to a malpractice lawsuit or ethical complaint.

Casemaker (CaseCheck+) and Fastcase (Bad Law Bot) offer citation services that *may* identify when a court has overruled or reversed a prior case. But Shepard's and KeyCite are the most respected and reliable citators. Use them, if humanly possible.

C. Search a Relevant Caselaw Database

The prior two methods will usually lead to the necessary cases applying the relevant statutes. To increase your confidence that all relevant cases have been uncovered, you could perform keyword searches in a caselaw database.[8]

After selecting the caselaw database for the controlling jurisdiction, you would enter the search terms into the global search box. You could run a natural language search or a terms and connectors (Boolean) search. Remember that a Boolean search is triggered when connectors or symbols are included in the search string, such as quotation marks or a proximity connector (*e.g.*, /5). Here are a few suggestions for performing keyword searches:

- Quote the words or phrases from a statute that are in dispute (*e.g.*, "vicious dog" or "careless management").

- Include the section number of the statute in the search string (*e.g.*, 347.22 and provocation).

- Limit the search to specific fields or segments of cases (*e.g.*, headnotes or summary or synopsis).

---

8. Searching by keywords is discussed in detail in Chapter 9 (keyword searching) and Chapter 15 (finding statutes).

- Use proximity connectors and root expanders for key phrases from a statute (*e.g.*, careless! /5 manage!).[9]

Performing keyword searches in a caselaw database has an advantage over filtering a KeyCite or Shepard's report by keywords. When filtering citator reports using the "search within results" box, natural language searching is not available; in other words, you cannot perform Google-like searches to filter those reports. Only a terms and connectors (Boolean) search is available.

D. Summary of Key Points

By the time you arrive at this **Step 7**, you should have found some cases cited in secondary authorities (**Step 2**). There are three other methods to find cases that interpret and apply your statutes:

1. Reviewing the case annotations in a code in print or online;

2. Cite checking a statute or case with a reliable citator like KeyCite or Shepard's; and

3. Performing keyword searches in a caselaw database.

Figure 19.7 recaps how to find interpretive cases on Lexis Advance and Westlaw using the three methods.

As you research cases during this **Step 7**, remember that all cases do not carry the same weight of authority. Ideally, you should find and rely on binding cases that interpret relevant statutes. Binding cases, however, do not always provide a reliable answer to a legal question. In that situation, you should expand your research to include persuasive cases. Determining which cases are binding and persuasive involves a two-step inquiry: (1) does federal law, state law, or both apply? and (2) what court will resolve the legal dispute?[10]

Although this determination can be complicated, you have assistance: **Table 1** (Binding vs. Nonbinding Cases) and **Table 2** (Choosing the Best Authority), in Appendix A and B, respectively.[11] **Table 1** informs you which cases are binding in various circumstances. And **Table 2** keeps you focused on locating judicial decisions in which the legal issues and facts are the same or similar to your client's situation. These "similar" cases fall within the "Best Authority" and "Good Authority" columns in **Table 2**. Cases in those columns will be the most helpful in predicting how a court will apply the relevant statutes to the client's issues.

---

9. Suppose a statute imposes liability on a dog owner for engaging in the "careless management" of the animal. By using proximity connectors and root expanders, you would retrieve cases containing variations of that phrase, such as "carelessly managed" and "careless in management of dog."

10. The two-step inquiry is discussed in depth in Chapter 2.

11. Navigating **Tables 1** and **2** is addressed in Chapter 2 (binding and nonbinding authorities) and Chapter 5 (research plan). Those chapters provide guidance on selecting the best cases for a legal issue.

Figure 19.7: Methods for Finding Interpretive Cases

Method	Process on Lexis Advance	Process on Westlaw
1. Review case annotations.	While viewing a code section (statute), scroll to the end of the statutory text.	While viewing a code section (statute), click the "Notes of Decisions" tab.
	Under "Case Notes," review the summaries of cases that discuss the statute.	Review the summaries of cases that discuss the statute. These summaries are usually the actual headnotes from the cited cases.
2. Use a reliable citator like KeyCite or Shepard's.	While viewing a code section (statute) or relevant case, click "Shepardize this document" in the right column; on the next screen, select "Citing Decisions" in the left column.	While viewing a code section (statute) or relevant case, click the "Citing References" tab, and then select "Cases."
	Then, you could: • filter the list of citing cases, such as by jurisdiction and keywords; and • click "Subsection reports by specific court citation" to limit results to cases that have cited a particular subsection of the statute.	Then, you could filter the list of citing cases, such as by jurisdiction and keywords.
3. Perform keyword searches.	Select the relevant caselaw database, and enter search terms into the global search box.	Same process as Lexis.
	Perform a natural language search or a terms and connectors (Boolean) search or both.	

Keyword Searching on Casemaker and Fastcase

If you do not have access to Westlaw or Lexis Advance, performing keyword searches for interpretive cases is necessary. On Casemaker and Fastcase, almost all codes do not contain case annotations. Additionally, although both Casemaker and Fastcase have citators, they are not as comprehensive as KeyCite and Shepard's.

E. Review Questions on Interpretive Cases

At this point, you should know how to find cases that interpret relevant statutes. To test your comprehension, answer the true-false and multiple-choice questions on this book's companion website, Core Knowledge. It will identify the correct answers and provide clear explanations for each question. The same questions are reproduced below.

1. Case annotations include the full text of cases that have cited an individual code section (statute).

   a. True

   b. False

2. Case annotations in a federal or state code are not drafted by legislatures.

   a. True

   b. False

3. A KeyCite or Shepard's report lists cases that have cited a statute at least once.

   a. True

   b. False

4. While researching interpretive cases, you should consult **Table 1** (Binding vs. Nonbinding Cases) and **Table 2** (Choosing the Best Authority).

   a. True

   b. False

5. Donnie found three great cases that discuss the controlling statute. He plans to validate each case using a citator. Identify the most reliable citator(s) for this task.

   a. KeyCite on Westlaw

   b. Shepard's on Lexis Advance

   c. CaseCheck+ on Casemaker

   d. Both A and B

6. Identify effective methods for finding cases that interpret a statute.

   a. Reviewing the case annotations in a code.

   b. Using a reliable citator like KeyCite or Shepard's.

   c. Performing keyword searches in a caselaw database.

   d. All of the above.

7. Hannah found a statute prohibiting entering a "dwelling place" with the intent to commit a theft. In reviewing just the case annotations for this burglary statute, what might she find?

    a. Rules of law from cases that define "dwelling place."

    b. Summaries of how courts have applied the burglary statute to various factual situations.

    c. Both A and B.

    d. None of the above.

8. A neighbor has sued Abby's client for injuries sustained by the client's dog, arguing that the client violated the animal-bite statute. Abby needs to research the meaning of the statutory phrase "the animal must cause serious injury" to determine the client's liability. What would be the most targeted method to find cases interpreting that statutory phrase?

    a. KeyCite the relevant statute and filter the KeyCite report by keywords using this search string: serious AND injury AND (animal OR dog OR pet)

    b. Shepardize the relevant statute and filter the Shepard's report by keywords using this search string: (serious! /5 injur!) /25 (animal OR dog OR pet)

    c. Perform a natural language search on Westlaw in the caselaw database for the controlling jurisdiction.

    d. Perform a natural language search on Lexis Advance in the caselaw database for the controlling jurisdiction.

F. Practice Researching Interpretive Cases

On this book's companion website, Core Knowledge, a few research assignments have been posted. The online assignments walk you through the steps for researching a statutory issue on Westlaw and Lexis Advance, including finding interpretive cases. For each assignment, you will research the law to resolve legal issues for your hypothetical client.

Step 1
(Research
Plan)

Step 2
(Secondary
Sources)

Step 3
(Find
Statutes)

Step 4
(Update
Statutes)

Step 5
(Read
Statutes)

Step 6
(Find
Regulations)

Step 7
(Find Cases)

Step 8
(Legislative
History)

Step 9
(Other States)

Step 10
(Validation)

Chapter 20

Step 8:
Research the Legislative History of Relevant Statutes, If Necessary

At this **Step 8**, you should consider researching the legislative history of a statute to discern legislative intent. Legislative history includes the statements of legislatures about a proposed bill that were made before the bill became law. It also includes the documents created at each stage of the legislative process.

For many research projects, you will not have to complete this **Step 8**. The starting point for discerning a legislature's intent is the "existing statutory text."[1] When the plain meaning of a statute reveals legislative intent, no further analysis is needed.[2] Thus, you should not resort to legislative history when the text of the statute answers your client's issue. And if judicial decisions that bind your court have addressed the client's specific legal issue, relying on legislative history is not necessary.

Nonetheless, you should consider researching a statute's legislative history when statutory language is unclear on its face or ambiguous as applied to a set of facts. For instance, if cases from the controlling jurisdiction do not provide sufficient insight into the meaning of an ambiguous statutory term, you could resort to legislative history. The legislative history may "shed a reliable light" on ambiguous terms.[3] The purpose of reviewing legislative history is to determine the intent of Congress or a state legislature in passing a particular statute.

---

1. *Lamie v. U.S. Tr.*, 540 U.S. 526, 527 (2004).
2. *See Good Samaritan Hosp. v. Shalala*, 508 U.S. 402, 409 (1993); *People v. Scott*, 324 P.3d 827, 829 (Cal. 2014) ("We begin by examining the statute's words, giving them a plain and commonsense meaning.").
3. *Exxon Mobil Corp. v. Allapattah Servs., Inc.*, 545 U.S. 546, 568 (2005).

Judges and scholars disagree on whether courts should rely on legislative history materials to interpret statutes.[4] Before researching a statute's legislative history, you should determine whether your judge would consider it. Your supervisor will probably know which judges in your jurisdiction rely on or reject legislative history materials.

This chapter first discusses the documents created throughout the life of a congressional bill. It then explains the process for researching a statute's legislative history, focusing on federal laws.[5]

A. Types of Federal Legislative History

As a proposed law works its way through Congress and to the President, five types of legislative history are usually created. They include the following documents:

- Legislative bills;
- Hearing materials;
- Committee and conference reports;
- Floor debate materials; and
- Presidential messages and statements.

1. Legislative Bills

Bills are legislative proposals to create new laws or to amend or repeal existing statutes. One or more members of the United States House of Representatives or the Senate must introduce a bill, which may be introduced in the House or Senate (or both simultaneously). Once proposed, the bill is assigned a number, such as "S. 5" for a Senate bill or "H.R. 5" for a House bill. Bills are numbered consecutively throughout a two-year session. Thus, a bill abbreviated "H.R. 5" is the fifth bill introduced in the House for that particular two-year session. A bill that does not pass during a specific Congress does not carry over to the next session.

Figure 20.1 shows the first page of bill "H.R. 3630" (Middle Class Tax Relief Job Creation Act of 2012). It was introduced in the first session of the 112th Congress, which two-year session spanned from 2011 through 2012.[6]

---

4. *Compare Lewis v. United States*, 523 U.S. 155, 170 (1998) (relying on the legislative history of a federal statute), *with Jerman v. Carlisle, McNellie, Rini, Kramer & Ulrich LPA*, 559 U.S. 573, 608 (2010) (Scalia, J., dissenting) (referring to reliance on legislative history as a "legal fiction").

5. A large portion of this chapter is taken from the CALI lesson "How to Research Federal Legislative History" by Eric P. Voigt and Nancy P. Johnson. It is used with permission from The Center for Computer-Assisted Legal Instruction.

6. The website of the Senate lists the beginning and ending dates of each session of Congress.

Figure 20.1: Excerpt of House Bill from the 112th Congress

112TH CONGRESS
1ST SESSION

H. R. 3630

To provide incentives for the creation of jobs, and for other purposes.

_____

IN THE HOUSE OF REPRESENTATIVES

DECEMBER 9, 2011

Mr. CAMP (for himself, Mr. BACHUS, Mr. DANIEL E. LUNGREN of California, Mr. LUCAS, Mr. UPTON, and Ms. ROS-LEHTINEN) introduced the following bill; which was referred to the Committee on Ways and Means, and in addition to the Committees on Energy and Commerce, Financial Services, Foreign Affairs, Transportation and Infrastructure, Agriculture, Oversight and Government Reform, House Administration, the Budget, Natural Resources, Rules, and Select Intelligence (Permanent Select), for a period to be subsequently determined by the Speaker, in each case for consideration of such provisions as fall within the jurisdiction of the committee concerned

_____

A BILL

To provide incentives for the creation of jobs, and for other purposes.

1   *Be it enacted by the Senate and House of Representa-*

2 *tives of the United States of America in Congress assembled,*

When a bill is introduced in the House or Senate, the bill is usually referred to at least one committee before the entire House or Senate votes on it. A committee may consider alternative versions or propose amendments to a bill before reporting or sending it to the entire chamber. (Or a bill may "die" in committee.) Further, if a committee approves a bill and sends it to the entire chamber for a vote, the bill could be amended again. As a result, there could be several versions of the same bill before the bill becomes enacted law.

You could compare amendments or different versions of a bill to infer the intent of Congress as to the bill. For example, an attorney could argue that Congress did not intend "to enact statutory language that it has earlier discarded in favor of other language."[7] The reasons for any changes to a bill, however, are not clear without referring to other legislative history materials.

---

7. *I.N.S. v. Cardoza-Fonseca*, 480 U.S. 421, 442–43 (1987).

2. Hearing Materials

Committees and subcommittees from the House and Senate hold hearings on referred bills to gather information. The committees invite experts from academia, trade and professional associations, lobbyists, and officials from the relevant regulatory agency to provide testimony. After these hearings, the House and Senate committees have transcripts created that reflect the oral and written testimony of witnesses who favored or opposed a bill.

Congress does not hold hearings on all pieces of federal legislation, and sometimes a committee holds a hearing but does not publish the oral or written testimony. Hearings may give insight into issues but are not persuasive for determining legislative intent. The testimony may reflect the biased positions of those testifying. The hearings may provide information that the members had available in making a decision on how to vote.

3. Committee and Conference Reports

Most often, a newly-introduced bill in the House or Senate is referred to one or more committees. The members of the committee discuss and debate the bill, may hold public hearings on the bill (as just discussed), and may amend the bill. If the committee approves the bill, it is "reported out of committee" and sent to the entire House or Senate for a vote. If the entire chamber where the bill was introduced passes the bill (known as an engrossed bill), the bill is then sent to the other chamber for approval. The other chamber often refers the engrossed bill to at least one committee. Thus, an enacted law may have one committee report from the House and one committee report from the Senate (or other combinations).

For example, bill "H.R. 3244" (Victims of Trafficking and Violence Protection Act of 2000) was introduced during the 106th Congress and then referred to the House Judiciary Committee and the House International Relations Committee. Each committee voted in favor of the bill and drafted a report.

Most federal courts agree that written reports that accompany a bill from a committee provide great insight into the purpose of the bill and the intent of Congress.[8] A committee report normally includes the following information: (1) the purpose, need, and scope of the bill; (2) a section-by-section analysis of the bill; (3) the reasons for recommending approval of the bill to the full chamber; (4) the text of any amendments to the bill and any changes to existing law; and (5) the views of any dissenting committee member.

Figure 20.2 displays the table of contents of a committee report (H.R. Rep. No. 115-215) for a bill (H.R. 2333) introduced in the House during the 115th Congress.

---

8. *See, e.g., Miccosukee Tribe of Indians of Fla. v. United States*, 566 F.3d 1257, 1274 (11th Cir. 2009) ("When considering the legislative history of enacted legislation, an authoritative source is the official congressional reports on the bill.").

Figure 20.2: First Page of House Report No. 115-215

SMALL BUSINESS INVESTMENT OPPORTUNITY ACT OF
2017

JULY 12, 2017.—Committed to the Committee of the Whole House on the State of
the Union and ordered to be printed

Mr. CHABOT, from the Committee on Small Business,
submitted the following

R E P O R T

[To accompany H.R. 2333]

The Committee on Small Business, to whom was referred the bill
(H.R. 2333) to amend the Small Business Investment Act of 1958
to increase the amount of leverage made available to small business investment companies, having considered the same, report fa-
vorably thereon with an amendment and recommend that the bill
as amended do pass.

CONTENTS

If the House and Senate pass different versions of a bill, then a conference committee convenes to work out a compromise. This committee is comprised of members
from both chambers, and it attempts to resolve the differences between the two bill
versions from both chambers. The conference committee issues a conference report
that explains what language differed between the two bills and what language the
committee agreed to. This report also discusses the committee's rationales for its
actions.

A conference committee report is an excellent source indicating the intent of Congress. This report shows the understanding of members from both the House and
Senate who worked closely on the bill that became law.

The excerpt in **Figure 20.3** is from a conference committee report (No. 112-399)
discussing the Middle Class Tax Relief Job Creation Act of 2012 (Pub. L. No. 112-
96). As shown, the conference committee rejected a tax provision that appeared in
the House bill but was absent from the Senate version. That tax provision, therefore,
did not appear in the final enacted law.

Figure 20.3: Excerpt from Conference Committee Report No. 112-399

PRESENT LAW

Gross income includes any unemployment compensation benefits received under the laws of the United States or any State, and is taxed at the applicable individual income tax rate.[49]

HOUSE BILL

The House bill imposes an excise tax equal to 100 percent on unemployment compensation benefits received by individuals with adjusted gross income above certain thresholds. The adjusted gross income threshold is $750,000 ($1,500,000 for married individuals filing joint returns). The excise tax is phased-in ratably over a $250,000 range ($500,000 for married individuals filing joint returns). Therefore unemployment compensation benefits are taxed at a 100 percent rate for individuals with $1,000,000 or more of adjusted gross income ($2,000,000 or more of adjusted gross income for married individuals filing joint returns).

The excise tax is not deductible in computing the taxpayer's taxable income.

Effective date.—The provision applies to taxable years beginning after December 31, 2011.

SENATE AMENDMENT

No provision.

CONFERENCE AGREEMENT

The conference agreement does not include the provision from the House bill.

4. Floor Debate Materials

After a committee approves a bill, it is usually sent to the floor of the House or Senate for debate and discussion. During debates, the legislators may propose amendments, argue for or against the pending bill, explain ambiguous language, and take a final vote. The *Congressional Record* publishes the debates and proceedings before both chambers.

Federal courts sometimes give weight to statements made during floor debates to show legislative intent. Courts consider whether the sponsor of the bill or the chairperson of the reviewing committee made the remarks.[9]

---

9. *See, e.g., Nat'l Credit Union Admin. Bd. v. Nomura Home Equity Loan, Inc.*, 764 F.3d 1199, 1232 (10th Cir. 2014) ("In interpreting a statute, we accord substantial weight to statements by its sponsors concerning purpose and scope.").

> **Scope Notes on Lexis Advance and Westlaw**
>
> The materials in the legislative history databases on Westlaw and Lexis Advance vary greatly. Before browsing or searching a database, you should determine its content and coverage. The databases on these platforms have a scope note (indicated with an "i" icon) that provides this important information. A scope note is usually located next to the name of a database or near the top of the screen after selecting a database.

5. Presidential Messages and Statements

A bill that passes both the House and Senate is known as an enrolled bill and sent to the President. The President may sign the bill into law, veto the entire bill and return it to Congress, or take no action. If the President vetoes the bill, it will not become law unless two-thirds of both the House and Senate vote to override the veto. When vetoing a bill, the President may deliver a message to Congress that explains the reasons for the veto. And when signing a bill, the President may issue statements about its purpose and, if relevant, how the regulatory agency should implement the law.

Judges and commentators generally agree that the persuasive value of presidential messages and statements is low. Nonetheless, some courts have relied on them for background information on a statute.[10]

B. Researching a Federal Legislative History

Now, you are ready to research the legislative history of a federal statute using Congress.gov, Westlaw, or Lexis Advance.

Congress.gov is available to the public and contains a wealth of information on federal bills and laws. For the 93rd Congress (1973–74) to the present, Congress.gov provides the text and number of all bills introduced in the House and Senate, and it identifies the public law numbers for enacted laws. And for the 104th Congress (1995–96) to the present, this website allows you to search the *Congressional Record*, and it provides the full text of committee reports.

Both Westlaw and Lexis have databases for the same materials and information available on Congress.gov. Two important differences between Congress.gov and the fee-based services is that they provide more historical coverage of legislative documents and contain compiled legislative histories (discussed below).

---

10. *See, e.g., United States v. Reitano*, 862 F.2d 982, 985 (2d Cir. 1988) (analyzing a presidential message to construe a statutory term).

The following hypothetical will help you understand how to research a legislative history. Assume that you represent an applicant with a disability who applied for a director position with a company. Although the company admitted that the client was qualified for the vacancy, it filled the vacancy with a non-disabled applicant who was slightly more qualified. On appeal, you want to argue that one purpose of the Americans with Disabilities Act (ADA) was to require employers to prefer applicants with a disability over non-disabled applicants.

You plan to research the documents created during the ADA's passage. When researching a legislative history for a federal statute, you have two options: finding a compiled legislative history or compiling the documents on your own.

1. Compiled Legislative Histories

Before compiling your own legislative history, you should check whether another source has already done the work. Individuals and organizations have compiled legislative histories for certain federal statutes, especially major ones. A compiled legislative history may contain the actual documents created during a bill's passage, such as transcripts of floor debates and committee reports. Or a compiled legislative history may provide only a list of citations to the documents. Either way, a compiled legislative history will save you time.

Figure 20.4 identifies sources and databases containing compiled legislative histories, as well as their availability.

Figure 20.4: Compiled Legislative Histories

Sources & Databases	Availability
Sources of Compiled Legislative Histories: A Bibliography of Government Documents, Periodical Articles, and Books (by Nancy P. Johnson)	Print HeinOnline (U.S. Federal Legislative History Library database)
Federal Legislative Histories: An Annotated Bibliography and Index to Officially Published Sources (by Bernard D. Reams, Jr.)	Print
LLSDC's Legislative Source Book, Legislative Histories of Selected U.S. Laws on the Internet: Free Sources	Website of the Law Librarians' Society of Washington, D.C.
Legislative Insight	ProQuest
Arnold & Porter Legislative Histories	Westlaw
U.S. GAO Federal Legislative Histories	Westlaw

To locate a compiled legislative history for a particular statute, you need more information than just a citation to the *United States Code*. You may need the popular name of the act. Or you may need the bill number, public law number, or citation to the *United States Statutes at Large*. Recall that every enacted law is assigned a public law number that identifies which Congress enacted the law and the order of passage.

And the *Statutes at Large* is a collection of all public laws for a particular session of Congress.[11]

Returning to the ADA hypothetical, imagine you decided to research a highly persuasive source of legislative history: Congressional committee reports. Often, a compiled legislative history in print or online contains committee reports. On Westlaw, you could locate a compiled history for the ADA using these steps:

1. From the home page, enter "Arnold & Porter Legislative Histories" in the global search box, and select this source from the drop-down list.

2. Click "Americans with Disabilities Act of 1990" on the next screen.

3. Select "Reports" on the next screen.

You now have a list of nine reports from House and Senate committees. Assume that you found relevant language in the report by the Committee on Education and Labor (H.R. Rep. No. 101-485, part II). According to this report in **Figure 20.5**, employers have "no obligation under this legislation to prefer applicants with disabilities over other applicants on the basis of disability."

Figure 20.5: Excerpt from House Report No. 101-485 (Part II)

**338 *56 Thus, under this legislation an employer is still free to select applicants for reasons unrelated to the existence or consequence of a disability. For example, suppose an employer has an opening for a typist and two persons apply for the job, one being an individual with a disability who types 50 words per minute and the other being an individual without a disability who types 75 words per minute. The employer is permitted to choose the applicant with the higher typing speed, if typing speed is necessary for successful performance on the job.

On the other hand, if the two applicants are an individual with a hearing impairment who requires a telephone headset with an amplifier and an individual without a disability, both of whom have the same typing speed, the employer is not permitted to choose the individual without a disability because of the need to provide the needed reasonable accommodation to the person with the disability.

In the above example, the employer would be permitted to reject the applicant with a disability and choose the other applicant for reasons not related to the disability or to the accommodation or otherwise not prohibited by this legislation. In other words, the employer's obligation is to consider applicants and make decisions without regard to an individual's disability, or the individual's need for a reasonable accommodation. But, the employer has no obligation under this legislation to prefer applicants with disabilities over other applicants on the basis of disability.

---

11. Public law numbers and the *Statutes at Large* are discussed in Chapter 4.

2. Compiling a Legislative History on Your Own

If a compiled legislative history is unavailable or incomplete, you could compile your own legislative history. Most often, you can locate materials that comprise a legislative history by knowing the public law number for the enacted law in dispute. As explained in Chapter 16, the history notes or source credits for an individual code section identify its public law number. These notes or credits are located at the end of the statutory text in an annotated code in print or online.

Pretend for a few moments that a compiled legislative history did not exist for the ADA. To find committee reports related to preferences for job applicants under the ADA, you could start by obtaining the ADA's public law number. To do that, you could retrieve 42 U.S.C. § 12112, which prohibits covered employers from discriminating on the basis of a disability. Under "Credit(s)" on Westlaw, you would see that section 12112 was enacted by Public Law Number 101-336 on July 26, 1990 (see **Figure 20.6**). And under "History" on Lexis Advance, you would find the same public law number (see **Figure 20.7**). The number "101-336" means that the ADA was the 336th law enacted during the 101st Congress.

Figure 20.6: Source Credits on Westlaw for 42 U.S.C.A. § 12112

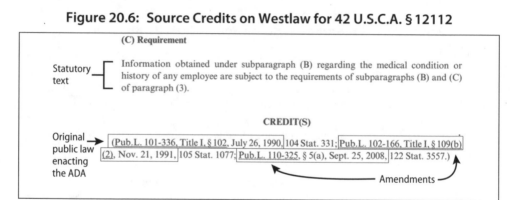

Figure 20.7: History Notes on Lexis Advance for 42 U.S.C.S. § 12112

a. Westlaw

With the public law number in hand, you can find committee reports associated with the ADA. You could follow these steps on Westlaw to locate committee reports:

1. From the home page, select "Content Types" and then click "Legislative History."

2. Click "U.S. Code Congressional & Administrative News" on the next screen.

3. Select "Congressional Committee Reports" on the next screen.

4. In the search template, find the field "Reports on Public Law No.," enter "101-336" (the public law number for the ADA), and click search.

This database provides access to the full text of multiple reports issued when the ADA was reported out of different committees. You would find the same report by the Committee on Education and Labor (H.R. Rep. No. 101-485, part II) that you located earlier from a compiled legislative history. That report states that the ADA does not require employers to treat applicants with a disability preferentially.

b. Lexis Advance and Congress.gov

The process for locating committee reports on Lexis Advance differs from the process on Westlaw. On Lexis, while you could perform a keyword search, a more structured approach would be to use the public law number and the bill number. Because you know that Public Law Number 101-336 created the ADA, you could find the bill number on Congress.gov. That site, by default, arranges public laws in reverse chronological order for each Congressional session. As shown in **Figure 20.8**, the ADA was introduced in the 101st Congress and assigned bill number "S. 933."

Next, you could complete the following steps on Lexis Advance to locate committee reports related to the ADA:

1. From the home page, select "Content Type" and then click "Statutes and Legislation."

2. Click "Legislative Histories" on the next screen.

3. Select "Committee Reports" on the next screen.

4. In the global search box, place the phrase "S. 933" in quotation marks and click search.

The results include a citation to the same committee report (H.R. Rep. No. 101-485, part II) you found on Westlaw that addresses the ADA and preferences for job applicants.

Figure 20.8: Public Laws from 101st Congress on Congress.gov

PL 101-337	H.R.2844 - To improve the ability of the Secretary of the Interior to properly manage certain resources of the National Park System.	07/27/1990
PL 101-336	S.933 - Americans with Disabilities Act of 1990	07/26/1990
PL 101-335	H.R.2514 - Thrift Savings Plan Technical Amendments Act of 1990	07/17/1990
PL 101-334	H.R.4525 - Ethics in Government Act Amendment of 1990	07/16/1990
PL 101-333	H.R.4252 - To authorize the Secretary of the Air Force to purchase certain property at Pease Air Force Base, New Hampshire.	07/16/1990

C. Researching a State Legislative History

When a state statute is unclear, you should consider resorting to its legislative history to discern the intent of the legislature. The path from bill to law at the state level is similar to the federal process, and the documents created during a state bill's passage are comparable to federal materials. And finding legislative histories in some states may be easier than locating them for federal laws. The legislative websites of some states, for instance, compile all or most of the legislative history for a particular statute, especially recent laws. Nonetheless, researching a state statute's legislative history in other jurisdictions may prove more challenging because legislative materials may not be readily available.

Before diving into the deep end of the "legislative history pool," seek outside assistance! First, review a guide explaining how a bill becomes law in your state. Second, review a guide on researching legislative histories for statutes in the controlling jurisdiction. The state legislature or a law library in your state has probably created these types of online guides. The following searches on the internet should produce relevant results:

[name of your state] legislative process LibGuide

[name of your state] legislature how a bill becomes law

[name of your state] researching legislative history

While scrolling through the results, look for research guides on ".edu" and ".gov" websites.

D. Summary of Key Points

The legislative history of a statute means the documents created by the legislature during the life of a bill. You should consider researching legislative history when statutory language is unclear and binding cases have not resolved the ambiguity. To research a federal legislative history, you need the bill number, public law number, citation to the *Statutes at Large*, popular name of an act, or some combination of that information. For state laws, you usually need the number for the session law that created or amended the statute and the bill number.

Figure 20.9 recaps the federal legislative process; the documents created during the process; and their availability on government websites, Lexis Advance, and Westlaw.[12]

---

12. This figure is based in large part on the chart set forth in Mary G. Algero, et al., *Federal Legal Research* 127–28 (2014). This figure simplifies the process; a bill does not always follow the path described in the chart.

Figure 20.9: Sources of Legislative History and Their Availability

Legislative Action	Source of Legislative History	Availability Online[1]
A proposed law is introduced in the House or Senate, numbered, read on the floor of the chamber, and usually referred to a committee.	Bills	Govinfo.gov
		Congress.gov
		Lexis Advance (Congressional Full Text of Bills database)
		Westlaw (Congressional Bills database)
The committee holds public hearings and studies the bill. The bill may be amended.	Hearing Materials	Govinfo.gov
		House and Senate Committees websites
		Lexis Advance (CQ Congressional Testimony database)
		Westlaw (U.S. Congressional Testimony database)
The committee votes on the bill, resulting in a favorable or unfavorable report.	Committee Reports	Lexis Advance (Committee Reports database)
		Westlaw (U.S. Code Congressional & Administrative News database)
A bill with a favorable report is sent to the floor of the House or Senate for readings and debates. The bill may be amended.	Floor Debate Materials	Govinfo.gov
		Congress.gov
		Lexis Advance (Congressional Record database)
		Westlaw (Congressional Record database)
If approved by vote of one chamber, the bill is sent as an engrossed bill to the other chamber. If the other chamber amends the bill and approves it, the bill is sent back to the originating chamber. If the originating chamber rejects the amended version, a conference committee is appointed to negotiate matters in dispute. If the conference committee agrees on terms, a unified bill is created, which includes amendments by the committee.	Conference Committee Report	Lexis Advance (Committee Reports database)
		Westlaw (U.S. Code Congressional & Administrative News database)
If the bill (or unified bill) passes both chambers, it is sent as an enrolled bill to the President. The President has ten days to act. If the President signs the bill, it becomes law. If the President does not sign or veto it within ten days, the bill becomes law automatically. If the President vetoes the bill, the House and Senate may override it by a two-thirds vote.	Presidential Messages and Statements	The White House website
		Govinfo.gov
		Lexis Advance
		Westlaw

[1] To access a relevant database on Lexis Advance or Westlaw, enter its name in the global search box; from the drop-down list, select the appropriate source (Lexis) or content page (Westlaw).

E. Review Questions on Legislative History

At this point, you should have a basic understanding of a statute's legislative history. To test your comprehension, answer the true-false and multiple-choice questions on this book's companion website, Core Knowledge. It will identify the correct answers and provide clear explanations for each question. The same questions are reproduced below.

1. Before researching a statute's legislative history, you should determine whether your judge would consider it.

   a. True

   b. False

2. Some courts give weight to statements made during debates before the entire Senate or House of Representatives.

   a. True

   b. False

3. Courts never rely on Presidential statements or messages.

   a. True

   b. False

4. A compiled legislative history may contain the actual documents created during a bill's passage.

   a. True

   b. False

5. Who may introduce bills in Congress?

   a. The President

   b. Members of Congress

   c. Lobbyists

   d. Judges

6. What is a proper use of the legislative history of a statute?

   a. Judges may refer to legislative history materials to find cases.

   b. Judges may refer to legislative history materials when statutory language is clear.

   c. Judges may refer to legislative history materials when statutory language is ambiguous.

   d. None of the above.

7. Identify the materials that could be created during and after a hearing before a Congressional committee

a. Transcripts of oral testimony before a House committee

b. Transcripts of oral testimony before a Senate committee

c. Written testimony from a witness before a House committee

d. All of the above

8. Generally, what information is included in a Congressional committee report?

a. Purpose and need for the bill

b. The committee's reasons for recommending approval of the bill to the full chamber

c. Both A and B

d. A statute's public law number

9. Identify the materials that may comprise the federal legislative history of a statute.

a. Statutes in the *United States Code*

b. Committee reports

c. Legislative bills

d. Both B and C

10. Which source of legislative history is usually the most authoritative on discerning the intent of Congress?

a. Hearing Materials

b. Committee Reports

c. Floor Debate Materials

d. Legislative Bills

F. Practice Researching a Legislative History

On this book's companion website, Core Knowledge, a few research assignments have been posted. The online assignments walk you through the steps for researching a statutory issue on Westlaw and Lexis Advance, including researching a legislative history. For each assignment, you will research the law to resolve legal issues for your hypothetical client.

Step 1
(Research Plan)

Step 2
(Secondary Sources)

Step 3
(Find Statutes)

Step 4
(Update Statutes)

Step 5
(Read Statutes)

Step 6
(Find Regulations)

Step 7
(Find Cases)

Step 8
(Legislative History)

Step 9
(Other States)

Step 10
(Validation)

Chapter 21

Step 9:
Research Comparable Statutes and Cases from Other Jurisdictions, If Necessary

You are almost at the finish line of the research race for a statutory issue. For this **Step 9**, you should consider researching comparable statutes from other, non-controlling jurisdictions and cases interpreting those statutes. By broadening the scope of your research, you may find additional authority that increases the reliability of the answer to the client's question.

You should consider completing **Step 9** in two primary circumstances. First, you should research primary authority from other states when the controlling statutes and cases do not provide sufficient rules of law. For instance, suppose the governing statute applies only to "vehicles," but no statute and no case in the controlling jurisdiction has defined that term. You could find a statute in another jurisdiction that applies to "vehicles" and determine how cases in that state have interpreted its meaning.

Second, researching out-of-state authority would be helpful when legally and factually similar cases in the governing jurisdiction do not exist. Courts in your jurisdiction may rely on out-of-state cases that interpret an identical term appearing in your statute and the other statute. To illustrate, assume your client, a consumer, has alleged that a business violated the statute prohibiting "unfair practices" by price gouging consumers after a natural disaster. Further assume that no binding case has addressed whether an "unfair" practice covers price gouging. You could then find cases in other jurisdictions that have interpreted the same "unfair practices" term. If an out-of-state case has held that "unfair practices" include price gouging after a natural disaster, you would have at least one authority supporting the client's position. One authority is always better than none.

In sum, consider researching out-of-state authority when the prior research steps do not yield sufficient authority from the controlling jurisdiction. Out-of-state research could be time consuming. Thus, you should consult with your professor or supervisor before starting this **Step 9**.

A. Researching Primary Authorities Outside Your Jurisdiction

When researching out-of-state authorities to provide clarity to the meaning of a controlling statute, you should follow two steps. The first step is to locate at least one comparable statute from another state. The second step is to find judicial decisions that interpret the comparable statute.

1. Researching Comparable Statutes

Before researching cases from other jurisdictions, you must find one or more comparable statutes. A **comparable statute** is one containing the same term as the disputed term from the controlling statute, and the same terms from both statutes should be used in a similar context. For example, suppose a Georgia statute requires an animal to be "vicious" to impose liability on a dog owner, and suppose the client's sole issue is whether her dog is "vicious." A comparable statute would include a statute from another jurisdiction that also requires a pet owner's animal to be "vicious" for an injured party to recover damages from the owner.

a. Uniform Laws

One good method to find a comparable statute is to determine whether the controlling statute is based on a **uniform law.** Other state legislatures may have enacted the same uniform law with the same or similar language contained in the controlling statute. The organization, the Uniform Law Commission (ULC), drafts uniform laws to promote uniformity in certain areas of state law.[1] The ULC attempts to persuade state legislatures across jurisdictions to enact its uniform laws. It has written over 200 uniform laws, such as the Uniform Commercial Code, Uniform Probate Code, and Uniform Arbitration Act. Each state legislature determines whether to reject a uniform law, approve it in whole, or approve a uniform law in part and reject it in part. In short, no uniform law represents the actual law in any jurisdiction until—and unless—a legislature has enacted it.

To discover which other states have adopted a uniform law, visit the ULC's website (www.uniformlaws.org), and click the "Acts" tab to view a list of all uniform laws. This site provides the full text of final uniform laws, as well as identifying which states have adopted each law. The site, however, does not provide citations to the versions enacted in other states. Because legislatures may modify any language of a uniform law, you need to find the exact version enacted in another jurisdiction and compare its language to the controlling statute.

---

1. This organization is also known as the National Conference of Commissioners on Uniform State Laws. It is comprised of attorneys, judges, legislators, and law professors. Although not the only one, this organization drafts the most uniform laws.

A few good methods are available to identify where a uniform law has been codified in other state codes. The free database hosted by Cornell's Legal Information Institute (www.law.cornell.edu/uniform) provides statutory citations for many enacted uniform laws. Additionally, you can retrieve the exhaustive "Uniform Laws Annotated" database on Westlaw by entering its name in the global search box. You would then select the appropriate uniform law and click the first listed hyperlink in the table of contents to access the annotations (see **Figure 21.1**). As shown in **Figure 21.2**, the annotations for the Uniform Arbitration Act identify which states have adopted it, as well as providing citations to the codified versions in the adopting states. Last, you could find codified versions of a uniform law by following the methods set forth in Chapter 15 (finding statutes).

Figure 21.1: Tables of Contents for Westlaw's Uniform Laws Annotated Database and Uniform Arbitration Act

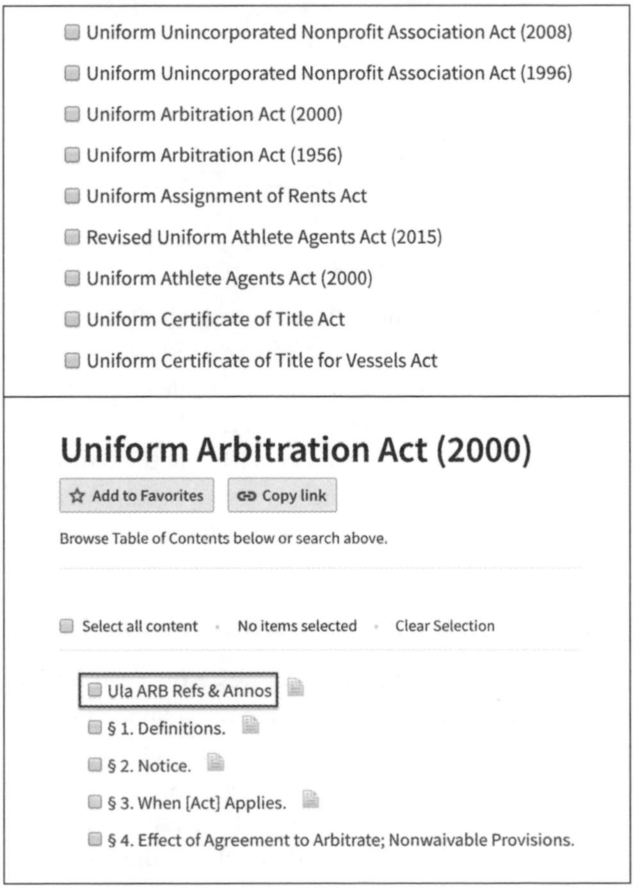

Figure 21.2: Citations to Uniform Arbitration Act in Adopting States

Editors' Notes			
TABLE OF JURISDICTIONS WHEREIN ACT HAS BEEN ADOPTED			
Jurisdiction	**Laws**	**Effective Date**	**Statutory Citation**
Alaska[1]	2004, c. 170	1-1-2005	AS 09.43.300 to 09.43.595.
Arizona[1]	2010, c. 139	1-1-2011	A.R.S. §§ 12-3001 to 12-3029.
Arkansas[1]	2011, No. 695		A.C.A. §§ 16-108-201 to 16-108-230.
Colorado	2004, c. 363	8-4-2004	West's C.R.S.A. §§ 13-22-201 to 13-22-230.
District of Columbia	D.C. Law 17-111	2-27-2008	D.C. Official Code, 2001 Ed. §§ 16-4401 to 16-4432.
Florida	2013, c. 232	7-1-2013	F.S.A. §§ 682.01 to 682.25.

b. Databases and Sources for Multi-State Research

In addition to finding uniform laws, there are several other options for researching statutes across multiple jurisdictions. Some sources and databases survey the laws of the fifty states on multiple topics, but others compile only the laws on a specific subject (*e.g.*, consumer protection laws or trade secrets). **Figure 21.3** sets forth sources and databases that collect statutes from various jurisdictions or that reference other secondary sources compiling statutes from across jurisdictions. This figure also describes the content of the listed sources and databases and how to navigate them.

2. Researching Cases Interpreting Comparable Statutes

After finding one or more comparable statutes, you need to research cases that have interpreted them. These interpretive cases may explain a disputed statutory term in more detail than the cases discussing the controlling statute. For instance, imagine that the governing statute requires a dog to be "vicious," but no court has addressed the client's issue of whether the controlling statute requires a prior bite of a human. Courts from another jurisdiction may have defined "vicious" in a comparable statute and required a prior human attack.

The good news is that you already know how to find cases interpreting statutes. (The "bad" news, however, is that this task takes time, a precious commodity for

Figure 21.3: Options to Locate the Laws Across Jurisdictions

Source or Database	Description	Navigating
50-State Survey Databases on Westlaw and HeinOnline[1]	These online databases provide citations for state statutes covering many topics, such as consumer protection, criminal, employment, family, and property laws. For many topics and statutes, the databases also have charts identifying the statutes' similarities and differences.	1. On Westlaw, enter "50 state surveys" in the global search box, and select the proper database under "Content Pages." 2. On HeinOnline, browse all databases by name, and then click the title "National Survey of State Laws."
50-State Survey Databases on Lexis Advance	This Lexis database covers similar topics as the 50-state survey database on Westlaw. It provides charts for many topics, and the charts usually compare and contrast the statutes from the fifty states.	On Lexis Advance, enter "50 state surveys" in the global search box, and select the proper database under "Sources."
Subject Compilations of State Laws Database on HeinOnline	This database provides citations to secondary sources that have collected state laws, and it organizes the sources into over 200 subjects. It also summarizes the content of the secondary sources.	On HeinOnline, browse all databases by name, and then select the title "Subject Compilations of State Laws."
Annotated State Codes	For some code sections (statutes), an annotated code cross-references similar statutes from other jurisdictions.	Retrieve the controlling statute with an annotated code. Then do the following for a print or online code: • On Lexis Advance and in print, any cross-referenced statutes would be cited after the statutory text. • On Westlaw, any cross-referenced statutes would be located under the tab "Context & Analysis."
Online Research Guides	Law librarians create free research guides (*e.g.*, LibGuides) that list sources and databases that have compiled statutes from all states on various topics.	Search the internet for a research guide with keywords like the following: • LibGuide 50 state surveys sources [your topic]
National Conference of State Legislatures Website	This website identifies state statutes on multiple subjects, including crimes, education, and labor and employment.	From the home page (www.ncsl.org), click the "Research" tab for a list of covered subjects.

[1] The 50-state survey databases on Westlaw and HeinOnline contain the same surveys. The surveys in both databases are drawn from the book, *National Survey of State Laws*, by Richard A. Leiter.

students and attorneys.) The three methods for researching interpretive cases are explained in detail in Chapter 19 and summarized below.

First, you should consult an annotated code from the outside jurisdiction and scan the case annotations—an excellent place to find interpretive cases. These annotations, whether in print or online, include summaries of, and citations to, judicial decisions interpreting the codified statutes. Case annotations are known as "Notes of Decisions" on Westlaw, but referred to as "Case Notes" on Lexis Advance.

Second, you could use a comprehensive citator like KeyCite (Westlaw) or Shepard's (Lexis) or use a basic citator on Casemaker or Fastcase. By this chapter, you should know what a citator does. If your memory has momentarily escaped you, here is a reminder: a citator will return a list of cases that have cited your statute. You can filter a citator report so that only the potentially relevant cases are displayed in the search results. For example, KeyCite and Shepard's reports can be filtered by jurisdiction, level of court, and date.

Third, you could perform keyword searches in the caselaw database for the outside (non-controlling) jurisdiction. After selecting the proper database, a natural language search or Boolean search could be performed.

B. Summary of Key Points

Completing this **Step 9** for a statutory issue is not necessary for many assignments. But when statutes and interpretive cases from the controlling jurisdiction do not yield a reliable answer, consider reaching outside your jurisdiction. Researching outside the controlling jurisdiction involves two steps.

You must first find at least one comparable statute from another jurisdiction. The out-of-state statute should contain the same wording as the terms at issue in the governing statute. The following sources and databases will help save you time:

- Uniform laws on the Uniform Law Commission's website;

- 50-state survey databases on Westlaw, Lexis Advance, and HeinOnline;

- Subject Compilations of State Laws database on HeinOnline;

- Annotated state codes in print or online;

- Online LibGuides; and

- National Conference of State Legislatures website.

The next step is to research cases that discuss the comparable statute. Three good approaches are available:

1. Reviewing the case annotations in an annotated code in print or online;

2. Using an online citator; and

3. Performing keyword searches in a caselaw database.

Keep in mind that this chapter has focused on researching statutes and cases from other jurisdictions for the purpose of understanding terms in the controlling statute from one jurisdiction. For some assignments, however, the controlling statutes may encompass multiple states. You, for instance, may have to survey the laws of many states on a single topic when a corporate client's business plan would adversely affect its consumers or dealers across jurisdictions. For that type of project, the 50-state survey databases on HeinOnline, Westlaw, and Lexis Advance would lead you to citations to statutes across states—and save you time.

C. Review Questions for Out-of-State Statutory Research

At this point, you should know how to research statutes and interpretive cases from outside the controlling jurisdiction. To test your comprehension, answer the true-false and multiple-choice questions on this book's companion website, Core Knowledge. It will identify the correct answers and provide clear explanations for each question. The same questions are reproduced below.

1. Before researching primary authority outside the governing jurisdiction, you should consult your professor or supervisor.

    a. True

    b. False

2. You should consider researching out-of-state authority when the statute and interpretive cases from the controlling jurisdiction do not yield a reliable answer.

    a. True

    b. False

3. Each uniform law drafted by the Uniform Law Commission represents the actual law.

    a. True

    b. False

4. For a statutory issue, identify the first step in researching primary authority from another jurisdiction.

    a. Find judicial decisions from another jurisdiction.

    b. Use an online citator like KeyCite or Shepard's.

    c. Find at least one comparable statute from another jurisdiction.

    d. Review the case annotations in a code from another jurisdiction.

5. Angela needs to find a comparable statute from outside the controlling jurisdiction. Which sources and databases should Angela consult?

   a. 50-state survey database on Lexis Advance

   b. Online Research Guides

   c. Both A and B

   d. Only A

D. Practice Researching Out-of-State Statutes and Interpretive Cases

On this book's companion website, Core Knowledge, a few research assignments have been posted. The online assignments walk you through the steps for researching a statutory issue on Westlaw and Lexis Advance, including finding statutes and interpretive cases from outside the controlling jurisdiction. For each assignment, you will research the law to resolve legal issues for your hypothetical client.

Chapter 22

Step 10:
Use a Reliable Citator to
Re-Confirm the Validity of
Each Relevant Authority

Step 1
(Research
Plan)

Step 2
(Secondary
Sources)

Step 3
(Find
Statutes)

Step 4
(Update
Statutes)

Step 5
(Read
Statutes)

Step 6
(Find
Regulations)

Step 7
(Find Cases)

Step 8
(Legislative
History)

Step 9
(Other States)

Step 10
(Validation)

Because of the many research steps and complexity of statutory issues, the process sometimes moves at the speed of a glacier. But it is far better to be thorough and right than fast *and wrong*. For this final **Step 10**, you must re-confirm that every rule or other legal proposition from every relevant primary authority remains good law. So you must validate each statute, administrative regulation, and interpretive case that forms the basis of any legal argument.

The citators Shepard's on Lexis Advance and KeyCite on Westlaw are the most reliable tools available to determine the validity of primary authorities. (Citators are discussed in detail in Chapter 8 and Chapter 16.) These citators indicate that a statute or regulation has negative treatment by tagging it with a red or yellow signal. For instance, both Shepard's and KeyCite inform you whether a statute has become invalid in the following circumstances:

- The legislature repealed the entire statute;

- The legislature amended the statute, repealing part of it;

- A court held that a state statute was preempted in whole or in part by federal law; or

- A court declared the statute unconstitutional in whole or in part.

As you completed the prior steps, you should have been validating all potentially relevant authority using Shepard's or KeyCite. A newly-enacted statute, however, may have repealed a statute you found at the beginning of your research. At **Step 10**, therefore, you must re-confirm the validity of each primary authority that you rely on and cite in any legal document. Relying on a statute or case that no longer reflects current law could subject you to an ethical complaint or malpractice claim.

Appendix A

Table 1: Binding vs. Nonbinding Cases

	1	2	3
	(1) State or Federal Issue (2) State or Federal Court	Binding (Mandatory) Cases	Nonbinding (Persuasive) Cases
A	State issue in state trial court	• That state's highest court • That state's intermediate appellate courts	• U.S. Supreme Court • Federal circuit courts • Federal district courts • That state's trial courts
B	State issue in state intermediate appellate court	• That state's highest court • That state's intermediate appellate courts	• U.S. Supreme Court • Federal circuit courts • Federal district courts • That state's trial courts
C	State issue in state's highest court	• That state's highest court	• U.S. Supreme Court • Federal circuit courts • Federal district courts • That state's intermediate appellate courts • That state's trial courts
D	State issue in federal district court	• That state's highest court • That state's intermediate appellate courts (limited circumstances) • Federal circuit court encompassing the district court (limited circumstances)	• U.S. Supreme Court • Other federal circuit courts • Federal district courts • That state's trial courts
E	State issue in federal circuit court	• That state's highest court • That state's intermediate appellate courts (limited circumstances) • That federal circuit court (limited circumstances)	• U.S. Supreme Court • Other federal circuit courts • Federal district courts • That state's trial courts
F	State issue in U.S. Supreme Court	• That state's highest court • That state's intermediate appellate courts (limited circumstances)	• U.S. Supreme Court • Federal circuit courts • Federal district courts • That state's trial courts

Table 1: Binding vs. Nonbinding Cases, *continued*

	1 (1) State or Federal Issue (2) State or Federal Court	2 Binding (Mandatory) Cases	3 Nonbinding (Persuasive) Cases
G	Federal issue in federal district court	• U.S. Supreme Court • Federal circuit court encompassing the district court	• Other federal circuit courts • That federal district court • Other federal district courts • All state courts
H	Federal issue in federal circuit court	• U.S. Supreme Court • That federal circuit court	• Other federal circuit courts • Federal district courts • All state courts
I	Federal issue in U.S. Supreme Court	• U.S. Supreme Court	• Federal circuit courts • Federal district courts • All state courts
J	Federal issue in state trial court	• U.S. Supreme Court • That state's highest court (limited circumstances) • That state's intermediate appellate courts (limited circumstances)	• Federal circuit courts • Federal district courts • That state's trial courts
K	Federal issue in state intermediate appellate court	• U.S. Supreme Court • That state's highest court (limited circumstances) • That state's intermediate appellate courts (limited circumstances)	• Federal circuit courts • Federal district courts • That state's trial courts
L	Federal issue in state's highest court	• U.S. Supreme Court • That state's highest court (limited circumstances)	• Federal circuit courts • Federal district courts • That state's intermediate appellate courts • That state's trial courts

Appendix B

Table 2: Choosing the Best Authority

		1	2	3
		Best Authority	**Good Authority**	**Fair/Weak Authority**
	Weight of Authority (Refer to Table 1)[1]	**Higher Row in Same Column = Better Authority** **Better Reasoned Cases = Better Authority** **Recent Cases = Better Authority** **Published Cases = Better Authority**		
A	**Binding:** Caselaw	Legal Issue: Same or similar Facts: Same or similar legally relevant facts	Legal Issue: Same or similar Facts: Different[2]	Legal Issue: Different but same area of law[3] Facts: Different
B	**Nonbinding: Highly to Moderately Persuasive** Caselaw	Legal Issue: Same or similar Facts: Same or similar legally relevant facts	Legal Issue: Same or similar Facts: Different[4]	Legal Issue: Different but same area of law Facts: Different
C	**Nonbinding: Slightly Persuasive** Caselaw	Legal Issue: Same or similar Facts: Same or similar legally relevant facts	Legal Issue: Same or similar Facts: Different	Legal Issue: Different but same area of law Facts: Different

[1] Review Table 1 in Appendix A to determine which authorities are binding and nonbinding (persuasive).

[2] For an example of when a case falling in this cell is better authority than a nonbinding decision in the "Best Authority" column, review Chapter 5, Section A.3.

[3] For an example of the type of case falling in this cell, review Chapter 5, Section A.3.

[4] For an example of the type of case falling in this cell, review Chapter 5, Section A.3.

Appendix C

Research Action Plan Form

Name of client and matter number:
Final work product (*e.g.*, memo, motion, or oral report) and due date:
Part One: Review the Client's Facts
Who: Who are the parties? What is their relationship to each other? Is client the plaintiff or defendant?
What: What happened? Who was injured?
Where: Location of events and injury?
When: Date (and time) of events and injury?
Why: Why is this being litigated? What relief does the plaintiff seek?
Part One (Continued): Identify the Governing Law
Federal or state law (or both):
Common law or statutory issue (or both):
Part Two: Identify the Legal Issues and Keywords
Draft an initial issue statement (include controlling law, legal question, and legally relevant facts):
Initial keywords (*i.e.*, search terms) to use:
Additional keywords (*i.e.*, search terms) uncovered during the research process:

Research Action Plan Form, *continued*

Part Three: Identify Binding Authorities and the Most Relevant Authorities
Court deciding client's issue (*e.g.*, state trial court?):
Binding authorities (*e.g.*, decisions from intermediate appellate court?):
Highly to moderately persuasive authorities (*e.g.*, decisions from federal circuit court?):
Most relevant authorities (similar legal issue and facts):
Part Four: Consider the Relevant Research Tools and Databases to Use:
Print sources (*e.g.*, West's Digest System or annotated code):
Online research platforms (*e.g.*, Westlaw, Lexis, Casemaker, or Fastcase):
Online databases (*e.g.*, Georgia Code, Alabama state cases, or Eleventh Circuit cases):
Part Five: Identify Any Constraints
Limitations on research expenses and your time:
Track Your Research
Relevant Secondary Sources Found   Legal encyclopedias: Treatises and practice manuals: American Law Report (A.L.R.) annotations: Legal articles: Jury instructions:
Online: Databases searched and search strings used:
Print: Sources reviewed and terms looked up:
Relevant statutes and other enacted laws found:
Relevant binding cases found:
Relevant nonbinding (persuasive) cases found:
Relevant Digest Topics and Key Numbers:
Irrelevant authorities—statutes, other enacted laws, and cases:

Index